A GENERAL THAN

Almighty God, Fat.
we your unworthy servants
give you most humble and hearty thanks
for all your goodness and loving kindness
to us and to all people.
We bless you for our creation, preservation,
and all the blessings of this life;
but above all for your immeasurable love
in the redemption of the world
by our Lord Jesus Christ,
for the means of grace,
and for the hope of glory.
And give us, we pray,
such a sense of all your mercies
that our hearts may be unfeignedly thankful,
and that we show forth your praise,
not only with our lips but in our lives,
by giving up ourselves to your service,
and by walking before you
in holiness and righteousness all our days;
through Jesus Christ our Lord,
to whom, with you and the Holy Spirit,
be all honour and glory,
for ever and ever. Amen.

(ASB)

BAPTIST PRAISE
AND
WORSHIP

Music Edition

Published by Oxford University Press
on behalf of the Psalms and Hymns Trust

OXFORD
UNIVERSITY PRESS

Great Clarendon Street, Oxford OX2 6DP

Oxford University Press is a department of the University of Oxford.
It furthers the University's objective of excellence in research, scholarship,
and education by publishing worldwide in

Oxford New York

Athens Auckland Bangkok Bogotá Buenos Aires Calcutta
Cape Town Chennai Dar es Salaam Delhi Florence Hong Kong Istanbul
Karachi Kuala Lumpur Madrid Melbourne Mexico City Mumbai
Nairobi Paris São Paulo Singapore Taipei Tokyo Toronto Warsaw

with associated companies in Berlin Ibadan

Oxford is a registered trade mark of Oxford University Press
in the UK and in certain other countries

Not for Sale in the USA

ISBN 0-19-143931-2

First published 1991
Reprinted 1992 (twice), 1995, 1998

Printed in Great Britain on acid-free paper by
Richard Clay Ltd., Bungay, Suffolk

A Words Edition and a Large Print Words Edition are also available

CONTENTS

PREFACE

The production of hymn-books for use in Baptist churches goes back at least 200 years. *The Baptist Church Hymnal* appeared in 1900, *The Revised Baptist Church Hymnal* in 1933, and *The Baptist Hymn Book* (which the compilers claimed was 'a completely new book') in 1962. In each case the initiative was taken by the Psalms and Hymns Trust, whose object is to assist worship in Baptist churches in each generation by producing a hymn-book and then applying the profits from its sales to assist the widows and orphans of Baptist ministers and missionaries. Since almost another 30 years had elapsed, it was hardly surprising that a committee was appointed in 1984 to produce a hymn-book by the early 90s. At the same time two sub-committees were set up, one to handle the music and the other to prepare readings, prayers, and responses.

As soon as the Editorial Committee met, it was aware how very different the scene was from that which had confronted the compilers in the late 1950s. Experimental forms of worship and changed emphases in theology had taken place as early as the mid-60s. The ecumenical and charismatic movements had challenged many of the more rigid traditions of worship, and there had been an explosion of hymn writing. All the influences which had led to a proliferation of Bible translations and the modernization of language in worship over a quarter of a century had resulted in a similar proliferation of hymn-books, with many hymns in the modern idiom. In 1962 many churches would have refused to use more than one book; in 1985 many were refusing to be restricted to one. These factors together meant that any new book would have to face stiff competition, and there were those who were quick to ask why, with so many hymn-books on the market, yet another was needed.

After careful consideration, the Trustees took the view that to fulfil their objective of assisting worship in Baptist churches it was necessary to proceed. There were two reasons for this. One was that the 'explosion' could not continue for ever; it was thought that before long churches would be looking for a book that was balanced, with hymns that were solid and enduring, which gave adequate expression to the gospel, and at the same time reflected the breadth of traditions within our Baptist heritage. The other reason was that in the view of the Trustees there was no other hymn-book already in existence which did so. Furthermore, the Trustees recognized the danger of churches using only those books which reflected their own particular convictions, and so depriving themselves of being stretched and challenged.

It was against this background that the Editorial Committee set to work. Their first step was to select the best of the old. A survey showed that less than half the hymns in *The Baptist Hymn Book* were in regular use, and in the event this is about the proportion which has been retained. In general, the Committee has kept the great classical hymns of the Church which have proved their worth and which people still enjoy singing. Selecting the new hymns proved more difficult at a time when the explosion in hymnody was at its height: it was not easy to determine how much would stand the test of time, but this is what they have tried to do.

It was then necessary to marry the old with the new, so as to avoid the impression that one half was from the eighteenth century and the other half from the twentieth. Inevitably this meant changes in language. To mention only two of the problems, most of the older hymns use 'thou' rather than 'you', and many of them are dominated by masculine concepts. The Committee rejected the idea of a slavish uniformity, but has modified language wherever possible and appropriate. In some of the well-known traditional hymns, where hymns are essentially poetry or where any changes in language would be so extensive as to make a hymn barely recognizable, it has concluded that most worshippers would prefer to continue with the familiar.

In general, *Baptist Praise and Worship* continues the traditions of earlier books. Naturally, expression has been given to those emphases which are distinctively Baptist (though not sectarian), but at the same time the selection includes hymns and tunes from a wide variety of Christian traditions and from many nations. The 1962 Committee dispersed children's hymns throughout the book, though retaining a section of Hymns for Younger Children; this Committee has gone further in that there is no children's section at all. In every major section, however, at least one or two hymns are there because in addition to their relevance and meaning for young people they are also capable of being sung by people of all ages. These are listed in the Index of Hymns for Family Worship.

Each Baptist hymn-book has sought to respond to and reflect changes in Baptist Church life, and *Baptist Praise and Worship* is no exception. In the last thirty years many Baptists have paid more attention to the Christian Year, and this change is reflected in the different arrangement of the hymns. During the same period many Baptists have moved further towards informality and spontaneity in their worship, and the inclusion of popular songs and choruses is also intended to help them. If the mixture of both emphases in one book helps each group of worshippers to explore what is best in the other, the Committee will be satisfied. Because many hymns can be used in different situations the custom of cross-referencing the sections has also been continued, though these can now be found in the separate Index of Sectional Cross-References.

The Music Advisory Committee has tried to include all those tunes which Baptists would expect to have available, whilst selectively introducing new ones. It has tried to recognize the varied musical tastes within our Baptist family. Practical consideration has been given to the vocal range of the average congregation and the musical aptitudes of most accompanists, and choirs and professional musicians will be able to find their own ways of enriching what is offered. Likewise, guitar chords (which are usually designed to match the harmonies of the keyboard accompaniment) can be simplified or adapted at will.

The Baptist Hymn Book broke new ground for Baptists by its inclusion of responsive readings for ministers and congregations. This has enriched worship for so many people that there was no doubt that it should be continued. But for *Baptist Praise and Worship* it was thought better to disperse this material throughout the book at the end of each appropriate section, rather than placing it all together at the very end. Chants are not widely used today, though the reading of psalms is frequent: hence the inclusion of some 60 psalms for responsive reading.

Previous Baptist hymn-books have always been published directly by the Psalms and Hymns Trust. But here too changes have taken place, and the Trustees are pleased to be able to publish *Baptist Praise and Worship* with the full co-operation of the Oxford University Press, to whom the Trustees record their thanks for the benefit of their professional experience and for many further services during the compilation. There is, however, no intention of changing the arrangement whereby the returns from the sale of the book will be applied by the Trust to denominational purposes, the major part being for the benefit of the widows and orphans of Baptist ministers and missionaries.

INTRODUCTORY NOTE

Prayers and responsive readings are to be found at the end of individual sections of the book as appropriate, and their item numbers are listed on the title pages for each of the first four main parts of the book.

Hymns can generally be sung in either unison or harmony, unless '*Unison*' is specified.

Small notes are for organ only, unless otherwise specified.

Guitar chords are generally (though not always) intended to be used alongside the harmonies of the keyboard accompaniments, and they can be simplified or adapted at will.

Refrains are printed in *italic*.

adpt. = adapted by

altd. = altered (see introduction to Copyright Acknowledgements)

arr. = arranged by

attrib. = attributed to

cent. = century

harm. = harmonized by

para. = paraphrased by

tr. = translated by

v(v). = verse(s)

COPYRIGHT ACKNOWLEDGEMENTS

Prayers and responsive readings

In the acknowledgements that follow, italic letters indicate specific paragraphs or sections of the item listed. Texts from the following sources are acknowledged:

BIBLICAL TEXTS, INCLUDING PSALMS

Authorized King James Version of the Holy Bible (all rights vested in the Crown in the United Kingdom and controlled by Royal Letters Patent): 26, 240*c*, 264*c*, 458*b*

Good News Bible (published by the Bible Societies/Collins, © New Testament: American Bible Society New York, 1966, 1971 and 4th edn. 1976, reproduced by permission of the publishers): 79, 91, 92, 154*a*, 154*c*, 193, 212, 213, 237, 267, 304, 305, 399, 417, 492, 493, 503, 646, 647, 656, 660, 663, 664, 665, 666, 667, 669, 670, 671, 674, 675, 677, 679, 680, 681, 682, 683, 685, 686, 687, 699, 701, 702, 703

New English Bible (2nd edn. © 1970, by permission of Oxford and Cambridge University Presses): 24*a*, 27*a*, 80, 82, 150, 151, 154*e*(*i*), 183, 187, 214, 418, 459, 468, 501, 502, 518, 519, 688

New International Version (© 1973, 1978, 1984 by International Bible Society, used with permission): 77, 136, 184, 185, 364, 365, 366, 495, 645, 653, 658, 662, 668, 672, 673, 676, 678, 684, 689, 691, 693, 695, 696, 698, 700, 704, 705, 706, 707, 708, 709, 710, 711

Revised Standard Version (© 1946, 1952, 1971 by the Division of Christian Education of the National Council of Churches of Christ in the USA, used by permission): 235, 240*b*, 240*d*, 263, 264*b*, 264*d*, 277 (adpt.), 458*a*, 458*c*

The Psalms: A New Translation for Worship (Collins, © 1976, 1977 David L. Frost, John A. Emerton, Andrew A. Macintosh): 25, 93, 654, 659

The following psalm texts © The Grail, used by permission of A. P. Watt Ltd.: 655, 657, 661, 690, 692, 694, 697

OTHER TEXTS

Alternative Service Book (© Central Board of Finance of the Church of England and reproduced by permission): 152, 153, 461 (adpt. from *BCP*); 423, 466, The Lord's Prayer, A General Confession, A General Thanksgiving, Sursum Corda

Book of Common Prayer, 1662 (all rights vested in the Crown in the United Kingdom and controlled by Royal Letters Patent): 278 (adpt.) (as in the *Daily Office Revised*, SPCK), 424, The Lord's Prayer

Church Missionary Society (Reproduced by permission of Hodder & Stoughton from *New Parish Prayers*, © 1982 ed. Frank Colquhoun): 494

1. THE CALL TO WORSHIP

1

ANGEL VOICES   85 85 843

E. G. MONK (1819–1900)

ANGEL voices ever singing
round thy throne of light,
angel-harps for ever ringing,
rest not day nor night;
thousands only live to bless thee
and confess thee
Lord of might.

2 Thou, who art beyond the farthest
mortal eye can scan,
can it be that thou regardest
songs of sinful man?
Can we know that thou art near us
and wilt hear us?
Yes, we can.

3 Yes, we know that thou rejoicest
o'er each work of thine;
thou didst ears and hands and voices
for thy praise design;
craftsman's art and music's measure
for thy pleasure
all combine.

4 In this house, great God, we offer
of thine own to thee;
and for thine acceptance proffer,
all unworthily,
hearts and minds and hands and voices
in our choicest
psalmody.

5 Honour, glory, might and merit,
thine shall ever be:
Father, Son and Holy Spirit,
Blessed Trinity:
Of the best that thou hast given,
earth and heaven
render thee.

FRANCIS POTT (1832–1909)

2

OLD 100th   LM

Genevan Psalter, 1551

ALL people that on earth do dwell,
   sing to the Lord with cheerful voice;
serve him with joy, his praises tell;
   come now before him and rejoice.

2 Know that the Lord is God indeed;
   without our aid he did us make;
we are his folk, he will us feed,
   and for his sheep he does us take.

3 O enter then his gates with praise,
   approach with joy his courts unto;
praise him and bless his name always,
   for it is seemly so to do.

4 Because the Lord our God is good;
   his mercy is for ever sure;
his truth at all times firmly stood,
   and shall from age to age endure.

WILLIAM KETHE (*c.*1550–1600)
based on Psalm 100

3

AS WE ARE GATHERED   99 99 99

Words and music by
JOHN DANIELS

4

AT YOUR FEET   10 11 10 11 with refrain   DAVE FELLINGHAM

AT your feet we fall, mighty risen Lord,
as we come before your throne to worship you.
By your Spirit's power you now draw our hearts,
and we hear your voice in triumph ringing clear.

I am he that liveth, that liveth and was dead,
behold I am alive for evermore.

2 There we see you stand, mighty risen Lord,
clothed in garments pure and holy shining bright,
eyes of flashing fire, feet like burnished bronze,
and the sound of many waters is your voice.

3 Like the shining sun in its noonday strength,
we now see the glory of your wondrous face.
Once that face was marred, but now you're glorified,
and your words like a two-edged sword have mighty power.

DAVE FELLINGHAM

5

DAVID EVANS
arr. GEOFF BAKER

BE STILL   96 66 66 96

Be still,
for the presence of the Lord,
  the holy one, is here;
come bow before him now
  with reverence and fear:
    in him no sin is found—
    we stand on holy ground.
Be still,
for the presence of the Lord,
  the holy one, is here.

2 Be still,
for the glory of the Lord
  is shining all around;
he burns with holy fire,
  with splendour he is crowned:
    how awesome is the sight—
    our radiant King of light!
Be still,
for the glory of the Lord
  is shining all around.

3 Be still,
for the power of the Lord
  is moving in this place:
he comes to cleanse and heal,
  to minister his grace—
    no work too hard for him,
    in faith receive from him.
Be still,
for the power of the Lord
  is moving in this place.

DAVID EVANS

6

FIRST TUNE

NATIVITY CM

H. LAHEE (1826–1912)

SECOND TUNE

LYNGHAM CM

T. JARMAN (1782–1862)

COME let us join our cheerful songs
    with angels round the throne;
ten thousand thousand are their tongues,
    but all their joys are one.

2 'Worthy the Lamb that died!' they cry,
    'to be exalted thus;'
'Worthy the Lamb!' our lips reply,
    'for he was slain for us.'

3 Jesus is worthy to receive
    honour and power divine;
and blessings more than we can give
    be, Lord, for ever thine.

4 Let all that dwell above the sky,
    and air, and earth, and seas,
combine to lift thy glories high,
    and speak thine endless praise.

5 The whole creation joins in one,
    to bless the sacred name
of him who sits upon the throne,
    and to adore the Lamb.

ISAAC WATTS (1674–1748)

7

GRÖNINGEN   668 668 33 66   J. NEANDER (1650–80)

GOD is in his temple,
the almighty Father,
  round his footstool let us gather:
him with adoration
serve, the Lord most holy,
  who has mercy on the lowly:
    let us raise
    hymns of praise,
for his great salvation:
  God is in his temple.

2 Christ comes to his temple:
we, his word receiving,
  are made happy in believing.
For, from sin delivered,
he has turned our sadness,
  our deep gloom, to light and gladness!
    Let us raise
    hymns of praise,
for our bonds are severed:
  Christ comes to his temple!

3 Come and claim your temple,
gracious Holy Spirit.
  In our hearts your home inherit:
make in us your dwelling,
your high work fulfilling,
  into ours your will instilling,
    till we raise
    hymns of praise,
beyond mortal telling,
  in the eternal temple.

W. T. MATSON (1833–99)

8

LAUS DEO   87 87   RICHARD REDHEAD (1820–1901)

AT your feet, our God and Father,
who has blessed us all our days,
we, with grateful hearts, now gather,
to begin the *day** with praise:

2 Praise for light so brightly shining
on our steps from heaven above,
praise for mercies daily twining
round us golden cords of love.

3 Jesus, for your love most tender,
on the cross for sinners shown,
we would praise you, and surrender
all our hearts to be your own.

4 With so blest a friend provided,
we upon our way can go,
sure of being safely guided,
guarded well from every foe.

5 Every day will be the brighter
as your gracious face we view;
every burden will be lighter
if we bear it, Lord, with you.

6 Spread your love's bright banner o'er us;
give us strength to serve and wait,
till the glory breaks before us,
through the city's open gate.

JAMES DRUMMOND BURNS (1823–64)

*substitute *year, month, (etc.)*, as required.

14

9

TRURO   LM

Psalmodia Evangelica, 1789

GOD of the morning, at whose voice
  the cheerful sun makes haste to rise,
and like a giant does rejoice
  to run his journey through the skies!

2 So like the sun, may I fulfil
  the appointed duties of the day,
with ready mind and active will
  march on, and keep my heavenly way.

3 But I shall rove and lose the race
  if God, my sun, should disappear,
and leave me in this world's wide maze
  to follow every wandering star.

4 Lord! your commands are clean and pure,
  enlightening our beclouded eyes;
your threatenings just, your promise sure;
  your gospel makes the simple wise.

5 Give me your counsel for my guide;
  and then receive me to your bliss:
all my desires and hopes beside
  are faint and cold compared with this.

ISAAC WATTS (1674–1748)
based on Psalms 19: 4, 8; 73: 24

10

ASCALON   668 D

Silesian folk melody

For this tune in F major see no. 334.

How pleased and blest was I
to hear the people cry,
'Come, let us seek our God today!'
Yes, with a cheerful zeal
we haste to Zion's hill,
and there our vows and honours pay.

2　Zion, thrice happy place,
adorned with wondrous grace,
and walls of strength embrace you round;
there all the tribes appear,
to pray and praise and hear
the sacred gospel's joyful sound.

3　There David's greater Son
has fixed his royal throne,
he sits for grace and judgement there:
he bids the saints be glad,
he makes the sinner sad,
and humble souls rejoice with fear.

4　May peace attend your gates,
and joy within them wait,
to bless the soul of every guest;
all who come seeking peace,
and wishing God's increase,
a thousand blessings on them rest!

5　My tongue repeats her vows,
peace to this sacred house!
For here my friends and kindred dwell;
and, since my glorious God
makes here his blest abode,
my soul shall ever love you well.

ISAAC WATTS (1674–1748)
based on Psalm 122

11

I WILL ENTER HIS GATES Irregular

Words and music by
LEONA VON BRETHORST

I will en-ter his gates with thanks-giv-ing in my heart, I will en - ter his courts with praise, I will say this is the day that the Lord has__ made, I will re - joice for he has made me glad.

12

JESUS CALLS US   87 87 D

Gaelic melody
adpt. and arr. JOHN BELL (b. 1949)
and GRAHAM MAULE (b. 1958)

JESUS calls us here to meet him
    as, through word and song and prayer,
we affirm God's promised presence
    where his people live and care.
Praise the God who keeps his promise;
    praise the Son who calls us friends;
praise the Spirit who, among us,
    to our hopes and fears attends.

2 Jesus calls us to confess him
    Word of life and Lord of all,
sharer of our flesh and frailness
    saving all who fail or fall.
Tell his holy human story;
    tell his tales that all may hear;
tell the world that Christ in glory
    came to earth to meet us here.

3 Jesus calls us to each other:
    found in him are no divides.
Race and class and sex and language:
    such are barriers he derides.
Join the hands of friend and stranger;
    join the hands of age and youth;
join the faithful and the doubter
    in their common search for truth.

4 Jesus calls us to his table
    rooted firm in time and space,
where the Church in earth and heaven
    finds a common meeting place.
Share the bread and wine, his body;
    share the love of which we sing;
share the feast for saints and sinners
    hosted by our Lord and King.

Iona Community

13

JUBILATE DEO

MICHAEL PRAETORIUS (1571–1621)
as sung at Taizé

Ju - bi - la - te De-o, ju-bi-la - te De - o, al - le-lu - ia.

This is a six–part round, the voices entering as indicated.

14

JUBILATE DEO

FRED DUNN

Ju - bi - la - te, ev - 'ry - bo - dy,

serve the Lord_ in___ all your ways, and

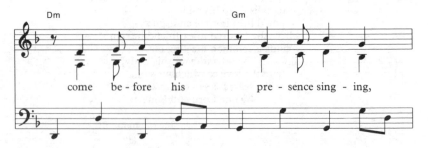

come be - fore his pre - sence sing - ing,

15

SING HOSANNA   10 8 10 9 with refrain

Traditional melody
arr. GERALD L. BARNES (b. 1935)

Praise   our   ma - ker,   praise   our   Sa - viour,

praise the Lord our e-ver-last-ing king! Ev - ery throne must

bow be-fore him, God is Lord of ev-ery-thing!

LET us sing to the God of salvation,
let us sing to the Lord our rock!
let us come to his house with thanksgiving,
let us come before the Lord and sing!

Praise our maker,
praise our Saviour,
praise the Lord our everlasting king!
Every throne must bow before him,
God is Lord of everything!

2 In his hand are the earth's deepest places
and the strength of the hills is his!
All the sea is the Lord's, for he made it,
by his hands the solid rock was formed:

3 Let us worship the Lord our maker,
let us kneel to the Lord our God;
for we all are the sheep of his pasture,
he will guide us by his powerful hand:

4 Let today be the time when you hear him!
May our hearts not be hard or cold,
lest we stray from the Lord in rebellion,
as his people did in time of old:

RICHARD BEWES (b. 1934)
based on Psalm 95

16

OLDOWN   84 84 84   BASIL HARWOOD (1859–1949)

SECOND TUNE

WENTWORTH   84 84 84   F. C. MAKER (1844–1927)

LORD Christ whose love has brought us here,
  our Saviour King,
within these walls, so dear to us,
  your praise shall ring.
Today, with joy and peace and hope,
  your people sing.

2 With joy we meet the friends we love,
    before your throne,
  our voices raised with one accord
    your name to own;
  whilst those we miss are still your care,
    nor are alone.

3 The peace which lifts us near to you
    is ours today;
  the sacred calm of trustful faith
    drives care away;
  that you will free from every fear,
    your servants pray.

4 With hope we face the paths untrod
    which none can view;
  for you will guide our stumbling feet,
    be near us too;
  may each year's service find us still
    nearer to you.

H. WHEELER ROBINSON (1872–1945) altd.

17

MARYTON   LM

H. P. SMITH (1825–98)

O LORD, how lovely is the sight:
   how beautiful your courts appear!
My soul is fainting with delight:
   the living God is present here.

2 The swallow and the brooding dove
   have settled in these eaves to nest:
about the altars which I love
   they also find a place of rest.

3 How blest are those who linger here
   to sing your praises day by day!
How blest are those who persevere
   along the stony pilgrim way!

4 For them the dry ravine will flow,
   and autumn rains refresh the wells:
from height to height the pilgrims go
   towards the mountain where God dwells.

5 No wonder that they laugh and sing!
   Lord, turn and listen to my prayer:
look down on your anointed king,
   and keep us in your watchful care.

6 O better spend a single day
   with glimpses of your courts within,
than laze luxurious years away
   where silken curtains cover sin.

7 Lord God, our rampart and our shield,
   you prosper all your servants do;
your grace and glory are revealed
   to those who put their trust in you.

M. HODGETTS (b. 1936)
based on Psalm 84

18

ST MATTHEW   DCM

Probably later form of melody
by WILLIAM CROFT (1678–1727)

O SEND your light forth and your truth;
    let them be guides to me,
and bring me to your holy hill,
    even where your dwellings be.
Then will I to God's altar go,
    to God my chiefest joy:
yes, God, my God, your name to praise
    my harp I will employ.

2 Why are you then cast down, my soul?
    why so discouraged be?
and why with vexing thoughts are you
    disquieted in me?
Still trust in God; for him to praise
    good cause I yet shall have:
he of my countenance is the health,
    my God who will me save.

FRANCIS ROUS (1579–1659)
WILLIAM BARTON (1597–1678)
based on Psalm 43: 3–5

19

LAUDATE OMNES GENTES   76 76

JACQUES BERTHIER
as sung at Taizé

Lau - da - te om - nes gen - tes, lau -

-da - te Do - mi - num! Lau - da - te om - nes

gen - tes, lau - da - te Do - mi - num!

(All peoples praise the Lord)

20

THE KING IS AMONG US   65 65

GRAHAM KENDRICK (b. 1950)
arr. S. CARROLL (b. 1949)

THE King is among us,
  his Spirit is here!
Let's draw near and worship,
  let songs fill the air.

2 He looks down upon us,
    delight in his face,
  enjoying his children's love,
    enthralled by our praise.

3 For each child is special,
    accepted and loved;
  a love gift from Jesus
    to his Father above.

4 And now he is giving
    his gifts to us all;
  for no one is worthless,
    and each one is called.

5 The Spirit's anointing
    on all flesh comes down,
  and we shall be channels
    for works like his own.

6 We come now believing
    your promise of power,
  for we are your people
    and this is your hour.

GRAHAM KENDRICK (b. 1950)

21

THIS IS THE DAY   Irregular

LES GARRETT (b. 1944)

THIS is the day,
   this is the day that the Lord has made,
   that the Lord has made.
We will rejoice,
   we will rejoice and be glad in it,
   and be glad in it.
This is the day that the Lord has made,
   we will rejoice and be glad in it.
This is the day,
   this is the day that the Lord has made.

2 This is the day . . . when he rose again.
   We will rejoice . . . and be glad in it.

3 This is the day . . . when the Spirit came.
   We will rejoice . . . and be glad in it.

LES GARRETT (b. 1944)
based on Psalm 118: 24

22

SANCTISSIMUS   12 10 12 10   W. H. COOKE (1820–1912)

SECOND TUNE

WAS LEBET   12 10 12 10   *Reinhardt MS*, Üttingen 1754

WORSHIP the Lord in the beauty of holiness,
bow down before him, his glory proclaim;
gold of obedience and incense of lowliness
bring, and adore him; the Lord is his name!

2 Low at his feet lay your burden of carefulness,
high on his heart he will bear it for you,
comfort your sorrows, and answer your prayerfulness,
guiding your steps in the best way for you.

3 Fear not to enter his courts in the slenderness
of the poor wealth you would reckon to own;
truth in its beauty, and love in its tenderness,
these are the offerings to bring to his throne.

4 These, though we bring them in trembling and fearfulness,
he will accept for the name that is dear;
mornings of joy give for evenings of tearfulness,
trust for our trembling, and hope for our fear.

5 Worship the Lord in the beauty of holiness,
bow down before him, his glory proclaim;
gold of obedience and incense of lowliness
bring, and adore him; the Lord is his name!

J. S. B. MONSELL (1811–75)

23

DARWALL   66 66 44 44   J. DARWALL (1731–89)

You holy angels bright,
　who wait at God's right hand,
or through the realms of light
　fly at your Lord's command,
　　assist our song,
　　　for else the theme
　　　too high does seem
　　　for mortal tongue.

2 You blessed souls at rest,
　who ran this earthly race,
and now, from sin released,
　behold the Saviour's face,
　　God's praises sound,
　　　as in his light
　　　with sweet delight
　　　you do abound.

3 You saints, who toil below,
　adore your heavenly King,
and onward as you go
　some joyful anthem sing;
　　take what he gives
　　　and praise him still,
　　　through good or ill,
　　　who ever lives!

4 My soul, bear now your part,
　triumph in God above:
and with a well-tuned heart
　sing out the songs of love!
　　Let all your days
　　　till life shall end,
　　　whate'er he send,
　　　be filled with praise.

RICHARD BAXTER (1615–91) altd.
v. 3 by J. H. GURNEY (1802–62)

24

Truly, my heart waits silently for God.

> **Father, it takes time for us to get to know one another:**
> **there has to be waiting.**
> **We wait on you now in silence**
> **so that your presence and love may be made known to us.**
> **In the name of Jesus. Amen.**

25

In your presence is the fullness of joy.

> **Lord God, we thank you that you are always with us**
> **to enrich our lives;**
> **not to take away from our human enjoyment of being with**
> **others at a time like this,**
> **but to add an eternal dimension to it.**
> **Give to us now, we pray, the fullness of your joy.**
> **In the name of Jesus. Amen.**

26

Come to me, all who labour and are heavy-laden,
and I will give you rest.

> **Father, into your hands,**
> **into your generous forgiveness and peace,**
> **we place ourselves.**
> **In the name of Jesus. Amen.**

27

Lord, to whom shall we go?
Your words are words of eternal life.

> **Lord God, we come here in all kinds of moods**
> **and from a variety of situations.**
> **You know what these are**
> **and what each of us needs to hear at this time.**
> **Make us ready for the word that will bring us life.**
> **In the name of Jesus. Amen.**

28

LASST UNS ERFREUEN
88 44 88 with refrain

Melody from
Geistliche Kirchengesäng, Cologne, 1623
arr. R. VAUGHAN WILLIAMS (1872–1958)

REFRAIN

Now— praise him, now— praise him, al - le -

-lu - ia, al-le - lu - ia, al-le - lu - ia!

ALL creatures of our God and King,
lift up your voice and with us sing,
  alleluia, alleluia!
O burning sun with golden beam,
and silver moon with softer gleam,

Now praise him, now praise him,
alleluia, alleluia, alleluia!

2 O rushing wind that is so strong,
and clouds that sail in heaven
  along,
  now praise him, alleluia!
O rising morn, in praise rejoice,
and lights of evening, find a voice,

3 O flowing water, pure and clear,
make music for your Lord to hear,
  alleluia, alleluia!
O fire so masterful and bright,
giving to all both warmth and light,

4 Dear mother earth, who day by day
unfolds rich blessings on our way,
  now praise him, alleluia!
The flowers and fruits that
  bloom and grow
let them his glory also show,

5 People and nations take your part,
love and forgive with all your heart;
  sing praise now, alleluia!
All who long pain and sorrow bear,
praise God and on him cast your care,

6 And now, most kind and gentle death,
waiting to hush our fading breath,
  now praise him, alleluia!
And leading home the child of God,
along the way our Lord has trod,

7 Let all things their creator bless,
and worship him in humbleness,
  now praise him, alleluia!
Praise, praise the Father, praise the Son,
and praise the Spirit, three in one,

W. H. DRAPER (1855–1933)
based on ST FRANCIS OF ASSISI (1182–1226)
altd.

41

29

First Tune

DIADEM 86 86 extended | J. ELLOR (1819–99)

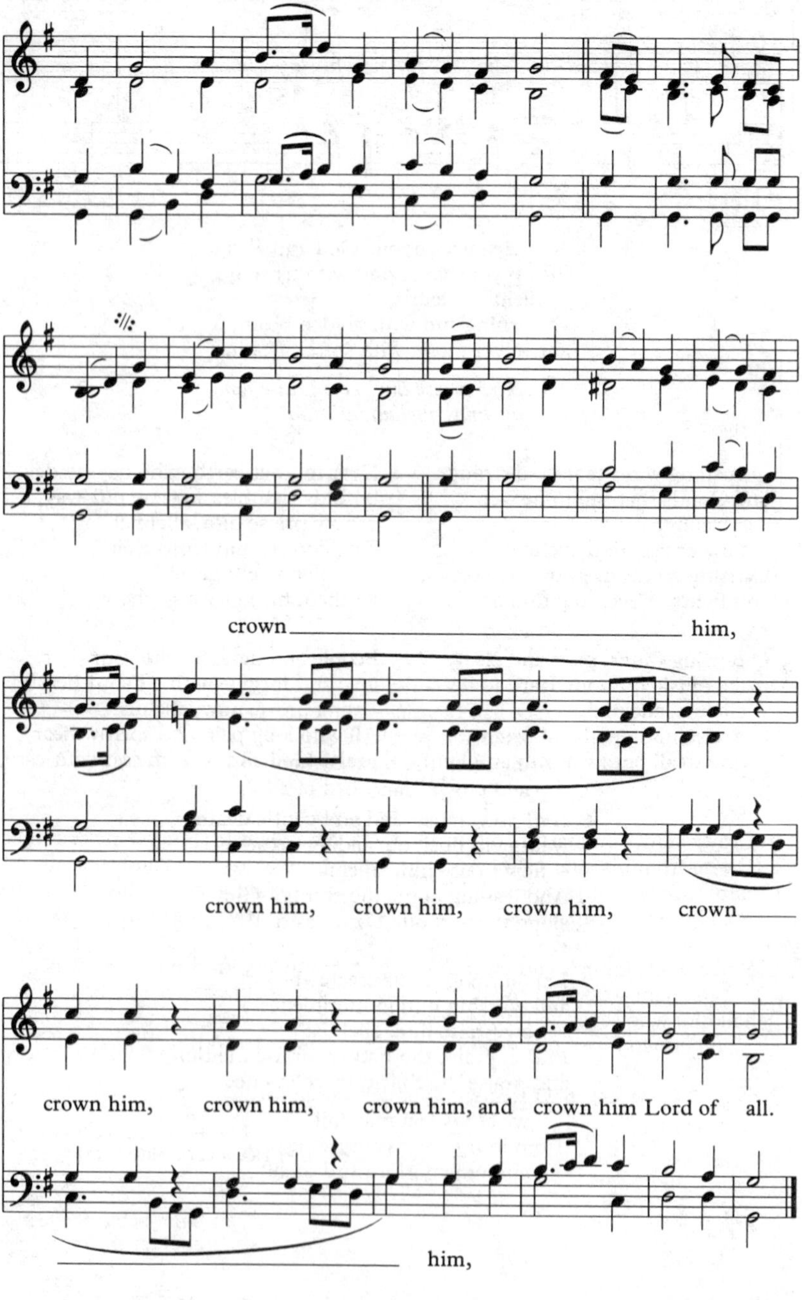
crown him,
crown him, crown him, crown him, crown
crown him, crown him, crown him, and crown him Lord of all.
him,

SECOND TUNE

MILES LANE   86 86 extended

Later form of melody by
W. SHRUBSOLE (*c.*1759–1806)

May also be sung to LADYWELL, no. 276 (*ii*).

ALL hail the power of Jesus' name;
let angels prostrate fall;
bring forth the royal diadem,
and crown him Lord of all.

2 Crown him, you martyrs of our God,
who from his altar call;
extol the stem of Jesse's rod,
and crown him Lord of all.

3 You seed of Israel's chosen race,
a remnant weak and small,
hail him who saves you by his grace,
and crown him Lord of all.

4 You Gentile sinners, ne'er forget
the wormwood and the gall;
go, spread your trophies at his feet,
and crown him Lord of all.

5 Let every kindred, every tribe,
on this terrestrial ball,
to him all majesty ascribe,
and crown him Lord of all.

6 O that with yonder sacred throng
we at his feet may fall,
join in the everlasting song,
and crown him Lord of all!

EDWARD PERRONET (1726–92)
JOHN RIPPON (1751–1836)

30

JERUSALEM   DLM

C. H. H. PARRY (1848–1918)

1. Bring to the Lord   a glad new song,   child-ren of

grace ex-tol your   king;   your love and praise   to God be -

calls let prai-ses fit for God be given: with strings and brass and wind re-joice— then, join our song in full ac- cord all li-ving things with breath and voice: let ev-ery

allargando

rit.

cre_ture praise the Lord!

BRING to the Lord a glad new song,
   children of grace extol your king;
your love and praise to God belong—
   to instruments of music, sing!
Let those be warned who spurn God's name,
   let rulers all obey God's word;
for justice shall bring tyrants shame:
   let every creature praise the Lord!

2 Sing praise within these hallowed walls,
   worship beneath the dome of heaven;
by cymbals' sounds and trumpets' calls
   let praises fit for God be given:
with strings and brass and wind rejoice—
   then, join our song in full accord
all living things with breath and voice:
   let every creature praise the Lord!

MICHAEL PERRY (b. 1942)
based on Psalms 149 and 150

31

Words and music by DON FISHEL (b. 1928)
arr. BETTY PULKINGHAM (b. 1928)

ALLELUIA   88 with refrain

32

BLESS THE LORD

JACQUES BERTHIER, as sung at Taizé
Words based on Psalm 103

Bless the Lord, my soul, and bless his ho - ly name.

Bless the Lord, my soul; he res-cues me from death.

33

BLESS THE LORD, O MY SOUL

Music anon.
arr. MARGARET EVANS
Words based on Psalm 103

Unison

Bless the Lord, O my soul, bless the

Lord, O my soul, and all that is with -

PRAISE

*To be sung by a second group, divided into altos, tenors, and basses if preferred.

34

TRAVELLERS' REST   10 11 11 6   RICHARD LLOYD (b. 1933)

HARMONY VERSION

The original key of D♭ major may be preferred.

SECOND TUNE

CHRISTE SANCTORUM   10 11 11 6

Paris Antiphoner, 1681
harm. DAVID EVANS (1874–1948)

CHRIST is the world's light, he and none other;
born in our darkness, he became our brother.
If we have seen him, we have seen the Father:
   Glory to God on high.

2 Christ is the world's peace, he and none other:
no man can serve him and despise his brother.
Who else unites us, one in God the Father?

3 Christ is the world's life, he and none other:
sold once for silver, murdered here, our brother—
he who redeems us, reigns with God the Father:

4 Give God the glory, God and none other:
give God the glory, Spirit, Son and Father:
give God the glory, God in man my brother:

F. PRATT GREEN (b. 1903)

53

35

ST ANDREW 87 87   E. H. THORNE (1834–1916)

SECOND TUNE

COME REJOICE 87 87   NOËL TREDINNICK (b. 1949)

COME, rejoice before your maker
  all you peoples of the earth;
serve the Lord your God with gladness,
  come before him with a song!

2 Know for certain that Jehovah
  is the true and only God:
we are his, for he has made us;
  we are sheep within his fold.

3 Come with grateful hearts before him,
  enter now his courts with praise;
show your thankfulness towards him,
  give due honour to his name.

4 For the Lord our God is gracious—
  everlasting in his love;
and to every generation
  his great faithfulness endures.

MICHAEL BAUGHEN (b. 1930)
based on Psalm 100

36

FIRST TUNE

SPEAN   11 10 11 10

J. F. BRIDGE (1844–1924)

SECOND TUNE

EPIPHANY HYMN   11 10 11 10

J. F. THRUPP (1827–67)

For this tune in D major see no. 190.

COME, worship God who is worthy of honour,
    enter his presence with thanks and a song!
He is the rock of his people's salvation,
    to whom our jubilant praises belong.

2 Ruled by his might are the heights of the mountains,
    held in his hands are the depths of the earth;
his is the sea, his the land, for he made them,
    king above all gods, who gave us our birth.

3 We are his people, the sheep of his pasture,
    he is our maker and to him we pray;
gladly we kneel in obedience before him—
    great is the God whom we worship this day!

4 Now let us listen, for God speaks among us,
    open our hearts and receive what he says:
peace be to all who remember his goodness,
    trust in his word and rejoice in his ways!

MICHAEL PERRY (b. 1942)
based on Psalm 95

37

DIADEMATA   DSM

G. J. ELVEY (1816–93)

CROWN him with many crowns,
    the Lamb upon his throne;
hark! how the heavenly anthem drowns
    all music but its own:
      awake my soul and sing
        of him who died for me,
      and hail him as your chosen King
        through all eternity.

2 Crown him the Son of God
    before the worlds began;
and you who tread where he has trod,
    crown him the Son of Man,
      who every grief has known
        that wrings the human breast,
      and takes and bears them
        for his own,
    that all in him may rest.

3 Crown him the Lord of life,
    triumphant from the grave,
who rose victorious in the strife,
    for those he came to save:
      his glories now we sing,
        who died and rose on high,
      who died eternal life to bring,
        and lives that death may die.

4 Crown him the Lord of love,
    who shows his hands and side—
those wounds yet visible above
    in beauty glorified.
      No angel in the sky
        can fully bear that sight,
      but downward bends his burning eye
        at mysteries so bright.

5 Crown him the Lord of peace—
    his kingdom is at hand;
from pole to pole let warfare cease
    and Christ rule every land!
      A city stands on high,
        his glory it displays,
      and there the nations 'Holy' cry
        in joyful hymns of praise.

6 Crown him the Lord of heaven,
    enthroned in worlds above;
crown him the King to whom is given
    the wondrous name of Love:
      all hail, Redeemer, hail!
        for you have died for me:
      your praise shall never, never fail
        throughout eternity.

MATTHEW BRIDGES (1800–94)
GODFREY THRING (1823–1903) altd.

38

PHILIPPINES   55 55 55 54

ELENA C. MAQUISO
arr. DAVID TRAFFORD (b. 1950)

FATHER in heaven,
grant to your children
mercy and blessing,
songs never ceasing,
love to unite us,
grace to redeem us—
 Father in heaven,
 Father, our God.

2 Jesus Redeemer,
may we remember
your gracious passion,
your resurrection.
Worship we bring you,
praise we shall sing you—
 Jesus Redeemer,
 Jesus, our Lord.

3 Spirit descending,
whose is the blessing,
strength for the weary,
help for the needy,
sealed in our sonship
yours be our worship—
 Spirit descending,
 Spirit adored.

D. T. NILES (1908–70)

39

FATHER WE ADORE YOU

Unison

TERRYE COELHO (b. 1952)

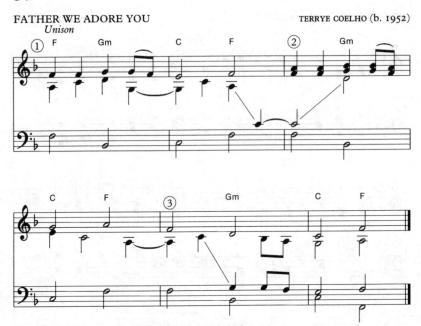

May also be sung as a three-part round,
the accompaniment *ad lib.* and the voices entering where indicated.

FATHER, we adore you,
lay our lives before you:
how we love you!

2 Jesus, we adore you,
lay our lives before you:
how we love you!

3 Spirit, we adore you,
lay our lives before you:
how we love you!

TERRYE COELHO (b. 1952)

40

FIRST TUNE

REGENT SQUARE   87 87 87

HENRY SMART (1813–79)

SECOND TUNE

LAUS ET HONOR   87 87 87

GORDON HARTLESS (b. 1913)

FILL your hearts with joy and gladness,
    sing and praise your God and mine!
Great the Lord in love and wisdom,
    might and majesty divine!
He who framed the starry heavens
    knows and names them as they shine.

2 Praise the Lord, his people, praise him!
    wounded souls his comfort know;
those who fear him find his mercies,
    peace for pain and joy for woe;
humble hearts are high exalted,
    human pride and power laid low.

3 Praise the Lord for times and seasons,
    cloud and sunshine, wind and rain;
spring to melt the snows of winter
    till the waters flow again;
grass upon the mountain pastures,
    golden valleys thick with grain.

4 Fill your hearts with joy and gladness,
    peace and plenty crown your days;
love his laws, declare his judgements,
    walk in all his words and ways;
he the Lord and we his children—
    praise the Lord, all people, praise!

TIMOTHY DUDLEY-SMITH (b. 1926)
based on Psalm 147

41

FATHER WE LOVE YOU

Words and music by
DONNA ADKINS

1. Fa - ther,
2. Je - sus, we love you, we wor - ship and a - dore you,
3. Spi - rit,

glo - ri - fy your name in all the earth.

Glo - ri - fy your name, *glo - ri - fy your name,*

glo - ri - fy your name in all the earth.

42

ST DENIO   11 11 11 11 Anapaestic

Welsh hymn melody, 1839
founded on a folk-tune

For beauty of meadows, for grandeur of trees,
for flowers of woodlands, for creatures of seas,
for all you created and trusted to man,
we praise you, Creator, extolling your plan.

2 As stewards of beauty received at your hand,
as creatures who hear your most urgent command,
we turn from our wasteful destruction of life,
confessing our failures, confessing our strife.

3 Teach us once again to be gardeners in peace;
all nature around us is ours but on lease;
your name we would hallow in all that we do,
fulfilling our calling, creating with you.

WALTER HENRY FARQUHARSON (b. 1936)

43

FROM THE RISING OF THE SUN

Words and music by PAUL DEMING
based on Psalm 113

From the ri-sing of the sun to the go-ing down of the same,___ the Lord's name is to be praised. From the ri-sing of the

Praise ye the Lord,

44

GLORIA

JACQUES BERTHIER
as sung at Taizé

May be sung as a four-part round, the voices entering where indicated.

45

THEODORIC (PERSONENT HODIE)
666 66 with refrain

Melody from *Piae Cantiones*, 1582
arr. GUSTAV HOLST (1874–1934)

Sing for joy, joy, joy! Sing for joy, joy, joy!

God is good! God is truth! God is beau-ty! Praise him!

GOD is love: his the care,
tending each, everywhere.
God is love—all is there!
Jesus came to show him,
that mankind might know him:

Sing for joy, joy, joy!
Sing for joy, joy, joy!
God is good! God is truth!
God is beauty! Praise him!

2 None can see God above;
neighbours here we can love;
thus may we Godward move
finding him in others,
sisters all, and brothers:

3 Jesus lived here for men,
strove and died, rose again,
rules our hearts, now as then;
for he came to save us
by the truth he gave us:

4 To our Lord praise we sing—
light and life, friend and king,
coming down love to bring,
pattern for our duty,
showing God in beauty:

PERCY DEARMER (1867–1936)
(refrain altd.)

69

46

GOD OF GODS   87 87 88 87

CHRISTIAN STROVER (b. 1932)

GOD of gods, we sound his praises,
 highest heaven its homage brings;
earth and all creation raises
 glory to the King of kings:
  holy, holy, holy, name him,
   Lord of all his hosts proclaim him;
  to the everlasting Father
every tongue in triumph sings.

2 Christians in their hearts enthrone him,
 tell his praises wide abroad;
prophets, priests, apostles own him
 martyrs' crown and saints' reward.
  Three in one his glory sharing,
   earth and heaven his praise declaring,
  praise the high majestic Father,
praise the everlasting Lord!

3 Hail the Christ, the King of glory,
 he whose praise the angels cry;
born to share our human story,
 love and labour, grieve and die:
  by his cross his work completed,
   sinners ransomed, death defeated;
  in the glory of the Father
Christ ascended reigns on high.

4 Lord, we look for your returning;
 teach us so to walk your ways,
hearts and minds your will discerning,
 lives alight with joy and praise:
  in your love and care enfold us,
   by your constancy uphold us;
  may your mercy, Lord and Father,
keep us now and all our days!

TIMOTHY DUDLEY-SMITH (b. 1926)
from Te Deum

47

RIMINGTON   LM

F. DUCKWORTH (1862–1941)

May also be sung to DUKE STREET, no. 313.

GIVE to our God immortal praise;
mercy and truth are all his ways:
wonders of grace to God belong,
repeat his mercies in your song.

2 Give to the Lord of lords renown;
the King of kings with glory crown:
his mercies ever shall endure,
when lords and kings are known no more.

3 He built the earth, he spread the sky,
and fixed the starry lights on high:
wonders of grace to God belong,
repeat his mercies in your song.

4 He fills the sun with morning light,
he bids the moon direct the night:
his mercies ever shall endure,
when suns and moons shall shine no more.

5 He sent his Son with power to save
from guilt and darkness and the grave:
wonders of grace to God belong,
repeat his mercies in your song.

ISAAC WATTS (1674–1748)
based on Psalm 136

48

HEATHLANDS   77 77 77   HENRY SMART (1813–79)

GOD of mercy, God of grace,
show the brightness of your face:
shine upon us, Saviour, shine;
fill your Church with light divine;
and your saving health extend
unto earth's remotest end.

2 Let the people praise you, Lord;
be by all that live adored;
let the nations shout and sing
glory to their Saviour King;
at your feet their tribute pay
and your holy will obey.

3 Let the people praise you, Lord;
earth shall then her fruits afford,
God to man his blessing give,
man to God devoted live;
all below, and all above,
one in joy and light and love.

H. F. LYTE (1793–1847)

49

RUSTINGTON   87 87 D

C. H. H. PARRY (1848–1918)

GOD, we praise you! God, we bless you!
  God, we name you sovereign Lord!
Mighty King whom angels worship
  Father, by your Church adored:
all creation shows your glory,
  heaven and earth draw near your throne
singing 'Holy, holy, holy,
  Lord of hosts, and God alone!'

2 True apostles, faithful prophets,
    saints who set their world ablaze,
  martyrs, once unknown, unheeded,
    join one growing song of praise,
  while your Church on earth confesses
    one majestic Trinity:
  Father, Son and Holy Spirit,
    God, our hope eternally.

3 Jesus Christ, the King of glory,
    everlasting Son of God,
  humble was your virgin mother,
    hard the lonely path you trod:
  by your cross is sin defeated,
    hell confronted face to face,
  heaven opened to believers,
    sinners justified by grace.

4 Christ, at God's right hand victorious,
    you will judge the world you made;
  Lord, in mercy help your servants
    for whose freedom you have paid:
  raise us up from dust to glory,
    guard us from all sin today;
  King enthroned above all praises,
    save your people, God, we pray.

CHRISTOPHER IDLE (b. 1938)
from Te Deum

50

QUEM PASTORES LAUDAVERE
888 7

14th-century German carol melody
arr. R. VAUGHAN WILLIAMS (1872–1958)

For this tune in F major (with guitar chords) see no. 192.

GOD the Father throned in splendour,
righteous, merciful and tender;
thankful songs your people render—
   sovereign Lord, we praise your name!

2 God the Son, in glory seated,
your redemptive act completed:
for your mercy we entreated,
   and you heard and loved and came.

3 God the Holy Spirit filling
every heart contrite and willing,
grace and holiness instilling,
   fruitful lives your constant aim.

4 Father, Son, and Holy Spirit,
source of riches we inherit:
glory, wisdom, truth and merit
   we ascribe to your great name!

BETTY STANLEY (b. 1921)

51

NICAEA   11 12 12 10   J. B. DYKES (1823–76)

HOLY, holy, holy, Lord God almighty,
    early in the morning our song shall rise to thee;
holy, holy, holy, merciful and mighty,
    God in three persons, blessed Trinity.

2 Holy, holy, holy! all the saints adore thee,
    casting down their golden crowns around the glassy sea;
cherubim and seraphim, falling down before thee,
    God ever living through eternity.

3 Holy, holy, holy! though the darkness hide thee,
    though the eye of sinful man thy glory may not see,
thou alone art holy, there is none beside thee,
    Perfect in power, in love, and purity.

4 Holy, holy, holy, Lord God almighty!
    All thy works shall praise thy name, in earth,
        and sky, and sea:
holy, holy, holy, merciful and mighty,
    God in three persons, blessed Trinity.

REGINALD HEBER (1783–1826)

52

JESUS, WE ENTHRONE YOU

Words and music by PAUL KYLE

Je - sus,_____ we en - throne_ you,_____

_ we pro - claim you our King,_____

stand-ing here_____ in the midst of us_____

_ we raise you up_ with our praise._____

And as we wor - ship, build_____ a throne;

and as we wor - ship, build_____ a throne;

and as we wor - ship, build_____ a throne; come, Lord

Je - sus, and take_____ your place._____

53

GWALCHMAI   74 74 D

J. D. JONES (1827–70)

KING of glory, King of peace,
    I will love you;
and that love may never cease,
    I will move you.
You have granted my request,
    you have heard me;
you have helped me when oppressed,
    you have spared me.

2 Therefore with my utmost art
    I will sing you;
deepest love within my heart
    I will bring you.
Though my sins against me cried,
    you did clear me;
and alone, when they replied,
    you did hear me.

3 Seven whole days, not one in seven,
    I will praise you;
in my heart, though not in heaven,
    I will raise you.
Small it is, in this poor sort
    to enrol you,
all eternity's too short
    to extol you.

GEORGE HERBERT (1593–1633)
altd. ANTHONY PETTI (1932–85)

54

LUCKINGTON   10 4 66 66 10 4   BASIL HARWOOD (1859–1949)

LET all the world in every corner sing,
    'My God and King!'
  The heavens are not too high;
  his praise may thither fly;
  the earth is not too low;
  his praises there may grow.
Let all the world in every corner sing,
    'My God and King!'

2 Let all the world in every corner sing,
    'My God and King!'
  The Church with psalms must shout,
  no door can keep them out:
  but, above all, the heart
  must bear the longest part.
Let all the world in every corner sing,
    'My God and King!'

GEORGE HERBERT (1593–1633)

55

JESUS, NAME ABOVE ALL NAMES

Words and music by NAIDA HEARN
arr. PATRICIA CAIN

Unison

Je - sus, name a-bove all names, beau-ti-ful Sa - viour, glo-ri-ous Lord;_____ Em - -man-u-el— God is with us, bless-ed Re- -deem - er, li - ving Word.

56

MONKLAND   77 77

JOHN ANTES (1740–1811)
arr. JOHN WILKES (d. 1882)

LET us gladly with one mind
praise the Lord, for he is kind:

for his mercy shall endure,
ever faithful, ever sure.

2 He has made the realms of space,
all things have their ordered place:

3 He created sky and sea,
field and mountain, flower and tree:

4 Every creature, great and small—
God alone has made them all:

5 Then he fashioned humankind,
Crown of all that he designed:

6 He has shaped our destiny—
heaven for all eternity:

7 Glory then to God on high,
'Glory!' let creation cry:

MICHAEL SAWARD (b. 1932)
after JOHN MILTON (1608–74)
based on Psalm 136

57

MAJESTY

Words and music by JACK W. HAYFORD

Ma - jes-ty,_____ wor-ship his ma - jes-ty,_____ un - to
Je - sus be glo - ry, hon-our and praise._____
Ma - jes-ty,_____ king-dom, au - tho - ri - ty,_____ flow from his
throne un - to his own, his an-them raise!_____ So ex -

58

MEEKNESS AND MAJESTY

Words and music by GRAHAM KENDRICK (b. 1950)
based on John 3: 13–16, Philippians 2: 6–11

1. Meek-ness and ma-jes-ty, man-hood and de-i-ty
2. Fa-ther's pure ra-di-ance, per-fect in in-no-cence,
3. Wis-dom un-search-a-ble, God the in-vi-si-ble,

1. in per-fect har-mo-ny – the man who is God:
2. yet learns o-be-di-ence to death on a cross:
3. love in-de-struc-ti-ble in frail-ty ap-pears:

1. Lord of e-ter-ni-ty dwells in hu-ma-ni-ty,
2. suf-fering to give us life, con-quering through sa-cri-fice –
3. Lord of in-fi-ni-ty, stoop-ing so ten-der-ly,

1. kneels in hu-mi-li-ty__ and_ wash-es our feet.
2. and, as they cru-ci-fy,__ prays, 'Fa-ther, for-give.'
3. lifts our hu-ma-ni-ty__ to the heights of his throne.

PRAISE

Oh what a my-ste-ry — meek-ness and ma-jes-ty: bow down and wor-ship, for this is your God, this is your God. God, this is your God.

59

UNIVERSITY   CM

C. COLLIGNON (1725–85)

Second Tune

LYDIA   CM

T. PHILLIPS (1735–1807)

May also be sung to LYNGHAM, no. 6.

O FOR a thousand tongues to sing
    my great Redeemer's praise,
the glories of my God and King,
    the triumphs of his grace!

2 Jesus! the name that charms our fears,
    that bids our sorrows cease;
it's music in the sinner's ears,
    it's life and health and peace.

3 He breaks the power of cancelled sin,
    he sets the prisoner free;
his blood can make the foulest clean;
    his blood availed for me.

4 He speaks, and, listening to his voice,
    new life the dead receive,
the mournful, broken hearts rejoice,
    the humble poor believe.

5 Hear him, you deaf; his praise, you dumb
    your loosened tongues employ;
you blind, behold your Saviour come;
    and leap, you lame, for joy.

6 My gracious master and my God,
    assist me to proclaim,
to spread through all the earth abroad,
    the honour of your name.

CHARLES WESLEY (1707–88)

60

Music by BASIL HARWOOD (1859–1949)
Words by DORIS M. WHITNEY (b. 1913)

THORNBURY   76 76 D

vv. 1, 3 *Unison*

1. O God of all cre - a - tion, the
3. In Christ's own strength and meek - ness we

Lord of heaven and earth,   the hope of ev - 'ry
see you face_ to face.   For all our times of

na - tion, who gave all life_ its birth,   we
weak - ness we ask for - giv - ing grace.   Help

come now to a - dore_ you and wor-ship as we
us_ to fight temp - ta - tion, let e - vil thoughts take

sing,　　　　　ac - cept the＿ praise we　of - fer, our
wing,　　　　　ac - cept the＿ lives we　of - fer, our

Lord,　　　our God,　our　King.＿＿＿＿
Lord,　　　our God,　our　King.＿＿＿＿

v. 2 *Harmony*

2. We　thank　you　for　all　la - bour,　with

toil　of　hand and　brain,＿＿　we　ask　to　serve　our

neigh - bour and not seek self - ish gain._____ For

health and hours of lei - sure our hearts with glad - ness_

ring,_____ ac - cept the__ joys we of - fer, our

Turn back for v. 3

King._____

Lord, our God, our King, our God, our King.

Organ

61

O GIVE THANKS TO THE LORD

Words and music by
JOANNE POND

62

HOW GREAT THOU ART
11 10 11 10 with refrain

Swedish folk melody
arr. STUART K. HINE (1899–1989)

Then sings my soul, my Sa-viour God, to thee, How great thou

art! How great thou art! Then sings my soul, my Sa-viour God, to

thee, How great thou art!__ How great thou__ art!

O LORD my God, when I in awesome wonder
   consider all the works thy hand hath made,
I see the stars, I hear the mighty thunder,
   thy power throughout the universe displayed;

> *Then sings my soul, my Saviour God, to thee,*
> *How great thou art! How great thou art!*
> *Then sings my soul, my Saviour God, to thee,*
> *How great thou art! How great thou art!*

2 When through the woods and forest glades I wander
   and hear the birds sing sweetly in the trees;
when I look down from lofty mountain grandeur,
   and hear the brook, and feel the gentle breeze;

3 And when I think that God his Son not sparing,
   sent him to die—I scarce can take it in,
that on the cross my burden gladly bearing,
   he bled and died to take away my sin:

4 When Christ shall come with shouts of acclamation
   and take me home—what joy shall fill my heart!
then shall I bow in humble adoration
   and there proclaim, my God, how great thou art!

Translated from the Russian
by STUART K. HINE (1899–1989)

63

HANOVER   10 10 11 11

Melody (and most of the bass) from
A Supplement to the New Version, 1708
probably by WILLIAM CROFT (1678–1727)

O WORSHIP the King,
  all-glorious above;
and gratefully sing
  his power and his love;
our shield and defender,
  the ancient of days,
surrounded with splendour,
  exalted with praise.

2 O tell of his might,
    and sing of his grace,
  whose robe is the light,
    whose canopy space;
  his chariots of wrath
    the deep thunder clouds form,
  and dark is his path
    on the wings of the storm.

3 Your bountiful care
    what tongue can recite?
  It breathes in the air,
    it shines in the light,
  it streams from the hills,
    it descends to the plain,
  and sweetly distils
    in the dew and the rain.

4 The earth, with its store
    of wonders untold,
  Almighty, your power
    has founded of old,
  established it fast
    by a changeless decree,
  and round it has cast
    like a garment, the sea.

5 O Lord of all might,
    how boundless your love!
  While angels delight
    to worship above,
  the humbler creation,
    though feeble their ways,
  with true adoration
    shall sing to your praise.

ROBERT GRANT (1779–1838) altd.

64

PRAISE HIM   10 6 10 6

E. R. BAILEY (1859–1938)
arr. A. EWART RUSBRIDGE (1917–69)

(Repeat the verse)

PRAISE him, praise him, everybody praise him,
    he is love, he is love.

2 Thank him, thank him, everybody thank him,
    he is love, he is love.

3 Love him, love him, everybody love him,
    he is love, he is love.

4 Crown him, crown him, everybody crown him,
    he is love, he is love.

5 Serve him, serve him, everybody serve him,
    he is love, he is love.

Anon. (c.1890), altd.

65

FIRST TUNE

Music by J. GOSS (1800–80)
Words by H. F. LYTE, (1793–1847) altd.

PRAISE MY SOUL   87 87 87

1. Praise, my soul, the King of hea - ven, to his feet your

tri-bute bring; ran-somed, healed, re - stored, for - gi - ven,

who like me his praise should sing? Praise him, praise him,

praise him, praise him, praise the e - ver - last - ing King.

Harmony

2. Praise him for his grace and fa - vour to our fa - thers

in dis - tress; praise him still the same for e - ver,

slow to blame, and swift to bless: praise him, praise him,

praise him, praise him, glor - ious in his faith - ful - ness.

3. Fa-ther - like he tends and spares us; all our weak-ness - -es he knows; in his hands he gent - ly bears us, res - cues us from all our foes; praise him, praise him, praise him, praise him, praise him, wide - ly as his mer - cy flows.

Unison

4. An-gels, help us to a - dore him, you be - hold him face to face, sun and moon bow down be - fore him, all that is in time and space; praise him, praise him, praise him, praise him, praise with us the God of grace.

65

REGENT SQUARE   87 87 87

HENRY SMART (1813–79)

PRAISE, my soul, the King of heaven,
to his feet your tribute bring;
ransomed, healed, restored, forgiven,
who like me his praise should sing?
Praise him, praise him,
praise him, praise him,
praise the everlasting King.

2 Praise him for his grace and favour
to our fathers in distress;
praise him still the same for ever,
slow to blame and swift to bless:
praise him, praise him,
praise him, praise him,
glorious in his faithfulness.

3 Father-like he tends and spares us;
all our weaknesses he knows;
in his hands he gently bears us,
rescues us from all our foes;
praise him, praise him,
praise him, praise him,
widely as his mercy flows.

4 Angels, help us to adore him,
you behold him face to face,
sun and moon bow down before him,
all that is in time and space;
praise him, praise him,
praise him, praise him,
praise with us the God of grace.

H. F. LYTE (1793–1847) altd.

66

GONFALON ROYAL   LM

P. C. BUCK (1871–1947)

O GOD of awesome majesty,
  our loving Father hid from sight;
most glorious uncreated one,
  renowned for holiness and might.

2 O God of peace and liberty,
  your love extends to every race;
your Son and Holy Spirit's power
  reveal to us your saving grace.

3 O God of immortality,
  through Christ we need not fear the grave;
death could not hold the King of kings,
  and your right hand is strong to save.

4 O God of awesome majesty,
  the only Lord of heaven and earth;
the supreme being we revere—
  majestic God, how great your worth!
                                    (Amen.)

BETTY STANLEY (b. 1921)

67

AUSTRIA   87 87 D   F. J. HAYDN (1732–1809)

LAUS DEO   87 87   RICHARD REDHEAD (1820–1901)

PRAISE the Lord, let heaven adore him,
   praise him, angels, in the height;
sun and moon, rejoice before him;
   praise him, all you stars of light.
Praise the Lord, for he has spoken;
   worlds his mighty voice obeyed;
laws which never shall be broken,
   for their guidance he has made.

2 Praise the Lord, for he is glorious;
   never shall his promise fail;
God has made his saints victorious;
   sin and death shall not prevail.
Praise the God of our salvation;
   hosts on high, his power proclaim;
heaven and earth, and all creation,
   praise and glorify his name.

Foundling Hospital Collection, 1796 altd.

68

LOBE DEN HERREN   14 14 47 8

Later form of melody in
Stralsund Gesangbuch, 1665 as given in
The Chorale Book for England, 1863

PRAISE to the Lord, the Almighty, the King of creation;
O my soul, praise him, for he is your health and salvation:
    all those who hear,
    brothers and sisters, draw near,
praise him in glad adoration.

2 Praise to the Lord, above all things so wondrously reigning,
bearing you high on his wings, and so gently sustaining:
    have you not seen?
    all you have needed has been
met by his gracious providing.

3 Praise to the Lord, who shall prosper your work and defend you!
Surely his goodness and mercy shall daily attend you:
    ponder anew
    what the Almighty can do,
who with his love will befriend you.

4 Praise to the Lord! O let all that is in me adore him!
All that has life and breath come now with praises before him!
    Let the amen
    sound from his people again:
gladly we praise and adore him.

JOACHIM NEANDER (1650–80)
tr. CATHERINE WINKWORTH (1827–78) and others

69

PRAISE TO GOD IN THE HIGHEST   Irregular

Words and music by
CHRISTOPHER HINKINS

Praise to God in the high - est, give him praise, all his peo - ple and his an - gel - cho - rus; praise to God in the high - est, from the earth to the hea-vens a re - sound-ing voice is heard.

PRAISE

1. Praise him sun and moon and stars,
2. Praise him bush-es, flowers and trees,

float-ing in the fir-ma-ment high,
grow-ing in the val-leys and hills,

Plu-to, Sa-turn, Ve-nus and Mars,
e-le-phants with ea-gles and bees,

v. 1 REFRAIN *D.C.*
v. 2 Straight on

let the hea-vens wor-ship him in sounds of ju-bi-la-tion.
let the whole earth wor-ship him and shout a-loud in cho-rus.

THE CALL TO WORSHIP

Glo - ry be to the Fa - ther, to the Fa - ther, the Son and to the Ho - ly Spi - rit; as it was in the be - gin - ning, as it was, is___ now___ and___ shall be e - ver - more.

(2 parts)

70

LAUDATE DOMINUM   10 10 11 11   C. H. H. PARRY (1848–1918)

Sing praise to the Lord!
  Praise him in the height;
rejoice in his word,
  you angels of light:
you heavens adore him
  by whom you were made,
and worship before him,
  in brightness arrayed.

2 Sing praise to the Lord!
  Praise him upon earth
in tuneful accord,
  you saints of new birth:
praise him who has brought you
  his grace from above;
praise him who has taught you
  to sing of his love.

3 Sing praise to the Lord!
  All things that give sound,
each jubilant chord
  re-echo around:
loud organs, his glory
  proclaim in deep tone,
and sweet harp, the story
  of what he has done.

4 Sing praise to the Lord!
  Thanksgiving and song
to him be outpoured
  all ages along:
for love in creation,
  for heaven restored,
for grace of salvation,
  sing praise to the Lord!

H. W. BAKER (1821–77)

71

LAUS DEO   87 87   RICHARD REDHEAD (1820–1901)

BRIGHT the vision that delighted
once the sight of Judah's seer;
sweet the countless tongues united
to entrance the prophet's ear.

2 Round the Lord in glory seated
cherubim and seraphim
filled his temple, and repeated
each to each the alternate hymn:

3 'Lord, your glory fills the heaven:
  earth is with its fullness stored;
  unto you be glory given,
  holy, holy, holy Lord.'

4 Heaven is still with glory ringing,
  earth takes up the angels' cry,
  'Holy, holy, holy,' singing,
  'Lord of hosts, the Lord most high.'

5 With his seraph train before him,
  with his holy Church below,
  thus conspire we to adore him,
  bid we thus our anthem flow:

6 'Lord, your glory fills the heaven;
  earth is with its fullness stored;
  unto you be glory given,
  holy, holy, holy Lord.'

RICHARD MANT (1776–1848)
based on Isaiah 6: 1–3

72

CROFT'S 136th   66 66 88

Melody and bass by
WILLIAM CROFT (1678–1727)

For a different version of this tune see no. 557.

WE give immortal praise
  to God the Father's love
for all our comforts here
  and better hopes above:
    he sent his own
    eternal Son,
  to die for sins
  that we have done.

2 To God the Son belongs
  immortal glory too,
who bought us with his blood
  from everlasting woe:
    and now he lives,
    and now he reigns,
  and sees the fruit
  of all his pains.

3 To God the Spirit's name
  immortal worship give,
whose new-creating power
  makes the dead sinner live:
    his work completes
    the great design,
  and fills the soul
  with joy divine.

4 To God the Trinity
  be endless honours done,
the undivided three,
  and the mysterious one:
    where reason fails
    with all her powers,
  there faith prevails,
  and love adores.

ISAAC WATTS (1674–1748)

73

LAUDES DOMINI   666 D

J. BARNBY (1838–96)

WHEN morning gilds the skies,
my heart awakening cries,
    'May Jesus Christ be praised!'
Alike at work and prayer
I know my Lord is there:
    'May Jesus Christ be praised!'

2 When sadness fills my mind
my strength in him I find:
    'May Jesus Christ be praised!'
When earthly hopes grow dim
my comfort is in him:
    'May Jesus Christ be praised!'

3 The night becomes as day
when from the heart we say:
    'May Jesus Christ be praised!'
The powers of darkness fear
when this glad song they hear:
    'May Jesus Christ be praised!'

4 Be this, while life is mine,
my canticle divine:
    'May Jesus Christ be praised!'
Be this the eternal song
through all the ages long:
    'May Jesus Christ be praised!'

from the German
EDWARD CASWALL (1814–78)

74

YOU ARE THE KING OF GLORY

Words and music by MAVIS FORD

75

YOU ARE WORTHY

Words and music by PAULINE MICHAEL MILLS
arr. DAVID TRAFFORD (b. 1950)

You are wor-thy, you are wor-thy, you are wor-thy, O Lord; you are wor-thy to re-ceive glo-ry, glo-ry and hon-our and power: for

you have cre - a - ted, have all things cre - a - ted, for

you have cre - a - ted all things,

and for your plea - sure they are cre - a - ted:

you are wor - thy, O Lord!

76

LAUDATE DOMINUM   10 10 11 11   C. H. H. PARRY (1848–1918)

You servants of God, your master proclaim,
and publish abroad his wonderful name;
the name all-victorious of Jesus extol,
his kingdom is glorious, and rules over all.

2 God rules in the height, almighty to save—
though hid from our sight, his presence we have;
the great congregation his triumph shall sing,
ascribing salvation to Jesus our King.

3 'Salvation to God who sits on the throne!'
let all cry aloud, and honour the Son;
the praises of Jesus the angels proclaim,
fall down on their faces and worship the Lamb.

4 Then let us adore and give him his right:
all glory and power, all wisdom and might,
all honour and blessing—with angels above—
and thanks never ceasing, and infinite love.

CHARLES WESLEY (1707–88) altd.

77

Do you not know?
Have you not heard?
The Lord is the everlasting God,
  the creator of the ends of the earth.
He will not grow tired or weary,
  and his understanding no one can fathom.
He gives strength to the weary
and increases the power of the weak.
  Even youths grow tired and weary,
  and young men stumble and fall;
but those who hope in the Lord
will renew their strength.
  They will soar on wings like eagles;
they will run and not grow weary,
  they will walk and not be faint.

78

This is the time to worship God:
  he brings us life.
This is the time to sing his praise:
  he brings us joy.
This is the time to pray to him:
  he brings us forgiveness and renewal.
This is the time to hear his word:
  he brings us guidance and hope.
This is the time to show your love for him:
  he brings us love beyond our deserving.

79

O God, you are my God,
and I long for you.
  My whole being desires you;
like a dry, worn-out, and waterless land,
my soul is thirsty for you.
  Let me see you in the sanctuary;
  let me see how mighty and glorious you are.
Your constant love is better than life itself,
and so I will praise you.

80

Praise be to the God and Father of our Lord Jesus Christ,
who in his great mercy gave us new birth into a living hope
by the resurrection of Jesus Christ from the dead!
The inheritance to which we are born
is one that nothing can destroy or spoil or wither.
It is kept for you in heaven, and you, because you put your faith in God,
are under the protection of his power until salvation comes—
the salvation which is even now in readiness
and will be revealed at the end of time.

81

This is the place
and this is the time;
here and now,
God waits
to break into our experience;
to change our minds,
to change our lives,
to change our ways;
to make us see the world
and the whole of life
in a new light;
to fill us with hope,
joy and certainty
for the future.

This is the place
as are all places;
this is the time
as are all times.
Here and now
let us praise God.

[*see also no. 469*]

82

Blessed be God's name from age to age,
for all wisdom and power are his.
How great are his signs,
and his marvels overwhelming!

His kingdom is an everlasting kingdom,
his sovereignty stands to all generations.
He is the living God, the everlasting,
whose kingly power shall not be weakened;
whose sovereignty shall have no end.

83

DUNDEE   CM

Melody from *Scottish Psalter*, 1615
Harmony from T. RAVENSCROFT'S *Psalmes*, 1621

'FORGIVE our sins as we forgive,'
    you taught us, Lord, to pray,
but you alone can grant us grace
    to live the words we say.

2 How can your pardon reach and bless
    the unforgiving heart
that broods on wrongs and will not let
    old bitterness depart?

3 In blazing light your cross reveals
    the truth we dimly knew,
how small the debts men owe to us,
    how great our debt to you!

4 Lord, cleanse the depths within our souls
    and bid resentment cease;
then, reconciled to God and man,
    our lives will spread your peace.

ROSAMOND E. HERKLOTS (1905–87)

84

REPTON   86 886

C. H. H. PARRY (1848–1918)

Harmony (vv. 3, 4) *

O calm of hills a - bove,

O   calm____   of   hills a - bove,

*Can be accompanied by the version above.

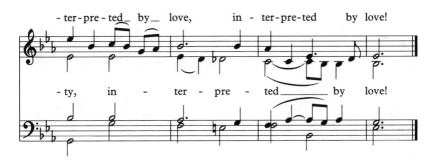

DEAR Lord and Father of mankind,
    forgive our foolish ways;
reclothe us in our rightful mind;
in purer lives thy service find,
    in deeper reverence, praise.

2 In simple trust like theirs
      who heard,
    beside the Syrian sea,
the gracious calling of the Lord,
let us, like them, without a word
    rise up and follow thee.

3 O sabbath rest by Galilee!
    O calm of hills above,
where Jesus knelt to share with thee
    the silence of eternity,
    interpreted by love!

4 Drop thy still dews of quietness,
    till all our strivings cease;
take from our souls the strain and stress,
and let our ordered lives confess
    the beauty of thy peace.

5 Breathe through the heats of our desire
    thy coolness and thy balm;
let sense be dumb, let flesh retire;
speak through the earthquake, wind and fire,
    O still small voice of calm.

J. G. WHITTIER (1807–92)

85

NEWCASTLE   86 886   H. L. MORLEY (1830–1916)

ETERNAL light! Eternal light!
   How pure the soul must be,
which placed within your searching sight,
returns your gaze with calm delight,
   and does not shrink or flee.

2 The spirits that surround your throne
   may bear the burning bliss,
but that is surely theirs alone,
since they have never, never known
   a fallen world like this.

3 O how shall I, whose native sphere
   is dark, whose mind is dim,
before your mystery appear,
and on my naked spirit bear
   the uncreated beam?

4 There is a way for all to rise
   to that sublime abode;—
Christ's offering and his sacrifice,
the Holy Spirit's energies,
   an advocate with God.

5 These, these prepare us for the sight
   of holiness above;
those born in ignorance and night
can dwell in the eternal light,
   through the eternal love.

THOMAS BINNEY (1798–1874) altd.
based on 1 John 1: 5; 2: 1–2

86

First Tune

DAY'S *English Psalter*, 1562
adpt. RICHARD REDHEAD (1820–1901)

ST FLAVIAN   CM

Second Tune

FINGAL   CM

JAMES SMITH ANDERSON (1853–1945)

How can we sing with joy to God,
  how can we pray to him,
when we are far away from God
  in selfishness and sin?

2 How can we claim to do God's will
  when we have turned away
from things of God to things of earth,
  and willed to disobey?

3 How can we praise the love of God
  which all his works make known,
when all our works turn from his love
  to choices of our own?

4 God knows how often we have sinned
  and joined with godless men,
yet in his love he calls to us
  to win us back again.

5 So we will turn again to God—
  his ways will be our ways,
his will our will, his love our love,
  and he himself our praise!

BRIAN FOLEY (b. 1919)

87

KILMARNOCK   CM

NEIL DOUGALL (1776–1862)

SECOND TUNE

GORING   CM

ERIC H. THIMAN (1900–75)

Now let us see your beauty, Lord,
   as we have seen before;
and by your beauty quicken us
   to love you and adore.

2 When with uncomplicated mind
   your loveliness we see,
we gladly give ourselves again
   to serve you loyally.

3 Our every feverish mood is cooled
   and gone is every load,
when we can lose the love of self,
   and find the love of God.

4 When we have wandered far away,
   your beauty draws us home;
and thus restored, your children true,
   more human we become.

5 Lord, we are coming to ourselves
   when we return to be
in bondage to your loveliness—
   the life completely free.

6 So now we come to ask again
   what you have often given,
the vision of that loveliness
   which is the life of heaven.

BENJAMIN WAUGH (1839–1908) altd.
based on Psalm 27: 4–6; 90: 17

88

LINTON   65 65

W. K. STANTON (1891–1978)

SECOND TUNE

CASWALL (BEMERTON)   65 65

Melody by F. FILITZ (1804–76)

JESUS stand among us
in your risen power;
let this time of worship
be a hallowed hour.

2 Breathe the Holy Spirit
  into every heart;
  bid the fears and sorrows
  from each soul depart.

3 Then with eager footsteps
  we'll pursue our way,
  watching for the dawning
  of eternal day.

WILLIAM PENNEFATHER (1816–73)
based on John 20: 19–23

89

RIVAULX   LM

J. B. DYKES (1823–76)

YOU gave us, Lord, by word and deed
the way of love your Father willed,
that those who go where'er you lead
may find in you a life fulfilled.

2 It was your joy to call them blest
who poor in spirit choose to be,
and find themselves of earth possessed,
the gentle heirs of all they see.

3 And blessèd too are those who mourn,
the merciful, the pure of heart,
and those by thirst and hunger torn
that justice hold its rightful part.

4 Your blessing, Lord, embraces too
all those who strive that peace may reign,
who right uphold and justice do
and face withal contempt and pain.

5 We humbly ask your pardon, Lord;
the ones who hear are all too few,
so speak again your healing word,
our sin forgive, our heart renew.

DENIS HURLEY
based on Matthew 5: 1–12

135

90

Awaken us, O Lord,
  awaken us to a sense of your presence.
Lord, we have faith:
  help us in doubt and uncertainty.
Your love goes before us:
  help us to follow with joy.

91

God, be merciful to us and bless us;
look on us with kindness,
    so that the whole world may know your will;
    so that all nations may know your salvation.

May the peoples praise you, O God;
may all the peoples praise you!
    May the nations be glad and sing for joy,
    because you judge the people with justice
    and guide every nation on earth.

May the peoples praise you, O God;
    may all the peoples praise you!

92

Where could I go to escape from you?
Where could I get away from your presence?

    If I went up to heaven, you would be there;
    if I lay down in the world of the dead,
    you would be there.

If I flew away beyond the east
or lived in the farthest place in the west,
    you would be there to lead me,
    you would be there to help me.

I could ask the darkness to hide me
or the light round me to turn into night,
    but even the darkness is not dark for you,
    and the night is as bright as the day.
    Darkness and light are the same to you.

93

Have mercy on me, O God, in your enduring goodness:
according to the fullness of your compassion
blot out my offences.

Wash me thoroughly from my wickedness:
and cleanse me from my sin.

Hide your face from my sins:
and blot out all my iniquities.

Create in me a clean heart, O God:
and renew a right spirit within me.

Do not cast me out from your presence:
do not take your Holy Spirit from me.

The sacrifice of God is a broken spirit:
a broken and contrite heart, O God, you will not despise.

94   A PRAYER OF CONFESSION

O Lord, we have tried so hard to live better lives:
to be good-tempered and considerate;
to work hard instead of being lazy;
to watch our tongues and not speak hastily;
to be cheerful even when things go wrong;
to act kindly to people we find it hard to like.

But it is always the same story. Trying is not enough.
Help us to catch your Spirit,
through prayer and worship,
fellowship and service,
so that the fruit of the Spirit will grow in us,
to your glory.

95 ASSURANCE OF PARDON

Let us confess our sins to God and ask his forgiveness.

If we say we have no sin, we deceive ourselves and there is no truth in us. But if we confess our sins to God, he will keep his promise and do what is right: he will forgive us our sins and purify us from all wrongdoing.

In humble repentance let us rest our hearts and minds in the forgiving and rescuing love of God and take the pardon he offers us.

Silence

God has forgiven us. Go in peace.

**Thanks be to God for the assurance of pardon.
Thanks be to God for the promise to set us free in Christ from condemnation and from the power of sin to dominate our lives.
Thanks be to God for the victory he gives us through Jesus Christ our Lord.**

96 A PRAYER FOR THE FORGIVENESS OF OTHERS

Jesus teaches us that if we wish to follow him we must be ready to forgive without qualification or calculation—to seventy times seven. Let us forgive from our hearts all who have sinned against us, and forgive yet again those who have wronged us in ways that we are finding difficult to forget.

**Lord, forgive us the wrongs we have done,
as we forgive the wrongs that others have done to us.**

97

ST STEPHEN   CM

WILLIAM JONES (1726–1800)

COME, Holy Ghost, our hearts inspire;
   let us thine influence prove,
source of the old prophetic fire,
   fountain of light and love.

2 Come, Holy Ghost, for moved by thee
   thy prophets wrote and spoke;
unlock the truth, thyself the key,
   unseal the sacred book.

3 Expand thy wings, celestial dove,
   brood o'er our nature's night;
on our disordered spirits move,
   and let there now be light.

4 God, through himself, we then shall know,
   if thou within us shine;
and sound, with all thy saints below,
   the depths of love divine.

CHARLES WESLEY (1707–88)

98

LATHBURY   64 64 D

WILLIAM F. SHERWIN (1826–88)

Second Tune

GOTTLIEB   64 64

F. C. MAKER (1844–1927)

BREAK now the bread of life,
    dear Lord to me,
as once you broke the loaves
    beside the sea:
beyond the sacred page
    I seek you, Lord;
my spirit longs for you,
    the living word!

2 You are the bread of life,
    dear Lord to me,
your holy word, the truth,
    is saving me;
give me to eat and live
    with you above;
teach me to love your truth,
    for you are love.

3 Show me the truth concealed
    within your word,
that in your book revealed
    I see you, Lord;
so send your Spirit, now,
    dear Lord, to me
that he may break my bonds
    and set me free.

MARY LATHBURY (1842–1913)
vv. 2 and 3 ALEXANDER GROVES (1843–1909)
altd.

99

ABERGELE   CM

J. AMBROSE LLOYD (1815–74)

ARDEN   CM

GEORGE THALBEN-BALL (1896–1987)

FATHER of mercies, in your word
 what endless glory shines!
For ever be your name adored
 for these celestial lines.

2 Here may the blind and hungry come
 and light and food receive;
here shall the humble guest find room,
 and taste, and see, and live.

3 Here the Redeemer's welcome voice
 spreads heavenly peace around,
and life and everlasting joys
 attend the glorious sound.

4 Here springs of consolation rise
 to cheer the fainting mind,
and thirsty souls receive supplies
 and sweet refreshment find.

5 Divine instructor, gracious Lord,
 be now and always near:
teach us to love your sacred word
 and view our Saviour here.

ANNE STEELE (1717–78)

100

FIRST TUNE

MEAD HOUSE 87 87 D

CYRIL V. TAYLOR (1907–91)

SECOND TUNE

DEERHURST 87 87 D

JAMES LANGRAN (1835–1909)

THE WORD

May also be sung to EBENEZER, no. 563.

GOD has spoken by his prophets,
  spoken his unchanging word;
each from age to age proclaiming
  God the one, the righteous Lord;
in the world's despair and turmoil
  one firm anchor holding fast,
God is on his throne eternal,
  he alone the first and last.

2 God has spoken by Christ Jesus,
  Christ, the everlasting Son,
brightness of the Father's glory,
  with the Father ever one;
spoken by the Word incarnate,
  God before all time began,
Light of light, to earth descending,
  man, revealing God to man.

3 God is speaking by his Spirit,
  speaking to the hearts of men,
in the age-long word declaring
  God's own message, now as then.
Through the rise and fall of nations
  one sure faith is standing fast:
God abides, his word unchanging,
  God alone the first and last.

G. W. BRIGGS (1875–1959)

101

CLEVELAND 87 87 9

CHRISTOPHER JOHNSON

Lord, you some-times speak in won - ders, un - mi - sta - ka - ble and clear; migh-ty signs to prove your pre - sence, o-ver - com-ing doubt and fear. O___ Lord, you some-times speak in won - ders.

LORD, you sometimes speak in wonders,
    unmistakable and clear;
mighty signs to prove your presence,
    overcoming doubt and fear.
O Lord, you sometimes speak in wonders.

2 Lord, you sometimes speak in whispers,
    still and small and scarcely heard;
only those who want to listen
    catch the all-important word.
O Lord, you sometimes speak in whispers.

3 Lord, you sometimes speak in silence,
    through our loud and noisy day;
we can know and trust you better
    when we quietly wait and pray.
O Lord, you sometimes speak in silence.

4 Lord, you often speak in Scripture—
    words that summon from the page,
shown and taught us by your Spirit
    with fresh light for every age.
O Lord, you often speak in Scripture.

5 Lord, you always speak in Jesus,
    always new yet still the same:
teach us now more of our Saviour;
    make our lives display his name.
O Lord, you always speak in Jesus.

CHRISTOPHER IDLE (b. 1938)

The original version of this text comprises the first four lines of each verse.
The fifth line was added by the composer to fit this particular musical setting.

102

RAVENSHAW 66 66 (Trochaic)

From a melody in M. WEISSE'S
Ein Neu Gesengbuchlen, 1531
arr. W. H. MONK (1823–89)

LORD, your word shall guide us
and with truth provide us:
teach us to receive it
and with joy believe it.

2 When our foes are near us,
then your word shall cheer us;
word of consolation,
message of salvation.

3 When the storms distress us,
and dark clouds oppress us,
then your word protects us
and its light directs us.

4 Who can tell the pleasure,
who recount the treasure
by your word imparted
to the simple-hearted?

5 Word of mercy, giving
courage to the living;
word of life, supplying
comfort to the dying.

6 O that we, discerning
its most holy learning,
Lord, may love and fear you—
evermore be near you!

H. W. BAKER (1821–77)

103

OPEN   10 10 10 10

A. S. COX (b. 1918)

Open this book that we may see your word
  embodied in the drama of our earth—
stories of people that your Spirit stirred,
  glimpses of hope and visions of new birth.

2 Open this book that we may meet the one
    who came as word-made-flesh for all to see;
  show us his life, all that was said and done,
    that we might see ourselves as we could be.

3 Open our ears that we may hear you still;
    teach us to live as well as speak your word.
  Open our eyes that we might face your will—
    the word-made-flesh in those who call you 'Lord'.

CHRISTOPHER ELLIS (b. 1949)

104

MIT FREUDEN ZART   87 87 887

Hymn melody of the
Bohemian Brethren, 1566

Our Father God, thy name we praise,
   to thee our hymns addressing,
and joyfully our voices raise
   thy faithfulness confessing;
     assembled by thy grace, O Lord,
     we seek fresh guidance from thy word;
   now grant anew thy blessing.

2 Touch, Lord, the lips that speak for thee;
   set words of truth before us,
that we may grow in constancy,
   the light of wisdom o'er us.
     Give us this day our daily bread;
     may hungry souls again be fed;
   may heavenly food restore us.

3 As with our brethren here we meet,
   thy grace alone can feed us.
As here we gather at thy feet,
   we pray that thou wilt heed us.
     The power is thine, O Lord divine,
     the kingdom and the rule are thine,
   may Jesus Christ still lead us!

from the Anabaptist *Ausbund*, 16th century
tr. E. A. PAYNE (1902–80)

105

QUIETUDE   65 65

H. GREEN (1871–1930)

SECOND TUNE

GREEN HILL   65 65

ROBIN SHELDON (b. 1932)

SPEAK, Lord, in the stillness,
    speak your word to me;
help me now to listen
    in expectancy.

2 Speak, O gracious Master,
    in this quiet hour;
let me see your face, Lord,
    feel your touch of power.

3 For the words you give me,
    they are life indeed;
living bread from heaven,
    now my spirit feed.

4 Speak, your servant listens—
    I await your word;
let me know your presence,
    let your voice be heard!

5 Fill me with the knowledge
    of your glorious will;
all your own good pleasure
    in my life fulfil.

EMILY M. CRAWFORD (1864–1927)

106   First Tune

KINGLEY VALE   87 87 47   H. P. ALLEN (1869–1946)

Second Tune

ST HELEN   87 87 87   GEORGE C. MARTIN (1844–1916)

THE WORD

Small notes are for organ only.
May also be sung to REGENT SQUARE, no. 631.

THANKS to God whose word was spoken
   in the deed that made the earth.
His the voice that called a nation,
   his the fires that tried her worth.
      God has spoken:
   praise him for his open word.

2 Thanks to God whose word incarnate
   glorified the flesh of man.
Deeds and words and death and rising
   tell the grace in heaven's plan.
      God has spoken:
   praise him for his open word.

3 Thanks to God whose word was written
   in the Bible's sacred page,
record of the revelation
   showing God to every age.
      God has spoken:
   praise him for his open word.

4 Thanks to God whose word is published
   in the tongues of every race.
See its glory undiminished
   by the change of time or place.
      God has spoken:
   praise him for his open word.

5 Thanks to God whose word is answered
   by the Spirit's voice within.
Here we drink of joy unmeasured,
   life redeemed from death and sin.
      God is speaking:
   praise him for his open word.

R. T. BROOKS (1918–85)

107

PETERSHAM DCM

C. W. POOLE (1828–1924)

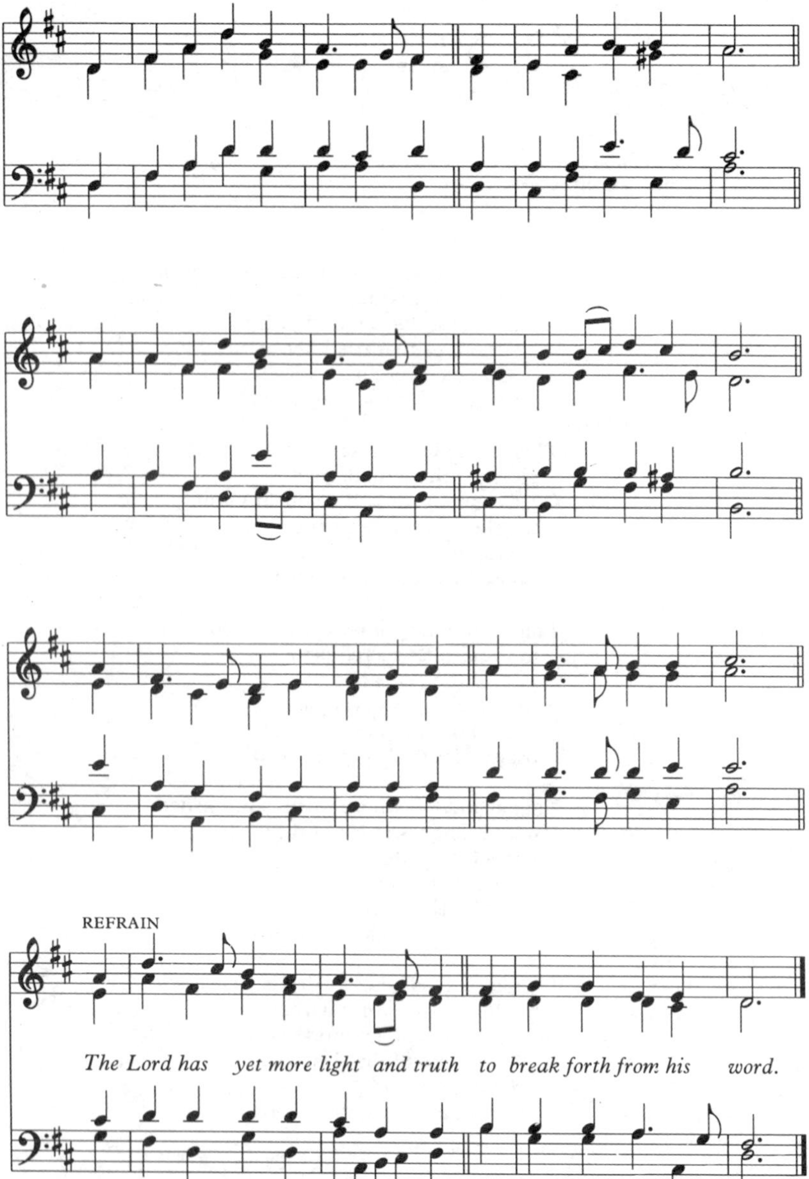
REFRAIN
The Lord has yet more light and truth to break forth from his word.

WE limit not the truth of God
    to our poor reach of mind,
by notions of our day and sect,
    crude, partial and confined;
no, let a new and better hope
    within our hearts be stirred:

    The Lord has yet more light and truth
    to break forth from his word.

2 Who dares to bind to his dull sense
    the oracles of heaven,
for all the nations, tongues and climes,
    and all the ages given?
That universe, how much unknown!
    That ocean unexplored!

3 In faith our great forefathers went
    the first steps of the way;
it was the dawning, yet to grow
    into the perfect day.
And grow it shall; our glorious sun
    more fervid rays afford:

4 O Father, Son and Spirit, send
    us increase from above;
enlarge, expand all Christian souls
    to comprehend your love:
and make us to go on to know,
    with nobler powers conferred,

GEORGE RAWSON (1807–89)

108

TALLIS'S CANON   LM

THOMAS TALLIS (c.1510–85)
adpt. in T. RAVENSCROFT *Psalmes*, 1621

GLORY to you my God, this night
for all the blessings of the light;
keep me, O keep me, King of kings,
beneath your own almighty wings.

2 Forgive me, Lord, through your dear Son,
the wrong that I this day have done,
that peace with God and man may be,
before I sleep, restored to me.

3 O may my soul on you repose
and restful sleep my eyelids close;
sleep that shall me more vigorous make
to serve my God when I awake.

4 If in the night I sleepless lie,
my mind with peaceful thoughts supply;
let no dark dreams disturb my rest,
no powers of evil me molest.

5 Praise God from whom all blessings flow;
praise him, all creatures here below;
praise him above, you heavenly host;
praise Father, Son and Holy Ghost.

THOMAS KEN (1637–1711)

109

PRESENCE   11 11 10 11   Iona Community

Lo, I am with you to the end of the world,
lo, I am with you to the end of the world;
lo, I am with you, lo, I am with you,
lo, I am with you to the end of the world.

2 Lo, I am with you when you leave self behind, (*etc.*)

3 Lo, I am with you in the struggle for peace,

4 Lo, I am with you when you suffer for love,

5 Lo, I am with you in the way of the cross,

6 Lo, I am with you in the darkness of death,

7 Lo, I am with you to the end of the world,

                                Iona Community

110

SHARON   87 87

Adpt. from W. BOYCE (1711–79)

For a different version of this tune (in E♭) see no. 497.

MERTON   87 87

W. H. MONK (1823–89)

May the grace of Christ our Saviour,
  and the Father's boundless love,
with the Holy Spirit's favour,
  rest upon us from above.

2 Thus may we abide in union
  with each other and the Lord;
and possess in sweet communion
  joys which earth cannot afford.

JOHN NEWTON (1725–1807)

111

VIENNA   77 77

Melody from J. H. KNECHT (1752–1817)

Now may he, who from the dead
    brought the shepherd of the sheep,
Jesus Christ, our King and head,
    all our souls in safety keep.

2 May he teach us to fulfil
    what is pleasing in his sight;
perfect us in all his will,
    and preserve us day and night.

3 To that dear Redeemer's praise,
    who the covenant sealed with blood,
let our hearts and voices raise
    loud thanksgivings to our God.

JOHN NEWTON (1725–1807)

112

PEACE, PERFECT PEACE   11 11 10 11   KEVIN MAYHEW

Unison

Peace, per-fect peace, is the gift of Christ our Lord,

peace, per-fect peace, is the gift of Christ our Lord.

Thus, says the Lord, will the world know my friends;

peace, per-fect peace, is the gift of Christ our Lord.

PEACE, perfect peace,
   is the gift of Christ our Lord,
peace, perfect peace,
   is the gift of Christ our Lord.
Thus, says the Lord,
   will the world know my friends;
peace, perfect peace,
   is the gift of Christ our Lord.

2 Hope, perfect hope,
   is the gift of Christ our Lord.

3 Joy, perfect joy,
   is the gift of Christ our Lord.

4 Faith, perfect faith,
   is the gift of Christ our Lord.

5 Love, perfect love,
   is the gift of Christ our Lord.

KEVIN MAYHEW

113

FIRST TUNE

OLD 100th LM

Genevan Psalter, 1551

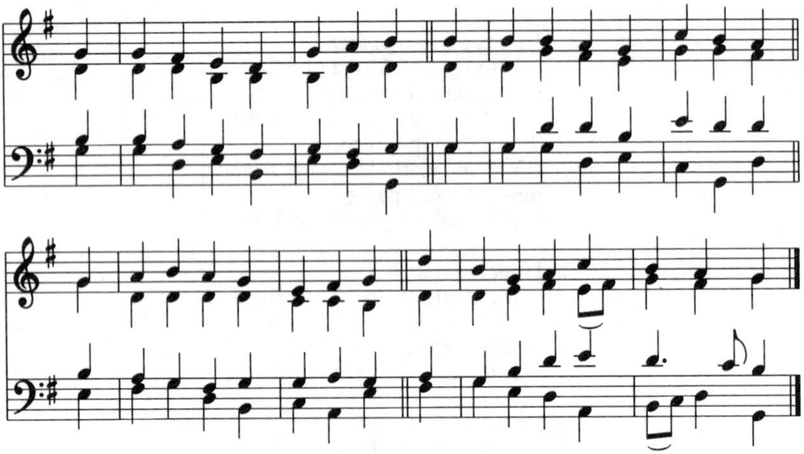

SECOND TUNE

COME TOGETHER LM

JIMMY OWENS
arr. DAVID PEACOCK (b. 1949)

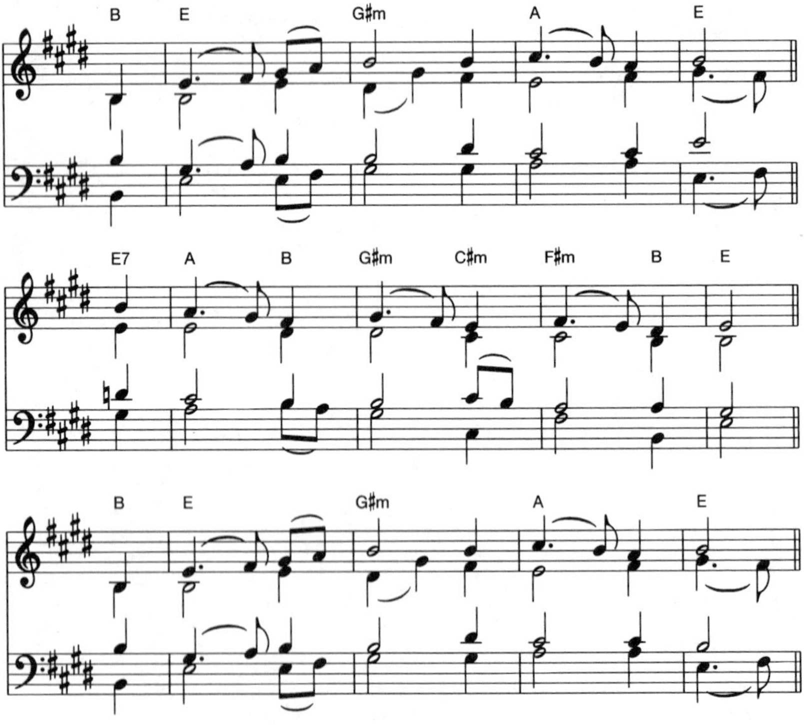

PRAISE GOD from whom all blessings flow,
praise him, all creatures here below,
praise him above, you heavenly host,
praise Father, Son, and Holy Ghost.

THOMAS KEN (1637–1711)

114

SHALOM 84 84

Traditional melody
arr. MICHAEL METCALFE (b. 1937)

Sha-lom, my friends, God's peace, my friends, go with you now and stay with you, in all you do, sha-lom, sha-lom.

*Or

Traditional
adpt. by MICHAEL LEHR

sha - lom!

May also be sung as a four-part round, the voices entering as indicated
and the accompanist playing a chord of D minor throughout.

115

NOW UNTO HIM

RACHEL E. MORTISHIRE

sempre coll' 8va ad lib.

Unison

Now un-to him who is a - ble to keep you, a - ble to keep you,

keep you from fall-ing, and to pre-sent you fault-less be-fore the

pre-sence of his glo - ry, with ex-ceed-ing joy,

Now unto him who is able to keep you,
    able to keep you, keep you from falling,
    and to present you faultless
    before the presence of his glory,
    with exceeding joy, with exceeding joy,
    in the presence of his glory with exceeding joy,
    with exceeding joy, with exceeding joy,
    faultless in the presence of his glory;
to the only God our Saviour,
    able to keep you, keep you from falling,
    be glory and majesty, dominion and power,
    both now and for ever. Amen.

based on Jude: 24–5

2. PROCLAIMING THE GOSPEL

116

ALL THINGS BRIGHT AND BEAUTIFUL

W. H. MONK (1823–89)

7 6 7 6 with refrain

REFRAIN

All things bright and beau-ti-ful, all__ crea-tures great and small,__

all things wise and won-der-ful, the_ Lord God made them all.

VERSES

All things bright and beautiful,
all creatures great and small,
all things wise and wonderful,
the Lord God made them all.

EACH little flower that opens,
each little bird that sings,
he made their glowing colours,
he made their tiny wings.

2 The purple-headed mountain,
the river running by,
the sunset, and the morning
that brightens up the sky:

3 The cold wind in the winter,
the pleasant summer sun,
the ripe fruits in the garden,
he made them every one.

4 He gave us eyes to see them,
and lips that we might tell
how great is God almighty,
who has made all things well.

CECIL FRANCES ALEXANDER (1818–95)

116

SECOND TUNE

ROYAL OAK   7 6 7 6 with refrain

17th-century English traditional melody
arr. MARTIN SHAW (1875–1958)

All things bright and beau-ti - ful, all crea-tures great and small,

all things wise and won - der - ful, the Lord God made them all.

All things bright and beautiful,
all creatures great and small,
all things wise and wonderful,
the Lord God made them all.

EACH little flower that opens,
    each little bird that sings,
he made their glowing colours,
    he made their tiny wings.

2 The purple-headed mountain,
    the river running by,
the sunset, and the morning
    that brightens up the sky:

3 The cold wind in the winter,
    the pleasant summer sun,
the ripe fruits in the garden,
    he made them every one.

4 He gave us eyes to see them,
    and lips that we might tell
how great is God almighty,
    who has made all things well.

CECIL FRANCES ALEXANDER (1818–95)

117

FINLANDIA   11 10 11 10   JEAN SIBELIUS (1865–1957)

May also be sung to INTERCESSOR, no. 641.

By gracious powers so wonderfully sheltered
  and confidently waiting, come what may,
we know that God is with us night and morning,
  and never fails to meet us each new day.

2 Yet are our hearts by their old foe tormented
  still evil days bring burdens hard to bear;
O give our frightened souls the sure salvation
  for which, O Lord, you taught us to prepare.

3 And when the cup you give is filled to brimming
  with bitter suffering, hard to understand,
we take it gladly, trusting though with trembling,
  out of so good and so beloved a hand.

4 If once again, in this mixed world, you give us
  the joy we had, the brightness of your sun,
we shall recall what we have learned through sorrow,
  and dedicate our lives to you alone.

5 Now as your silence deeply spreads around us,
  open our ears to hear your children raise
from all the world, from every nation round us,
  to you their universal hymn of praise.

DIETRICH BONHOEFFER (1906–45)
(written for the New Year, 1945)
tr. F. PRATT GREEN (b. 1903)
and Compilers

118

CARPENTER, CARPENTER

MARION PAYTON

Some - bo - dy great - er than   you   or   me,___

put the ap - ple on the ap - ple - tree; __ the flower in the earth and the fish in the sea, are by some-bo - dy great - er than you or me. __

CARPENTER, carpenter, make me a tree,
that's the work of somebody far greater than me;
gardener, gardener, shape me a flower,
that's the work of somebody with far greater power.

Somebody greater than you or me,
put the apple on the apple-tree;
the flower in the earth and the fish in the sea,
are by somebody greater than you or me.

2 Builder, now raise up a coloured rainbow,
that's something far greater than people could know;
farmer, I ask you design me some corn,
that's somebody greater than any man born.

3 Now, electrician, will you light a star,
that's the work of somebody who's greater by far;
plumber, connect up the river and sea,
that's the work of somebody far greater than me.

MARION PAYTON

119

CHILEAN VENITE   66 66 44 44

Chilean folk melody
adpt. and arr. MICHAEL PAGET

*In the second half of verses 2, 3, and 4, soprano voices may sing the small notes as echoes.

COME, let us praise the Lord,
  with joy our God proclaim,
his greatness tell abroad,
  and bless his saving name.
    Lift high your songs
    before his throne
    to whom alone
    all praise belongs.

2 Our God of matchless worth,
  our King beyond compare,
the deepest bounds of earth,
  the hills, are in his care.
    He all decrees,
    who by his hand
    prepared the land
    and formed the seas.

3 In worship bow the knee,
  our glorious God confess;
the great creator, he,
  the Lord our righteousness.
    He reigns unseen:
    his flock he feeds
    and gently leads
    in pastures green.

4 Come, hear his voice today,
  receive what love imparts;
his holy will obey
  and harden not your hearts.
    His ways are best;
    and lead at last,
    all troubles past,
    to perfect rest.

TIMOTHY DUDLEY-SMITH (b. 1926)
based on Psalm 95

120

ST GEORGE'S, WINDSOR   77 77 D

G. J. ELVEY (1816–93)

COME, you thankful people, come,
raise the song of harvest-home!
Fruit and crops are gathered in,
safe before the storms begin;
God our maker will provide
for our needs to be supplied:
come with all God's people, come,
raise the song of harvest-home.

2 All the world is God's own field,
fruit unto his praise to yield;
wheat and weeds together sown,
unto joy or sorrow grown;
first the blade, and then the ear,
then the full corn shall appear:
Lord of harvest, grant that we
wholesome grain and pure may be.

3 For the Lord our God shall come,
and shall take his harvest home,
from his field shall in that day
all corruption purge away,
give his angels charge at last
in the fire the weeds to cast,
but the fruitful ears to store
in his care for evermore.

4 Even so, Lord, quickly come,
bring your final harvest home;
gather now your people in,
free from sorrow, free from sin;
there, together purified,
ever thankful at your side:
come, with all your angels, come,
raise the glorious harvest-home.

HENRY ALFORD (1810–71) altd.

121
FIRST TUNE

LUCERNA LAUDONIAE   77 77 77

DAVID EVANS (1874–1948)

Fa - ther,   un - to   you___   we___   raise   this   our   sac - ri - fice   of   praise.

SECOND TUNE

ENGLAND'S LANE   77 77 77

English traditional melody
adpt. GEOFFREY SHAW (1879–1943)

Fa-ther, un-to you we raise   this our   sac-ri-fice of praise.

FOR the beauty of the earth,
   for the beauty of the skies,
for the love which from our birth
   over and around us lies;

Father, unto you we raise
this our sacrifice of praise.

2 For the beauty of each hour
   of the day and of the night,
hill and vale, and tree and flower,
   sun and moon, and stars of light;

3 For the joy of human love,
   brother, sister, parent, child,
friends on earth, and friends above;
   for all gentle thoughts and mild;

4 For your greater gift of grace,
   Christ your Son to sinners given,
bringing to our human race
   all the hopes and joys of heaven;

5 For the Church that evermore
   lifts her holy hands above,
offering up on every shore
   her pure sacrifice of love;

F. S. PIERPOINT (1835–1917) altd.

122

IRISH   CM

Hymns and Sacred Poems
Dublin, 1749

Melody from *Scottish Psalter*, 1635
as given in PLAYFORD'S *Psalms*, 1671

LONDON NEW   CM

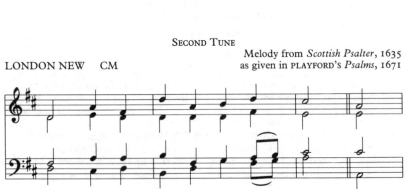

God moves in a mysterious way,
  his wonders to perform;
he plants his footsteps in the sea,
  and rides upon the storm.

2 Deep in unfathomable mines
  of never-failing skill
he treasures up his bright designs,
  and works his sovereign will.

3 You fearful saints, fresh courage take;
  the clouds you so much dread
are big with mercy, and shall break
  in blessings on your head.

4 Judge not the Lord by feeble sense,
  but trust him for his grace;
behind a frowning providence
  he hides a smiling face.

5 His purposes will ripen fast,
  unfolding every hour;
the bud may have a bitter taste,
  but sweet will be the flower.

6 Blind unbelief is sure to err,
  and scan his work in vain;
God is his own interpreter,
  and he will make it plain.

WILLIAM COWPER (1731–1800)

123

EAST ACKLAM   84 84 888 4   FRANCIS JACKSON (b. 1917)

FOR the fruits of his creation,
   thanks be to God;
for his gifts to every nation,
   thanks be to God;
for the ploughing, sowing, reaping,
silent growth while we are sleeping,
future needs in earth's safe keeping,
   thanks be to God.

2 In the just reward of labour,
   God's will is done;
  in the help we give our neighbour,
   God's will is done;
  in our world-wide task of caring
  for the hungry and despairing,
  in the harvest we are sharing,
   God's will is done.

3 For the harvest of his Spirit,
   thanks be to God;
  for the good we all inherit,
   thanks be to God;
  for the wonders that astound us,
  for the truths that still confound us,
  most of all, that love has found us,
   thanks be to God.

F. PRATT GREEN (b. 1903)

124

SHIPSTON   87 87

English traditional melody
arr. R. VAUGHAN WILLIAMS (1872–1958)

GOD, whose farm is all creation,
   take the gratitude we give;
take the finest of our harvest,
   crops we grow that all may live.

2 Take our ploughing, seeding, reaping,
   hopes and fears of sun and rain,
  all our thinking, planning, waiting,
   ripened in this fruit and grain.

3 All our labour, all our watching,
   all our calendar of care,
  in these crops of your creation,
   take, O God: they are our prayer.

JOHN ARLOTT (b. 1914)

125

HE MADE ME   86 86 86 83

ALAN PINNOCK

HE gave me eyes so I could see
the wonders of the world;
without my eyes I could not see
the other boys and girls.
He gave me ears so I could hear
the wind and rain and sea.
I've got to tell it to the world,
He made me!

2 He gave me lips so I could speak
　　and say what's in my mind;
　without my lips I could not speak
　　a single word or line.
　He made my mind so I could think,
　　and choose what I should be.
　I've got to tell it to the world,
　　He made me!

3 He gave me hands so I could touch
　　and hold a thousand things;
　I need my hands to help me write,
　　to help me fetch and bring.
　These feet he made so I could run,
　　he meant me to be free.
　I've got to tell it to the world,
　　He made me!

ALAN PINNOCK

126

DUNDEE　CM

Melody from *Scottish Psalter*, 1615
Harmony from T. RAVENSCROFT'S *Psalmes*, 1621

1 TO the hills will lift mine eyes:
　　from whence doth come mine aid?
　My safety cometh from the Lord,
　　who heaven and earth hath made.

2 Thy foot he'll not let slide, nor will
　　he slumber that thee keeps.
　Behold, he that keeps Israel,
　　he slumbers not, nor sleeps.

3 The Lord thee keeps; the Lord thy shade
　　on thy right hand doth stay;
　the moon by night thee shall not smite,
　　nor yet the sun by day.

4 The Lord shall keep thy soul; he shall
　　preserve thee from all ill;
　henceforth thy going out and in
　　God keep for ever will.

FRANCIS ROUS (1579–1659)
WILLIAM BARTON (1597–1678)
based on Psalm 121

127

MONMOUTH   888 D

G. DAVIS (*c*.1770–1824)

I'LL praise my maker while I've breath,
and when my voice is lost in death,
    praise shall employ my nobler powers:
my days of praise are never past,
while life and thought and being last,
    or immortality endures.

2 Happy the one whose hopes rely
    on Jacob's God! He made the sky
        and earth and seas, which life contain:
his truth for ever stands secure;
    he saves the oppressed, he feeds the poor,
        and none shall find his promise vain.

3 The Lord has eyes to give the blind;
    the Lord supports the fainting mind;
        he sends the labouring conscience peace:
he helps the stranger in distress,
    the widow and the fatherless,
        and grants the prisoner sweet release.

4 I'll praise him while he lends me breath;
    and when my voice is lost in death,
        praise shall employ my nobler powers:
my days of praise are never past,
    while life and thought and being last,
        or immortality endures.

ISAAC WATTS (1674–1748) altd.
based on Psalm 146

128

NUN DANKET   67 67 66 66

Adpt. from a melody by
J. CRÜGER (1598–1662)

Now thank we all our God,
   with hearts and hands and voices,
who wondrous things has done,
   in whom this world rejoices;
who, from our mother's arms,
   has blessed us on our way
with countless gifts of love,
   and still is ours today.

2 O may this bounteous God,
   through all our life be near us,
with ever joyful hearts
   and blessèd peace to cheer us;
and keep us in his grace,
   and guide us when perplexed,
and bring us in his love
   through this world to the next.

3 All praise and thanks to God
   the Father now be given,
the Son and him who reigns
   with them in highest heaven;
the one eternal God,
   whom earth and heaven adore;
for thus it was, is now,
   and shall be evermore.

MARTIN RINKART (1586–1649)
tr. CATHERINE WINKWORTH (1827–78) altd.

128 Second Tune

GRACIAS 67 67 66 66 Geoffrey Beaumont (1903–70)

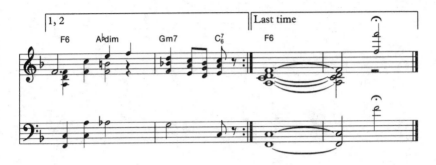

Now thank we all our God,
  with hearts and hands and voices,
who wondrous things has done,
  in whom this world rejoices;
who, from our mother's arms,
  has blessed us on our way
with countless gifts of love,
  and still is ours today.

2 O may this bounteous God,
  through all our life be near us,
with ever joyful hearts
  and blessèd peace to cheer us;
and keep us in his grace,
  and guide us when perplexed,
and bring us in his love
  through this world to the next.

3 All praise and thanks to God
  the Father now be given,
the Son and him who reigns
  with them in highest heaven;
the one eternal God,
  whom earth and heaven adore;
for thus it was, is now,
  and shall be evermore.

MARTIN RINKART (1586–1649)
tr. CATHERINE WINKWORTH (1827–78) altd.

129

TYTHERTON SM

L. R WEST (1753–1826)

SOUTHWELL SM

DAMON'S *Psalmes*, 1579

O BLESS the Lord, my soul,
  his saving grace proclaim,
and all that is within me join
  to bless his holy name.

2 O bless the Lord, my soul,
    his mercies bear in mind,
  forget not all his benefits:
    the Lord to me is kind.

3 He will not always chide;
    he will with patience wait;
  his wrath is ever slow to rise,
    and ready to abate.

4 He pardons all my sins,
    prolongs my feeble breath,
  he heals all my infirmities,
    and ransoms me from death.

5 He clothes me with his love,
    upholds me with his truth,
  and like the eagle he renews
    the vigour of my youth.

6 Then bless his holy name
    whose grace has made me whole,
  whose loving-kindness crowns my days;
    O bless the Lord, my soul.

attrib. JAMES MONTGOMERY (1771–1854) altd.
based on Psalm 103

130

First Tune

HIGHWOOD   11 10 11 10   R. R. TERRY (1865–1938)

Second Tune

STRENGTH AND STAY   11 10 11 10   J. B. DYKES (1823–76)

O Lord of every shining constellation
    that wheels in splendour through the midnight sky;
grant us your Spirit's true illumination
    to read the secrets of your work on high.

2 You, Lord, have made the atom's hidden forces,
    your laws its mighty energies fulfil;
teach us, to whom you give such rich resources,
    in all we use, to serve your holy will.

3 O Life, awaking life in cell and tissue,
    from flower to bird, from beast to brain of man;
help us to trace, from birth to final issue,
    the sure unfolding of your age-long plan.

4 You, Lord, have stamped your image on your creatures,
    and, though they mar that image, love them still;
lift up our eyes to Christ, that in his features
    we may discern the beauty of your will.

5 Great Lord of nature, shaping and renewing,
    you made us more than nature's sons to be;
you help us tread, with grace our souls enduing,
    the road to life and immortality.

ALBERT F. BAYLY (1901–84)

131

From a Hebrew melody
adpt. THOMAS OLIVERS (1725–99)

LEONI   66 84 D

THE GOD of Abraham praise,
  who reigns enthroned above,
ancient of everlasting days,
  and God of love.
Jehovah great I AM!
  by earth and heaven confessed;
we bow and bless the sacred name,
  for ever blest.

2 The God of Abraham praise,
  at whose supreme command
from earth we rise, and seek the joys
  at his right hand;
we all on earth forsake,
  its wisdom, fame and power;
and him our only portion make,
  our shield and tower.

3 The God of Abraham praise,
  whose all-sufficient grace
shall guide us all our happy days,
  in all our ways:
he is our faithful friend;
  he is our gracious God;
and he will save us to the end,
  through Jesus' blood.

4 He by himself has sworn—
  we on his oath depend—
we shall, on eagles' wings upborne,
  to heaven ascend:
we shall behold his face,
  we shall his power adore,
and sing the wonders of his grace
  for evermore.

5 The whole triumphant host
  give thanks to God on high:
'Hail, Father, Son and Holy Ghost!'
  they ever cry.
Hail Abraham's God and ours!
  We join the heavenly throng,
and celebrate with all our powers
  in endless song.

THOMAS OLIVERS (1725–99) altd.

132

BUNESSAN   55 54 D

Gaelic melody
harm. *New Church Praise*, 1975

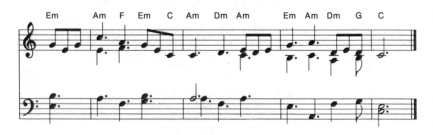

For an alternative arrangement of this tune (in D major) see no. 249.

MORNING has broken
  like the first morning,
blackbird has spoken
  like the first bird.
Praise for the singing!
  Praise for the morning!
Praise for them, springing
  fresh from the word!

2 Sweet the rain's new fall
   sunlit from heaven,
 like the first dewfall
   on the first grass.
 Praise for the sweetness
   of the wet garden,
 sprung in completeness
   where his feet pass.

3 Mine is the sunlight!
   Mine is the morning!
 Born of the one light
   Eden saw play!
Praise with elation,
   praise every morning,
God's re-creation
  of the new day!

ELEANOR FARJEON (1881–1965)

133

CREATOR GOD   CM   NORMAN L. WARREN (b. 1934)

THERE is no moment of my life,
    no place where I may go,
no action which God does not see,
    no thought he does not know.

2 Before I speak, my words are known,
      and all that I decide,
  to come or go: God knows my
        choice,
      and makes himself my guide.

3 If I should close my eyes to him,
      he comes to give me sight;
  if I should go where all is dark,
      he makes my darkness light.

4 He knew my days before all days,
      before I came to be;
  he keeps me, loves me, in my ways;
      no lover such as he.

BRIAN FOLEY (b. 1919)
based on Psalm 139

134

GENESIS   10 9 10 9 with refrain   GRAHAM WESTCOTT (b. 1947)

PART I

THINK of a world without any flowers,
    think of a wood without any trees,
think of a sky without any sunshine,
    think of the air without any breeze.
We thank you, Lord, for flowers and trees and sunshine;
we thank you, Lord, and praise your holy name.

2   Think of a world without any animals,
    think of a field without any herd,
think of a stream without any fishes,
    think of a dawn without any bird.
We thank you, Lord, for all your living creatures;
we thank you, Lord, and praise your holy name.

PART II

3   Think of a world without any paintings,
        think of a room where all the walls are bare,
    think of a rainbow without any colours,
        think of the earth with darkness everywhere.
    We thank you, Lord, for paintings and for colours;
    we thank you, Lord, and praise your holy name.

4   Think of a world without any poetry,
        think of a book without any words,
    think of a song without any music,
        think of a hymn without any verse.
    We thank you, Lord, for poetry and music:
    we thank you, Lord, and praise your holy name.

5   Think of a world without any science,
        think of a journey with nothing to explore,
    think of a quest without any mystery,
        nothing to seek and nothing left in store.
    We thank you, Lord, for miracles of science;
    we thank you, Lord, and praise your holy name.

6   Think of a world without any people,
        think of a street with no-one living there,
    think of a town without any houses,
        no-one to love and nobody to care.
    We thank you, Lord, for families and friendships;
    we thank you, Lord, and praise your holy name.

PART III

7   Think of a world without any worship,
        think of a God without his only Son,
    think of a cross without a resurrection,
        only a grave and not a victory won.
    We thank you, Lord, for showing us our Saviour;
    we thank you, Lord, and praise your holy name.

8   Thanks to our Lord for being here among us,
        thanks be to him for sharing all we do,
    thanks for our church and all the love we find here,
        thanks for this place and all its promise true.
    We thank you, Lord, for life in all its richness;
    we thank you, Lord, and praise your holy name.

                              BUNTY NEWPORT (b. 1927)

135

WIR PFLÜGEN   76 76 D with refrain   J. A. P SCHULZ (1747–1800)

All good gifts a - round us are sent from heaven a - bove,

then thank the Lord, O thank the Lord, for all____ his love.

WE plough the fields and scatter
    the good seed on the land,
but it is fed and watered
    by God's almighty hand;
he sends the snow in winter,
    the warmth to swell the grain,
the breezes and the sunshine
    and soft refreshing rain.

All good gifts around us
are sent from heaven above,
then thank the Lord, O thank the Lord,
for all his love.

2 He only is the maker
    of all things near and far;
he paints the wayside flower,
    he lights the evening star;
the wind and waves obey him,
    by him the birds are fed;
much more to us, his children,
    he gives our daily bread.

3 We thank you then, our Father,
    for all things bright and good,
the seed-time and the harvest,
    our life, our health, our food.
Accept the gifts we offer
    for all your love imparts,
and what you find more precious,
    our humble, thankful hearts.

MATTHIAS CLAUDIUS (1740–1815)
tr. JANE MONTGOMERY CAMPBELL (1817–78)

136

The heavens declare the glory of God;
the skies proclaim the work of his hands.
Day after day they pour forth speech;
night after night they display knowledge.

The law of the Lord is perfect, reviving the soul.
**The statutes of the Lord are trustworthy,
making wise the simple.**

The commands of the Lord are radiant,
giving light to the eyes.
**The fear of the Lord is pure,
enduring for ever.**

137

Lord God, creator of all things, you continually sustain the
life of the universe and all that is within it.
**We thank you that you have called us
to share in the work of caring for what you have made.**

You have made us your partners and led us into the secrets and
mysteries of your universe.
**You have revealed to us the secrets hidden in your creation
and, through the skills of scientists, physicists and engineers,
you have taught us how to use them effectively.**

You have placed us in a position of great responsibility within
the animal kingdom.
**Lord God,
accept our thanks for this green and fertile planet
and for the place you have given us within it.**

138

**O Lord, whose way is perfect,
help us always to trust in your goodness,
that walking with you
and following you in all simplicity,
we may possess quiet and contented minds
and may cast all our care on you,
for you care for us.
Grant this, O Lord, for the sake of your Son, Jesus Christ.
Amen.**

139

STUTTGART   87 87   Melody by C. F. WITT (1660–1716)

May also be sung to CROSS OF JESUS, no. 285.

COME, thou long-expected Jesus,
  born to set thy people free;
from our fears and sins release us;
  let us find our rest in thee.

2 Israel's strength and consolation,
    hope of all the earth thou art;
  dear desire of every nation,
    joy of every longing heart.

3 Born thy people to deliver;
    born a child, and yet a king;
  born to reign in us for ever;
    now thy gracious kingdom bring.

4 By thine own eternal Spirit
    rule in all our hearts alone:
  by thine all-sufficient merit
    raise us to thy glorious throne.

CHARLES WESLEY (1707–88)

140

ES IST EIN' ROS'   76 76 676

German melody
harm. MICHAEL PRAETORIUS (1571–1621)

A GREAT and mighty wonder:
    redemption drawing near!
the virgin bears the infant,
    the Prince of peace is here:
repeat the hymn again:

To God on high be glory,
and peace on earth. Amen.

2 The Word becomes incarnate
    and yet remains on high;
the shepherds hear the anthem
    as glory fills the sky:
repeat the hymn again:

3 The angels sing the story:
    rejoice, O distant lands!
you valleys, forests, mountains,
    and oceans, clap your hands!
repeat the hymn again:

4 He comes to save all nations:
    let all now hear his word!
approach and bring him worship,
    the Saviour and the Lord:
repeat the hymn again:

J. M. NEALE (1818–66)

141

PICARDY   87 87 87

French traditional carol

ORIEL   87 87 87

C. ETT, *Cantica Sacra*, 1840

EARTH was waiting, spent and
   restless,
  with a mingled hope and fear;
and the faithful few were sighing,
  'Surely, Lord, the day is near;
the desire of all the nations,
  it is time he should appear.'

2 Still the gods were in their temples,
  but the ancient faith had fled;
and the priests stood by their altars
  only for a piece of bread;
and the oracles were silent,
  and the prophets all were dead.

3 In the sacred courts of Zion,
  where the Lord had his abode,
there the money-changers trafficked,
  and the sheep and oxen trod;
and the world, because of wisdom,
  knew not either Lord or God.

4 Then the Spirit of the Highest
  on a virgin meek came down,
and he burdened her with blessing,
  and he pained her with renown;
for she bore the Lord's anointed,
  for his cross and for his crown.

5 Earth for him had groaned and travailed
  since the ages first began;
for in him was hid the secret
  that through all the ages ran—
Son of Mary, Son of David,
  Son of God, and Son of Man.

W. C. SMITH (1824–1908)

142

CRÜGER   76 76 D

J. CRÜGER (1598–1662)
adpt. W. H. MONK (1823–89)

HAIL to the Lord's anointed,
   great David's greater Son!
Hail, in the time appointed,
   his reign on earth begun!
He comes to break oppression,
   to set the captive free,
to take away transgression,
   and rule in equity.

2 He comes with comfort speedy
      to those who suffer wrong;
   to help the poor and needy,
      and bid the weak be strong;
   to give them songs for sighing,
      their darkness turn to light,
   whose souls, condemned and dying,
      are precious in his sight.

3 Before him on the mountains,
      shall peace the herald go,
   and righteousness in fountains
      from hill to valley flow.
   Kings shall fall down before him,
      and gold and incense bring;
   all nations shall adore him,
      his praise all people sing.

4 In all the world victorious,
      he on his throne shall rest;
   from age to age more glorious,
      all-blessing and all-blest;
   the tide of time shall never
      his covenant remove;
   his name shall stand for ever,
      his changeless name of love.

JAMES MONTGOMERY (1771–1854) altd.

143

BRISTOL   CM RAVENSCROFT'S *Psalmes*, 1621

ST SAVIOUR   CM F. G. BAKER (1839–1919)

HARK the glad sound! The Saviour comes,
  the Saviour promised long;
let every heart prepare a throne,
  and every voice a song.

2 He comes the prisoners to release
    from fear and greed and shame,
  each prison wall that evil builds
    shall fall before his name.

3 He comes into a darkened world
    to be its truth and light,
  that those whose eyes are closed to God
    may yet regain their sight.

4 He comes to bind the broken heart,
    to comfort the distressed,
  to pour the treasures of his grace
    on outcast and oppressed.

5 Our glad hosannas, Prince of peace,
    your coming shall proclaim;
  and heaven's eternal arches ring
    with your belovèd name.

PHILIP DODDRIDGE (1702–51) altd.
based on Luke 4: 18–19

144

VENI EMMANUEL   88 88 88

From a 15th-century French Missal
adpt. T. HELMORE (1811–90)

O COME, O come, Immanuel,
and ransom captive Israel,
that mourns in lonely exile here
until the Son of God appear.

Rejoice! rejoice! Immanuel
shall come to thee, O Israel.

2 O come, O come, thou Lord of might,
who to thy tribes on Sinai's height
in ancient times didst give the law
in cloud and majesty and awe.

3 O come, thou rod of Jesse, free
thine own from Satan's tyranny;
from depths of hell thy people save,
and give them victory o'er the grave.

4 O come, thou dayspring, come and cheer
our spirits by thine advent here;
disperse the gloomy clouds of night,
and death's dark shadows put to flight.

5 O come, thou key of David, come
and open wide our heavenly home;
make safe the way that leads on high,
and close the path to misery.

Latin, 12th century
tr. J. M. NEALE (1818–66) altd.

145

DIVINUM MYSTERIUM   87 87 877   Melody from *Piae Cantiones*, 1582

SECOND TUNE

NEANDER   87 87 87   From Chorale *Unser Herrscher*
by J. NEANDER (1650–80)

With this tune the line 'Evermore and evermore' is omitted.

Of the Father's heart begotten
  when the worlds had yet to be,
he is Alpha and Omega,
  he the source, the ending he,
of the things that are, that have been,
  and that future years shall see:

  Evermore and evermore.

2 By his word was all created;
   he commanded; it was done!
earth and sky and boundless ocean,
   universe of three in one,
all that sees the moon's soft radiance,
   all that breathes beneath the sun.

3 This is he whom saints in old time,
   in their visions looked toward,
whom the voices of the prophets
   promised in their faithful word:
now he shines, the long-expected;
   let creation praise its Lord.

4 Now let old and young uniting
   sound, in music's richest ways,
all his wondrous grace and glory,
   infant lips their anthems raise,
sisters, brothers, parents singing
   with pure heart their song of praise.

5 All the heights of heaven adore him;
   angel hosts, his praises sing;
all dominions, bow before him,
   and extol our God and King;
let no tongue on earth be silent,
   every voice in concert sing.

AURELIUS PRUDENTIUS (348–413)
tr. J. M. NEALE (1818–66) altd.

146

CRUGYBAR   98 98 D

Welsh traditional melody

THE light of the morning is breaking,
   the shadows are passing away;
the nations of earth are awaking,
   new peoples are learning to pray.
Let wrong, great Redeemer, be righted,
   in knowing and doing your will;
and gather, one family united,
   the whole world to your cross on the hill.

2 Your love is the bond of creation,
   your love is the peace of mankind:
make safe with your love every nation
   in concord of heart and of mind.
Your pity alone can deliver
   the earth from her sorrows, dear Lord:
her pride and her hardness forgive her,
   your blood for her ransom was poured.

3 Your throne, great Redeemer, be founded
   in radiance of wisdom and love;
your name through the wide world be sounded
   till earth be as heaven above.
Though hills and high mountains should tremble,
   though all that is seen melt away,
your voice shall in triumph assemble
   your loved ones at dawning of day.

H. ELVET LEWIS (1860–1953)

147

WINCHESTER NEW   LM

From a chorale in the
Musikalisches Handbuch, Hamburg, 1690
arr. W. H. HAVERGAL (1793–1870)

ON Jordan's bank the Baptist's cry
announces that the Lord is nigh;
awake and hearken, for he brings
glad tidings from the King of kings.

2 Then cleansed be every life from sin,
make straight the way for God within.
Now let us each our heart prepare
for Christ to come and enter there.

3 For you are our salvation, Lord,
our refuge, and our great reward;
without your grace we waste away
like flowers that wither and decay.

4 To heal the sick stretch out your hand,
and bid the fallen sinner stand;
shine forth, and let your light restore
earth's own true loveliness once more.

5 All praise to you eternal Son,
whose work of freedom has begun,
whom, with the Father, we adore
and Holy Spirit evermore.

CHARLES COFFIN (1676–1749)
tr. JOHN CHANDLER (1806–76) and others
based on Luke 3: 1–18

148

WAIT FOR THE LORD

JACQUES BERTHIER
as sung at Taizé

WAIT for the Lord,
his day is near.
Wait for the Lord:
be strong, take heart!

Taizé Community

149

THERE'S A LIGHT UPON THE MOUNTAINS
15 15 15 15

M. L. WOSTENHOLM
(1887–1959)

THERE'S a light upon the mountains,
　　and the day is at the spring,
when our eyes shall see the beauty
　　and the glory of the King;
weary was our heart with waiting,
　　and the night watch seemed so long,
but his triumph day is breaking,
　　and we hail it with a song.

2 There's a hush of expectation,
　　and a quiet in the air;
and the breath of God is moving
　　in the fervent breath of prayer;
for the suffering, dying Jesus
　　is the Christ upon the throne,
and the travail of our spirits
　　is the travail of his own.

3 He is breaking down the barriers,
　　he is casting up the way;
he is calling for his angels
　　to build up the gates of day;
but his angels here are human,
　　not the shining hosts above,
for the drum-beats of his army
　　are the heart-beats of our love.

4 Hark! we hear a distant music,
　　and it comes with fuller swell;
it's the triumph song of Jesus,
　　of our king Immanuel;
Zion, go now forth to meet him,
　　and my soul, be swift to bring
all the sweetest and the dearest
　　for the triumph of our King.

HENRY BURTON (1840–1930)

150

Let the heavens rejoice and the earth exult,
   let the sea roar and all the creatures in it,
let the fields exult and all that is in them;
      then let all the trees of the forest shout for joy
      before the Lord when he comes to judge the earth.
He will judge the earth with righteousness
      and the peoples in good faith.

151

'I am the Alpha and the Omega,' says the Lord God,
      'who is and who was and who is to come,
      the sovereign Lord of all.'
He who gives this testimony speaks: 'Yes, I am coming soon!'
      Amen. Come, Lord Jesus!

152

Almighty God,
give us grace to cast away the works of darkness
and to put on the armour of light,
now in the time of this mortal life,
in which your Son Jesus Christ
      came to us in great humility:
so that, at the last day,
when he shall come in his glorious majesty
      to judge the living and the dead,
we may rise to the life immortal,
through him who is alive and reigns
      with you and the Holy Spirit,
one God, now and for ever.
Amen.

153   A PRAYER FOR BIBLE STUDY

Blessed Lord,
who caused all holy Scriptures
      to be written for our learning:
help us so to hear them,
to read, mark, learn, and inwardly digest them,
that, through patience, and the comfort
      of your holy word,
we may embrace and for ever hold fast
      the hope of everlasting life
which you have given us in our Saviour Jesus Christ.
Amen.

154   THE LIGHTING OF THE ADVENT CANDLES

Advent 1 · The First Candle

We light this first Advent Candle to remind us of the Advent hope—
Jesus is coming again!

**The Apostle Paul writes: The night is nearly over, the day is
almost here. Let us stop doing the things that belong to the dark,
and let us take up weapons for fighting in the light.**

Advent 2 · The Second Candle

We light this second Advent Candle to remind us of God's gift of the Bible—
the Bible points us to Jesus, the light of the world.

**The Apostle Peter writes: The word of prophecy was fulfilled
in our hearing! You should give that word your closest attention,
for it shines like a lamp amidst all the dirt and darkness
of the world, until the day dawns, and the morning star rises
in your hearts.**

Advent 3 · The Third Candle

We light this third Advent Candle to remind us of John the Baptist and of
all God's messengers who prepare the way of the Saviour's coming.

**The Apostle John writes: God sent his messenger,
a man named John, who came to tell people about the light,
so that all should hear his message and believe.**

Advent 4 · The Fourth Candle

We light this fourth Advent Candle to remind us of our calling to reflect
the light of Jesus in this dark world.

**Jesus said: You are the world's light . . . Let your light shine
in the sight of men. Let them see the good things you do
and praise your Father in heaven.**

Christmas Day · The Christmas Candle

We light this Christmas Candle to remind us that Jesus is the light of
the world.

**A boy has been born for us, a son given to us.
Glory to God in highest heaven!
Peace upon earth amongst people of goodwill!**

155

IRIS   87 87 with refrain

French traditional carol

Come _____ and wor - ship

Christ, the new-born King: __ wor-ship Christ the new - born King.

ANGELS from the realms of glory,
   wing your flight through all the earth;
heralds of creation's story
   now proclaim Messiah's birth!

   Come and worship
     Christ, the new-born King:
   come and worship,
     worship Christ the new-born King.

2 Shepherds in the fields abiding
   watching by your flocks at night,
God with us is now residing:
   see, there shines the infant light!

3 Wise men, leave your contemplations!
   brighter visions shine afar;
seek in him the hope of nations,
   you have seen his rising star:

4 Though an infant now we view him,
   he will share his Father's throne,
gather all the nations to him;
   every knee shall then bow down:

JAMES MONTGOMERY (1771–1854)

156

MARY'S CHILD   4 3 6 D

GEOFFREY AINGER (b. 1925)
arr. A. S. COX (b. 1918)

Born in the night,
    Mary's child,
a long way from your home;
    coming in need,
      Mary's child,
born in a borrowed room.

2   Clear shining light,
      Mary's child,
your face lights up our way;
    light of the world,
      Mary's child,
dawn on our darkened day.

3   Truth of our life,
      Mary's child,
you tell us God is good;
    prove it is true,
      Mary's child,
go to your cross of wood.

4   Hope of the world,
      Mary's child,
you're coming soon to reign;
    King of the earth,
      Mary's child,
walk in our streets again.

GEOFFREY AINGER (b. 1925)

157

CRADLE SONG   11 11 11 11 Anapaestic   W. J. KIRKPATRICK (1838–1921)

Away in a manger, no crib for a bed,
the little Lord Jesus laid down his sweet head.
The stars in the bright sky looked down where he lay,
the little Lord Jesus asleep on the hay.

2 The cattle are lowing, the baby awakes,
but little Lord Jesus no crying he makes.
I love you, Lord Jesus—look down from the sky,
and stay by my side until morning is nigh.

3 Be near me, Lord Jesus; I ask you to stay
close by me for ever, and love me, I pray.
Bless all the dear children in your tender care,
and fit us for heaven to live with you there.

vv. 1 & 2 Anon.
v. 3 J. T. McFARLAND

158

BUNESSAN   55 54 D

Gaelic melody
harm. *New Church Praise*, 1975

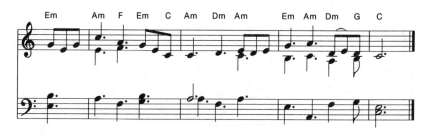

For an alternative arrangement of this tune (in D major) see no. 249.

CHILD in the manger,
  infant of Mary;
outcast and stranger,
  Lord of all;
child who inherits
  all our transgressions,
all our demerits
  on him fall.

2 Once the most holy
  child of salvation
gently and lowly
  lived below;
now as our glorious
  mighty Redeemer,
see him victorious
  over each foe.

3 Prophets foretold him
  infant of wonder;
angels behold him
  on his throne;
worthy our Saviour
  of all their praises;
happy for ever
  are his own.

MARY MACDONALD (1789–1872)
tr. LACHLAN MACBEAN (1853–1931)

159

YORKSHIRE   10 10 10 10 10 10   J. WAINWRIGHT (1723–68)

CHRISTIANS, awake! salute the happy morn,
on which the Saviour of mankind was born;
rise to adore the mystery of love
which hosts of angels chanted from above;
with them the joyful tidings first began
of God incarnate, of the virgin's son.

2 Then to the watchful shepherds it was told,
who heard the angelic herald's voice, 'Behold,
I bring good tidings of a Saviour's birth
to you and all the nations upon earth:
this day has God fulfilled his promised word,
this day is born a Saviour, Christ the Lord.'

3 He spoke; and straightway the celestial choir
in hymns of joy, unknown, before conspire.
The praises of redeeming love they sang,
and heaven's whole orb with alleluias rang:
God's highest glory was their anthem still,
'On earth be peace, and unto men goodwill.'

4 O may we keep and ponder in our mind
God's wondrous love in saving lost mankind;
trace we the babe, who has retrieved our loss,
from his poor manger to his bitter cross;
tread in his steps, assisted by his grace,
till our first heavenly state again takes place.

5 Then may we hope, the angelic hosts among,
to sing, redeemed, a glad triumphant song:
he that was born upon this joyful day
around us all his glory shall display;
saved by his love, incessant we shall sing
eternal praise to heaven's almighty King.

JOHN BYROM (1692–1763)
based on Luke 2: 10

160

CELEBRATIONS Irregular with refrain

VALERIE COLLISON (b. 1933)

Come and join the ce-le-bra-tion, it's a ve-ry spe-cial day; come and share our ju-bi-la-tion, there's a new king born_ to-day!

Come and join the celebration,
it's a very special day;
come and share our jubilation,
there's a new king born today!

SEE the shepherds hurry down to Bethlehem,
gaze in wonder at the Son of God who lay before them.

2 Wise men journey, led to worship by a star,
   kneel in homage, bringing precious gifts from lands afar, so,

3 'God is with us,' round the world the message bring,
   he is with us, 'Welcome' all the bells on earth are pealing.

VALERIE COLLISON (b. 1933)

161

AR HYD Y NOS   84 84 888 4

Welsh traditional melody
arr. JOHN BARNARD (b. 1948)

COME and sing the Christmas story
   this holy night!
Christ is born: the hope of glory
   dawns on our sight.
Alleluia! Earth is ringing
with a thousand angels singing—
hear the message they are bringing
   this holy night.

2 Jesus, Saviour, child of Mary
   this holy night,
in a world confused and weary
   you are our light.
God is in a manger lying,
manhood taking, self denying,
life embracing, death defying
   this holy night.

3 Lord of all! Let us acclaim him
   this holy night;
King of our salvation name him,
   throned in the height.
Son of Man—let us adore him,
all the earth is waiting for him;
Son of God—we bow before him
   this holy night.

MICHAEL PERRY (b. 1942)

162

EVERY STAR   87 87 with refrain   SYDNEY CARTER (b. 1915)

God a-bove,   man be-low,   ho-ly is the_ name I_ know.

EVERY star shall sing a carol;
   every creature, high or low,
come and praise the King of heaven
   by whatever name you know.

    God above, man below,
    holy is the name I know.

2 When the King of all creation
   had a cradle on the earth,
holy was the human body,
   holy was the human birth.

3 Who can tell what other cradle
   high above the milky way
still may rock the King of heaven
   on another Christmas Day?

4 Who can count how many crosses
   still to come or long ago
crucify the King of heaven?
   Holy is the name I know.

5 Who can tell what other body
   he will hallow for his own?
I will praise the son of Mary,
   brother of my blood and bone.

6 Every star and every planet,
   every creature high and low,
come and praise the King of heaven
   by whatever name you know.

SYDNEY CARTER (b. 1915)

163

GOD REST YOU MERRY, GENTLEMEN   English traditional carol
86 86 86 with refrain

O___ ti - dings of com - fort and joy, com-fort and

joil.— O— ti - dings of com - fort and joy!

GOD rest you merry, gentlemen,
　　let nothing you dismay,
for Jesus Christ our Saviour
　　was born on Christmas Day,
to save us all from Satan's power
　　when we had gone astray:

　　O tidings of comfort and joy.

2 At Bethlehem in Judah
　　this holy babe was born,
and laid within a manger
　　upon this happy morn;
at which his mother Mary
　　did neither fear nor scorn:

3 From God our heavenly Father
　　a holy angel came;
the shepherds saw the glory
　　and heard the voice proclaim
that Christ was born in Bethlehem—
　　and Jesus is his name:

4 The shepherds at these tidings
　　rejoiced in heart and mind,
and on the darkened hillside
　　they left their flocks behind,
and went to Bethlehem straightway
　　this holy child to find:

5 And when to Bethlehem they came
　　where Christ the infant lay;
they found him in a manger
　　where oxen fed on hay,
and there beside her newborn child
　　his mother knelt to pray:

6 Now to the Lord sing praises,
　　all people in this place!
with Christian love and fellowship
　　each other now embrace,
and let this Christmas festival
　　all bitterness displace.

Traditional

164

IN DULCI JUBILO   66 77 78 55   14th-century German carol melody

GOOD Christians all, rejoice
with heart and soul and voice;
listen now to what we say,
Jesus Christ is born today:
ox and ass before him bow,
and he is in the manger now.
Christ is born today!
Christ is born today!

2 Good Christians all, rejoice
with heart and soul and voice;
now you hear of endless bliss,
Jesus Christ was born for this;
he has opened heaven's door,
mankind is blest for evermore.
Christ was born for this!
Christ was born for this!

3 Good Christians all, rejoice
with heart and soul and voice;
now you need not fear the grave,
Jesus Christ was born to save;
come at his most gracious call
to find salvation, one and all:
Christ was born to save!
Christ was born to save!

J. M. NEALE (1818–66)

165

MENDELSSOHN   77 77 D with refrain

F. MENDELSSOHN (1809–47)
arr. W. H. CUMMINGS (1831–1915)

Hark! the he-rald-an-gels sing_ Glo-ry_ to   the new-born King.

HARK! the herald-angels sing
glory to the new-born King,
peace on earth, and mercy mild,
God and sinners reconciled.
Joyful, all you nations rise,
join the triumph of the skies;
with the angelic host proclaim,
'Christ is born in Bethlehem.'

Hark! the herald-angels sing
Glory to the new-born King.

2 Christ, by highest heaven adored,
Christ, the everlasting Lord,
late in time behold him come,
offspring of a virgin's womb.
Veiled in flesh the Godhead see!
Hail, the incarnate deity!
Pleased as man with men to dwell,
Jesus, our Immanuel.

3 Hail, the heaven-born Prince of peace!
Hail, the sun of righteousness!
Light and life to all he brings,
risen with healing in his wings,
mild, he lays his glory by;
born, that man no more may die;
born, to raise the sons of earth;
born, to give them second birth.

CHARLES WESLEY (1707–88)
based on Luke 2: 1–20

166

CRANHAM   Irregular

Words by CHRISTINA ROSSETTI (1830–94) altd.
Music by GUSTAV HOLST (1874–1934)

1. In the bleak mid - win - ter,
2. Our God, heav'n can - not hold him,
3. An - gels and arch - an - gels
4. What can I give him,

frost - y wind made moan,____
nor____ earth sus - tain,____
may have ga - thered there,____
poor____ as I am?____

earth stood hard as i - ron,
heav'n and earth shall flee a - way
che - ru - bim and se - ra - phim
If I were a shep - herd,

wa - ter like a stone;   snow had fall - en,
when he comes to reign: in the bleak mid -
thronged the___ air—   but his mo - ther
I would bring a lamb;   if I were a

snow on snow,   snow__ on__ snow,   in the bleak mid -
- win - ter a sta - ble-place suf - ficed the Lord__ God Al -
on - ly, in her maid-en bliss, wor-shipped the be -
wise__ man, I would do my part; yet what I can I

- win - ter,   long___ a - go.
- might - y,   Je - sus___ Christ.
- lov - èd with___ a___ kiss.
give him— give___ my___ heart.

167

Polish carol melody
arr. A. EWART RUSBRIDGE (1917–1969)

INFANT HOLY   87 87 88 77

INFANT holy,
  infant lowly,
for his bed a cattle stall;
  oxen lowing,
  little knowing
Christ the babe is Lord of all.
  Swift are winging
  angels singing,
  nowells ringing,
  tidings bringing,
Christ the babe is Lord of all.

2   Flocks were sleeping,
  shepherds keeping
vigil till the morning new
  saw the glory,
  heard the story,
tidings of a gospel true.
  Thus rejoicing,
  free from sorrow,
  praises voicing,
  greet the morrow,
Christ the babe was born for you!

Polish carol, tr. E. M. G. REED (1885–1933)

168

NOEL   DCM

English traditional melody
adpt. ARTHUR SULLIVAN (1842–1900)
arr. CARADOG ROBERTS (1878–1935)

IT came upon the midnight clear,
    that glorious song of old,
from angels bending near the earth
    to touch their harps of gold:
'Peace on the earth, goodwill to men,
    from heaven's all-gracious King;'
the world in solemn stillness lay
    to hear the angels sing.

2 Still through the cloven skies they come,
    with peaceful wings unfurled,
and still their heavenly music floats
    o'er all the weary world:
above its sad and lowly plains
    they bend on hovering wing,
and over all its Babel sounds
    the blessed angels sing.

3 Yet with the woes of sin and strife
    the world has suffered long,
beneath the angel-strain have rolled
    two thousand years of wrong;
and man, at war with man, hears not
    the love-song which they bring:
so hush the noise, you men of strife,
    and hear the angels sing.

4 And still the days are hastening on,
    by prophets once foretold,
when with the ever-circling years
    comes round the age of gold;
when peace shall over all the earth
    its ancient splendours fling,
and all the world send back the song
    which now the angels sing.

E. H. SEARS (1810–76)
based on Luke 2: 14

169

ADESTE FIDELES Irregular

Melody by J. F. WADE (*c.*1711–86)

O come, let us a - dore him, O come, let us a - dore him, O

come, let us a - dore __ him, __ Christ __ the Lord!

O COME, all you faithful,
  joyful and triumphant,
O come now, O come now to Bethlehem;
  come and behold him,
  born the King of angels:

  O come, let us adore him,
  Christ the Lord!

2   True God of God,
  light from light eternal,
maiden for mother, he was born for us all;
  only begotten,
  Son of God the Father:

3   See how the shepherds,
  summoned to his cradle,
leaving their flocks, draw near to gaze;
  we too will thither
  bend our joyful footsteps:

4   Sing choirs of angels,
  sing in exultation,
sing all you citizens of heaven above.
  'Glory to God,
  glory in the highest!'

CHRISTMAS DAY
5   Yes, Lord, we greet you,
  born this happy morning;
Jesus to you be glory given!
  Word of the Father,
  now in flesh appearing:

Latin, 17th century
tr. FREDERICK OAKELEY (1802–80)
based on Luke 2: 15

170

FIRST TUNE

FOREST GREEN   DCM

English traditional melody
harm. R. VAUGHAN WILLIAMS (1872–1958)

O LITTLE town of Bethlehem,
how still we see you lie!
Above your deep and dreamless sleep
the silent stars go by.
Yet, in your dark streets shining
the everlasting light,
the hopes and fears of all the years
are met in you tonight.

2 For Christ is born of Mary;
and, gathered all above,
while mortals sleep, the angels keep
their watch of wondering love.
O morning stars, together
proclaim the holy birth,
and praises sing to God the King,
and peace to men on earth.

3 How silently, how silently,
the wondrous gift is given!
So God imparts to human hearts
the blessings of his heaven.
No ear may hear his coming;
but in this world of sin,
where meek souls will receive him, still
the dear Christ enters in.

4 O holy child of Bethlehem,
descend to us, we pray;
cast out our sin, and enter in;
be born in us today.
We hear the Christmas angels
the great glad tidings tell;
O come to us, abide with us,
our Lord Immanuel.

PHILLIPS BROOKS (1835–93)

170

CHRISTMAS CAROL   DCM

H. WALFORD DAVIES (1869–1941)

O LITTLE town of Bethlehem,
  how still we see you lie!
Above your deep and dreamless sleep
  the silent stars go by.
Yet, in your dark streets shining
  the everlasting light,
the hopes and fears of all the years
  are met in you tonight.

2 For Christ is born of Mary;
    and, gathered all above,
  while mortals sleep, the angels keep
    their watch of wondering love.
  O morning stars, together
    proclaim the holy birth,
  and praises sing to God the King,
    and peace to men on earth.

3 How silently, how silently,
    the wondrous gift is given!
  So God imparts to human hearts
    the blessings of his heaven.
  No ear may hear his coming;
    but in this world of sin,
  where meek souls will receive him, still
    the dear Christ enters in.

4 O holy child of Bethlehem,
    descend to us, we pray;
  cast out our sin, and enter in;
    be born in us today.
  We hear the Christmas angels
    the great glad tidings tell;
  O come to us, abide with us,
    our Lord Immanuel.

PHILLIPS BROOKS (1835–93)

171

FIRST TUNE

GARTAN   67 67

Irish traditional melody
harm. DAVID EVANS (1874–1948)

SECOND TUNE

LOVE INCARNATE   67 67

C. E. PETTMAN (1865–1943)

LOVE came down at Christmas,
   love all lovely, love divine;
love was born at Christmas—
   star and angels gave the sign.

2 Worship we the Godhead,
   love incarnate, love divine;
worship we our Jesus:
   but wherewith for sacred sign?

3 Love shall be our token,
   love be yours and love be mine,
love to God and all men,
   love for plea and gift and sign.

CHRISTINA ROSSETTI (1830–94)

172

IRBY   87 87 77

H. J. GAUNTLETT (1805–76)
harm. A. H. MANN (1850–1929)

Once in royal David's city
  stood a lowly cattle shed,
where a mother laid her baby
  in a manger for his bed.
Mary was the mother mild,
Jesus Christ her little child.

2 He came down to earth from
    heaven,
    who is God and Lord of all;
and his shelter was a stable,
    and his cradle was a stall;
with the poor, despised and lowly,
lived on earth our Saviour holy.

3 So he is our life's true pattern,
    tears and smiles like us he knew.
From a baby, weak and helpless
    day by day like us he grew;
and he feels for all our sadness,
and he shares in all our gladness.

4 And our eyes at last shall see him,
    through his own redeeming love;
for that child so dear and gentle
    is our Lord in heaven above;
and he leads his children on
to the place where he has gone.

5 Not in that poor lowly stable,
    with the oxen standing by,
we shall see him, but in heaven
    set at God's right hand on high,
when his children gather round
bright like stars, with glory crowned.

CECIL FRANCES ALEXANDER (1818–95)

173

HUMILITY   77 77 with refrain   J. GOSS (1800–80)

Hail, the ev - er - bless-ed morn! Hail, re-demp-tion's hap - py dawn!

Sing through all Je - ru - sa - lem,_ Christ is born in Beth-le-hem!

SEE, amid the winter's snow,
born for us on earth below,
see, the tender lamb appears,
promised from eternal years!

Hail, the ever-blessèd morn!
Hail, redemption's happy dawn!
Sing through all Jerusalem,
Christ is born in Bethlehem!

2 Low within a manger lies
he who built the starry skies,
he who, throned in height sublime,
sits amid the cherubim!

3 Sacred infant, all divine,
grace and tender love combine,
bringing you from highest bliss
down to such a world as this!

4 Holy child with gentle face,
Saviour of our fallen race,
ever teach us so that we
learn your deep humility.

EDWARD CASWALL (1814–78)
based on Luke 2: 1–20

174

MICHAEL PERRY (b. 1942)
arr. STEPHEN COATES (b. 1952)

CALYPSO CAROL Irregular

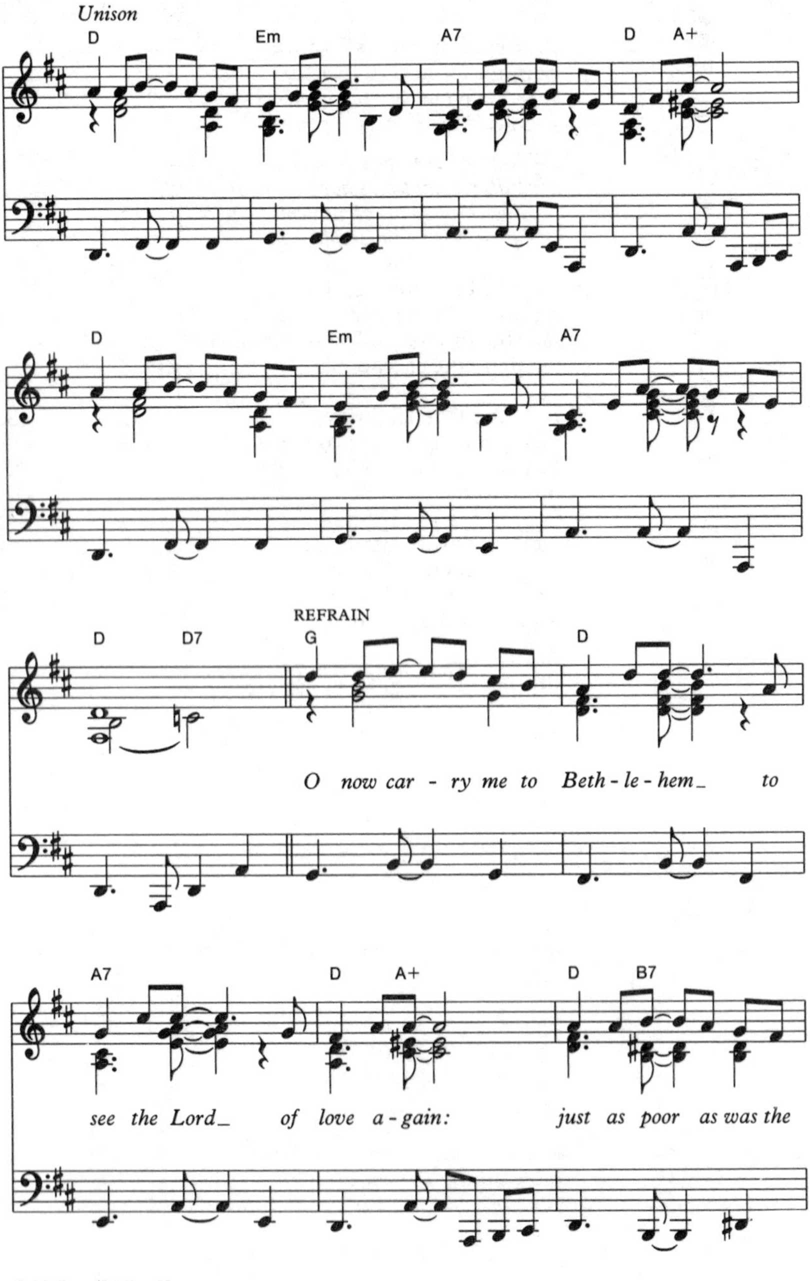
Unison
D Em A7 D A+
D Em A7
D D7
REFRAIN
G D
O now car - ry me to Beth - le - hem_ to
A7 D A+ D B7
see the Lord_ of love a - gain: just as poor as was the

sta-ble then,   the Prince of glo - ry when he came._____

sta-ble then,   the Prince of glo - ry when he came._____

SEE him lying on a bed of straw:
a draughty stable with an open door;
Mary cradling the babe she bore—
the Prince of glory is his name.

O now carry me to Bethlehem
to see the Lord of love again:
just as poor as was the stable then,
the Prince of glory when he came.

2 Star of silver, sweep across the skies,
show where Jesus in the manger lies;
shepherds swiftly from your stupor rise
to see the Saviour of the world!

3 Angels, sing again the song you sang,
sing the glory of God's gracious plan;
sing that Bethl'em's little baby can
be the Saviour of us all.

4 Mine are riches, from your poverty;
from your innocence, eternity;
mine, forgiveness by your death for me,
child of sorrow for my joy.

MICHAEL PERRY (b. 1942)

175

Traditional
arr. JOHN BELL (b. 1949)

SCARLET RIBBONS   87 87 D

SHEPHERDS watch and wise men wonder,
    monarchs scorn and angels sing;
such a place as none would reckon
    hosts a holy helpless thing;
stabled beasts and passing strangers
    watch a baby laid in hay;
God surprises earth with heaven
    coming here on Christmas Day.

2 Who would think that what was needed
    to transform and save the earth
might not be a plan or army,
    proud in purpose, proved in worth?
Who would think, despite derision,
    that a child should lead the way?
God surprises earth with heaven,
    coming here on Christmas Day.

Iona Community

176

STILLE NACHT   66 77 66   Melody by F. X. GRUBER (1787–1863)

SILENT night! holy night!
all is calm, all is bright
round the virgin and her child.
Holy infant, so gentle and mild,
   sleep in heavenly peace;
   sleep in heavenly peace!

2 Silent night! holy night!
shepherds quake at the sight,
glory streams from heaven afar:
heavenly hosts sing, 'Alleluia,
   Christ the Saviour is born,
   Christ the Saviour is born.'

3 Silent night! holy night!
Son of God, love's pure light:
radiant beams your holy face
with the dawn of saving grace,
   Jesus, Lord, at your birth,
   Jesus, Lord, at your birth.

after J. MOHR (1792–1848)
J. F. YOUNG (1820–85)

177

GABRIEL'S MESSAGE   10 10 12 7 3

Basque traditional carol melody
arr. C. EDGAR PETTMAN (1865–1943)

Glo - - - - ri - a!

The word 'Gloria' may be sung in unison.

THE angel Gabriel from heaven came,
his wings as drifted snow, his eyes as flame;
'All hail,' said he, 'thou lowly maiden Mary,
most highly favoured lady.'
   Gloria!

2 'For known a blessed mother thou shalt be,
all generations laud and honour thee,
thy son shall be Immanuel, by seers foretold;
most highly favoured lady.'
   Gloria!

3 Then gentle Mary meekly bowed her head,
'To me be as it pleaseth God,' she said,
'My soul shall laud and magnify his holy name.'
Most highly favoured lady.
   Gloria!

4 Of her, Immanuel, the Christ was born
in Bethlehem, all on a Christmas morn,
and Christian folk throughout the world will ever say,
'Most highly favoured lady.'
   Gloria!

Basque carol para. SABINE BARING-GOULD (1834–1924)

178

THE FIRST NOWELL   Irregular

W. SANDYS' *Christmas Carols*, 1833

THE first Nowell the angel did say,
was to certain poor shepherds in fields as they lay:
in fields where they lay keeping their sheep,
on a cold winter's night that was so deep.

Nowell, nowell, nowell, nowell,
born is the King of Israel.

2 And by the light of shining star,
   three wise men came from country far;
   to seek for a king was their intent,
   and to follow the star wherever it went.

3 The star drew nigh to the north-west,
   o'er Bethlehem it took its rest,
   and there it did both stop and stay,
   right over the place where Jesus lay.

4 Then entered in those wise men three;
   full reverently, they bent the knee,
   and offered there, in his presence,
   their gold, and myrrh, and frankincense.

5 Then let us all with one accord
   sing praises to our heavenly Lord,
   who brought forth heaven and earth from nought
   and with his blood mankind has bought.

Traditional
based on Luke 2: 10–11
and Matthew 2: 1–11

179

MARGARET   Irregular

T. R. MATTHEWS (1826–1910)

THOU didst leave thy throne and thy kingly crown
    when thou camest to earth for me;
but in Bethlehem's home there was found no room
    for thy holy nativity:
O come to my heart, Lord Jesus,
    there is room in my heart for thee.

2 Heaven's arches rang when the angels sang,
    proclaiming thy royal degree;
but of lowly birth cam'st thou, Lord, on earth
    and in great humility;
O come to my heart, Lord Jesus,
    there is room in my heart for thee.

3 The foxes found rest, and the birds their nest
    in the shade of the cedar tree;
but the earth was the bed for thy weary head,
    in the deserts of Galilee;
O come to my heart, Lord Jesus,
    there is room in my heart for thee.

4 Thou camest, O Lord, with the living word
    that should set thy people free;
but with mocking scorn, and with crown of thorn,
    they bore thee to Calvary;
O come to my heart, Lord Jesus,
    thy cross is my only plea.

5 When heaven's arches ring, and her choirs shall sing,
    at thy coming to victory,
let thy voice call me home, saying, 'Yet there is room,
    there is room at my side for thee;'
and my heart shall rejoice, Lord Jesus,
    when thou comest and callest for me.

EMILY ELLIOTT (1836–97)
based on Luke 2: 7

180

MOUNTAIN HEIGHTS   77 77 D

Anon.
arr. DAVID PEACOCK (b. 1949)

Arrangement © D. Peacock/Jubilate Hymns

WHERE do Christmas songs begin?
By the stable of an inn
where the song of hosts on high
mingled with a baby's cry.
There for joy and wonder smiled
man and maid and holy child.
Christmas songs begin with them,
sing the songs of Bethlehem!

2 Who is this, whose human birth
here proclaims him child of earth?
He it is who formed the skies,
saw the new-made stars arise;
life immortal, light divine,
blinking in the candle-shine;
born our darkness to dispel,
God with us, Emmanuel.

3 Only love can answer why
he should come to grieve and die,
share on earth our pain and loss,
bear for us the bitter cross.
Love is come to seek and save,
life to master death and grave,
so in Christ is all restored,
risen and redeeming Lord!

4 Praise we then, in Christmas songs,
him to whom all praise belongs.
Here the angel host reply,
'Glory be to God on high,
joy and peace to mortals given,
peace on earth and peace with heaven!'
Join we now, as one with them;
sing the songs of Bethlehem!

TIMOTHY DUDLEY-SMITH (b. 1926)

181

German carol melody
arr. GEOFFREY SHAW (1879–1943)

PUER NOBIS   76 77

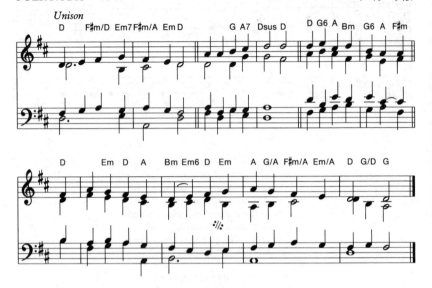

UNTO us a boy is born!
  King of all creation,
came he to a world forlorn,
  the Lord of every nation.

2 Cradled in a stall was he
  with sleepy cows and asses;
but the very beasts could see
  that he all men surpasses.

3 Herod then with fear was filled:
  'A prince,' he said. 'in Jewry!'
All the little boys he killed
  at Bethlem in his fury.

4 Now may Mary's son, who came
  so long ago to love us,
lead us all with hearts aflame
  unto the joys above us.

5 Alpha and Omega he!
  let the organ thunder,
while the choir with peals of glee
  loud rends the air asunder.

Latin, 15th century
tr. PERCY DEARMER (1867–1936)

278

182

WINCHESTER OLD   CM

T. ESTE'S *Psalmes*, 1592

WHILE shepherds watched their flocks by night,
all seated on the ground,
the angel of the Lord came down,
and glory shone around:

2 'Fear not!' said he (for mighty dread
had seized their troubled mind),
'Glad tidings of great joy I bring
to you and all mankind.

3 'To you in David's town, this day
is born, of David's line,
a Saviour, who is Christ the Lord;
and this shall be the sign:

4 'The heavenly babe you there shall find
to human view displayed,
all meanly wrapped in swaddling clothes
and in a manger laid.'

5 Thus spoke the seraph; and forthwith
appeared a shining throng
of angels, praising God, who thus
addressed their joyful song:

6 'All glory be to God on high,
and to mankind be peace;
goodwill henceforth from heaven to earth
begin and never cease.'

NAHUM TATE (1652–1715)
based on Luke 2: 8–20

183 THE MAGNIFICAT

Tell out, my soul, the greatness of the Lord,
rejoice, rejoice, my spirit, in God my Saviour;
so tenderly has he looked upon his servant,
humble as she is.
    For, from this day forth,
    all generations will count me blessèd,
    so wonderfully has he dealt with me,
    the Lord, the Mighty One.
His name is holy;
his mercy sure from generation to generation
toward those who fear him;
    the deeds his own right arm has done
    disclose his might:
The arrogant of heart and mind he has put to rout;
    he has torn imperial powers from their thrones,
    but the humble have been lifted high.
The hungry he has satisfied with good things,
    the rich sent empty away.
He has ranged himself at the side of Israel his servant;
firm in his promise to our forefathers,
he has not forgotten to show mercy to Abraham
and his children's children, for ever.

184

For to us a child is born, to us a son is given
    and the government will be upon his shoulders,
    and his name will be called Wonderful Counsellor,
    Mighty God, Everlasting Father, Prince of Peace.

185

Do not be afraid;
I bring you good news of great joy
that will be for all the people:
    today in the town of David
    a Saviour has been born to you;
    he is Christ the Lord.

186   A PRAYER AT CHRISTMAS EVE COMMUNION

The Lord be with you!
And also with you!
Lift up your hearts!
We lift them up to the Lord.
Let us give thanks to the Lord our God!
It is right to give him thanks and praise.

It is not only right, it is our duty and our joy, at all times and
in all places to give you thanks and praise, holy Father, heavenly
King, almighty and eternal God, through Jesus Christ, your only
Son, our Lord.

> **For the birth of Jesus your Son, our Saviour,**
> **cradled in the manger at Bethlehem,**
>   **we thank you, heavenly Father.**

For the love and gentle care of Mary, his mother,
most blessed of all women,
  we thank you, heavenly Father.

> **For shepherds keeping watch over their flocks by night,**
> **who came with haste to worship Christ, the new-born King,**
>   **we thank you, heavenly Father.**

For wise men from the East, who followed the star
and presented their gifts of gold, frankincense and myrrh,
  we thank you, heavenly Father.

> **For the light and love of this Christmas season,**
> **in our hearts and in our homes,**
> **bringing joy and gladness to all,**
>   **we thank you, heavenly Father.**

And in all our joyful gratitude we join our voices with the angels
who are always singing to you:
Holy, holy, holy!
God of power and might,
heaven and earth are full of your glory.
Glory be to you, O Lord most high.
Blessèd is he that comes in the name of the Lord!
Hosanna in the highest!

Lord God, Holy Spirit,
may that Word who was made flesh
now be born again amongst us,
in the faithful hearts of his people,
and in these gifts of bread and wine,
that, here on earth, we may share his risen life
and come, at the last, to his eternal kingdom.
Through Jesus Christ our Lord.
Amen.

187

When all things began, the Word already was.
The Word dwelt with God,
and what God was, the Word was.
The Word, then, was with God at the beginning,
and through him all things came to be;
no single thing was created without him.
All that came to be was alive with his life,
and that life was the light of men.
The light shines on in the dark,
and the darkness has never mastered it.

He was in the world;
but the world, though it owed its being to him,
did not recognize him.
He entered into his own realm,
and his own would not receive him.
But to all who did receive him,
to those who have yielded him their allegiance,
he gave the right to become children of God,
not born of any human stock,
or by the fleshly desire of a human father,
but the offspring of God himself.

So the Word became flesh;
he came to dwell among us, and we saw his glory,
such glory as befits the Father's only Son,
full of grace and truth.

188   PRAYER OF PETITION

O Lord Jesus Christ,
willing to be made like us in your humanity:
   the sharer of our sorrows,
   the companion of our journeys,
   the light of our darkness,
   the remedy for our ills,
so fill us with your Spirit and your grace
that as you have been made like us,
we may grow to be more like you.
For your mercy's sake. Amen.

189

DIX   77 77 77

C. KOCHER (1786–1872)
adpt. W. H. MONK (1823–89)

1 As with gladness men of old
did the guiding star behold;
as with joy they hailed its light,
leading onward, beaming bright,
so, most gracious God, may we
evermore your glory see.

2 As with joyful steps they sped,
Saviour, to your lowly bed,
there to bend the knee before
one whom heaven and earth adore,
so may we with willing feet
ever seek your mercy-seat.

3 As they offered gifts most rare
at your cradle rude and bare,
so may we with holy joy,
pure, and free from sin's alloy,
all our costliest treasures bring,
Christ, to you, our heavenly King.

4 Holy Jesus, every day
keep us in the narrow way;
and, when earthly things are past,
bring our ransomed souls at last
where they need no star to guide,
where no clouds your glory hide.

5 In the heavenly country bright
need they no created light;
you its light, its joy, its crown,
you its sun, which goes not down.
There for ever may we sing
Alleluias to our King.

W. C. DIX (1837–98)
based on Matthew 2: 1–11

190

EPIPHANY HYMN   11 10 11 10   J. F. THRUPP (1827–67)

BRIGHTEST and best of the sons of the morning,
  dawn on our darkness, and lend us your aid;
star of the east, the horizon adorning,
  guide where our infant Redeemer is laid.

2 Cold on his cradle the dew-drops are shining;
  low lies his head with the beasts of the stall;
angels adore him, in slumber reclining,
  maker and monarch, and Saviour of all.

3 Say, shall we yield him, in costly devotion,
  fragrance of Edom, and offerings divine;
gems of the mountain, and pearls of the ocean,
  myrrh from the forest, or gold from the mine?

4 Vainly we offer each ample oblation;
  vainly with gifts would his favour secure;
richer by far is the heart's adoration;
  dearer to God are the prayers of the poor.

5 Brightest and best of the sons of the morning,
  dawn on our darkness, and lend us your aid;
star of the east, the horizon adorning,
  guide where our infant Redeemer is laid.

REGINALD HEBER (1783–1826)
based on Matthew 2: 1–11

191

FIRST TUNE

FAWLEY LODGE   65 65   NORMAN L. WARREN (b. 1934)

© N. L. Warren/Jubilate Hymns

SECOND TUNE

EUDOXIA   65 65   S. BARING-GOULD (1834–1924)

FAITHFUL vigil ended,
    watching, waiting cease:
Master, grant your servant
    his discharge in peace.

2 All your Spirit promised,
    all the Father willed,
now these eyes behold it
    perfectly fulfilled.

3 This your great deliverance
    sets your people free;
Christ their light uplifted
    all the nations see.

4 Christ, your people's glory!
    watching, doubting cease:
grant to us your servants
    our discharge in peace.

TIMOTHY DUDLEY-SMITH (b. 1926)
based on Luke 2: 29–32

192

QUEM PASTORES LAUDAVERE
888 7

14th-century German carol melody
arr. R. VAUGHAN WILLIAMS (1872–1958)

For this tune in G major see no. 50.

SHEPHERDS came, their praises bringing,
who had heard the angels singing:
'Far from you be fear unruly,
   Christ is King of glory born.'

2 Wise men whom a star had guided
incense, gold, and myrrh provided,
made their sacrifices truly
   to the King of glory born.

3 Jesus born the King of heaven,
Christ to us through Mary given,
to your praise and honour duly
   be resounding glory done.

from *Quem pastores laudavere* (15th century)
tr. G. B. CAIRD (1917–84)

193 THE NUNC DIMITTIS

**Now, Lord, you have kept your promise,
and you may let your servant go in peace.
With my own eyes I have seen your salvation,
which you prepared in the presence of all people:
a light to reveal your will to the Gentiles
and bring glory to your people Israel.**

194

King Jesus,
we bring you our gold:
  **talents your Father gave us,
  skills we have acquired,
  a little money, a little power,
  a little success perhaps,
  and plenty of ambition.
  These we offer to you,
  so that you may make them really worth something
  in your kingdom.**

Jesus, great High Priest,
we bring you our frankincense:
  **deep needs and longings,
  which are sometimes easier to admit in church:
  the need for forgiveness and peace,
  the need for friendship and love,
  the wish to do good
  and the knowledge that we must have help
  if we are to do it.
  Lord, help us,
  pray for us.**

Jesus, crucified Saviour
we bring you our myrrh:
  **shadows on our path,
  weakness, illness, limitations,
  grief for ourselves and others,
  our knowledge of parting and pain.
  These we offer to you
  so that what we bear
  may be touched with the holiness
  of what you bore for us;
  and so that, by your grace,
  we may have part
  in the world's redemption.**

195

ST ALBINUS   78 78 4   H. J. GAUNTLETT (1805–76)

Al - le - lu - ia!

For this tune in B♭ major see no. 253.

CHRIST upon the mountain peak
   stands alone in glory blazing;
let us, if we dare to speak,
   with the saints and angels praise
      him:
      Alleluia!

2 Trembling at his feet, we saw
   Moses and Elijah speaking:
all the prophets and the law
   shout through them their joyful
      greeting:
      Alleluia!

3 Swift the cloud of glory came,
   God proclaiming in its thunder
Jesus as his Son, by name;
   nations, cry aloud in wonder:
      Alleluia!

4 This is God's beloved Son,
   law and prophets fade before him,
first and last, and only one:
   Let creation now adore him:
      Alleluia!

BRIAN A. WREN (b. 1936)
based on Matthew 17: 1–8,
Mark 9: 2–8 and Luke 9: 28–36

196

FISHER'S SONG

DEBORAH ROOKE (b. 1962)

Fish-er-man, come and fish for men, Fish-er-man, fish for me.

VERSES 1–4

1. Pe-ter was a fish-er-man, Fish-er-man, come and fish for men, be-side the sea of Ga-li-lee, Fish-er-man, fish for me.

VERSES 5–8

5. Yet from death the Sav-iour rose, Fish-er-man, come and fish for men, and Pe-ter was the

one_ he chose. *Fish-er-man, fish for me._*

Fish-er-man, come and fish for men, Fish-er-man, fish for me._

This song may be sung either as a congregational hymn, or as a solo with unison refrain.
When sung as a solo, melodic variations may be improvised.

Fisherman, come and fish for men,
Fisherman, fish for me.

PETER was a fisherman,
Fisherman, come and fish for men,
beside the sea of Galilee,
Fisherman, fish for me.

2 Heard the voice of the Saviour call,
Fisherman, come . . .
turned to follow him, leaving all,
Fisherman, fish . . .

3 Loved and served his Saviour friend,
swore to follow him to the end.

4 But on a cross his master died,
and he denied the crucified.

5 Yet from death the Saviour rose,
and Peter was the one he chose.

6 The rock on which to build his
Church,
giving us new life and birth.

7 And still today the Saviour calls,
'Leave your nets upon the shore.'

8 Will you hear his call today,
or will you simply turn away?

Fisherman, come and fish for men,
Fisherman, fish for me.

DEBORAH ROOKE (b. 1962)
based on Matthew 16: 18 and Luke 5: 11

197

FIRST TUNE

ALSTONE LM

C. E. WILLING (1830–1904)

SECOND TUNE

WAREHAM LM

WILLIAM KNAPP (1698–1768)

How blest the poor who love the Lord
   and hold his kingdom in their hearts;
for they perceive with inner sight
   the wealth that only God imparts!

2 How blest are those who hunger now—
   they shall not go unsatisfied;
because they seek for righteousness,
   their needs will always be supplied.

3 How blest are those who weep and mourn,
   for in their sorrow Christ appears
to share their grief and bring them hope—
   till joy shall drive away their tears.

4 How blest are those who, for his sake,
   know pain and insult, hate and scorn;
for he will turn the darkest night
   to great reward in heaven's dawn.

5 How blest are those who have refused
   to live for selfish gain alone;
though now they feel distress and pain
   they soon shall reap as they have sown.

6 How blest are those who seek and find
   the precious pearl of countless price,
and in God's kingdom taste the fruit
   of Jesus' perfect sacrifice!

MOLLIE KNIGHT

198

FIRST TUNE
Melody by C. HUTCHESON (1792–1860)
harm. DAVID EVANS (1874–1948)

STRACATHRO   CM

SECOND TUNE

BISHOPTHORPE   CM

JEREMIAH CLARKE (1670–1707)

IMMORTAL love, for ever full,
   for ever flowing free,
for ever shared, for ever whole,
   a never-ebbing sea.

2 We may not climb the heavenly steeps
   to bring the Lord Christ down;
in vain we search the lowest deeps
   for him no depths can drown.

3 And not for signs in heaven above
   or earth below, they look,
who know with John his smile of
      love,
   with Peter his rebuke.

4 In joy of inward peace, or sense
   of sorrow over sin,
God is his own best evidence;
   his witness is within.

5 So warm, sweet, tender, even yet
   a present help is he;
and faith has still its Olivet,
   and love its Galilee.

6 The healing of his seamless dress
   is by our beds of pain;
we touch him in life's throng and
      press,
   and we are whole again.

7 In love alone, too great to tell,
   his saving name is given;
to turn aside from him is hell,
   to walk with him is heaven.

J. G WHITTIER (1807–92) altd.

199

WILD MOUNTAIN THYME   78 78 6 77 86

Irish traditional melody
arr. Iona Community

And he's   here   when   we   call   him,___

_bring-ing   health,   love   and   laugh-ter_____   to   life   now   and_
_e - ver   af - ter,_____   for   the   good   of   us   all._____

IN a byre near Bethlehem,
passed by many a wandering stranger,
the most precious Word of life
was heard gurgling in a manger,
for the good of us all.

> _And he's here when we call him,_
> _bringing health, love and laughter_
> _to life now and ever after,_
> _for the good of us all._

2 By the Galilean lake
where the people flocked for teaching,
the most precious Word of life
fed their mouths as well as preaching,
for the good of us all.

3 Quiet was Gethsemane,
camouflaging priest and soldier;
the most precious Word of life
took the world's weight on his shoulder,
for the good of us all.

4 On the hill of Calvary—
place to end all hope of living—
the most precious Word of life
breathed his last and died, forgiving,
for the good of us all.

5 In a garden, just at dawn,
near the grave of human violence,
the most precious Word of life
cleared his throat and ended silence,
for the good of us all.

J. BELL (b. 1949) and G. MAULE (b. 1958)

297

200

THE STORY OF JESUS   10 9 10 8

C. B. JUTSON (1870–1930)

GOD has given us a book full of stories,
    which was made for his people of old,
it begins with the tale of a garden,
    and ends with the city of gold.

2 But the best is the story of Jesus,
    of the babe with the ox in the stall,
of the song that was sung by the angels,
    the most beautiful story of all.

3 There are stories for parents and children,
    for the old who are ready to rest,
but for all who can read them or listen,
    the story of Jesus is best.

4 For it tells how he came from the Father,
    his far-away children to call,
to bring the lost sheep to their shepherd—
    the most beautiful story of all.

MARIA PENSTONE (1859–1910)

201

ST GEORGE   SM

H. J. GAUNTLETT (1805–76)

May also be sung to CARLISLE, no. 282.

IT's good, Lord, to be here!
 your glory fills the night;
your face and garments, like the sun,
 shine with unborrowed light.

2 It's good, Lord, to be here!
 your beauty to behold,
where Moses and Elijah stand,
 your messengers of old.

3 Fulfiller of the past!
 promise of things to be!
we hail your body glorified,
 and our redemption see.

4 Before we taste of death,
 we see your kingdom come;
we long to hold the vision bright,
 and make this hill our home.

5 It's good, Lord, to be here!
 yet we may not remain;
but since you bid us leave the mount
 come with us to the plain.

J. ARMITAGE ROBINSON (1858–1933)
based on Matthew 17: 1–8,
Mark 9: 2–8, and Luke 9: 28–36

202

YISU NE KAHA   99 99 99

Urdu melody
harm. F. B. WESTBROOK (1903–75)

JESUS the Lord said: 'I am the bread,
the bread of life for mankind am I.
   The bread of life for mankind am I,
      the bread of life for mankind am I.
Jesus the Lord said: 'I am the bread,
the bread of life for mankind am I.'

2 Jesus the Lord said: 'I am the life,
the resurrection and the life am I.'

3 Jesus the Lord said: 'I am the vine,
and you are the branches of the vine,' said he.

vv. 1 & 2 Anon., tr. from Urdu by
DERMOTT MONAHAN (1906–57)
v. 3 MICHAEL BALL (b. 1938)
based on John 6: 35, 48–51; 11: 25; 15: 5

203

SANDYVALE 10 9 11 9

MIKE SAMMES

Unison

Jesus, transfigured, we scarcely can look
    on your face, like the sun, shining bright;
you talk with Elijah and Moses of old
    in the splendour and radiance of light.

2 Awestruck and dazed, Peter speaks for us all,
    'It is good, Lord, to be on this hill;
for Moses, Elijah and you, let us build
    shrines of honour where nature is still.'

3 Round us the cloud, and with awesome acclaim
    comes the voice of the Lord from above;
we hear through the cloud-thickened sky, 'It's my Son,
    listen well to my Son whom I love.'

4 Jesus, transfigured, the splendour has passed,
    we must go from this hill to the plain;
the cries of the world and the call of the cross
    lie below in the valley again.

DAVID M. OWEN
based on Matthew 17: 1–8, Mark 9: 2–8, and Luke 9: 28–36

204

LOVE UNKNOWN   66 66 88   JOHN IRELAND (1879–1962)

For a unison version of this tune see no. 510.

My song is love unknown,
  my Saviour's love to me:
love to the loveless shown,
  that they might lovely be.
    O who am I,
      that for my sake
      my Lord should take
    frail flesh, and die?

2 He came from his blest throne
  salvation to bestow;
but men refused, and none
  the longed-for Christ would know.
    But O my friend,
      my friend indeed,
      who at my need
    his life did spend.

3 Sometimes they strew his way,
  and his sweet praises sing;
resounding all the day
  hosannas to their king.
    Then 'Crucify!'
      is all their breath,
      and for his death
    they thirst and cry.

4 Why, what has my Lord done?
  What makes this rage and spite?
He made the lame to run,
  he gave the blind their sight.
    Such injuries!
      Yet this is why
      they hate my Lord
    and speak their lies.

5 They rise and needs will have
  my dear Lord made away.
A murderer they save,
  the Prince of life they slay.
    Yet patient he
      to suffering goes,
      that he his foes
    from death might free.

6 In life, no house, no home
  my Lord on earth might have:
in death, no friendly tomb,
  but what a stranger gave.
    What may I say?
      Heaven was his home;
      but mine the tomb
    wherein he lay.

7 Here might I stay and sing,
  no story so divine;
never was love, dear King!
  Never was grief like thine.
    This is my friend
      in whose glad praise
      I all my days
    could gladly spend.

SAMUEL CROSSMAN (1624–83)

204

SECOND TUNE

ST JOHN   66 66 88

J. B. CALKIN (1827–1905)

MY song is love unknown,
    my Saviour's love to me:
love to the loveless shown,
    that they might lovely be.
        O who am I,
            that for my sake
            my Lord should take
        frail flesh, and die?

2 He came from his blest throne
    salvation to bestow;
but men refused, and none
    the longed-for Christ would know.
        But O my friend,
            my friend indeed,
            who at my need
        his life did spend.

3 Sometimes they strew his way,
    and his sweet praises sing;
resounding all the day
    hosannas to their king.
        Then 'Crucify!'
            is all their breath,
            and for his death
        they thirst and cry.

4 Why, what has my Lord done?
    What makes this rage and spite?
He made the lame to run,
    he gave the blind their sight.
        Such injuries!
            Yet this is why
            they hate my Lord
        and speak their lies.

5 They rise and needs will have
    my dear Lord made away.
A murderer they save,
    the Prince of life they slay.
        Yet patient he
            to suffering goes,
            that he his foes
        from death might free.

6 In life, no house, no home
    my Lord on earth might have:
in death, no friendly tomb,
    but what a stranger gave.
        What may I say?
            Heaven was his home;
            but mine the tomb
        wherein he lay.

7 Here might I stay and sing,
    no story so divine;
never was love, dear King!
    Never was grief like thine.
        This is my friend
            in whose glad praise
            I all my days
        could gladly spend.

SAMUEL CROSSMAN (1624–83)

205

BRESLAU   LM

Melody in *As Hymnodus Sacer*, Leipzig, 1625
adpt. and harm. F. MENDELSSOHN (1809–47)

MY dear Redeemer and my Lord,
I read my duty in your word;
but in your life the law appears
drawn out in living characters.

2 Such was your truth, and such your zeal,
such deference to your Father's will,
such love, and meekness so divine,
I would transcribe and make them mine.

3 Cold mountains and the midnight air
witnessed the fervour of your prayer;
the desert your temptations knew,
your conflict, and your victory too.

4 Be now my pattern; make me bear
more of your gracious image here;
then God the judge shall own my name
among the followers of the Lamb.

ISAAC WATTS (1674–1748)
based on Mark 1: 12–13

206

BELMONT   CM

W. GARDINER (1770–1853)

O CHANGELESS Christ, for ever new,
    who walked our earthly ways,
still draw our hearts as once you drew
    the hearts of other days.

2 As once you spoke by plain and hill
    or taught by shore and sea,
so be today our teacher still,
    O Christ of Galilee.

3 As wind and storm their master heard
    and his command fulfilled,
may troubled hearts receive your word,
    the tempest-tossed be stilled.

4 And as of old to all who prayed
    your healing hand was shown,
so be your touch upon us laid,
    unseen but not unknown.

5 In broken bread, in wine outpoured,
    your new and living way
proclaim to us, O risen Lord,
    O Christ of this our day.

6 O changeless Christ, till life is past
    your blessing still be given;
then bring us home, to taste at last
    the timeless joys of heaven.

TIMOTHY DUDLEY-SMITH (b. 1926)

207

EISENACH   LM

J. H. SCHEIN (1586–1630)
arr. J. S. BACH (1685–1750)

O LOVE, how deep, how broad, how high!
It fills the heart with ecstasy,
    that God, the Son of God, should take
    our mortal form for mortals' sake.

2 For us he was baptized, and bore
    his holy fast, and hungered sore;
    for us temptations sharp he knew;
    for us the tempter overthrew.

3 For us he prayed, for us he taught,
    for us his daily works he wrought,
    by words and signs and actions, thus
    still seeking not himself but us.

4 For us to wicked men betrayed,
    scourged, mocked, in purple robe arrayed,
    he bore the shameful cross and death;
    for us at length gave up his breath.

5 For us he rose from death again,
    for us he went on high to reign,
    for us he sent his Spirit here,
    to guide, to strengthen and to cheer.

Anon. Latin, 15th century
tr. BENJAMIN WEBB (1820–85)

208

DISCOVERY   11 10 11 10 88 7

MICHAEL BALL (b. 1938)

PULL back the veil on the dawn of creation;
 vanish the mists from the sources of time;
echo the bird that broods over the waters,
 singing the secret of grace in its prime.
  Love's the secret! Love's the secret!
 Love is God's risk and God's reason,
 God's rule and God's rhyme, God's rhyme.

2 Pull back the curtain on Bethlehem's stable;
 strip off the tinsel and peer through the dark;
look at the child who's a threat yet in danger,
 homeless and helpless he first makes his mark.
  Love's the secret! Love's the secret!
 Love is God's cradle, God's table,
 God's cup and God's ark, God's ark.

3 Pull back the veil on each parable's story,
 be it of virgins or talents forlorn;
find in the kernel a core of compassion,
 planted in minds yet in flesh to be born.
  Love's the secret! Love's the secret!
 Love is God's madness, God's sadness,
 God's feast and God's corn, God's corn.

4 Pull back the curtain that hides what is holy;
 tear it in two as Christ did from the hill;
see at the centre of Good and bad Friday
 something no mob or marauder can kill.
  Love's the secret! Love's the secret!
 Love is God's way and God's witness,
 God's worth and God's will, God's will.

5 Pull back the stone that conceals what is buried;
 pull back the veil and the curtain of doom;
pull back the centuries' doubts and delusions,
 look through the mystery into the tomb.
  Love's the secret! Love's the secret!
 Love is surprising, God's rising,
 God's wealth and God's womb, God's womb.

Iona Community

209

SEARCH FOR THE INFANT   10 9 10 9 8 7 10 9   PAUL CARTER

SEARCH for the infant born in a stable,
    search where it's humble, search where it's poor.
Man's search for God finds rest in a stable,
    there in the smell and warmth of the straw.
See the infant, what a wonder!
    See the mother's tender care.
Cow and ass stand close together,
    while their bodies warm the air.

2 Search for the man who travels the country,
    feeding the hungry, healing the blind.
Man's search for God finds rest in the needy,
    there with the outcasts of every kind.
There the word of love is spoken,
    there the truth of God made clear,
in the country, up on the hillside,
    people in thousands jostle to hear.

3 Search for the man who hangs on a gallows,
    nailed there by hatred, nailed there by fear.
Man's search for God finds rest at the gallows,
    there at the cross the answer is near.
Hear the mocking, hear the scorning,
    see the blood and feel the pain.
On the hilltop, nailed to the gallows,
    love meets rejection, all seems in vain.

4 Search for the man who's risen for ever,
    out on the highway, down by the shore.
Man's search for God finds truth in his spirit,
    still with the needy, still with the poor.
Where there's hunger, where there's hatred,
    where injustice, where there's pain,
out of the stable, out of the country,
    down from the gallows, Jesus does reign.

ROY WARD

210

HAREWOOD   66 66 88   S. S. WESLEY (1810–76)

May also be sung to ST JOHN, no. 204.

SON of the Lord most high
  who gave the worlds their birth,
he came to live and die
  the Son of Man on earth.
    In Bethlehem's stable born was he
    and humbly bred in Galilee.

2 Born in so low estate,
    schooled in a workman's trade,
  not with the high and great
    his home the highest made:
      but labouring by good Joseph's side,
      life's common lot he glorified.

3 Then, when his hour had come,
    he heard his Father's call;
  and leaving friends and home,
    he gave himself for all;
      glad news to bring, the lost to find,
      to heal the sick, the lame, the blind.

4 Toiling by night and day,
    himself with burdens sore,
where hearts in bondage lay,
    their burdens too he bore:
      till, scorned by those he died to **save**
      himself in death, as life, he gave.

5 O lowly majesty,
    lofty in lowliness!
Blest Saviour, who am I
    to share your blessedness?
      Servant divine, you have called me
      a loyal follower now to be.

G. W. BRIGGS (1875–1959) altd.

211

HATCHLANDS   76 86   ANGELA BARKER

WE love the Jesus stories
    of what was lost and found,
and how he teaches us to see
    God's kingdom all around.

2 He tells of hidden treasure,
    of sheep and goats and seeds,
of birds that nest in leafy trees,
    and corn and wheat and weeds.

3 We learn of guests and banquets,
    of talents and of debts,
of houses built on sand and rock,
    and pearls and fishing-nets.

4 He teaches love for others,
    that God forgives our sin,
that what we do for those in need
    we do it all for him.

DAVID M. OWEN

212

Think of Jesus, whom God sent to be the high priest of the faith
we profess, who for a little while was made lower than the angels.
**He had to become like his brothers in every way, in order to be
their faithful and merciful high priest in his service to God,
so that his people's sins can be forgiven.**

And now he can help those who are tempted, because he himself
was tempted and suffered.
**Our high priest is not one who cannot feel sympathy for our
weaknesses.**
**On the contrary, we have a high priest who was tempted
in every way that we are, but did not sin.**

Let us be brave then, and approach God's throne, where there is grace.
There we will receive mercy and find grace to help us just when we need it.

213

Jesus said:
I am the bread of life.
He who comes to me will never be hungry;
he who believes in me will never be thirsty.

Jesus said:
I am the light of the world.
**Whoever follows me will have the light of life
and will never walk in darkness.**

Jesus said:
I am the gate.
Whoever comes in by me will be saved;
he will come in and go out and find pasture.

Jesus said:
**I am the good shepherd,
who is willing to die for the sheep.
I have come in order that you might have life—
life in all its fullness.**

Jesus said:
I am the resurrection and the life.
Whoever believes in me will live, even though he dies;
and whoever lives and believes in me will never die.

Jesus said:
**I am the way, the truth and the life;
no one goes to the Father except by me.**

Jesus said:
I am the vine, and you are the branches.
Whoever remains in me, will bear much fruit;
for you can do nothing without me.

214

How blest are those who know their need of God;
the kingdom of heaven is theirs.

How blest are the sorrowful;
they shall find consolation.

How blest are those of a gentle spirit;
they shall have the earth for their possession.

How blest are those who hunger and thirst to see right prevail;
they shall be satisfied.

How blest are those who show mercy;
mercy shall be shown to them.

How blest are those whose hearts are pure;
they shall see God.

How blest are the peacemakers;
God shall call them his children.

How blest are those who have suffered for the cause of right;
the kingdom of heaven is theirs.

215

HERZLIEBSTER JESU   11 11 11 5

Later form of a melody by
J. CRÜGER (1598–1662)
harm. adpt. from
J. S. BACH (1685–1750)

Ah, holy Jesus, how have you offended
that man to judge you has in hate pretended?
by foes derided, by your own rejected,
    O most afflicted!

2 Who was the guilty? Who brought this upon you?
It is my treason, Lord, that has undone you;
and I, O Jesus, it was I denied you,
    I crucified you.

3 See how the shepherd for the sheep is offered,
the slave has sinned and yet the Son has suffered;
for our atonement hangs the Saviour bleeding,
    God interceding.

4 For me, kind Jesus, was your incarnation,
your dying sorrow and your life's oblation,
your bitter passion and your desolation,
    for my salvation.

5 O mighty Saviour, I cannot repay you.
I do adore you and will here obey you.
Recall your mercy and your love unswerving,
    not my deserving.

JOHANN HEERMANN (1585–1647)
tr. ROBERT BRIDGES (1844–1930)

216

ST THEODULPH   76 76 D

Melody by MELCHIOR TESCHNER (c.1615)
harm. from J. S. BACH (1685–1750)

REFRAIN

All glo-ry, praise and hon - our, to you, Re-deem-er, King,

(*Fine*)

to whom the lips of chil - dren made sweet ho-san-nas ring.

VERSES

D.C.

All glory, praise and honour,
to you, Redeemer, King,
to whom the lips of children
made sweet hosannas ring.

YOU are the King of Israel,
great David's greater Son;
you ride in lowly triumph,
the Lord's anointed one!

2 The company of angels
are praising you on high,
and we with all creation
together, make reply:

3 The people of the Hebrews
with palms before you went;
our praise and prayer and anthems
before you we present:

4 To you before your Passion
they sang their hymns of praise;
to you, now high exalted,
our melody we raise:

5 As you received their praises,
accept the prayers we bring,
for you delight in goodness
O good and gracious King!

J. M. NEALE (1818–66)
based on Matthew 21: 9

217

ST MARY   CM

Melody from E. PRYS's *Llyfr y Psalmau*, 1621

SECOND TUNE

DAY's *English Psalter*, 1562
adpt. RICHARD REDHEAD (1820–1901)

ST FLAVIAN   CM

ALONE now going forth, O Lord,
   in sacrifice to die;
is all your sorrow naught to us
   who pass unheeding by?

2 Our sins, not yours, you bear, dear Lord;
   make us your sorrow feel,
till through our pity and our shame
   love answers love's appeal.

3 This is earth's darkest hour, but you
   can light and life restore;
then let all praise be given to you
   who lives for evermore.

4 Grant us to suffer with you, Lord,
   that, as we share this hour,
your cross may bring us to your joy
   and resurrection power.

PETER ABELARD (1079–1142)
tr. F. BLAND TUCKER (1895–1984) altd.

218

FIRST TUNE

HEINLEIN   77 77

Melody from the
Nürnbergisches Gesangbuch, 1676–77, altd.
attrib. MARTIN HERBST (1654–81)

SECOND TUNE

BUCKLAND   77 77

L. G. HAYNE (1836–83)

The tune HEINLEIN may be used for verses 1–3, and BUCKLAND for verse 4.

FORTY days and forty nights
　　you were fasting in the wild;
forty days and forty nights
　　tempted and yet undefiled.

2 Burning heat throughout the day,
　　bitter cold when light had fled;
prowling beasts around your way,
　　stones your pillow, earth your bed.

3 Let us your endurance share
　　and from earthly greed abstain,
with you watching unto prayer
　　with you strong to suffer pain.

4 Then if evil on us press,
　　flesh or spirit to assail,
Victor in the wilderness,
　　help us not to swerve or fail!

G. H. SMYTTAN (1822–70) altd.
based on Mark 1: 12–13

219

English traditional melody
arr. R. VAUGHAN WILLIAMS (1872–1958)

HERONGATE   LM

Second Tune

BROOKFIELD   LM

T. B. SOUTHGATE (1814–68)

It is a thing most wonderful,
  almost too wonderful to be,
that God's own Son should come from heaven
  and die to save a child like me.

2 And yet I know that it is true;
    he came to this poor world below,
  and wept, and toiled, and mourned, and died,
    only because he loved us so.

3 I cannot tell how he could love
    someone so weak and full of sin;
  his love must be most wonderful
    if he could die my love to win.

4 It is most wonderful to know
    his love for me so free and sure;
  but it's more wonderful to see
    my love for him so faint and poor.

5 And yet I want to love you, Lord;
    O teach me how to grow in grace,
  and I will love you more and more,
    until I see you face to face.

W. W. HOW (1823–97)
based on Romans 5: 8

220

WAREHAM   55 11 D   WILLIAM KNAPP (1698–1768)

ALL you that pass by,
   to Jesus draw nigh;
to you is it nothing that Jesus
      should die?
   Your ransom and peace,
   your surety he is,
come, see if there ever was sorrow
      like his.

2   He dies to atone
      for sins not his own.
   Your debt he has paid, and your
         work he has done:
      you all may receive
      the peace he did leave,
   who made intercession, 'My
         Father, forgive.'

3   For you and for me
      he prayed on the tree:
   the prayer is accepted, the sinner
         is free.
      The sinner am I,
      who on Jesus rely,
   and come for the pardon God
         cannot deny.

4   His death is my plea;
      my advocate see,
   and hear the blood speak that has
         answered for me:
      he purchased the grace
      which now I embrace;
   O Father, you know he has died
         in my place!

CHARLES WESLEY (1707–88)
based on Lamentations 1: 12

221

JESUS, REMEMBER ME   68 68

JACQUES BERTHIER
as sung at Taizé
Words based on Luke 23: 42

Je - sus,   re - mem-ber me   when you come in - to your

king - dom.   Je - sus,   re - mem-ber me

when   you   come   in - to   your   king - dom.

222

FIRST TUNE

SHEILA CARROLL (b. 1949)
arr. A. S. COX (b. 1918)

SHOUT WITH JOY   87 87 D

LISTEN to the shouts of praises!
  someone great is coming here,
riding to the holy city,
  nearer now—the people cheer.
Jesus Christ, the King, is coming;
  crowds are pouring down the street.
Raise your branches, all you children,
  shout with joy and stamp your feet.

2 Now we see him—gentle Jesus,
    healer of the lame and blind,
  humbly riding on a donkey,
    friend of children, good and kind.
  Look, he comes, the promised Saviour;
    round him loud hosannas ring:
  welcome him, you waiting people,
    welcome Christ, your Lord and King!

MOLLIE KNIGHT
based on Matthew 21: 7–9

222

LUX EOI   87 87 D

ARTHUR SULLIVAN (1842–1900)

LISTEN to the shouts of praises!
  someone great is coming here,
riding to the holy city,
  nearer now—the people cheer.
Jesus Christ, the King, is coming;
  crowds are pouring down the street.
Raise your branches, all you children,
  shout with joy and stamp your feet.

2 Now we see him—gentle Jesus,
  healer of the lame and blind,
humbly riding on a donkey,
  friend of children, good and kind.
Look, he comes, the promised Saviour;
  round him loud hosannas ring:
welcome him, you waiting people,
  welcome Christ, your Lord and King!

MOLLIE KNIGHT
based on Matthew 21: 7–9

223

PASSION CHORALE 76 76 D

Melody by H. L. HASSLER (1564–1612)
harm. J. S. BACH (1685–1750)

O SACRED head, sore wounded,
    with grief and pain weighed down,
how scornfully surrounded
    with thorns thine only crown:
how pale art thou with anguish,
    with sore abuse and scorn,
how does that visage languish,
    which once was bright as morn!

2 What thou, my Lord, hast suffered,
    was all for sinners' gain:
mine, mine was the transgression,
    but thine the deadly pain.
I bow my head, my Saviour,
    for I deserve thy place;
O grant to me thy favour,
    surround me with thy grace.

3 What language shall I borrow
    to thank thee, dearest friend,
for this thy dying sorrow,
    thy pity without end?
Lord, make me thine for ever,
    and should I fainting be,
Lord, let me never, never
    outlive my love to thee!

4 Be near me when I'm dying,
    O show thy cross to me,
and, my last need supplying,
    come, Lord, and set me free!
These eyes, new faith receiving,
    from Jesus shall not move;
for they who die believing,
    die safely through thy love.

BERNARD OF CLAIRVAUX (1091–1153)
tr. PAUL GERHARDT (1607–76)
tr. J. W. ALEXANDER (1804–59)

335

224

DANIEL LM

Irish traditional melody
harm. MARTIN SHAW (1875–1958)

Lord Jesus, for my sake you come,
  the Son of Man, and God most high;
you leave behind your Father's home
  to live and serve, to love and die.

2 Your eyes seek out our world's distress
    through insult, grief and agony;
  they meet our tears with tenderness
    yet blaze upon our blasphemy.

3 Are these the robes that make men proud,
    is this the crown that you must wear?
  Your face is set, your head is bowed,
    and silently you persevere.

4 You never grasped at selfish gain,
    and yet your hands are marked with blood;
  transfixed by nails, they cling in pain
    to sorrow on a cross of wood.

5 Lord Jesus, come to me anew;
    your hands, your eyes, your thoughts be mine,
  until I learn to love like you
    and live on earth the life divine.

MICHAEL PERRY (b. 1942)

225

WINCHESTER NEW   LM

From a chorale in the
Musikalisches Handbuch, Hamburg, 1690,
arr. W. H. HAVERGAL (1793–1870)

RIDE on! ride on in majesty!
In lowly pomp ride on to die!
O Christ, your triumphs now begin
to capture death and conquer sin.

2 Ride on! ride on in majesty!
While all the tribes 'Hosanna' cry,
they cast their garments at your feet
and wave the palms their King to greet.

3 Ride on! ride on in majesty!
your last and fiercest strife is nigh!
The Father on his sapphire throne
awaits his own anointed Son.

4 Ride on! ride on in majesty!
In lowly pomp ride on to die!
Bow down your head to mortal pain,
then take, O God, your power and reign!

H. H. MILMAN (1791–1868)
based on Matthew 21: 8–9

226

GRAFTON   87 87 87

French church melody
from *Chants Ordinaires de l'Office Divin*
Paris, 1881

SING, my tongue, the glorious battle,
  sing the ending of the fray;
now above the cross, the trophy,
  sound the loud triumphant lay:
tell how Christ, the world's redeemer,
  as a victim won the day.

2 Tell how, when at length the fullness
  of the appointed time was come,
he, the Word, was born of woman,
  left for us his Father's home,
showed to us the perfect manhood,
  shone as light amidst the gloom.

3 Thus, with thirty years accomplished,
   went he forth from Nazareth,
destined, dedicate and willing,
   wrought his work, and met his death;
like a lamb he humbly yielded
   on the cross his dying breath.

4 Faithful cross, the sign of triumph,
   now for man the noblest tree,
none in foliage, none in blossom,
   none in fruit thy peer may be;
symbol of the world's redemption,
   for the weight that hung on thee!

5 Unto God be praise and glory:
   to the Father and the Son,
to the eternal Spirit, honour
   now and evermore be done;
praise and glory in the highest,
   while the timeless ages run.

VENANTIUS FORTUNATUS (*c.*530–609)
tr. PERCY DEARMER (1867–1936)

227

STAY WITH ME

JACQUES BERTHIER as sung at Taizé
Words based on Matthew 26: 36, 41

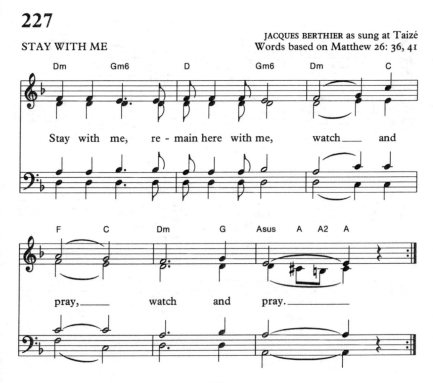

Stay with me, re - main here with me, watch___ and pray,___ watch and pray.___

228

GONFALON ROYAL   LM

P. C. BUCK (1871–1947)

THE royal banners forward go;
the cross shines forth in mystic glow,
where he in flesh, our flesh who made,
our sentence bore, our ransom paid.

2 There, whilst he hung, his sacred side
by soldier's spear was opened wide,
to cleanse us in the precious flood
of water mingled with his blood.

3 Fulfilled is now what David told
in true prophetic song of old,
how God the nations' king should be;
for God is reigning from the tree.

4 O tree of glory, tree most fair,
ordained those holy limbs to bear,
how bright in purple robe it stood,
the purple of a Saviour's blood!

5 Upon its arms, so widely flung,
the weight of this world's ransom hung:
the price of humankind to pay
and spoil the spoiler of his prey.

6 To you, eternal three in one,
let homage meet by all be done;
as by the cross you now restore,
so rule and guide us evermore.
                              (Amen.)

VENANTIUS FORTUNATUS (*c*.530–609)
tr. J. M. NEALE (1818–66)

229

YELLOW BITTERN   LM

ADRIAN BEECHAM (1904–82)

SEE, Christ was wounded for our sake,
    and bruised and beaten for our sin,
so by his sufferings we are healed,
    for God has laid our guilt on him.

2 Look on his face, come close to him—
    see, you will find no beauty there:
despised, rejected, who can tell
    the grief and sorrow he must bear?

3 Like sheep that stray, we leave God's path,
    to choose our own and not his will;
like sheep to slaughter he has gone,
    obedient to his Father's will.

4 Cast out to die by those he loved,
    reviled by those he died to save,
see how sin's pride has sought his death,
    see how sin's hate has made his grave.

5 For on his shoulders God has laid
    the weight of sin that we should bear;
so by his passion we have peace,
    through his obedience and his prayer.

BRIAN FOLEY (b. 1919)
based on Isaiah 53

230

HORSLEY   CM

W. HORSLEY (1774–1858)

THERE is a green hill far away,
  outside a city wall,
where the dear Lord was crucified,
  who died to save us all.

2 We may not know, we cannot tell,
    what pains he had to bear,
  but we believe it was for us
    he hung and suffered there.

3 He died that we might be forgiven,
    he died to make us good,
  that we might go at last to heaven,
    saved by his precious blood.

4 There was no other good enough
    to pay the price of sin;
  he only could unlock the gate
    of heaven, and let us in.

5 O dearly, dearly has he loved,
    and we must love him too,
  and trust in his redeeming blood,
    and try his works to do.

CECIL FRANCES ALEXANDER (1818–95)
based on Mark 15: 22–24

231

WARRINGTON   LM

R. HARRISON (1748–1810)

WE sing the praise of him who died,
   of him who died upon the cross;
the sinner's hope let men deride,
   for this we count the world but loss.

2 Inscribed upon the cross we see,
   in shining letters, 'God is love';
he bears our sins upon the tree,
   he brings us mercy from above.

3 The cross, it takes our guilt away,
   it holds the fainting spirit up;
it cheers with hope the gloomy day,
   and sweetens every bitter cup.

4 It makes the coward spirit brave,
   and nerves the feeble arm for fight;
it takes the terror from the grave,
   and gilds the bed of death with light.

5 The balm of life, the cure of woe,
   the measure and the pledge of love;
the sinner's refuge here below,
   the angels' theme in heaven above.

THOMAS KELLY (1769–1855)

232

WERE YOU THERE

Afro–American spiritual
arr. F. B. WESTBROOK (1903–75)

(were you there?) (when they cru - ci - fied my Lord?) Oh! Oh! Some-times it cau - ses me to trem-ble, trem-ble, trem-ble;

WERE you there when they crucified my Lord?
Were you there when they crucified my Lord?
Oh! Sometimes it causes me to tremble, tremble, tremble;
Were you there when they crucified my Lord?

2 Were you there when they nailed him to the tree?

3 Were you there when they laid him in the tomb?

4 Were you there when God raised him from the dead?

American folk hymn

233

ROCKINGHAM   LM

E. MILLER (1731–1807)

WHEN I survey the wondrous cross
    where the young Prince of glory died,
my richest gain I count but loss,
    and pour contempt on all my pride.

2 Forbid it, Lord, that I should boast,
    save in the death of Christ my God:
all the vain things that charm me most,
    I sacrifice them to his blood.

3 See from his head, his hands, his feet,
    sorrow and love flow mingled down:
did e'er such love and sorrow meet,
    or thorns compose so rich a crown?

4 Were the whole realm of nature mine,
    that were an offering far too small,
love so amazing, so divine,
    demands my soul, my life, my all.

ISAAC WATTS (1674–1748)
based on Galatians 6: 14

234

American folk hymn, *Southern Harmony*, 1835
arr. CARLTON R. YOUNG

CHARLESTOWN   87 87

WHEN he was baptized in Jordan
   Jesus knew his chosen role:
ready now for time of testing
   in the desert of the soul.

2 Starved of bread to feed the body,
   starved of rest to feed the brain,
   starved of friends to feed the spirit,
   Jesus daily bore the strain.

3 During six long weeks of trial
   evil masquerades as good:
   points false roads to instant lordship,
   tempts him with the word of God.

4 He attacks the great impostor:
   evil shall not win this day!
   Ready now to serve his calling,
   sets his face Jerusalem way.

5 In the hour of our temptation,
   as we meet each vital choice,
   make us wise and make us willing,
   Lord of life, to heed your voice.

BERNARD BRALEY (b. 1924)
based on Mark 1: 9–13

235

Hosanna! Blessed is he who comes in the name of the Lord!
Hosanna in the highest! God save the King!

Hosanna to the Son of David, great David's greater Son!
Jesus, Son of David, have mercy on me.

Who is this Son of David,
whom David himself calls 'Lord'?

He is the King of glory, the Lord strong and mighty.
Hosanna to the Son of David, the Lord who is our shepherd.

Behold your King, humble, and riding on an ass.
Come, let us worship, and bow down,

for the Lord is King!
Jesus is King! Hosanna to his name!

236

Saviour, we thank you
that on the first Palm Sunday
you rode as the King who comes in peace,
but unmistakably as the King.
**O Christ, who once rode humbly into Jerusalem,
we salute you in your heavenly majesty.**

For those who followed your royal progress that day
and for those who follow it still,
your royalty is unforgettable.
**O Christ, who once rode humbly into Jerusalem,
we salute you in your heavenly majesty.**

Even while, in faith and hope,
we must wait for your coronation at the end of time.
**O Christ, who once rode humbly into Jerusalem,
we salute you in your heavenly majesty.**

237

It is a true saying,
to be completely accepted and believed:
Christ Jesus came into the world to save sinners.
I am the worst of them, but God was merciful to me.

Everyone has sinned
and is far away from God.
But by the free gift of God's grace
all are put right with him
through Jesus Christ.

**God offered him, so that by his death he should become
the means by which people's sins are forgiven
through their faith in him.**

He endured the suffering that should have been ours,
the pain that we should have borne.
**We are healed by the punishment he suffered,
made whole by the blows he received.**

The Son of Man came to serve and to give his life
to redeem many people.
**To him be honour and glory
for ever and ever. Amen.**

238

O God, we commend to your blessing
all who suffer:
**we pray for those who feel themselves forsaken or betrayed,
and for any who, having worked and struggled,
have nothing to show for it
except the signs and penalties of failure;**

we pray for the victims of injustice,
for all who must endure the scorn and mockery of lesser men and women,
and for all who suffer alone;
**we pray for any who face a martyr's death.
We remember all who watch and weep,
and all who thirst.**

May they know
that the suffering of Christ
has transfigured all suffering,
that the death of Christ
has transfigured all death,
and may the victory of Christ
be their victory,
through his grace. Amen.

239

Today he who hung the earth upon the waters
is hung upon the cross;
he who is the King of the angels
is arrayed in a crown of thorns;
he who wraps the heavens in clouds
is wrapped in the purple of mockery;

the Bridegroom of the Church
is transfixed with nails;
the Son of the Virgin
is pierced with a spear;
we venerate your Passion, O Christ,
show us also your glorious resurrection.

240

We have a high priest who in every respect has been tempted as we
are, yet is without sin.
Salvation is in Christ Jesus.
Let us then with confidence draw near to the throne of grace,
that we may receive mercy and help.

Jesus also suffered outside the gate to sanctify the people
through his own blood.
Salvation is in Christ Jesus.
Therefore let us go forth to him outside the camp,
bearing abuse for him.

Christ our Passover is sacrificed for us.
If we have died with him, we shall also live with him.
Lord, we believe,
help our unbelief.

The spirit is willing, but the flesh is weak.
Lord, have mercy.
Christ, have mercy.
Lord, have mercy.

241

God our Father, today, in remembrance and awe, we tread the holy
ground of Calvary:
this place of abandonment,
that has become the scene of our adoration;
this place of suffering,
that has become the source of our peace;
this place of violence,
that has become the battlefield on which love is victorious.

Father, as we re-live the events of this day it is with awe that we
count the cost of our salvation.
Words cannot be found to utter our thanksgiving.
Accept our silent adoration.
In Jesus' name. Amen.

242

NETTLETON   87 87 D

American folk hymn

For this tune in E♭ major see no. 433.

AT the dawning of salvation,
   in the morning of the world,
Christ is raised, a living banner
   by the love of God unfurled.
Through the daylight, through the darkness,
   Christ leads on his great array:
all the saints and all the sinners
   he has gathered on his way.

2 He is risen in the morning,
   he is risen from the dead;
he is laughter after sadness,
   he is light when night has fled.
He has suffered, he has triumphed,
   life is his alone to give:
as he gave it once he gives it
   evermore, that we may live.

3 For the glory of salvation
   in the dawn of Easter Day
we will praise you, loving Father;
   we rejoice to sing and pray
with the Son and with the Spirit.
   Lead us on, your great array,
saints and sinners celebrating
   your triumphant love today.

JOCK CURLE

243

EASTER SKIES   10 10

JOHN MARSH (b. 1947)

May also be sung to SONG 46, no. 561.

ALL shall be well!
    for on our Easter skies
see Christ the Sun
    of righteousness arise.

2 All shall be well!
    the sacrifice is made;
the sinner freed,
    the price of pardon paid.

3 All shall be well!
    The cross and passion past;
dark night is done,
    bright morning come at last.

4 All shall be well!
    within our Father's plan
death has no more
    dominion over man.

5 Jesus alive!
    rejoice and sing again,
'All shall be well
    for evermore, Amen!'

TIMOTHY DUDLEY-SMITH (b. 1926)
based on Romans 6: 5–14

244

TRURO   LM

Psalmodia Evangelica, 1789

CHRIST is alive! Let Christians sing;
    the cross stands empty to the sky;
let streets and homes with praises ring;
    love drowned in death shall never die.

2 Christ is alive! No longer bound
    to distant years in Palestine;
but saving, healing, here and now,
    and touching every place and time.

3 Not throned afar, remotely high,
    untouched, unmoved by human pains,
but daily, in the midst of life,
    our Saviour in the Godhead reigns.

4 In every insult, rift and war,
    where colour, scorn or wealth divide,
he suffers still, yet loves the more,
    and lives where even hope has died.

5 Christ is alive and comes to bring
    new life to this and every age,
till earth and all creation ring
    with joy, with justice, love and praise.

BRIAN A. WREN (b. 1936)

245

MORGENLIED   87 87 D with refrain

F. C. MAKER (1844–1927)

REFRAIN

Christ is ris-en! al - le - lu - ia!   ris - en our vic - tor-ious head;

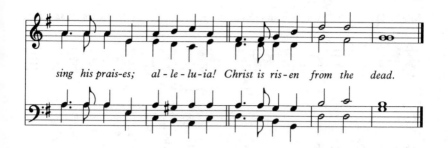

sing his prais-es; al - le - lu - ia! Christ is ris-en from the dead.

CHRIST is risen! alleluia!
　　risen our victorious head.
Sing his praises; alleluia!
　　Christ is risen from the dead.
Gratefully our hearts adore him,
　　as his light once more appears;
bowing down in joy before him,
　　rising up from griefs and tears.

Christ is risen! alleluia!
　　risen our victorious head;
　　sing his praises; alleluia!
　　　Christ is risen from the dead.

2 Christ is risen! all the sadness
　　of his earthly life is o'er;
through the open gates of gladness
　　he returns to life once more.
Death and hell before him bending,
　　he is raised the victor now,
angels on his steps attending,
　　glory round his wounded brow.

3 Christ is risen! henceforth never
　　death nor hell shall us enthral;
we are Christ's, in him for ever
　　we have triumphed over all;
all the doubting and dejection
　　of our trembling hearts have ceased;
on his day of resurrection;
　　let us rise and keep the feast.

J. S. B. MONSELL (1811–75)

246

LLANFAIR   77 77 with alleluias   R. WILLIAMS (1781–1821)

'CHRIST the Lord is risen today!'
   Alleluia!
All creation joins to say:
   Alleluia!
raise your joy and triumph high;
   Alleluia!
sing now heaven, and earth reply:
   Alleluia!

2 Love's redeeming work is done,
   fought the fight, the battle won:
   vain the stone, the watch, the seal;
   Christ has burst the gates of hell.

3 Lives again our glorious King:
   where, O death, is now your sting?
   once he died our souls to save;
   where your victory, O grave?

4 Soar we now where Christ has led,
   following our exalted head;
   made like him, like him we rise;
   ours the cross, the grave, the skies.

5 King of glory! Soul of bliss!
   Everlasting life is this:
   you to know, your power to prove,
   thus to sing, and thus to love.

CHARLES WESLEY (1707–88)

247

SONG OF RESURRECTION
11 11 11 11 Anapaestic

DAVID TURNER

STOWEY   11 11 11 11 Anapaestic   English traditional melody

COME, sing of the springtime, God's pledge of new birth.
The snows are all melted which shrouded the earth;
old root-ends, deep hidden, send shoots to the light;
and long-dormant insects burst out into flight.
   Alleluia!

2 Come, sing of Christ's rising, the joyful surprise,
which lifted low spirits and opened blind eyes,
reviving numb hope with its heart-warming call:
'My love is not dead; it is stronger than all.'

3 Come, sing of the son who struck out on his own,
but came to his senses when lost and alone;
and sing of the father's delight to forgive,
for he who was dead is back home and alive.

4 Come, sing of the countless disciples today
who live in Christ's spirit and walk in his way,
who sometimes laid low by life's hardships and pains,
yet rise above self with its deadening chains.

DAVID TURNER

When sung to the tune STOWEY the 'Alleluia!' is omitted.

248

AVE VIRGO VIRGINUM   76 76 D

Medieval melody from
J. HORN'S *Gesangbuch*, 1544

For a different harmonization of this tune (in F major) see no. 407(*i*).
May also be sung to GOOD KING WENCESLAS, no. 407(*ii*).

COME, you faithful, raise the strain
   of triumphant gladness;
God has brought his people now
   into joy from sadness;
it's the spring of souls today;
   Christ has burst his prison,
and from three days' sleep in death
   as a sun has risen.

2 Now the queen of seasons, bright
   with the day of splendour,
with the royal feast of feasts,
   comes its joy to render;
comes to gladden Christians, who
   with sincere affection
welcome in unwearied strains
   Jesus' resurrection.

3 Alleluia now to you,
   Christ, our King immortal,
who triumphant burst the bars
   of the tomb's dark portal.
Alleluia, with the Son
   God the Father praising.
Alleluia, yet again,
   to the Spirit raising.

JOHN OF DAMASCUS (c.675–749)
tr. J. M. NEALE (1818–66)

249

Gaelic melody
harm. JOHN HUGHES (1896–1968)

BUNESSAN   55 54 D

For another arrangement of this tune (in C major) see no. 158.

EARLY on Sunday,
Mary comes running.
Says to the gardener,
  'Where is my Lord?'
Mary, stop crying:
this is no gardener.
Look at your master,
  to life restored.

2 Later on Sunday,
  two, slowly walking,
  tell their companion,
    'Jesus is dead.'
  Sitting at supper,
  warmed by his presence,
  they know their master
    as he breaks bread.

3 Sunday by Sunday,
  as the first Easter,
  Jesus comes to us,
    makes himself known.
  Joy of your people,
  life, resurrection,
  Jesus, our master,
    we are your own.

J. WOOLFORD
based on Luke 24: 1–35 and John 20: 1–18

250

VULPIUS 888 with alleluias

Melody from M. VULPIUS'S *Gesangbuch*, 1609
harm. HENRY G. LEY (1887–1962)

Al - le - lu - ia, al - le - lu - ia, al - le - lu - ia!

For a different arrangement of this tune (in D major) see no. 475.

GOOD Christians all, rejoice and sing!
Now is the triumph of our King!
To the whole world glad news we
    bring:
    Alleluia!

2 The Lord of life is risen today;
bring flowers of song to strew his
    way;
let everyone rejoice and say:
    Alleluia!

3 Praise we in songs of victory
that love, that life which cannot die,
and sing with hearts uplifted high:
    Alleluia!

4 Your name we bless, O risen Lord,
and sing today with one accord
the life laid down, the life restored:
    Alleluia!

C. A. ALINGTON (1872–1955) altd.

251

First Tune

PHILIPPINE   LM

R. E. ROBERTS (1878–1940)

SECOND TUNE

CHURCH TRIUMPHANT   LM   J. W. ELLIOTT (1833–1915)

I KNOW that my Redeemer lives!
What joy the blest assurance gives!
He lives, he lives, who once was dead;
he lives, my everlasting head!

2 He lives, to bless me with his love;
he lives to plead for me above;
he lives, my hungry soul to feed;
he lives, to help in time of need.

3 He lives, and grants me daily breath;
he lives, and I shall conquer death:
he lives, my mansion to prepare;
he lives, to lead me safely there.

4 He lives, all glory to his name;
he lives, my Saviour, still the same;
what joy the blest assurance gives!
I know that my Redeemer lives!

SAMUEL MEDLEY (1738–99)
based on Job 19: 25 and Mark 16: 6

252

EASTER HYMN   77 77 with alleluias

Adapted from a melody
in *Lyra Davidica*, 1708

JESUS CHRIST is risen today,
    Alleluia!
our triumphant holy day,
    Alleluia!
who did once upon the cross,
    Alleluia!
suffer to redeem our loss.
    Alleluia!

2 Hymns of praise then let us sing,
  unto Christ, our heavenly King,
  who endured the cross and grave,
  sinners to redeem and save.

3 For the pains which he endured,
  our salvation have secured,
  now above all powers he's King,
  where the angels ever sing.

                    Lyra Davidica, 1708

253

ST ALBINUS   78 78 4

H. J. GAUNTLETT (1805–76)

Al - le - lu - ia!

For this tune in C major see no. 195.

JESUS lives! your terrors now
  can, O death, no more appal us;
Jesus lives! by this we know,
  you, O grave, cannot enthral us.
    Alleluia!

2 Jesus lives! henceforth is death
  but the gate of life immortal;
this shall calm our trembling breath,
  when we pass its gloomy portal.
    Alleluia!

3 Jesus lives! for us he died;
  then, alone to Jesus living,
pure in heart may we abide,
  glory to our Saviour giving.
    Alleluia!

4 Jesus lives! our hearts know well,
  nought from us his love shall sever;
life, nor death, nor powers of hell,
  tear us from his keeping ever.
    Alleluia!

5 Jesus lives! to him the throne
  over all the world is given:
may we go where he is gone,
  rest and reign with him in heaven.
    Alleluia!

CHRISTIAN F. GELLERT (1715–69)
tr. FRANCES ELIZABETH COX (1812–97)
based on Romans 8: 11

254

LIKE A LAMB

Words and music by
GRAHAM KENDRICK (b. 1950)
based on Isaiah 53: 4–7 and John 20: 11–16

Unison

VERSES

1. Led like a lamb to the slaugh-ter, in si-lence and shame,
2. At break of dawn, poor Ma - ry, still weep-ing she came,
3. At the right hand of the Fa - ther, now seat-ed on high,

there on your back you__ car - ried a world of
when through her grief she__ heard your__ voice now
you have be - gun your e - ter - nal__ reign of

vio-lence and pain. Bleed-ing,__
speak-ing her name. *Ma-ry!__
jus - tice and joy. Glo-ry,__

dy - ing,__ bleed-ing,__
Mas-ter!__ Ma - ry!__
glo - ry,__ glo - ry,__

*It is effective if the men sing 'Mary!' and the women reply 'Master!'

PROCLAIMING THE GOSPEL

dy - ing. ___
Mas - ter! ___
glo - ry. ___

You're a - live, you're a-live, you have ri-sen,

al - le - lu - ia! ___
(al - le - lu - ia! al - le - lu - ia!)

And the

power and the glo-ry are gi-ven,   al-le-lu-ia, ___
(al-le-lu-ia! al-le-lu-ia!)

Je-sus to

Last time

you.

*The word 'alleluia' can be sung antiphonally, as indicated,
the people having been divided into three equal groups.

255

ADORATION (ST JOHN'S) 66 66 88 W. H. HAVERGAL (1793–1870)

Now lives the Lamb of God,
our Passover, the Christ,
who once with nails and wood
for us was sacrificed:

*Come, keep the feast, the anthem sing
that Christ indeed is Lord and King!*

2 Now risen from the dead
   Christ never dies again;
in us, with Christ as head,
   sin nevermore shall reign:

3 In Adam all must die,
   forlorn and unforgiven;
in Christ all come alive,
   the second Man from heaven.

4 Give praise to God alone
   who life from death can bring;
whose mighty power can turn
   the winter into spring.

DAVID MOWBRAY (b. 1938)
based on 1 Corinthians 5: 7–8; 15: 20–22

256

CHRIST AROSE   65 64 with refrain

R. LOWRY (1826–99)
arr. G. F. BROCKLESS (1887–1957)

Up from the grave he a - rose,_____ with a might-y tri-umph o'er his

foes;_____ he a-rose a vic-tor from the dark do-main, and he

lives for e - ver with his saints to reign: he a - rose!_____ He a-rose!_____ Al - le - lu - ia! Christ a - rose!

Low in the grave he lay,
  Jesus, my Saviour;
waiting the coming day,
  Jesus, my Lord.

  Up from the grave he arose,
  with a mighty triumph o'er his foes;
  he arose a victor from the dark domain,
  and he lives for ever with his saints to reign:
  He arose! He arose!
  Alleluia! Christ arose!

2 Vainly they watch his bed,
    Jesus, my Saviour;
  vainly they seal the dead,
    Jesus, my Lord.

3 Death cannot keep his prey,
    Jesus, my Saviour;
  he tore the bars away,
    Jesus, my Lord.

ROBERT LOWRY (1826–99)

257

NOËL NOUVELET   11 11 10 11

French traditional carol
arr. MARTIN SHAW (1875–1958)

Love is come a - gain,   like   wheat that springs up   green.

For a different arrangement of this tune (in E minor) see no. 534.

Now the green blade rises
   from the buried grain,
wheat that in dark earth
   many days has lain;
love lives again,
   that with the dead has been:

   Love is come again,
      like wheat that springs up green.

2 In the grave they laid him,
   Love whom men had slain,
thinking that never
   he would wake again,
laid in the earth
   like grain that sleeps unseen:

3 Forth he came at Easter,
   like the risen grain,
he that for three days
   in the grave had lain,
quick from the dead
   my risen Lord is seen:

4 When our hearts are wintry,
   grieving, or in pain,
your touch can call us
   back to life again,
fields of our hearts
   that dead and bare have been:

J. M. C. CRUM (1872–1958)

258

VRUECHTEN   67 67 with refrain   17th-century Dutch melody

REFRAIN

Come,   share our Eas - ter__ joy   that death could   not im - pri -

- son, nor a - ny power de - stroy, our___
Christ, who is a - ri - sen,__ a - ri - sen, a -
- ri - sen, a - ri - - - sen!

THIS joyful Eastertide
   what need is there for grieving?
Cast all your cares aside
   and be not unbelieving:

   Come, share our Easter joy
      that death could not imprison,
   nor any power destroy,
      our Christ, who is arisen!

2 No work for him is vain,
   no faith in him mistaken,
for Easter makes it plain
   his kingdom is not shaken:

3 Then put your trust in Christ,
   in waking or in sleeping:
his grace on earth sufficed;
   he'll never quit his keeping:

F. PRATT GREEN (b. 1903)

259

ALMSGIVING   888 4

J. B. DYKES (1823–76)

WHEN fear and grief had barred the door,
   and sick with failure, raw with shame,
the lost disciples met once more,
     their master came.

2 What joy dispelled their sorrow then,
   as faith reborn drove out their fear;
what transformation in those men;
     their Lord was near!

3 They saw his hand, the wound-prints there,
   and knew that he, though risen again
and Lord of all, would always share
     all human pain.

4 As Jesus had himself been sent,
   so with his Spirit they would go
to raise dead souls, to call 'Repent!
     Love's freedom know!'

5 Lord Christ, you meet us in this hour;
   break through our sorrow, fear and doubt;
reveal your wounds, bestow your power;
     then send us out!

BASIL E. BRIDGE (b. 1927)
based on John 20: 19–23

260

MACCABAEUS   10 11 11 11 with refrain   G. F. HANDEL (1685–1759)

Yours be the glo - ry! ri - sen, conquer-ing Son:

end - less_ is the vic - tory o - ver death you won.

Yours be the glory! risen, conquering Son;
endless is the victory over death you won;
angels robed in splendour rolled the stone away,
kept the folded grave clothes, where your body lay:

Yours be the glory! risen, conquering Son:
endless is the victory over death you won.

2 See! Jesus meets us, risen from the tomb,
lovingly he greets us, scatters fear and gloom;
let the church with gladness hymns of triumph sing,
for her Lord is living, death has lost its sting:

3 No more we doubt you, glorious Prince of life:
what is life without you? Aid us in our strife;
make us more than conquerors through your deathless love,
bring us safe through Jordan to your home above:

EDMOND BUDRY (1854–1932)
tr. R. BIRCH HOYLE (1875–1939)

261

VICTORY   888 with alleluia

G. P. DA PALESTRINA (1525–94)
adpt. W. H. MONK (1823–89)

Al-le - lu - ia!

THE strife is o'er, the battle done;
the victory of life is won;
now be the song of praise begun,
  Alleluia!

2 The powers of death have done their worst,
by Christ their legions were dispersed;
let shouts of holy joy outburst,
  Alleluia!

3 The three sad days have quickly sped;
he rises glorious from the dead;
all glory to our risen head!
  Alleluia!

4 He conquered hell, its power defied,
the way to heaven he opened wide;
sing praise to him the crucified,
  Alleluia!

5 Lord, by the stripes which wounded thee,
from death's dread sting thy servants free,
that we may live, and sing to thee,
  Alleluia!

Latin, 17th century
tr. FRANCIS POTT (1832–1909) altd.

262

The Lord is risen!
He is risen indeed! Alleluia!

263

Blessed be the God and Father of our Lord Jesus Christ!
By his great mercy we have been born anew
to a living hope through the resurrection
of Jesus Christ from the dead.

Christ has been raised from the dead.
In Christ shall all be made alive.
Alleluia! Praise the Lord!

264

Worthy is the Lamb who was slain,
to receive power and wealth and wisdom and might
and honour and glory and blessing!
He emptied himself, and took the form of a servant,
he became obedient unto death, even death on a cross.
But God did not leave his soul in hell.
Christ rose again the third day, as the scriptures said.
Christ is risen!
Risen indeed. Alleluia!
Alleluia! Praise the Lord!

265   EASTER MORNING

The congregation can be divided into groups 1 and 2, L/R if there is
a central aisle, or M/F.

It is Easter and we celebrate life.
   (1) **The trumpets of the angels,**
   (2) **the singing of the springtime birds,**
   (1) **and the alleluias of the Church,**
  (All) **all say: Christ is risen! Jesus lives!**

It is Easter and we celebrate victory.
   (1) **The Christ who died for sin**
   (2) **is risen in glory;**
   (1) **the devil is done for,**
   (2) **the cross rises over the field of battle,**
   (1) **as empty as the tomb,**
  (All) **and stands for ever as the sign of our conquering King.**

It is Easter and we celebrate hope.
   (1) **If Christ has been raised,**
   (2) **anything can happen**
   (1) **and no good thing is impossible.**
  (All) **Alleluia!**

266 EASTER EVENING

Risen Lord and Master:
we ask you to meet us on the road we travel.
    (1) **Meet us in conversation that opens up the scriptures;**
    (2) **meet us in the supplying of our needs;**
    (1) **meet us in those people whose needs we can supply;**
  (All) **be made known to us in the breaking of bread.**

When days or moods are dark,
and the one in whom we had hoped seems far away,
  (All) **meet and walk with us,**
       for your name's sake.

267

I passed on to you what I received, which is of the greatest importance:
that Christ died for our sins.
  As written in the scriptures: that he was buried and raised
    to life three days later.
  As written in the scriptures: that he appeared to Peter
    and then to all the apostles.
Then he appeared to more than five hundred of his followers at once.
Then he appeared to James, and afterwards to all the apostles.
  The truth is that Christ has been raised from death, as the
    guarantee that those who sleep in death will also be raised.
This is how it will be when the dead are raised to life.
When the body is buried, it is mortal; when raised, it will be immortal.
When buried, it is ugly and weak; when raised, it will be beautiful and
strong.
  Where, Death, is your victory?
  Where, Death, is your power to hurt?
  Thanks be to God,
    who gives us the victory through our Lord Jesus Christ!
So then, my dear brothers and sisters, stand firm and steady.
Keep busy always in your work for the Lord,
since you know that nothing you do in the Lord's service is ever useless.

268

Lord God, keep us convinced of the victory of Christ your Son,
which became so vivid for us in the Easter alleluias.
  Sustain in our mind the peace renewed in garden or countryside
    as we return to the world of our daily responsibilities,
and in your Church may the joy of high festival still echo
in the habitual services, meetings and appointments.
  May your Holy Spirit turn each week into a holy week,
    each Sunday into the Lord's day of resurrection and new life.

269

NEANDER 87 87 87

From Chorale *Unser Herrscher*
by J. NEANDER (1650–80)

COME, you people, raise the anthem,
　cleave the sky with shouts of praise;
sing to him, the mighty Saviour,
　who from death the world does raise;
shepherd, prophet, word incarnate,
　him the heart of man obeys.

2 Lo, for us and our salvation
　hatred, scorn, and death he bore;
he, to bring mankind to freedom,
　died that we might die no more;
then, arising, showed his glory,
　Prince of life for evermore.

3 Now in that celestial country
　his the honour, his the might,
'mid the circling alleluias
　welling from the sons of light;
he the King and he the captain,
　victor in the hard-won fight.

4 Praise and honour to the Father,
　praise and honour to the Son,
praise and honour to the Spirit,
　in the Godhead ever one.
God of life and resurrection,
　honour, praise, to you be done.

JOB HUPTON (1762–1849) altd.

391

270

HYFRYDOL   87 87 D

R. H. PRICHARD (1811–87)

For this tune in G major see no. 273.

ALLELUIA! sing to Jesus,
    his the sceptre, his the throne;
alleluia! his the triumph,
    his the victory alone;
hark! the songs of peaceful Sion
    thunder like a mighty flood;
Jesus out of every nation
    has redeemed us by his blood.

2 Alleluia! bread of angels,
    you on earth our food, our stay;
alleluia! here the sinful
    flee to you from day to day;
alleluia! not as orphans
    are we left in sorrow now;
alleluia! he is near us,
    faith believes, nor questions how.

3 Alleluia! alleluia!
    glory be to God on high;
to the Father, and the Saviour,
    who has gained the victory;
glory to the Holy Spirit,
    fount of love and sanctity.
Alleluia! alleluia!
    to the triune Majesty.

W. C. DIX (1837–98) altd.
based on Acts 1: 3–11,
Revelation 5: 6–14

271

MARCHING THROUGH GEORGIA
13 13 13 8 with refrain

American folk melody
arr. DAVID TRAFFORD (b. 1950)

A - men,   he comes!   to

bring his own re-ward! A - men, praise God! for jus-tice now re-stored;

394

ASCENSION

king-doms of the world be-come the king-doms of the Lord:

Love has the vic-tory for e-ver!

COME and see the shining hope
    that Christ's apostle saw;
on the earth, confusion,
    but in heaven an open door,
where the living creatures
    praise the Lamb for evermore:
Love has the victory for ever!

Amen, he comes! to bring his own reward!
Amen, praise God! for justice now restored;
kingdoms of the world become
the kingdoms of the Lord:
Love has the victory for ever!

2 All the gifts you send us, Lord,
    are faithful, good, and true;
holiness and righteousness
    are shown in all you do:
who can see your greatest Gift
    and fail to worship you?
Love has the victory for ever!

3 Power and salvation all
    belong to God on high!
So the mighty multitudes
    of heaven make their cry,
singing, 'Alleluia' where
    the echoes never die:
Love has the victory for ever!

CHRISTOPHER IDLE (b. 1938)
based on Revelation 4–5

272

ASCENSION   77 77 with alleluias   Melody by W. H. MONK (1823–89)

Al - le - lu - ia!

Al - le - lu - ia!

Al - le - lu - ia!

Al - le - lu - ia!

May also be sung to LLANFAIR, no. 246.

HAIL the day that sees him rise,
  Alleluia!
to his throne above the skies;
  Alleluia!
Christ, awhile to mortals given,
  Alleluia!
enters now the highest heaven.
  Alleluia!

2 There for him high triumph waits;
  lift your heads, eternal gates!
  Christ has vanquished death and sin;
  take the King of glory in!

3 See! the heaven its Lord receives,
  yet he loves the earth he leaves:
  though returning to his throne,
  still he calls mankind his own.

4 See! he lifts his hands above;
  see! he shows the prints of love;
  hark! his gracious lips bestow
  blessings on his church below.

5 Still for us he intercedes;
  his prevailing death he pleads;
  near himself prepares our place,
  he the first fruits of our race.

6 Lord, though parted from our sight
  far above the starry height,
  grant our hearts may thither rise,
  seeking you beyond the skies.

CHARLES WESLEY (1707–88)
THOMAS COTTERILL (1779–1823)

273

HYFRYDOL   87 87 D

R. H. PRICHARD (1811–87)

For this tune in F major see no. 270.

HAIL, thou once despisèd Jesus,
 hail, thou Galilean King!
thou didst suffer to release us;
 thou didst free salvation bring:
hail, thou agonising Saviour,
 bearer of our sin and shame;
by thy merits we find favour;
 life is given through thy name.

2 Paschal Lamb, by God appointed,
 all our sins on thee were laid;
by almighty love anointed,
 thou hast full atonement made:
all thy people are forgiven
 through the virtue of thy blood;
opened is the gate of heaven;
 man is reconciled to God.

3 Jesus, hail! enthroned in glory,
 there for ever to abide;
all the heavenly host adore thee,
 seated at thy Father's side:
there for sinners thou art pleading;
 there thou dost our place prepare;
ever for us interceding,
 till in glory we appear.

4 Worship, honour, power and blessing,
 thou art worthy to receive;
loudest praises, without ceasing,
 meet it is for us to give:
help, ye bright angelic spirits,
 bring your sweetest, noblest lays;
help to sing our Saviour's merits,
 help to chant Immanuel's praise.

JOHN BAKEWELL (1721–1819) altd.

274

ST MAGNUS   CM

Melody and bass (slightly altered)
probably by JEREMIAH CLARKE (1670–1707)

THE head that once was crowned with thorns
   is crowned with glory now:
a royal diadem adorns
   the mighty victor's brow.

2 The highest place that heaven affords
   is his by sovereign right:
the King of kings and Lord of lords,
   he reigns in perfect light.

3 The joy of all who dwell above,
   the joy of all below,
to whom he manifests his love,
   and grants his name to know.

4 To them the cross, with all its shame,
   with all its grace, is given:
their name an everlasting name,
   their joy the joy of heaven.

5 They suffer with their Lord below;
   they reign with him above;
their profit and their joy, to know
   the mystery of his love.

6 The cross he bore is life and health,
   though shame and death to him;
his people's hope, his people's wealth,
   their everlasting theme.

THOMAS KELLY (1769–1855)
based on Revelation 17: 14; 19: 12, 16

275

ST STEPHEN   CM

WILLIAM JONES (1726–1800)

WITH joy we meditate the grace
   of our high priest above;
his heart is made of tenderness,
   it overflows with love.

2 Touched with a sympathy within,
   he knows our feeble frame;
he knows what sore temptations mean,
   for he has felt the same.

3 He, in the days of feeble flesh,
   poured out his cries and tears;
and now exalted feels afresh
   what every member bears.

4 He'll never quench the smoking flax,
   but raise it to a flame;
the bruisèd reed he never breaks,
   nor scorns the meanest name.

5 Then let our humble faith address
   his mercy and his power;
we shall obtain delivering grace
   in the distressing hour.

ISAAC WATTS (1674–1748) altd.
based on Isaiah 42: 3 and Hebrews 4: 15–16

276

ST GEORGE'S, EDINBURGH   DCM with Coda   A. M. THOMSON (1778–1831)

1. You gates, lift up your heads on high; you doors that last for-
2. You gates, lift up your heads; you doors, doors that do last for-

aye,__ be lift-ed up, that so the King of__ glo-ry en-ter-
aye,__ be lift-ed up, that so the King of__ glo-ry en-ter-

may! But who of glo-ry is the King? The
may! But who is he that is the

King, the King of

might-y Lord is this, e'en that same Lord that
glo-ry? Who is this? The Lord of hosts and

*Small notes for organ

great in __ might and strong in bat - tle is, e'en
none but __ he, __ the King of glo - ry is, the

that same Lord that great in __ might and strong in __ bat - tle
Lord of hosts and none but __ he, __ the King of __ glo - ry

D.C.

is.
is.

CODA (after verse 2)

Al - le - lu-ia! Al - le - lu-ia! Al - le-lu-ia!

Al - le - lu - ia! Al - le - lu-ia! A-men, a-men, a — men.

Words by FRANCIS ROUS (1579–1659)
and WILLIAM BARTON (1597–1678)
based on Psalm 24: 7–10

276

SECOND TUNE

LADYWELL   DCM

W. H. FERGUSON (1874–1950)

You gates, lift up your heads on high;
    you doors that last for aye,
be lifted up, that so the King
    of glory enter may!
But who of glory is the King?
    The mighty Lord is this,
e'en that same Lord that great in might
    and strong in battle is.

2 You gates, lift up your heads; you doors,
    doors that do last for aye,
be lifted up, that so the King
    of glory enter may!
But who is he that is the King
    of glory? Who is this?
The Lord of hosts and none but he,
    the King of glory is.

FRANCIS ROUS (1579–1659)
WILLIAM BARTON (1597–1678)
based on Psalm 24: 7–10

276

FRIENDS REMEMBERED   DCM

JOHN LOCK (b. 1937)

You gates, lift up your heads on high;
   you doors that last for aye,
be lifted up, that so the King
   of glory enter may!
But who of glory is the King?
   The mighty Lord is this,
e'en that same Lord that great in
      might
   and strong in battle is.

2 You gates, lift up your heads; you
      doors,
   doors that do last for aye,
be lifted up, that so the King
   of glory enter may!
But who is he that is the King
   of glory? Who is this?
The Lord of hosts and none but he,
   the King of glory is.

FRANCIS ROUS (1579–1659)
WILLIAM BARTON (1597–1678)
based on Psalm 24: 7–10

277

We see Jesus,
   crowned with glory and honour.
Jesus, for a little while, was made lower than the angels
   and suffered death among men.
Because he suffered death,
   God has crowned him with glory and honour.
God's living word of life was made flesh
   and dwelt among us, full of grace and truth.
He alone, he the first of men to ascend into heaven,
   was the first and only-begotten Son of God who had come down.
He is given to us, but not to grasp for ourselves,
   since he ascends to his Father and to our Father.
He did not grasp for himself his own divinity,
   but humbled himself,
he took the form of a servant,
   was born in the likeness of men,
   and become obedient unto death.
Therefore, God has highly exalted him,
   that at the name of Jesus every knee should bow.

To the glory of God the Father,
let us confess that Jesus Christ is Lord,
as did the first apostles,
whose first act was to see him ascend.
   Like them, let us wait upon the Father
   for the keeping of Christ's promise to send the Holy Spirit.

278

Almighty God,
as we believe your only-begotten Son our Lord Jesus Christ
   to have ascended into heaven,
so may also we, in heart and mind, there ascend
and with him continually dwell;
who is alive and reigns with you and the Holy Spirit,
one God, now and for ever. Amen.

279

ARDWICK   555 11   H. J. GAUNTLETT (1805–76)

AWAY with our fears,
our troubles and tears,
the Spirit is come,
the witness of Jesus returned to his home.

2 The pledge of our Lord
to his heaven restored,
is sent from the sky,
and tells us our head is exalted on high.

3 Our glorified head
his Spirit has shed,
with his people to stay,
and never again will he take him away.

4 Our heavenly guide
with us shall abide,
his comforts impart,
and set up his kingdom of love in the heart.

5 The heart that believes
his kingdom receives,
his power and his peace,
his life, and his joy's everlasting increase.

CHARLES WESLEY (1707–88)
based on John 14

280

BE STILL AND KNOW   888

Anon.
arr. DAVID TRAFFORD (b. 1950)

Be still and know that I am God,
be still and know that I am God,
be still and know that I am God.

2 I am the Lord that healeth thee.

3 In thee, O Lord, do I put my trust.

Anon.
based on Psalm 46: 10

281

WHITSUN PSALM   LM

NOËL TREDINNICK (b. 1949)

© N. Tredinnick/Jubilate Hymns

SECOND TUNE

ANTWERP   LM

W. SMALLWOOD (1831–97)

May also be sung to FULDA (WALTON), no. 585.

BORN by the Holy Spirit's breath,
loosed from the law of sin and death;
now cleared in Christ from every claim,
no judgement stands against our name.

2 In us the Spirit makes his home
that we in him may overcome;
Christ's risen life, in all its powers,
its all-prevailing strength, is ours.

3 Children and heirs of God most high,
we by his Spirit 'Father' cry;
that Spirit with our spirit shares
to frame and breathe our wordless prayers.

4 One is his love, his purpose one:
to form the likeness of his Son
in all who, called and justified,
shall reign in glory at his side.

5 Nor death nor life, nor powers unseen,
nor height nor depth can come between;
we know through peril, pain and sword,
the love of God in Christ our Lord.

TIMOTHY DUDLEY-SMITH (b. 1926)
based on Romans 8

282

CARLISLE   SM

C. LOCKHART (1745–1815)

TRENTHAM   SM

R. JACKSON (1840–1914)

BREATHE on me, breath of God,
    fill me with life anew,
that I may love what thou dost love,
    and do what thou wouldst do.

2 Breathe on me, breath of God,
    until my heart is pure,
until with thee I will one will,
    to do or to endure.

3 Breathe on me, breath of God,
    till I am wholly thine,
until this earthly part of me
    glows with thy fire divine.

4 Breathe on me, breath of God,
    so shall I never die,
but live with thee the perfect life
    of thine eternity.

EDWIN HATCH (1835–89)
based on Job 33: 4

283

DOWN AMPNEY   66 11 D

R. VAUGHAN WILLIAMS (1872–1958)

COME down, O love divine!
seek out this soul of mine
and visit it with your own ardour glowing;
O Comforter, draw near,
within my heart appear,
and kindle it, your holy flame bestowing.

2　O let it freely burn
till earthly passions turn
to dust and ashes in its heat consuming;
and let your glorious light
shine ever on my sight,
and clothe me round, while still my path illuming.

3　Let holy charity
my outward vesture be,
and lowliness become my inner clothing;
true lowliness of heart
which takes the humbler part,
and for its own shortcomings weeps with loathing.

4　And so the yearning strong
with which the soul will long
shall far surpass the power of human telling;
for none can guess its grace
till we become the place
in which the Holy Spirit makes his dwelling.

BIANCO DA SIENA (d. 1434)
tr. R. F. LITTLEDALE (1833–90)
based on John 14: 16, 26

284

CROSS DEEP   LM

BARRY ROSE (b. 1934)

May also be sung to TALLIS'S CANON, no. 108.

COME, dearest Lord, descend and dwell
 by faith and love in every breast;
then shall we know, and taste, and feel
 the joys that cannot be expressed.

2 Come, fill our hearts with inward strength;
 make our enlightened souls possess
and learn the height and breadth and length
 of your immeasurable grace.

3 Now to the God whose power can do
 more than our thoughts or wishes know,
be everlasting honours done
 by all the Church, through Christ his Son.

ISAAC WATTS (1674–1748)
based on Ephesians 3: 14–20

285

CROSS OF JESUS   87 87   J. STAINER (1840–1901)

COME now, everlasting Spirit,
    bring to every thankful mind
all the Saviour's dying merit,
    all his sufferings for mankind.

2 True recorder of his Passion,
    now the living faith impart,
now reveal his great salvation,
    preach his gospel to our heart.

3 Come, the witness of his dying;
    come, remembrancer divine,
let us feel your power, applying
    Christ to every soul, and mine.

CHARLES WESLEY (1707–88)
based on John 14: 26

286

First Tune

CAREY (SURREY)   88 88 88

H. CAREY (1692–1743)

CREATOR Spirit, by whose aid
the world's foundations first were laid,
come, visit every waiting mind,
come, pour thy joys on humankind;
from sin and sorrow set us free
and make thy temples worthy thee.

2 O source of uncreated light,
the Father's promised paraclete,
thrice holy fount, thrice holy fire,
our hearts with heavenly love inspire;
come, and thy sacred unction bring,
to sanctify us while we sing.

3 Plenteous of grace, descend from high,
rich in thy sevenfold energy:
thou strength of his almighty hand
whose power doth heaven and earth command,
give us thyself, that we may see
the Father and the Son by thee.

4 Immortal honour, endless fame,
attend the almighty Father's name;
the Saviour Son be glorified,
who for lost man's redemption died;
and equal adoration be,
eternal Paraclete, to thee!

Latin hymn, 9th century
tr. JOHN DRYDEN (1631–1700) altd.

286

SECOND TUNE

ABINGDON   88 88 88

ERIK ROUTLEY (1917–82)

CREATOR Spirit, by whose aid
the world's foundations first were laid,
come, visit every waiting mind,
come, pour thy joys on humankind;
from sin and sorrow set us free
and make thy temples worthy thee.

2 O source of uncreated light,
the Father's promised paraclete,
thrice holy fount, thrice holy fire,
our hearts with heavenly love inspire;
come, and thy sacred unction bring,
to sanctify us while we sing.

3 Plenteous of grace, descend from high,
rich in thy sevenfold energy:
thou strength of his almighty hand
whose power doth heaven and earth command,
give us thyself, that we may see
the Father and the Son by thee.

4 Immortal honour, endless fame,
attend the almighty Father's name;
the Saviour Son be glorified,
who for lost man's redemption died;
and equal adoration be,
eternal Paraclete, to thee!

Latin hymn, 9th century
tr. JOHN DRYDEN (1631–1700) altd.

287

RAIN SONG   88 85 with refrain

BETTY PULKINGHAM (b. 1928)
arr. DAVID TRAFFORD (b. 1950)

Unison
REFRAIN

Fall - ing,   fall - ing,

gent - ly   fall - ing,   rain from heaven so   gent - ly   fall - ing:

sim.

on   the   earth,   so parched   and thir-sty,   God sends down his

Last time

rain.   rain.

Ped.

THE HOLY SPIRIT

Falling, falling, gently falling,
rain from heaven so gently falling:
on the earth, so parched and thirsty,
God sends down his rain.

EVEN so, Lord, send your Spirit—
fall upon the poor and weary,
those who come to you sincerely
you'll not turn away.

2 'In those latter days,' the Lord says,
'I'll pour out my Spirit on all flesh,
I shall come with power among you,
you shall know my name.'

3 Even so, Lord, come among us;
lead and guide and purify us
in the fire of your refining,
in the Spirit's flame.

4 Thank you, Jesus, Lord of heaven,
for the gift you've freely given,
gift of love and gift of living
in the Spirit's power.

BETTY PULKINGHAM (b. 1928)
based on Joel 2: 28 and Acts 2: 17

288

CAPETOWN 777 5

Adpt. F. FILITZ (1804–76)

CHARITY 777 5

J. STAINER (1840–1901)

GRACIOUS Spirit, Holy Ghost,
taught by you we covet most
of your gifts at Pentecost,
    holy, heavenly love.

2 Faith that mountains could remove,
tongues of earth or heaven above,
knowledge, all things, empty prove
    without heavenly love.

3 Love is kind, and suffers long;
love is meek, and thinks no wrong;
love, much more than death, is strong:
    therefore give us love.

4 Prophecy will fade away,
melting in the light of day;
love will ever with us stay:
    therefore give us love.

5 Faith and hope and love we see
joining hand in hand agree;
but the greatest of the three,
    and the best, is love.

CHRISTOPHER WORDSWORTH (1807–85)
based on 1 Corinthians 13

289

First Tune

HARTLEY WINTNEY   87 87   GERALD L. BARNES (b. 1935)

Second Tune

ALL FOR JESUS   87 87   J. STAINER (1840–1901)

HOLY Spirit, come confirm us
    in the truth that Christ makes known;
we have faith and understanding
    through your helping gifts alone.

2 Holy Spirit, come console us,
    come as advocate to plead,
loving Spirit from the Father,
    grant in Christ the help we need.

3 Holy Spirit, come renew us,
    come yourself to make us live:
holy, through your loving presence,
    holy, through the gifts you give.

4 Holy Spirit, come possess us,
    you the love of three in one.
Holy Spirit of the Father,
    Holy Spirit of the Son.

BRIAN FOLEY (b. 1919)

290

HOLY MANNA   87 87 D

American folk hymn-tune
harm. ERIK ROUTLEY (1917–82)

HOLY Spirit, ever dwelling
   in the holiest realms of light;
Holy Spirit, ever brooding
   o'er a world of gloom and night;
Holy Spirit, ever raising
   sons of earth to thrones on high;
living, life-imparting Spirit,
   you we praise and magnify.

2 Holy Spirit, ever living
   as the Church's very life;
Holy Spirit, ever striving
   through her in a ceaseless strife;
Holy Spirit, ever forming
   in the Church the mind of Christ;
you we praise with endless worship
   for your fruit and gifts unpriced.

3 Holy Spirit, ever working
   through the Church's ministry;
quickening, strengthening and
      absolving,
   setting captive sinners free;
Holy Spirit, ever binding
   age to age, and soul to soul,
in a fellowship unending,
   you we worship and extol.

TIMOTHY REES (1874–1939)
based on Romans 8: 26–27
and Ephesians 4: 1–16

291

LINTON   65 65

W. K. STANTON (1891–1978)

HOLY Spirit, hear us;
   help us while we sing;
breathe into the music
   of the praise we bring.

2 Holy Spirit, prompt us
   when we kneel to pray;
nearer come, and teach us
   what we ought to say.

3 Holy Spirit, shine now
   on the book we read;
gild its holy pages
   with the light we need.

4 Holy Spirit, give us
   each a lowly mind;
make us more like Jesus,
   gentle, pure and kind.

5 Holy Spirit, help us
   daily by your might,
what is wrong to conquer,
   and to choose the right.

W. H. PARKER (1845–1929)
based on Romans 8: 26–27

292

LÜBECK   77 77

FREYLINGHAUSEN'S *Gesangbuch*, 1704

HOLY Spirit, truth divine,
dawn upon this soul of mine;
word of God, and inward light,
wake my spirit, clear my sight.

2 Holy Spirit, love divine,
glow within this heart of mine;
kindle every high desire;
perish self in your pure fire.

3 Holy Spirit, power divine,
fill and nerve this will of mine;
boldly may I strongly live,
bravely bear, and nobly strive.

4 Holy Spirit, peace divine,
still this restless heart of mine;
speak to calm this tossing sea,
stayed in your tranquillity.

5 Holy Spirit, joy divine,
gladden now this heart of mine;
in the desert ways I'll sing,
spring, O well, for ever spring!

SAMUEL LONGFELLOW (1819–92)
based on Galatians 5: 22

293

SPIRITUS VITAE   98 98   MARY J. HAMMOND (1878–1964)

O BREATH of love, come breathe within us,
  renewing thought and will and heart;
come, love of Christ, afresh to win us,
  revive your Church in every part!

2 O wind of God, come bend us, break us
   till humbly we confess our need;
then, in your tenderness remake us,
   revive, restore—for this we plead.

3 O breath of life, come sweeping through us,
   revive your Church with life and power;
O breath of life, come, cleanse, renew us
   and fit your Church to meet this hour.

ELIZABETH A. P. HEAD (1850–1936) altd.

431

294

O HOLY SPIRIT BREATHE ON ME
88 66 8

NORMAN WARREN (b. 1934)

O HOLY Spirit breathe on me,
O Holy Spirit breathe on me
and cleanse away my sin;
fill me with love within:
O Holy Spirit breathe on me!

2 O Holy Spirit fill my life,
O Holy Spirit fill my life,
take all my pride from me,
give me humility:
O Holy Spirit breathe on me!

3 O Holy Spirit make me new,
O Holy Spirit make me new,
make Jesus real to me,
give me his purity:
O Holy Spirit breathe on me!

4 O Holy Spirit, wind of God,
O Holy Spirit, wind of God,
give me your power today,
to live for you always:
O Holy Spirit breathe on me!

NORMAN WARREN (b. 1934)

295

SKYE BOAT SONG   86 86 with refrain

Scottish traditional melody
arr. D. COOMBES

Unison

Spirit of God, unseen as the wind,
gentle as is the dove:
teach us the truth and help us believe,
show us the Saviour's love!

You spoke to us—long, long ago—
gave us the written word;
we read it still, needing its truth,
through it God's voice is heard.

2 Without your help we fail our Lord,
we cannot live his way;
we need your power, we need your
strength,
following Christ each day.

MARGARET OLD
based on Acts 2: 2

296

LIVING FLAME 76 86 86 86

NORMAN WARREN (b. 1934)

Music © N. L. Warren/Jubilate Hymns

SPIRIT of God within me,
 possess my human frame;
fan the dull embers of my heart,
 stir up the living flame:
strive till that image Adam lost,
 new minted and restored,
in shining splendour brightly bears
 the likeness of the Lord.

2 Spirit of truth within me,
 possess my thought and mind;
lighten anew the inward eye
 by Satan rendered blind:
shine on the words that wisdom speaks
 and grant me power to see
the truth made known to men in Christ,
 and in that truth be free.

3 Spirit of love within me,
 possess my hands and heart;
break through the bonds of self-concern
 that seeks to stand apart:
grant me the love that suffers long,
 that hopes, believes and bears;
the love fulfilled in sacrifice,
 that cares as Jesus cares.

4 Spirit of life within me,
 possess this life of mine;
come as the wind of heaven's breath,
 come as the fire divine!
Spirit of Christ, the living Lord,
 reign in this house of clay,
till from its dust with Christ I rise
 to everlasting day.

TIMOTHY DUDLEY-SMITH (b. 1926)
based on John 16: 13

297

ELLACOMBE   76 76 D   Mainz *Gesangbuch*, 1833

THE Spirit came, as promised,
   in God's appointed hour;
and now to each believer
   he comes in love and power:
and by his Holy Spirit,
   God seals us as his own;
and through the Son and Spirit
   makes access to his throne.

2 The Spirit makes our bodies
   the temple of the Lord;
he binds us all together
   in faith and true accord:
the Spirit in his greatness,
   brings power from God above;
and with the Son and Father
   dwells in our hearts in love.

3 He bids us live together
   in unity and peace,
employ his gifts in blessing,
   and let base passions cease:
we should not grieve the Spirit
   by open sin or shame;
nor let our words and actions
   deny his holy name.

4 The word, the Spirit's weapon,
   will bring all sin to light;
and prayer, by his directing,
   will add new joy and might:
be filled then with his Spirit,
   live out God's will and word;
rejoice with hymns and singing,
   make music to the Lord!

JAMES E. SEDDON (1915–83)

298 & 299

SPIRIT OF THE LIVING GOD

DANIEL IVERSON (1890–1972)
arr. GERALD L. BARNES (b. 1935)

298

SPIRIT of the living God,
fall afresh on me;
Spirit of the living God,
fall afresh on me:
break me, melt me,
mould me, fill me.
Spirit of the living God,
fall afresh on me!

DANIEL IVERSON (1890–1972)

Words and music © 1935, 1963 Moody Bible
Institute of Chicago, USA

299

SPIRIT of the living God,
move among us all;
make us one in heart and mind,
make us one in love:
humble, caring,
selfless, sharing.
Spirit of the living God,
fill our lives with love!

MICHAEL A. BAUGHEN (b. 1930)

Words © M. Baughen/Jubilate Hymns

300

LAUDS 77 77

JOHN WILSON (b. 1905)

1. THERE'S a spirit in the air,
   telling Christians everywhere:
   'Praise the love that Christ revealed,
   living, working, in our world.'

2. Lose your shyness, find your tongue,
   tell the world what God has done:
   God in Christ has come to stay.
   Live tomorrow's life today!

3. When believers break the bread,
   when a hungry child is fed,
   praise the love that Christ revealed,
   living, working, in our world.

4. Still his Spirit gives us light,
   seeing wrong and setting right:
   God in Christ has come to stay.
   Live tomorrow's life today!

5. When a stranger's not alone,
   where the homeless find a home,
   praise the love that Christ revealed,
   living, working, in our world.

6. May his Spirit fill our praise,
   guide our thoughts and change
      our ways.
   God in Christ has come to stay.
   Live tomorrow's life today!

7. There's a Spirit in the air,
   calling people everywhere:
   praise the love that Christ revealed,
   living, working, in our world.

BRIAN A. WREN (b. 1936)

439

301

O God, the Holy Spirit,
   (*Voice 1*) **come to us, and among us;**
   (*Voice 2*) **come as the wind, and cleanse us;**
        (*1*) **come as the fire, and burn;**
        (*2*) **come as the dew, and refresh.**

Convict, convert and consecrate many hearts and lives
        (*1*) **to our great good**
        (*2*) **and your greater glory,**
    (*All*) **and this we ask for Jesus Christ's sake.**

302

Creator Spirit, moving upon the primal sea to calm and order it,
   breathe your grace into our life.
Divine helper, strengthen our hearts by your anointing
   and set them on fire with your love.
By your gifts, complete our imperfect minds,
   that we may think wisely and speak truth.
Recall our bodies, nerve, sinew and sense, to holy use,
   that we may welcome, love and do that which is good.
Shield us from the influence of evil: grant inward peace,
   as your impulses prompt our actions.
The Son's promise, the Father's gift, eternally their companion
   and newly ours,
teach us what we may know of God, and what we must know
   to believe, to be blessed and to be saved.

303

O Holy Spirit, giver of light and life,
impart to us thoughts higher than our own thoughts,
   (*Voice 1*) **and prayers better than our own prayers,**
   (*Voice 2*) **and powers beyond our own powers,**
that we may spend and be spent
in the ways of love and goodness,
      (*All*) **after the perfect image**
           of our Lord and Saviour, Jesus Christ.

304

Jesus said: I am telling you the truth: whoever believes in me
will do what I do—yes, he will do even greater things,
because I am going to the Father.

**I will ask the Father, and he will give you another Helper,
   who will stay with you for ever.**

The Helper, the Holy Spirit, whom the Father will send in my name,
will teach you everything and make you remember all that I have told you.

> **The Helper will come—the Spirit, who reveals the truth about
> God and who comes from the Father.
> I will send him to you from the Father, and he will speak about
> me.**

I am telling you the truth; it is better for you that I go away,
because if I do not go, the Helper will not come to you.
But if I do go away, then I will send him to you.

> **And when he comes, he will prove to the world that they are
> wrong about sin and about what is right and about God's
> judgement.**

They are wrong about sin, because they do not believe in me;
they are wrong about what is right, because I am going to the Father
and you will not see me any more; and they are wrong about
judgement, because the ruler of this world has already been judged.

> **When the Spirit comes, who reveals the truth about God,
> he will lead you into all truth.
> He will not speak on his own authority, but he will speak of what
> he hears, and will tell you of things to come.**

He will give me glory, because he will take what I say and tell it to you.

305

The Spirit produces love, joy, peace, patience, kindness,
goodness, faithfulness, humility, and self-control.
> **There is no law against such things as these.**

And those who belong to Christ Jesus
have put to death their human nature with all its passions and desires.
> **The Spirit has given us life; he must also control our lives.**

We must not be proud, or irritate one another,
or be jealous of one another.
> **Those who live as the Spirit tells them to have their minds
> controlled by what the Spirit wants.**

To be controlled by human nature results in death;
to be controlled by the Spirit results in life and peace.
> **So then we have an obligation, but it is not to live as human
> nature wants us to.**

For if you live according to your human nature, you are going to die;
but if by the Spirit you put to death your sinful actions, you will live.
> **Those who are led by God's Spirit are God's children.**

The Spirit makes you God's children,
and by the Spirit's power we cry out to God, 'Father! my Father!'
> **God's Spirit joins himself to our spirits to declare that we are
> God's children.**

306

CHRIST TRIUMPHANT
88 85 with refrain

MICHAEL BAUGHEN (b. 1930)

Yours   the   glo - ry   and   the   crown,_____   the   high

GOD'S REIGN

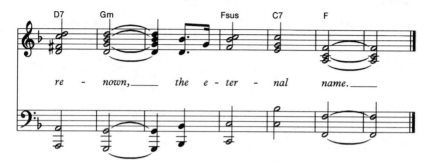

CHRIST triumphant, ever reigning,
　　Saviour, Master, King!
Lord of heaven, our lives sustaining,
　　hear us as we sing:

Yours the glory and the crown,
　　the high renown,
　　　the eternal name!

2 Word incarnate, truth revealing,
　　Son of Man on earth!
Power and majesty concealing
　　by your humble birth:

3 Suffering servant, scorned, ill-treated,
　　victim crucified!
Death is through the cross defeated,
　　sinners justified:

4 Priestly King, enthroned for ever
　　high in heaven above!
Sin and death and hell shall never
　　stifle hymns of love:

5 So our hearts and voices raising
　　through the ages long,
ceaselessly upon you gazing,
　　this shall be our song:

MICHAEL SAWARD (b. 1932)

307

BEATITUDO   CM

J. B. DYKES (1823–76)

For this tune in G major see no. 405.

SECOND TUNE

SAN ROCCO   CM

DEREK WILLIAMS (b. 1945)

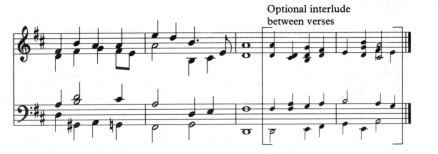

Optional interlude
between verses

GIVE me the wings of faith to rise
    within the veil, and see
the saints above, how great their joys,
    how bright their glories be.

2 Once they were mourning here below,
    with sighing and with tears;
they wrestled hard, as we do now,
    with sins, and doubts, and fears.

3 I ask them whence their victory came:
    they, with united breath,
ascribe their victory to the Lamb,
    their triumph to his death.

4 They marked the footsteps where he trod,
    his zeal inspired their breast;
and, following their incarnate God,
    possess the promised rest.

5 Our glorious leader claims our praise
    for his own pattern given;
while the great cloud of witnesses
    show the same path to heaven.

ISAAC WATTS (1674–1748)

308

DAMBUSTERS' MARCH   77 75 77 11

ERIC COATES (1886–1958)
arr. ROBIN SHELDON (b. 1932)

Music © 1954 Chappell Music Ltd./International Music Publications

GOD is our strength and refuge,
our present help in trouble;
and we therefore will not fear,
though the earth should change!
Though mountains shake and tremble,
though swirling floods are raging,
God the Lord of hosts is with us evermore!

2 There is a flowing river,
within God's holy city;
God is in the midst of her—
she shall not be moved!
God's help is swiftly given,
thrones vanish at his presence—
God the Lord of hosts is with us evermore!

3 Come, see the works of our maker,
learn of his deeds all-powerful;
wars will cease across the world
when he shatters the spear!
Be still and know your creator,
uplift him in the nations—
God the Lord of hosts is with us evermore!

RICHARD BEWES (b. 1934)
based on Psalm 46

309

Later form of melody
in *Paris Antiphoner*, 1681

O QUANTA QUALIA   11 10 11 10

HERE from all nations, all tongues, and all peoples,
    countless the crowd but their voices are one;
vast is the sight and majestic their singing—
    'God has the victory: he reigns from the throne!'

2 These have come out of the hardest oppression,
    now they may stand in the presence of God,
serving their Lord day and night in his temple,
    ransomed and cleansed by the Lamb's precious blood.

3 Gone is their thirst and no more shall they hunger,
    God is their shelter, his power at their side;
sun shall not pain them, no burning will torture,
    Jesus the Lamb is their shepherd and guide.

4 He will go with them to clear living water
    flowing from springs which his mercy supplies;
gone is their grief and their trials are over—
    God wipes away every tear from their eyes.

5 Blessing and glory and wisdom and power
    be to the Saviour again and again;
might and thanksgiving and honour for ever
    be to our God: Alleluia! Amen.

CHRISTOPHER IDLE (b. 1938)
based on Revelation 7: 9–17

310

OUR GOD REIGNS

LEONARD SMITH JNR.

Verse 1 is the same in both versions. In the original version, rhythms need to be adjusted to fit the words.

GOD'S REIGN

POPULAR VERSION

1 How lovely on the mountains are the feet of him
who brings good news, good news,
announcing peace, proclaiming news of happiness:
our God reigns, our God reigns!
Our God reigns!

2 You watchmen, lift your voices joyfully as one,
shout for your King, your King.
See eye to eye the Lord restoring Zion:
your God reigns, your God reigns!

3 Waste places of Jerusalem, break forth with joy,
we are redeemed, redeemed.
The Lord has saved and comforted his people:
your God reigns, your God reigns!

4 Ends of the earth, see the salvation of your God,
Jesus is Lord, is Lord.
Before the nations he has bared his holy arm:
your God reigns, your God reigns!

LEONARD SMITH JNR.
based on Isaiah 52: 7–10

(Original version overleaf)

ORIGINAL VERSION

How lovely on the mountains are the feet of him
who brings good news, good news,
announcing peace, proclaiming news of happiness:
our God reigns, our God reigns!
Our God reigns!

2 He had no stately form, he had no majesty,
that we should be drawn to him.
He was despised and we took no account of him,
yet now he reigns with the most high.
Now he reigns
with the most high!

3 It was our sin and guilt that bruised and wounded him,
it was our sin that brought him down.
When we like sheep had gone astray, our shepherd came
and on his shoulders bore our shame.
On his shoulders
he bore our shame.

4 Meek as a lamb that's led out to the slaughterhouse,
dumb as a sheep before its shearer,
his life ran down upon the ground like pouring rain,
that we might be born again.
That we might be
born again.

5 Out from the tomb he came with grace and majesty,
he is alive, he is alive.
God loves us so, see here his hands, his feet, his side,
yes, we know he is alive.
He is alive!

6 How lovely on the mountains are the feet of him
who brings good news, good news,
announcing peace, proclaiming news of happiness:
our God reigns, our God reigns!
Our God reigns!

LEONARD SMITH JNR.
based on Isaiah 52: 7–10; 53

311

LITTLE CORNARD   66 66 88   MARTIN SHAW (1875–1958)

HILLS of the north, rejoice,
  river and mountain-spring,
hark to the advent voice;
  valley and lowland, sing.
Christ comes in righteousness and love,
he brings salvation from above.

2 Isles of the southern seas,
  sing to the listening earth;
carry on every breeze
  hope of a world's new birth:
in Christ shall all be made anew;
his word is sure, his promise true.

3 Lands of the east, arise!
  He is your brightest morn;
greet him with joyous eyes,
  let praise his path adorn:
your seers have longed to know their Lord;
to you he comes, the final word.

4 Shores of the utmost west,
  lands of the setting sun,
welcome the heavenly guest
  in whom the dawn has come:
he brings a never-ending light,
who triumphed o'er our darkest night.

5 Shout, as you journey home;
  songs be in every mouth!
Lo, from the north they come,
  from east and west and south:
in Jesus all shall find their rest,
in him the universe be blest.

CHARLES E. OAKLEY (1832–65)
Editors of *English Praise*, 1975 altd.

312

BENTLEY   76 76 D

JOHN HULLAH (1812–84)

For this tune in D♭ major see no. 609.

JERUSALEM the golden
  in glory high above;
O city of God's presence,
  O vision of God's love:
how wonderful the pleasures
  and joys awaiting there;
what radiancy of glory,
  what peace beyond compare!

2 They stand, those halls of Zion,
  all jubilant with song;
and bright with many an angel,
  and all the martyr throng:
the Prince is ever in them,
  the daylight is serene;
the tree of life and healing
  has leaves of richest green.

3 There is the throne of David;
  and there from pain released,
the shout of those who triumph,
  the song of those who feast:
and all who with their leader
  have conquered in the fight,
are garlanded with glory
  and robed in purest white.

4 How lovely is that city!
  the home of God's elect;
how beautiful the country
  that eager hearts expect!
Jesus, in mercy bring us
  to that eternal shore
where Father, Son and Spirit
  are worshipped evermore.

after BERNARD OF CLUNY *c.*1140
J. M. NEALE (1818–66)
based on Revelation 7: 14; 21: 1–7

313

DUKE STREET   LM   JOHN HATTON (d. 1793)

SECOND TUNE

TRURO   LM   *Psalmodia Evangelica,* 1789

JESUS shall reign where'er the sun
does his successive journeys run;
his kingdom stretch from shore to shore
till moons shall rise and set no more.

2 People and realms of every tongue
declare his love in sweetest song,
and children's voices shall proclaim
their early blessings on his name.

3 Blessings abound where Jesus reigns—
the prisoner leaps to lose his chains,
the weary find eternal rest,
the hungry and the poor are blessed.

4 To him shall endless prayer be made,
and princes throng to crown his head;
his name like incense shall arise
with every morning sacrifice.

5 Let all creation rise and bring
the highest honours to our King;
angels descend with songs again
and earth repeat the loud 'Amen!'

ISAAC WATTS (1674–1748)
based on Psalm 72

314

HELMSLEY   87 87 47 extended

Adpt. from an 18th-century
English melody

Lo! He comes, with clouds descending,
   once for sinners crucified:
thousand thousand saints attending
   sing with triumph at his side.
      Alleluia!
   Jesus now shall ever reign.

2 Every eye shall now behold him
   robed in awesome majesty;
those who set at nought and sold him,
   pierced, and nailed him to the tree,
      deeply wailing,
   shall the true Messiah see.

3 Every island, sea, and mountain,
   heaven and earth, shall flee away;
all who hate him must, defeated,
   hear his voice proclaim the day.
      Come to judgement!
   Come to judgement! Come away.

4 Yea, amen! Let all adore thee,
   high on thine eternal throne:
Saviour, take the power and glory,
   claim the kingdom for thine own.
      O come quickly.
   Alleluia! Come, Lord, come!

CHARLES WESLEY (1707–88)
based on JOHN CENNICK (1718–55)
based on Revelation 1: 7

315

ANTIOCH   CM

G. F. HANDEL (1685–1759)
arr. LOWELL MASON (1792–1872)

and heaven, and heaven and na-ture sing

Joy to the world! the Lord is come;
　　let earth receive her King,
let every heart prepare him room,
　　and heaven and nature sing.

2　Joy to the earth! the Saviour reigns;
　　　let men their songs employ;
　　while fields and floods, rocks, hills, and plains
　　　repeat the sounding joy.

3　No more let sins and sorrows grow,
　　　nor thorns infest the ground;
　　he comes to make his blessings flow
　　　far as sin's curse is found.

4　He rules the world with truth and grace,
　　　and makes the nations prove
　　the glories of his righteousness,
　　　and wonders of his love.

ISAAC WATTS (1674–1748)
based on Psalm 98 and Zechariah 9: 9

316

WOODACRE   66 65 D

GRAHAM K. BISHOP-HUNT (b. 1953)

O LORD of the kingdom where losing is winning
   and love has a strength which gives promise of dawn;
teach us in our doubting to know resurrection
   and live in your world as a people reborn.

2 O living Lord Jesus we share in your triumph,
   the world may be dark but we live by your word;
death has no dominion for Jesus is risen,
   away with our grieving, rejoice in the Lord.

3 O Lord in your kingdom the poorest is welcome,
   the homeless find lodging, the outcast belong;
fill us with your loving and free us Lord Jesus
   to worship and serve you all ages along.

EDMUND BANYARD

317

GOPSAL   66 66 88

G. F. HANDEL (1685–1759)

⊕ Optional organ coda for final verse.

Coda taken from the complete version realized from Handel's MS by John Wilson.

REJOICE! the Lord is King.
    Your Lord and King adore;
mortals, give thanks and sing,
    and triumph evermore.
Lift up your heart, lift up your voice.
    Rejoice; again I say, rejoice.

2 Jesus the Saviour reigns,
    the God of truth and love;
when he had purged our stains,
    he took his seat above.
Lift up your heart, lift up your voice.
    Rejoice; again I say, rejoice.

3 His kingdom cannot fail:
    he rules o'er earth and heaven;
the keys of death and hell
    are to our Jesus given.
Lift up your heart, lift up your voice.
    Rejoice; again I say, rejoice.

4 He sits at God's right hand
    till all his foes submit,
and bow to his command
    and fall before his feet.
Lift up your heart, lift up your voice.
    Rejoice; again I say, rejoice.

5 Rejoice in glorious hope.
    Jesus the judge shall come,
and take his servants up
    to their eternal home.
We soon shall hear the archangel's voice;
    God's trumpet shall sound out, Rejoice!

CHARLES WESLEY (1707–88) altd.
based on Philippians 4: 4

317

DARWALL   66 66 88

J. DARWALL (1731–89)

REJOICE! the Lord is King.
　　Your Lord and King adore;
mortals, give thanks and sing,
　　and triumph evermore.
Lift up your heart, lift up your voice.
　　Rejoice; again I say, rejoice.

2　Jesus the Saviour reigns,
　　the God of truth and love;
when he had purged our stains,
　　he took his seat above.
Lift up your heart, lift up your voice.
　　Rejoice; again I say, rejoice.

3　His kingdom cannot fail:
　　he rules o'er earth and heaven;
the keys of death and hell
　　are to our Jesus given.
Lift up your heart, lift up your voice.
　　Rejoice; again I say, rejoice.

4　He sits at God's right hand
　　till all his foes submit,
and bow to his command
　　and fall before his feet.
Lift up your heart, lift up your voice.
　　Rejoice; again I say, rejoice.

5　Rejoice in glorious hope.
　　Jesus the judge shall come,
and take his servants up
　　to their eternal home.
We soon shall hear the archangel's voice;
　　God's trumpet shall sound out, Rejoice!

CHARLES WESLEY (1707–88) altd.
based on Philippians 4: 4

318

THE GLORY SONG   10 10 10 10 with refrain   C. H. GABRIEL (1856–1932)

REFRAIN

Come let us sing: praise to our King,   Je-sus our

Come_____ let us sing: praise to our King,

Come let us sing: praise to our   King,_____ Je-sus our

SING we the King who is coming to reign,
glory to Jesus, the Lamb that was slain.
Life and salvation his empire shall bring,
joy to the nations when Jesus is King.

Come let us sing: praise to our King,
Jesus our King, Jesus our King:
this is our song, who to Jesus belong:
glory to Jesus, to Jesus our King.

2 All then shall dwell in his marvellous light,
races long severed his love shall unite,
justice and truth from his sceptre shall spring,
wrong shall be ended when Jesus is King.

3 All shall be well in his kingdom of peace,
freedom shall flourish and wisdom increase,
foe shall be friend when his triumph we sing,
sword shall be sickle when Jesus is King.

4 Kingdom of Christ, for your coming we pray,
hasten, O Father, the dawn of the day
when this new song your creation shall sing,
Satan is vanquished and Jesus is King.

C. SILVESTER HORNE (1865–1914)
based on Revelation 11: 15–17

319

ST CLEMENT   98 98   C. C. SCHOLEFIELD (1839–1904)

THE day you gave us, Lord, is ended,
    the darkness falls at your behest;
to you our morning hymns ascended,
    your praise shall hallow now our rest.

2 We thank you that your Church unsleeping,
    while earth rolls onward into light,
through all the world her watch is keeping
    and rests not now by day or night.

3 As o'er each continent and island
    the dawn leads on another day,
the voice of prayer is never silent,
    nor dies the strain of praise away.

4 The sun, that bids us rest, is waking
    God's children 'neath the western sky,
and hour by hour fresh lips are making
    your wondrous doings heard on high.

5 So be it, Lord; your throne shall never
    like earth's proud empires, pass away;
but stand, and rule, and grow for ever,
    till all your creatures own your sway.

JOHN ELLERTON (1826–93)

320

FIRST TUNE

CREDITON   CM

Melody from THOMAS CLARK'S
2nd Set of Psalm Tunes
[*for*] *Country Choirs* (*c.*1807)

SECOND TUNE

RICHMOND   CM

T. HAWEIS (1734–1820)
adpt. S. WEBBE (THE YOUNGER) (*c.*1770–1843)

THE King shall come when morning dawns,
    and light triumphant breaks;
when beauty gilds the eastern hills,
    and life to joy awakes.

2 He who was born a little child
    to suffer and to die
shall come with glory, like the sun
    that lights the morning sky.

3 Far brighter than the glorious day
    when he, victorious, rose,
and left the lonesome place of death,
    despite the rage of foes—

4 Far brighter than that glorious morn
    shall this fair morning be,
when Christ our King, in beauty comes,
    and we his face shall see.

5 The King shall come when morning dawns,
    and light and beauty brings:
hail, Christ the Lord! Your people pray,
    'Come quickly, King of kings.'

Greek hymn
tr. JOHN BROWNLIE (1857–1925) altd.

321

TETHERDOWN   10 10 11 11   GERALD L. BARNES (b. 1935)

THE kingdom of God
   is justice and joy,
for Jesus restores
   what sin would destroy;
God's power and glory
   in Jesus we know,
and here and hereafter
   that kingdom shall grow.

2 The kingdom of God
   is mercy and grace,
the lepers are cleansed,
   the sinners find place,
the outcast are welcomed
   God's banquet to share,
and hope is awakened
   in place of despair.

3 The kingdom of God
   is challenge and choice,
believe the good news,
   repent and rejoice!
His love for us sinners
   brought Christ to his cross,
our crisis of judgement
   for gain or for loss.

4 God's kingdom is come,
   the gift and the goal,
in Jesus begun,
   in heaven made whole;
the heirs of the kingdom
   shall answer his call,
and all things cry glory
   to God all in all!

BRYN AUSTIN REES (1911–83)
based on Romans 14: 17

322

NIAGARA   LM

R. JACKSON (1840–1914)

CHURCH TRIUMPHANT   LM

J. W. ELLIOTT (1833–1915)

THE Lord is King! lift up your voice,
O earth and all the heavens rejoice;
from world to world the joy shall ring:
'The Lord omnipotent is King!'

2 The Lord is King! who then shall dare
resist his will, distrust his care,
or murmur at his wise decrees,
or doubt his royal promises?

3 The Lord is King! in him we trust,
the judge of all the earth is just;
holy and true are all his ways:
let every creature speak his praise.

4 He reigns! you saints exalt your strains;
your God is King, your Father reigns:
and he is at the Father's side,
the man of love, the crucified.

5 One Lord, one empire, all secures;
he reigns,— and life and death are yours,
through earth and heaven one song shall ring,
'The Lord omnipotent is King!'

JOSIAH CONDER (1789–1855)
based on Psalm 97

323

LLOYD CM

CUTHBERT HOWARD (1856–1927)

MENDIP CM

English traditional melody
adpt. CECIL SHARP (1859–1924)
harm. R. VAUGHAN WILLIAMS (1872–1958)

THERE is a land of pure delight,
 where saints immortal reign;
infinite day excludes the night,
 and pleasures banish pain.

2 There everlasting spring abides,
 and never-withering flowers:
death, like a narrow sea, divides
 this heavenly land from ours.

3 Sweet fields beyond the swelling flood
 stand dressed in living green;
so to the Jews old Canaan stood,
 while Jordan rolled between.

4 But timorous mortals start and shrink
 to cross this narrow sea,
and linger shivering on the brink,
 and fear to launch away.

5 O could we make our doubts remove,
 those gloomy doubts that rise,
and see the Canaan that we love
 with unbeclouded eyes,

6 Could we but climb where Moses stood,
 and view the landscape o'er,
not Jordan's stream, nor death's cold flood,
 should fright us from the shore.

ISAAC WATTS (1674–1748)
based on Deuteronomy 34

324

RESTORE, O LORD

GRAHAM KENDRICK (b. 1950)
and C. ROLINSON
arr. J. BRETT

RESTORE, O Lord, the honour of your name,
in works of sovereign power come shake the earth again,
that men may see and come with reverent fear
to the living God whose kingdom shall outlast the years.

2 Restore, O Lord, in all the earth your fame,
and in our time revive the church that bears your name.
And in your anger, Lord, remember mercy,
O living God, whose mercy shall outlast the years.

3 Bend us, O Lord, where we are hard and cold,
in your refiner's fire come purify the gold.
Though suffering comes and evil crouches near,
still our living God is reigning, he is reigning here.

4 Restore, O Lord, the honour of your name,
in works of sovereign power come shake the earth again,
that men may see and come with reverent fear
to the living God whose kingdom shall outlast the years.

GRAHAM KENDRICK (b. 1950)

3. CELEBRATING THE GOSPEL

325

TREWEN   88 88 D Anapaestic

D. EMLYN EVANS (1843–1913)

A SOVEREIGN protector I have,
  unseen, yet for ever at hand,
unchangeably faithful to save,
  almighty to rule and command.
He smiles, and my comforts abound;
  his grace as the dew shall descend,
and walls of salvation surround
  the soul he delights to defend.

2 Inspirer and hearer of prayer,
  the shepherd of all who believe,
my all to your covenant care,
  I sleeping and waking will leave.
If you are my shield and my sun,
  the night is no darkness to me;
and, fast as my moments roll on,
  they bring you Lord nearer to me.

A. M. TOPLADY (1740–78) altd.
based on Psalm 84 and Psalm 139: 5–12

326

ABBA FATHER   75 75 D

Words and music by DAVE BILBROUGH

RESPONSE IN FAITH

Ne - ver let my heart grow cold, ne - ver let___ me go.___ Ab - ba Fa - ther, let me be yours, and yours___ a - lone.___

327

MEINE HOFFNUNG   87 87 337

Melody from JOACHIM NEANDER'S
Alpha and Omega, 1680

SECOND TUNE

MICHAEL   87 87 337

HERBERT HOWELLS (1892–1983)

ALL my hope on God is founded;
  all my trust he does renew.
Through all change and chance he guides me,
  only good and only true.
    God unknown,
    he alone
  calls my heart to be his own.

2 Pride of man and earthly glory,
  sword and crown betray his trust;
all we build with care and labour,
  tower and temple, fall to dust.
    But God's power,
    hour by hour,
is my temple and my tower.

3 God's great goodness lasts for ever,
  deep his wisdom, passing thought:
splendour, light and life attend him,
  beauty springing out of nought.
    Evermore,
    from his store
new-born worlds rise and adore.

4 Day by day the almighty giver
  does his gracious gifts bestow;
God's good will is for our pleasure,
  leading us where'er we go.
    See love stand
    at his hand,
and joy wait on his command.

5 Still from man to God eternal
  sacrifice of praise be done,
high above all praises praising
  for the gift of Christ his Son.
    Hear Christ call
    one and all:
those who follow shall not fall.

ROBERT BRIDGES, (1844–1930) altd.
based on JOACHIM NEANDER (1650–80)

485

328

From *Bouquet*, 1825
publ. THOMAS CAMPBELL

SAGINA   88 88 88

Repeat lines 5 and 6

AND can it be that I should gain
    an interest in the Saviour's blood?
Died he for me, who caused his pain?
    for me, who him to death pursued?
Amazing love! how can it be
that thou, my God, shouldst die for me!

2 'Tis mystery all! The Immortal dies:
    who can explore his strange design?
In vain the first-born seraph tries
    to sound the depths of love divine.
'Tis mercy all! let earth adore,
let angel minds inquire no more.

3 He left his Father's throne above—
    so free, so infinite his grace—
emptied himself of all but love,
    and bled for Adam's helpless race.
'Tis mercy all, immense and free;
for, O my God, it found out me!

4 Long my imprisoned spirit lay
    fast bound in sin and nature's night;
thine eye diffused a quickening ray—
    I woke, the dungeon flamed with light;
my chains fell off, my heart was free.
I rose, went forth, and followed thee.

5 No condemnation now I dread;
    Jesus, and all in him, is mine!
Alive in him, my living head,
    and clothed in righteousness divine,
bold I approach the eternal throne,
and claim the crown, through Christ, my own.

CHARLES WESLEY (1707–88)
based on 1 Corinthians 3: 22–3; 11: 3; 15: 22

329

BLESSED ASSURANCE   99 99 D

PHOEBE P. KNAPP (1839–1908)
arr. GERALD L. BARNES (b. 1935)

This is my sto - ry, this is my song, prais-ing my

BLESSÈD assurance, Jesus is mine:
O what a foretaste of glory divine!
Heir of salvation, purchase of God;
born of his Spirit, washed in his blood.

This is my story, this is my song,
praising my Saviour all the day long.

2 Perfect submission, perfect delight,
visions of rapture burst on my sight;
angels descending, bring from above
echoes of mercy, whispers of love.

3 Perfect submission, all is at rest,
I in my Saviour am happy and blest;
watching and waiting, looking above,
filled with his goodness, lost in his love.

FRANCES VAN ALSTYNE (1820–1915)

330

WONDERFUL LOVE   10 4 10 7 4 10

F. L. WISEMAN (1858–1944)

COME let us sing of a wonderful love,
   tender and true;
out of the heart of the Father above,
   streaming to me and to you:
     wonderful love
   dwells in the heart of the Father above.

2 Jesus, the Saviour, this gospel to tell,
   joyfully came;
came with the helpless and hopeless to dwell,
   sharing their sorrow and shame;
     seeking the lost,
   saving, redeeming at measureless cost.

3 Jesus is seeking the wanderers yet;
   why do they roam?
love only waits to forgive and forget;
   home! weary wanderers, home!
     Wonderful love
   dwells in the heart of the Father above.

4 Come to my heart now, O wonderful love,
   come and abide,
lifting my life till it rises above
   envy and falsehood and pride;
     seeking to be
   lowly and humble, a learner of thee.

ROBERT WALMSLEY (1831–1905)
based on 1 John 4: 9–10

331

First Tune

MORNING LIGHT   76 76 D

G. J. WEBB (1803–87)

COME, praise the name of Jesus
for all his gracious powers,
our only God and Saviour
who makes his goodness ours;
he calls us to his kingdom,
the Lord of life and death,
to see his face in glory
and know him now by faith.

2 His virtue and his wisdom,
endurance, self-control,
his godliness and kindness,
his love which crowns them all—
this is his royal nature
that we are called to share,
his robe of perfect beauty
that we are given to wear.

3 We see his shining splendour
in every sunless place
where Christ, the light of nations,
appears in truth and grace.
Transfigured by his likeness
we make the vision known,
reflecting in our faces
the radiance of his own.

4 The King of grace inspires us
to love him more and more,
to grasp our hope more firmly
and make our calling sure.
Christ Jesus, Lord and Saviour,
to this dark world you came;
and for the dawn of heaven,
we praise your holy name.

CHRISTOPHER IDLE (b. 1938)
based on 2 Peter 1

331

Second Tune

STAND UP   76 76 D

GEORGE THALBEN-BALL (1896–1987)

COME, praise the name of Jesus
 for all his gracious powers,
our only God and Saviour
 who makes his goodness ours;
he calls us to his kingdom,
 the Lord of life and death,
to see his face in glory
 and know him now by faith.

2 His virtue and his wisdom,
 endurance, self-control,
his godliness and kindness,
 his love which crowns them all—
this is his royal nature
 that we are called to share,
his robe of perfect beauty
 that we are given to wear.

3 We see his shining splendour
 in every sunless place
where Christ, the light of nations,
 appears in truth and grace.
Transfigured by his likeness
 we make the vision known,
reflecting in our faces
 the radiance of his own.

4 The King of grace inspires us
 to love him more and more,
to grasp our hope more firmly
 and make our calling sure.
Christ Jesus, Lord and Saviour,
 to this dark world you came;
and for the dawn of heaven,
 we praise your holy name.

CHRISTOPHER IDLE (b. 1938)
based on 2 Peter 1

332

ALL FOR JESUS   87 87   J. STAINER (1840–1901)

ALL for Jesus, all for Jesus!
   this our song shall ever be:
you our only hope, our Saviour,
   yours the love that sets us free!

2 All for Jesus: you will give us
   strength to serve you hour by hour:
none can move us from your presence
   while we trust your grace and power.

3 All for Jesus—you have loved us,
   all for Jesus—you have died,
all for Jesus—you are with us;
   all for Jesus crucified.

4 All for Jesus, all for Jesus,
   all our talents and our powers,
all our thoughts and words and actions,
   all our passing days and hours.

5 All for Jesus, all for Jesus!
   This the Church's song shall be
till at last her children gather,
   one in him eternally.

W. J. SPARROW-SIMPSON (1859–1952)
and Jubilate Hymns

333

SING HEY   11 11 11 11 D

JOHN BELL (b. 1949)

REFRAIN

Sing hey for the   car-pen-ter   leav-ing his tools! Sing

hey for the   Pha-ri-sees leav-ing their rules! Sing hey for the   fish-er-men

leav-ing their nets! Sing hey for the   peo-ple who leave their re - grets!

To be sung unaccompanied.

COME with me, come wander, come welcome the world
where strangers might smile or where stones may be hurled;
come leave what you cling to, lay down what you clutch
and find, with hands empty, that hearts can hold much.

> *Sing hey for the carpenter leaving his tools!*
> *Sing hey for the Pharisees leaving their rules!*
> *Sing hey for the fishermen leaving their nets!*
> *Sing hey for the people who leave their regrets!*

2 Come walk in my company, come sleep by my side,
come savour a lifestyle with nothing to hide;
come sit at my table and eat with my friends,
discovering that love which the world never ends.

3 Come share in my laughter, come close to my fears,
come find yourself washed with the kiss of my tears;
come stand close at hand while I suffer and die,
and find in three days how I never will lie.

4 Come leave your possessions, come share out your treasure,
come give and receive without method or measure,
come loose every bond that's resisting the Spirit,
enabling the earth to be yours to inherit.

J. BELL (b. 1949) and G. MAULE (b. 1958)

334

ASCALON   56 9 55 8

Silesian folk melody

For an alternative version of this tune (in E♭ major, and with metre 668 D) see no. 10.

FAIREST Lord Jesus,
Lord of all creation,
Jesus, of God and Mary the Son;
    you will I cherish,
    you will I honour,
Jesus, my soul's delight and crown.

2 Fair are the meadows,
    fairer still the woodlands,
robed in the verdure and bloom of spring.
    Jesus is fairer,
    Jesus is purer,
he makes the saddest heart to sing.

3 Fair are the flowers,
    fairer still the sons of men
in all the freshness of youth arrayed;
    yet is their beauty
    fading and fleeting;
my Jesus, yours will never fade.

4 Fair is the moonlight,
    fairer still the sunshine,
fair is the shimmering, starry sky:
    Jesus shines brighter,
    Jesus shines clearer
than all the heavenly host on high.

5 All fairest beauty,
    heavenly and earthly,
is found in you, Jesus, wondrously;
    none can be nearer,
    fairer or dearer,
than you, my Saviour, are to me.

Anon. German (1677)
tr. LILIAN STEVENSON (1870–1960)

335

ST MATTHIAS   88 88 88   W. H. MONK (1823–1889)

Give   us Christ's love, its___
depth and length, its___ heart and soul and   mind___ and strength.

FATHER of all, whose laws have stood
as signposts for our earthly good;
whose Son has come with truth and grace,
your likeness shining in his face:

Give us Christ's love, its depth and length,
its heart and soul and mind and strength.

2 The first and finest day is yours
to consecrate all other hours;
all other lords may we disown
and worship bring to you alone:

3 Surround our homes with joy and peace,
with loyalty and cheerfulness;
let partners live without pretence
and children grow in confidence:

4 May bitter hearts fresh mercy feel
and thieving hands no longer steal;
none damn their neighbour with a lie,
nor stoke the fires of jealousy:

5 Father of all, whose laws have stood
as signposts for our earthly good;
whose Son has come with truth and grace,
your likeness shining in his face:

DAVID MOWBRAY (b. 1938)

335   Second Tune

ST CATHERINE   88 88 88   Melody by H. F. HEMY (1818–88)

Give us Christ's love, its depth and length, its heart and soul and mind and strength.

FATHER of all, whose laws have stood
as signposts for our earthly good;
whose Son has come with truth and grace,
your likeness shining in his face:

Give us Christ's love, its depth and length,
its heart and soul and mind and strength.

2 The first and finest day is yours
to consecrate all other hours;
all other lords may we disown
and worship bring to you alone:

3 Surround our homes with joy and peace,
with loyalty and cheerfulness;
let partners live without pretence
and children grow in confidence:

4 May bitter hearts fresh mercy feel
and thieving hands no longer steal;
none damn their neighbour with a lie,
nor stoke the fires of jealousy:

5 Father of all, whose laws have stood
as signposts for our earthly good;
whose Son has come with truth and grace,
your likeness shining in his face:

DAVID MOWBRAY (b. 1938)

336

CARLISLE   SM

C. LOCKHART (1745–1815)

CAMBRIDGE   SM

R. HARRISON (1748–1810)

HAVE faith in God, my heart,
    trust and be unafraid;
God will fulfil in every part
    each promise he has made.

2 Have faith in God, my mind,
    although your light burns low;
God's mercy holds a wiser plan
    than you can fully know.

3 Have faith in God, my soul,
    his cross for ever stands;
and neither life nor death can pluck
    his children from his hands.

4 Lord Jesus, make me whole;
    grant me no resting place,
until I rest, heart, mind and soul,
    the captive of your grace.

BRYN AUSTIN REES (1911–83)
based on Mark 11: 22

337

HERONGATE LM

English traditional melody
arr. R. VAUGHAN WILLIAMS (1872–1958)

DEAR Master, in whose life I see
all that I long, but fail to be,
let your clear light for ever shine
to shame and guide this life of mine.

2 Though what I dream and what I do
in my poor days are always two,
help me, oppressed by things undone,
dear Lord, whose deeds and dreams were one.

JOHN HUNTER (1848–1917)

338

CELESTE   88 88 Anapaestic   *Lancashire Sunday School Songs,* 1857

How good is the God we adore!
   our faithful, unchangeable friend:
his love is as great as his power
   and knows neither measure nor end.

2 For Christ is the first and the last;
   his Spirit will guide us safe home;
we'll praise him for all that is past
   and trust him for all that's to come.

J. HART (1712–68)

339

FIRST TUNE

ST PETER   CM

A. R. REINAGLE (1799–1877)

SECOND TUNE

STRACATHRO   CM

Melody by C. HUTCHESON (1792–1860)
harm. DAVID EVANS (1874–1948)

How sweet the name of Jesus sounds
   in a believer's ear!
It soothes our sorrows, heals our wounds,
   and drives away our fear.

2 It makes the wounded spirit whole,
   and calms the troubled breast;
it's manna to the hungry soul,
   and to the weary, rest.

3 Dear name! the rock on which I build,
   my shield and hiding-place,
my never-failing treasury, filled
   with boundless stores of grace.

4 Jesus! my shepherd, brother, friend,
   my prophet, priest and king;
my Lord, my life, my way, my end,
   accept the praise I bring.

5 Weak is the effort of my heart,
   and cold my warmest thought;
but when I see you as you are,
   I'll praise you as I ought.

6 Till then I would your love proclaim
   with every fleeting breath;
and may the music of your name
   refresh my soul in death!

JOHN NEWTON (1725–1807)

340

BULLINGER   85 83   E. W. BULLINGER (1837–1913)

SECOND TUNE

CUTTLE MILLS   85 83   WILLIAM GRIFFITH (1867–1929)

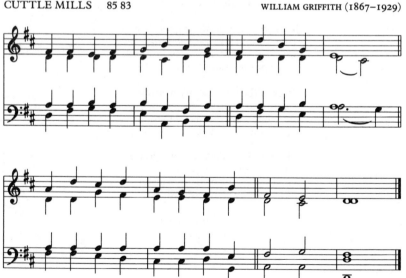

I AM trusting you, Lord Jesus,
    you have died for me,
trusting you for full salvation,
    great and free.

2 I am trusting you for pardon:
    at your feet I bow,
for your grace and tender mercy
    trusting now.

3 I am trusting you to guide me;
    you alone shall lead,
every day and hour supplying
    all my need.

4 I am trusting you for power:
    yours can never fail;
words which you yourself have given
    must prevail.

5 I am trusting you, Lord Jesus;
    never let me fall:
I am trusting you for ever,
    and for all.

FRANCES RIDLEY HAVERGAL (1836–79)

341

JANE   88 88 D Anapaestic

DAVID PEACOCK (b. 1949)

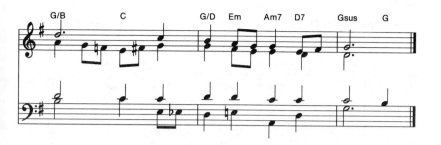

I LOVE you, O Lord, you alone,
my refuge on whom I depend;
my maker, my Saviour, my own,
my hope and my trust without end.
The Lord is my strength and my song,
defender and guide of my ways;
my master to whom I belong,
my God who shall have all my praise.

2 The dangers of death gathered round,
the waves of destruction came near;
but in my despairing I found
the Lord who released me from fear:
I called for his help in my pain,
to God my salvation I cried;
he brought me his comfort again,
I live by the strength he supplied.

3 The earth and the elements shake
with thunder and lightning and hail;
the cliffs and the mountain-tops break
and mortals are feeble and pale.
His justice is full and complete,
his mercy to us has no end;
the clouds are a path for his feet,
he comes on the wings of the wind.

4 My hope is the promise he gives,
my life is secure in his hand;
I shall not be lost, for he lives!
He comes to my aid—I shall stand!
Lord God, you are powerful to save,
your Spirit will spur me to pray;
your Son has defeated the grave:
I trust and I praise you today!

CHRISTOPHER IDLE (b. 1938)
based on Psalm 18

342

I RECEIVE YOUR LOVE

PAUL ARMSTRONG

I RECEIVE your love,
I receive your love,
in my heart I receive your love,
   O Lord.
I receive your love
by your Spirit within me,
I receive, I receive your love.

2 I confess your love,
I confess your love,
from my heart I confess your love,
   O Lord.
I confess your love
by your Spirit within me,
I confess, I confess your love.

PAUL ARMSTRONG

343

MARTYRDOM   CM

H. WILSON (1766–1824)
arr. R. A. SMITH (1780–1829)

I'M not ashamed to own my Lord,
    or to defend his cause;
maintain the honour of his word,
    the glory of his cross.

2 Jesus, my Lord, I know his name;
    his name is all my trust;
he will not put my soul to shame,
    nor let my hope be lost.

3 Firm as his throne his promise stands;
    and he can well secure
what I've committed to his hands
    till the decisive hour.

4 Then he will own my worthless name
    before his Father's face;
and in the new Jerusalem
    appoint for me a place.

ISAAC WATTS (1674–1748)
based on 2 Timothy 1: 12

344

ST OSWALD   87 87

J. B. DYKES (1823–76)

ALL FOR JESUS   87 87

J. STAINER (1840–1901)

In the cross of Christ I glory,
    towering o'er the wrecks of time:
all the light of sacred story
    gathers round its head sublime.

2 When the woes of life o'ertake me,
    hopes deceive, and fears annoy,
never shall the cross forsake me;
    lo! it glows with peace and joy.

3 When the sun of bliss is beaming
    light and love upon my way,
from the cross the radiance streaming
    adds more lustre to the day.

4 Bane and blessing, pain and pleasure,
    by the cross are sanctified;
peace is there that knows no measure,
    joys that through all time abide.

5 In the cross of Christ I glory,
    towering o'er the wrecks of time:
all the light of sacred story
    gathers round its head sublime.

JOHN BOWRING (1792–1872)
based on Galatians 6: 14

345

FIRST TUNE

ABERYSTWYTH   77 77 D

JOSEPH PARRY (1841–1903)

JESUS, lover of my soul,
    let me to your presence fly,
while the gathering waters roll,
    while the tempest still is high.
Hide me, O my Saviour, hide,
    till the storm of life is past;
safe into the haven, guide
    and receive my soul at last.

2 Other refuge have I none,
    all my hope in you I see:
leave, O leave me, not alone;
    still support and comfort me.
All my trust on you is stayed,
    all my help from you I bring:
cover my defenceless head
    with the shadow of your wing.

3 You, O Christ, are all I want,
    more than all in you I find:
raise the fallen, cheer the faint,
    heal the sick and lead the blind.
Just and holy is your name,
    I am all unworthiness;
false and full of sin I am,
    you are full of truth and grace.

4 Plenteous grace with you is found,
    grace to wash away my sin:
let the healing streams abound;
    make and keep me clean within.
Living fountain, now impart
    all your life and purity;
spring for ever in my heart,
    rise to all eternity!

CHARLES WESLEY (1707–88) altd.

345

HOLLINGSIDE   77 77 D

J. B. DYKES (1823–76)

JESUS, lover of my soul,
    let me to your presence fly,
while the gathering waters roll,
    while the tempest still is high.
Hide me, O my Saviour, hide,
    till the storm of life is past;
safe into the haven, guide
    and receive my soul at last.

2 Other refuge have I none,
    all my hope in you I see:
leave, O leave me, not alone;
    still support and comfort me.
All my trust on you is stayed,
    all my help from you I bring:
cover my defenceless head
    with the shadow of your wing.

3 You, O Christ, are all I want,
    more than all in you I find:
raise the fallen, cheer the faint,
    heal the sick and lead the blind.
Just and holy is your name,
    I am all unworthiness;
false and full of sin I am,
    you are full of truth and grace.

4 Plenteous grace with you is found,
    grace to wash away my sin:
let the healing streams abound;
    make and keep me clean within.
Living fountain, now impart
    all your life and purity;
spring for ever in my heart,
    rise to all eternity!

CHARLES WESLEY (1707–88) altd.

346

MISERICORDIA   888 6

HENRY SMART (1813–79)

SECOND TUNE

SAFFRON WALDEN   888 6

A. H. BROWN (1830–1926)

RESPONSE IN FAITH

WOODWORTH   888 6 extended   W. B. BRADBURY (1816–68)

O Lamb of God,— I come, I come.—

JUST as I am, without one plea,
but that your blood was shed for me,
and that you will me to be free,
    O Lamb of God, I come.

2 Just as I am, though tossed about
with many a conflict, many a doubt,
fightings within and fears without,
    O Lamb of God, I come.

3 Just as I am, poor, wretched, blind;
sight, riches, healing of the mind—
all that I need, in you to find,
    O Lamb of God, I come.

4 Just as I am; you will receive,
will welcome, pardon, cleanse,
    relieve:
because your promise I believe;
    O Lamb of God, I come.

5 Just as I am; your love unknown
has broken every barrier down:
now to be yours, yes, yours alone,
    O Lamb of God, I come.

6 Just as I am, of that free love
the breadth, length, depth and
    height to prove,
here for a time and then above,
    O Lamb of God, I come.

CHARLOTTE ELLIOTT (1789–1871)

347

LORD, THE LIGHT OF YOUR LOVE

Words and music by
GRAHAM KENDRICK (b. 1950)

1. Lord, the light of your love is shi - ning, in the midst of the
2. Lord, I come to your awe-some pres - ence, from the sha-dows in -
3. As we gaze on your king - ly bright-ness so our fa - ces dis -

dark - ness, shi - ning: Je - sus, light of the
- to your ra - diance; by your blood I may
- play your like - ness, ev - er chan - ging from

world, shine up - on___ us; set us free by the
en - ter your bright - ness: search me, try me, con -
glo - ry to glo - ry: mir - rored here, may our

RESPONSE IN FAITH

truth you now bring us—
-sume all my dark-ness—} shine on__ me, shine on__
lives tell your sto - ry—

me.

REFRAIN

Shine, Je - sus, shine,__ fill this land with the
Flow, ri - ver, flow,__ flood the na - tions with

Fa-ther's glo-ry; blaze, Spi - rit, blaze, set our hearts on
grace and mer-cy; send forth your word, Lord, and

fire. let there be light!

348

IN MY LIFE, LORD   48 46

BOB KILPATRICK
arr. A. S. COX (b. 1918)

IN my life, Lord,
  be glorified, be glorified;
in my life, Lord,
  be glorified today.

2 In your Church, Lord,
  be glorified, be glorified;
in your Church, Lord,
  be glorified today.

BOB KILPATRICK

349

TENHEAD   56 64

JOHN BARNARD (b. 1948)

May also be sung to SOMMERLIED, no. 377.

LORD, you need no house,
    no manger now, nor tomb;
yet come, I pray, to make
    my heart your home.

2 Lord, you need no gift,
    for all things come from you;
receive what you have given—
    my heart renew.

3 Lord, you need no skill
    to make your likeness known;
create your image here—
    my heart your throne.

CHRISTOPHER IDLE (b. 1938)
based on Acts 17: 24–31

350

GETHSEMANE   777 8   P. BLISS (1838–76)

'MAN of sorrows,' wondrous name
for the Son of God, who came
ruined sinners to reclaim!
　　Alleluia! what a Saviour!

2 Bearing shame and scoffing rude,
in my place condemned he stood;
sealed my pardon with his blood:
　　Alleluia! what a Saviour!

3 Guilty, lost and helpless we:
spotless Lamb of God was he:
'Full atonement!'— can it be?
　　Alleluia! what a Saviour!

4 'Lifted up' was he to die,
'It is finished!' was his cry;
now in heaven exalted high:
　　Alleluia! what a Saviour!

5 When he comes, our glorious King,
all his ransomed home to bring,
then anew this song we'll sing:
　　Alleluia! what a Saviour!

PHILIPP BLISS (1838–76)
based on Isaiah 53:3

351

NUN DANKET ALL   CM

J. CRÜGER (1598–1662)

O DEAREST Lord, thy sacred head
    with thorns was pierced for me;
O pour thy blessing on my head,
    that I may think for thee.

2 O dearest Lord, thy sacred hands
    with nails were pierced for me;
O shed thy blessing on my hands,
    that they may work for thee.

3 O dearest Lord, thy sacred feet
    with nails were pierced for me;
O pour thy blessing on my feet,
    that they may follow thee.

4 O dearest Lord, thy sacred heart
    with spear was pierced for me;
O pour thy Spirit in my heart,
    that I may live for thee.

FATHER ANDREW (1869–1946)

352

WOLVERCOTE   76 76 D

W. H. FERGUSON (1874–1950)

May be sung to THORNBURY, no 398.

O JESUS, I have promised
   to serve you to the end;
be now and ever near me,
   my master and my friend:
I shall not fear the battle
   if you are by my side,
nor wander from the pathway
   if you will be my guide.

2 O let me feel you near me:
   the world is ever near;
I see the sights that dazzle,
   the tempting sounds I hear;
my foes are ever near me,
   around me and within;
but, Jesus, draw still nearer,
   and shield my soul from sin.

3 O let me hear you speaking
   in accents clear and still,
above the storms of passion,
   the murmurs of self-will;
O speak to reassure me,
   to hasten or control;
O speak, and make me listen,
   O guardian of my soul.

4 O Jesus, you have promised
   to all who follow you,
that where you are in glory
   your servant shall be too;
and Jesus, I have promised
   to serve you to the end;
O give me grace to follow,
   my master and my friend.

5 O let me see your footmarks,
   and in them plant my own;
my hope to follow truly
   is in your strength alone:
O guide me, call me, draw me,
   uphold me to the end;
and then in heaven receive me,
   my Saviour and my friend!

J. E. BODE (1816–74)

352

DAY OF REST   76 76 D

J. W. ELLIOTT (1833–1915)

May also be sung to THORNBURY, no. 398.

O JESUS, I have promised
　　to serve you to the end;
be now and ever near me,
　　my master and my friend:
I shall not fear the battle
　　if you are by my side,
nor wander from the pathway
　　if you will be my guide.

2 O let me feel you near me:
　　the world is ever near;
I see the sights that dazzle,
　　the tempting sounds I hear;
my foes are ever near me,
　　around me and within;
but, Jesus, draw still nearer,
　　and shield my soul from sin.

3 O let me hear you speaking
　　in accents clear and still,
above the storms of passion,
　　the murmurs of self-will;
O speak to reassure me,
　　to hasten or control;
O speak, and make me listen,
　　O guardian of my soul.

4 O Jesus, you have promised
　　to all who follow you,
that where you are in glory
　　your servant shall be too;
and Jesus, I have promised
　　to serve you to the end;
O give me grace to follow,
　　my master and my friend.

5 O let me see your footmarks,
　　and in them plant my own;
my hope to follow truly
　　is in your strength alone:
O guide me, call me, draw me,
　　uphold me to the end;
and then in heaven receive me,
　　my Saviour and my friend!

J. E. BODE (1816–74)

353

WAVENEY   CM

RICHARD REDHEAD (1820–1901)

WARWICK   CM

S. STANLEY (1767–1822)

O JESUS, King most wonderful,
    O conqueror renowned,
O sweetness inexpressible,
    in whom all joys are found!

2 When once you come into the heart,
    then truth begins to shine;
then earthly vanities depart,
    then kindles love divine.

3 O Jesus, light of all below,
    the fount of life and fire,
surpassing all the joys we know,
    and all we can desire.

4 May every heart confess your name,
    and ever you adore;
and, seeking you, itself inflame
    to seek you more and more.

5 Our tongues shall ever bless you, Lord,
    our love be yours alone;
and ever may our lives express
    the image of your own.

6 Stay with us, Lord, and with your light
    illume the soul's abyss;
scatter the darkness of our night,
    and fill the world with bliss.

Latin, 12th century
tr. EDWARD CASWALL (1814–78)

354

LORD OF THE YEARS 11 10 11 10

MICHAEL BAUGHEN (b. 1930)
arr. DAVID ILIFF (b. 1939)

O LOVING Lord, you are for ever seeking
    those of your mind, intent to do your will,
strong in your strength, your power and grace bespeaking,
    faithful to you, through good report and ill.

2 To you we come, and humbly make confession,
    faithless so oft in thought and word and deed,
asking that we may have, in true possession,
    your free forgiveness in the hour of need.

3 In duties small become our inspiration,
    in larger tasks endue us with your might;
through faithful service shall come full salvation;
    so may we serve, your will our chief delight.

4 Not disobedient to the heavenly vision,
    faithful in all things, seeking not reward,
so, following you, may we fulfil our mission,
    true to ourselves, our neighbours and our Lord.

W. VAUGHAN JENKINS (1868–1920)
based on Philippians 2: 5–11

354

ST OSYTH   11 10 11 10

THOMAS WOOD (1892–1950)

O LOVING Lord, you are for ever seeking
    those of your mind, intent to do your will,
strong in your strength, your power and grace bespeaking,
    faithful to you, through good report and ill.

2 To you we come, and humbly make confession,
    faithless so oft in thought and word and deed,
asking that we may have, in true possession,
    your free forgiveness in the hour of need.

3 In duties small become our inspiration,
    in larger tasks endue us with your might;
through faithful service shall come full salvation;
    so may we serve, your will our chief delight.

4 Not disobedient to the heavenly vision,
    faithful in all things, seeking not reward,
so, following you, may we fulfil our mission,
    true to ourselves, our neighbours and our Lord.

W. VAUGHAN JENKINS (1868–1920)
based on Philippians 2: 5–11

355

HEREFORD   LM

S. S. WESLEY (1810–76)

WILTON   LM

S. STANLEY (1767–1822)

O THOU who camest from above
   the pure, celestial fire to impart,
kindle a flame of sacred love
   on the mean altar of my heart.

2 There let it for thy glory burn
   with inextinguishable blaze;
and, trembling, to its source return
   in humble love and fervent praise.

3 Jesus, confirm my heart's desire
   to work and speak and think for thee;
still let me guard the holy fire,
   and still stir up thy gift in me.

4 Ready for all thy perfect will,
   my acts of faith and love repeat,
till death thine endless mercies seal,
   and make the sacrifice complete.

CHARLES WESLEY (1707–88)

356

SOUTHCOTE   99 79 with refrain

SYDNEY CARTER (b. 1915)
arr. DONALD DAVISON

And it's from the old I tra-vel to the new; keep me tra-vel-ling a-long with you.

ONE more step along the world I go,
one more step along the world I go,
from the old things to the new
keep me travelling along with you:

And it's from the old I travel to the new;
keep me travelling along with you.

2 Round the corners of the world I turn,
more and more about the world I learn,
all the new things that I see
you'll be looking at along with me:

3 As I travel through the bad and good,
keep me travelling the way I should;
where I see no way to go
you'll be telling me the way, I know:

4 Give me courage when the world is rough,
keep me loving though the world is tough;
leap and sing in all I do,
keep me travelling along with you:

5 You are older than the world can be,
you are younger than the life in me;
ever old and ever new,
keep me travelling along with you.

SYDNEY CARTER (b. 1915)

357

SEEK YE FIRST THE KINGDOM OF GOD

KAREN LAFFERTY (b. 1948)

The refrain may be sung by soprano voices while others sing the verses.

SEEK ye first the kingdom of God,
and his righteousness,
and all these things shall be added unto you;
allelu-, alleluia.
   Alleluia, alleluia, alleluia, allelu-, alleluia!

2 Man shall not live by bread alone,
   but by every word,
   that proceeds from the mouth of God;
   allelu-, alleluia.

3 Ask and it shall be given unto you,
   seek and ye shall find,
   knock and the door shall be opened up to you;
   allelu-, alleluia.

4 Trust in the Lord with all thine heart,
   he shall direct thy path,
   in all thy ways acknowledge him;
   allelu-, alleluia.

5 Praise to the Father, praise to the Son,
   praise to the Spirit too,
   and to the Godhead, three in one;
   allelu-, alleluia.

KAREN LAFFERTY (b. 1948)
based on Matthew 6: 33, 7: 7–8
and Deuteronomy 8: 3

545

358

First Tune

ST BEES   77 77

J. B. DYKES (1823–76)

Second Tune

NOTTINGHAM   77 77

School of MOZART

TAKE my life, and let it be
consecrated, Lord, to thee;
take my moments and my days,
let them flow in ceaseless praise.

2 Take my hands, and let them move
at the impulse of thy love;
take my feet, and let them be
swift and beautiful for thee.

3 Take my voice, and let me sing
always, only, for my King;
take my lips, and let them be
filled with messages from thee.

4 Take my silver and my gold,
all by thee to be controlled;
take my intellect, and use
every power as thou shalt choose.

5 Take my will, and make it thine:
it shall be no longer mine.
Take my heart—it is thine own;
it shall be thy royal throne.

6 Take my love; my Lord, I pour
at thy feet its treasure-store;
take myself, and I will be,
ever, only, all for thee.

FRANCES RIDLEY HAVERGAL (1836–79)

359

OPEN OUR EYES, LORD

Words and music by BOB CULL
arr. DAVID PEACOCK (b. 1949)

O-pen our eyes, Lord, we want to see Je - sus, to reach out and touch him and say that we love him.

O-pen our ears, Lord, and help us to lis - ten; O o-pen our eyes, Lord, we want to see Je - sus.

360

LAND OF REST   75 75

American folk melody
adpt. MICHAEL BALL (b. 1938)

TAKE this moment, sign and space,
 take my friends around,
make our fellowship a place
 where your love is found.

2 Take me as you call my name,
 send your love to mend
who I am and what I've been,
 all I've failed to tend.

3 Take the tiredness of my days,
 take what I regret,
let your free forgiveness touch
 all I can't forget.

4 Take the little child in me
 scared of growing old,
help me now to find my worth
 made in Christ's own mould.

5 Take my talents, take my skill,
 take what's yet to be;
let my life be yours and yet
 be more truly me.

Iona Community

361

FIRST TUNE

Melody from *Scottish Psalter*, 1635
as given in PLAYFORD'S *Psalms*, 1671

LONDON NEW   CM

SECOND TUNE

CONTEMPLATION   CM   F. A. G. OUSELEY (1825–89)

WHEN all your mercies, O my God,
  my rising soul surveys,
enchanted with the view, I'm lost
  in wonder, love and praise.

2 Unnumbered comforts on my soul
    your tender care bestowed,
  before my infant heart conceived
    from whom those comforts flowed.

3 When in the slippery paths of youth
    with heedless steps I ran,
  your arm unseen conveyed me safe,
    and brought me up to man.

4 When worn with sickness many times
    your health renewed my face;
  and, when in sins and sorrows sunk,
    revived my soul with grace.

5 Ten thousand thousand precious gifts
    my daily thanks employ;
  nor is the least a cheerful heart
    that tastes those gifts with joy.

6 Through every period of my life
    your goodness I'll pursue;
  and after death, in distant worlds,
    the glorious theme renew.

7 Through all eternity to you
    a joyful song I'll raise:
  for Oh, eternity's too short
    to utter all your praise.

JOSEPH ADDISON (1672–1719)
based on Psalm 103: 1–3

362

MONKS GATE   65 65 66 65

English traditional melody
adpt. R. VAUGHAN WILLIAMS (1872–1958)

WHO would true valour see,
    let him come hither;
one here will constant be,
    come wind, come weather.
There's no discouragement
shall make him once relent
his first avowed intent
    to be a pilgrim.

2 Whoso beset him round
    with dismal stories,
do but themselves confound;
    his strength the more is.
No lion can him fright,
he'll with a giant fight,
but he will have a right
    to be a pilgrim.

3 Hobgoblin nor foul fiend
    can daunt his spirit:
he knows he at the end
    shall life inherit.
Then fancies fly away,
he'll fear not what men say,
he'll labour night and day
    to be a pilgrim.

JOHN BUNYAN (1628–88)

363

KELVINGROVE   76 76 77 76

Scottish traditional melody
harm. GERALD L. BARNES (b. 1935)

WILL you come and follow me,
    if I but call your name?
Will you go where you don't know
    and never be the same?
Will you let my love be shown,
will you let my love be known,
will you let my life be grown
    in you and you in me?

2 Will you leave yourself behind
    if I but call your name?
Will you care for cruel and kind
    and never be the same?
Will you risk the hostile stare
should your life attract or scare?
Will you let me answer prayer
    in you and you in me?

3 Will you let the blinded see
    if I but call your name?
Will you set the prisoners free
    and never be the same?
Will you kiss the leper clean,
and do such as this unseen,
and admit to what I mean
    in you and you in me?

4 Will you love the 'you' you hide
    if I but call your name?
Will you quell the fear inside
    and never be the same?
Will you use the faith you've found
to reshape the world around,
through my sight and touch and sound
    in you and you in me?

5 Lord, your summons echoes true
    when you but call my name.
Let me turn and follow you
    and never be the same.
In your company I'll go
where your love and footsteps show.
Thus I'll move and live and grow
    in you and you in me.

Iona Community

364

Seek the Lord while he may be found;
   call on him while he is near.
Let the wicked forsake his way,
   and the evil man his thoughts.
Let him turn to the Lord, and he will have mercy on him,
   and to our God, for he will freely pardon.

365

Jesus said to his disciples: If anyone would come after me,
he must deny himself and take up his cross and follow me.
   For whoever wants to save his life will lose it,
but whoever loses his life for me will find it.
   What good will it be for a man if he gains the whole world,
   yet forfeits his soul,
   or what can a man give in exchange for his soul?

366

If anyone is in Christ, he is a new creation;
   the old has gone, the new has come!
God was reconciling the world to himself in Christ.
   We implore you on Christ's behalf: be reconciled to God.
God made him who had no sin to be sin for us,
   so that in him we might become the righteousness of God.
Now is the time of God's favour,
   now is the day of salvation.

367

Lord Jesus Christ,
I know I have sinned in my thoughts, words and actions:
there are so many good things I have not done,
there are so many sinful things I have done.
I am sorry for my sins
and turn from everything I know to be wrong.
You gave your life upon the cross for me;
gratefully I give my life back to you.
Now I ask you to come into my life:
come in as my Saviour to cleanse me,
come in as my Lord to control me,
come in as my friend to be with me.
And I will serve you all the remaining years of my life,
in complete obedience. Amen.

368

Lord Jesus, you gave yourself for me upon the cross,
I now give myself to you:
    all that I have,
    all that I am,
    all that I hope to be.
Give me in return your forgiveness,
your love, your courage,
and send me forth in your name and in your service.

369

VISION   15 15 15 6

H. WALFORD DAVIES (1869–1941)
arr. JOHN WILSON (b. 1905)

Lord Je - sus, live in us!

(Harmony ad lib.)

Lord Je - sus, live in us! Live in me!

Organ

ALL who worship God in Jesus,
    all who serve the Son of Man,
in the kingdom he prepared for us
    before the world began,
know the purpose of his coming
    is the test of all we plan:
      Lord Jesus, live in us!

2 As the need of man increases
    in a world that grows afraid,
when the tempter finds a reason
    why the truth should be betrayed,
we who bear the name of Christian,
    we know who must be obeyed:
      Lord Jesus, live in us!

3 It's his deeper revolution
    that redeems us from the fall;
it's his reconciling Spirit
    shall make comrades of us all;
it's the joy of God within us
    cries in answer to his call:
      Lord Jesus, live in us!
        Live in me!

F. PRATT GREEN (b. 1903)

370

FIRST TUNE

EVELYNS   65 65 D

W. H. MONK (1823–89)

SECOND TUNE

CAMBERWELL   65 65 D

MICHAEL BRIERLEY (b. 1932)

CONFESSING THE FAITH

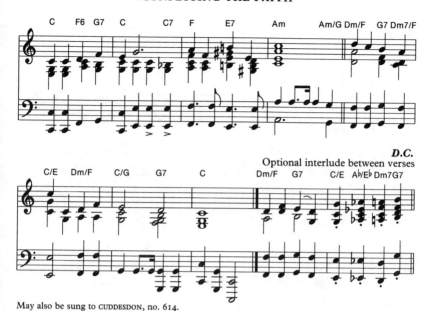

D.C.

Optional interlude between verses

May also be sung to CUDDESDON, no. 614.

AT the name of Jesus
  every knee shall bow,
every tongue confess him
  King of glory now.
It's the Father's pleasure
  we should call him Lord,
who from the beginning
  was the mighty Word:

2 Mighty and mysterious
  in the highest height,
God from everlasting,
  very light of light.
One with God the Father
  and the Spirit blest,
love in love eternal,
  rest in perfect rest.

3 Humbled for a season
  to receive a name
from the lips of sinners
  unto whom he came,
faithfully he bore it,
  spotless to the last,
brought it back victorious
  when from death he passed;

4 Bore it up triumphant
  with its human light,
through all ranks of creatures
  to the central height;
to the throne of Godhead,
  to the Father's breast,
filled it with the glory
  of that perfect rest.

5 Name him, Christians, name him,
  with love strong as death,
but with awe and wonder,
  and with bated breath;
he is God the Saviour,
  he is Christ the Lord,
ever to be worshipped,
  trusted and adored.

6 With his Father's glory
  Jesus comes again,
angel hosts attend him
  and announce his reign;
for all wreaths of empire
  meet upon his brow,
and our hearts confess him
  King of glory now.

CAROLINE NOEL (1817–77) altd.
based on Philippians 2: 5–11

371

ENGELBERG   10 10 10 with alleluias   C. V. STANFORD (1852–1924)

VERSES 1, 2, 4, 5, 6 *(Unison)*

vv. 1, 2, 4, 5   v. 6

Al - le - lu - ia!   Al - le - lu - ia!

VERSE 3 *(Harmony)*

Al - le - lu - ia!

May also be sung to SINE NOMINE, no. 478.

> FOR all the love that from our earliest days
> has gladdened life and guarded all our ways,
> we bring you, Lord, our song of grateful praise,
> > *Alleluia!*

> 2 For all the truth from wisdom's lighted page,
> undimmed and pure, that shines from age to age,
> God's holy word, our priceless heritage,
> > *Alleluia!*

> 3 For all the joy that childhood's days have brought,
> for healthful lives and purity of thought,
> for life's deep meaning to our spirits taught,
> > *Alleluia!*

> 4 For all the hope that sheds its glorious ray
> along the dark and unknown future way,
> and lights the path to God's eternal day,
> > *Alleluia!*

> 5 For all the strength that has been gained through prayer,
> to face life's tasks, its eager quests to share,
> till ampler powers fulfil its promise fair,
> > *Alleluia!*

> 6 For Christ the Lord, our Saviour and our friend,
> upon whose love and truth our lives depend,
> our hope, our strength, our joy that knows no end,
> > *Alleluia!*

L. J. EGERTON SMITH (1879–1958)

372

FOR THIS PURPOSE Words and music by GRAHAM KENDRICK (b. 1950)

1. For this pur-pose Christ was re-vealed, to de-stroy all the works of the e-vil one. Christ in us has o-ver-come,___ so with glad-ness we sing

2. In the name of Je-sus we stand, by the power of his blood we now claim this ground. Sa-tan has no au-tho-ri-ty here,___ powers of dark-ness must flee,___

CONFESSING THE FAITH

and wel-come his king-dom in. (MEN) O-ver
for Christ has the vic-to-ry.

sin he has con-quered, al-le-lu-ia, (WOMEN) he has con-quered; (MEN) o-ver

death vic-tor-ious, al-le-lu-ia, (WOMEN) vic-tor-ious; (MEN) o-ver

sick-ness he has tri-umphed, al-le-lu-ia, (WOMEN) he has tri-umphed: (ALL) Je - sus

reigns o-ver all!

565

373

RETIREMENT   78 78 77 77

G. F. BROCKLESS (1887–1957)

GOD is hope and God is now!
  Hope, despite distress and darkness,
    war and famine, woe and fear;
    hope though hearts are sick with sorrow,
      hope afar, yet richly near:
    heart, arise! your faith avow,
  God is hope, and God is now,
  God is hope, and God is now!

2 God is hope, and God is now!
  Hope not only for tomorrow—
    death defeated, heaven won—
    but for present needs and graces,
      ours today through Christ the Son.
    Spirit-wrought, we know not how,
  God is hope, and God is now,
  God is hope, and God is now!

3 God is hope, and God is now,
  Hope for earth, and hope for heaven,
    hope not meant for us alone:
    then to all God's human children
      we must make his gospel known.
    Up, my soul, make good your vow—
  take God's hope, and share it now!
  Take God's hope, and share it now.

MARGARET CLARKSON (b. 1915)

374

ABBOT'S LEIGH 87 87 D

CYRIL V. TAYLOR (1907–91)

GOD is love: let heaven adore him;
   God is love: let earth rejoice;
let creation sing before him,
   and exalt him with one voice.
He who laid the earth's foundation,
   he who spread the heavens above,
he who breathes through all creation,
   he is love, eternal love.

2 God is love, so he is holding
   all the world in one embrace,
with unfailing grasp enfolding
   every child of every race.
And when human hearts are breaking
   under sorrow's iron rod,
all the sorrow, all the aching,
   wrings with pain the heart of God.

3 God is love: and though with blindness
   sin afflicts the souls of men,
God's eternal loving-kindness
   holds and guides them even then.
Sin and death and hell shall never
   o'er us final triumph gain;
God is love, so love for ever
   o'er the universe must reign.

TIMOTHY REES (1874–1939) altd.
based on 1 John 4: 8

375

EIN' FESTE BURG   87 87 66 667

Later form of a melody by
MARTIN LUTHER (1483–1546)

GOD is our refuge and defence,
    whose shield and weapons round us,
ensure our safe deliverance
    from evils that confound us.
        The old foe still intends
        to gain his ruthless ends;
        determined on his course
        and armed with cunning force:
    on earth he has no equal.

2 Though we may strive with all our might,
    we face complete destruction;
the one true man takes up our fight,
    whom God himself has chosen.
        You ask us, 'Who is this?'
        Why, Jesus Christ, who is
        the Lord of hosts' own Son,
        our God, the only one!
    He triumphs in the battle.

3 If devils lurked on every side,
    all eager to devour us,
we still should not be terrified:
    they cannot overpower us!
        The peevish Prince of lies,
        however hard he tries,
        is impotent to hurt
        and has his just desert:
    the slightest word can fell him.

4 They must allow God's word to stand,
    and fall inert before it.
We trust the issue to his hand,
    who gives us his own Spirit.
        And though they take away
        all we hold dear today,
        wealth, honour, life or kin,
        we know they cannot win:
    the kingdom shall not fail us.

MARTIN LUTHER (1483–1546)
tr. ALAN GAUNT (b. 1935)

376

SHIPSTON   87 87

English traditional melody
arr. R. VAUGHAN WILLIAMS (1872–1958)

GOD the Father of creation,
  master of the realms sublime,
Lord of light and life's foundation:
  we believe and trust in him.

2 Christ who came from highest heaven,
  God from God before all time,
Son for our redemption given:
  we believe and trust in him.

3 Spirit, God in us residing,
  power of life and love supreme,
intercessor—pleading, guiding:
  we believe and trust in him.

4 Trinity of adoration!
  earth responds to heaven's theme;
one the Church's acclamation:
  we believe and trust in him!

MICHAEL PERRY (b. 1942)

377

SOMMERLIED   56 64   H. VON MÜLLER (CAREY BONNER) (1859–1938)

GOD who made the earth,
　the air, the sky, the sea,
who gave the light its birth,
　he cares for me.

2 God who made the grass,
　the flower, the fruit, the tree,
the day and night to pass,
　he cares for me.

3 God who made the sun,
　the moon, the stars, is he
who, when life's troubles come,
　will care for me.

4 God who sent his Son
　to die on Calvary,
he, if I trust in him,
　will care for me.

SARAH BETTS RHODES (1824–1904)

378

HE IS LORD   Irregular

MARVIN V. FREY
arr. DAVID TRAFFORD (b. 1950)
Words anon.
based on Philippians 2: 9–11

He is Lord, he is Lord; he is ri-sen from the dead, and he is Lord. Ev-ery knee shall bow, ev-ery tongue con - fess that Je - sus Christ is Lord.

379

HE LIVES

Words and music by A. H. ACKLEY (1887–1960)

He lives,____ he lives,____ Christ Je-sus lives to-day!__ He
He lives,____ he lives,____
walks with me and talks with me a-long life's nar-row way.__ He
lives,____ he lives,____ sal-va-tion to im-part!__ You
He lives,____ he lives,____
ask me how I know he lives? He lives with-in my heart.__

380

MONTGOMERY   11 11 11 11 Anapaestic

Melody probably by SAMUEL JARVIS
First published 1762

How firm a foundation, O saints of the Lord,
is laid for your faith in his excellent word;
what more can he say than already he's said,
to all who to Jesus for refuge have fled?

2 'In every condition, in sickness, in health,
in poverty's grip, or abounding in wealth;
at home and abroad, on the land, on the sea,
as your days may demand shall your strength ever be.

3 'Fear not, I am with you, so be not dismayed;
for I am your God, and will come to your aid:
I'll strengthen you, help you, and cause you to stand,
upheld by my righteous, omnipotent hand.

4 'When through the deep waters I call you to go,
you will not be swamped by the rivers of woe;
for I will be with you, your troubles to bless,
and sanctify to you life's deepest distress.

5 'When through fiery trials your pathway shall lie,
my grace all-sufficient shall be your supply;
the flame shall not hurt you; my only design
your dross to consume and your gold to refine.

6 'Down into old age all my people shall prove
my sovereign, eternal, unchangeable love;
though body and mind may decline and decay
your true inner self I renew day by day.

7 'The soul that on Jesus has leaned for repose
I cannot, I will not, desert to its foes:
that soul, though all hell should endeavour to shake,
I'll never abandon and never forsake.'

'K' in *Rippon's Selection*, 1787, altd.
based on Isaiah 43: 1–5 and 2 Corinthians 4: 16

381

LONDONDERRY AIR   11 10 11 10 D

Irish traditional melody
arr. JOHN BARNARD (b. 1948)

CONFESSING THE FAITH

For another arrangement of this tune see no. 486.

I CANNOT tell why he, whom angels worship,
    should set his love upon the sons of men,
or why, as shepherd, he should seek the wanderers,
    to bring them back, they know not how or when.
But this I know, that he was born of Mary,
    when Bethlehem's manger was his only home,
and that he lived at Nazareth and laboured,
    and so the Saviour of the world, is come.

2 I cannot tell how silently he suffered,
    as with his peace he graced this place of tears,
or how his heart upon the cross was broken,
    the crown of pain to three and thirty years.
But this I know, he heals the broken-hearted,
    and stays our sin, and calms our lurking fear,
and lifts the burden from the heavy-laden,
    for yet the Saviour of the world, is here.

3 I cannot tell how he will win the nations,
    how he will claim his earthly heritage,
how satisfy the needs and aspirations
    of east and west, of sinner and of sage.
But this I know, all flesh shall see his glory,
    and he shall reap the harvest he has sown,
and some glad day his sun shall shine in splendour
    when he the Saviour of the world, is known.

4 I cannot tell how all the lands shall worship,
    when, at his bidding, every storm is stilled,
or who can say how great the jubilation
    when every human heart with love is filled.
But this I know, the skies will thrill with rapture,
    and myriad, myriad human voices sing,
and earth to heaven, and heaven to earth, will answer,
    at last the Saviour of the world, is King!

W. Y. FULLERTON (1857–1932)

579

382

HYFRYDOL   87 87 D   R. H. PRICHARD (1811–87)

REFRAIN

Yes, I'll sing___ the won - drous sto - ry of ___ the

Christ who died for me, sing it with his saints in glo - ry, ga - thered by the cry - stal sea.

I WILL sing the wondrous story
    of the Christ who died for me,
how he left the realms of glory
    for the cross on Calvary.

    Yes, I'll sing the wondrous story
        of the Christ who died for me,
    sing it with his saints in glory,
        gathered by the crystal sea.

2 I was lost: but Jesus found me,
    found the sheep that went astray,
raised me up and gently led me
    back into the narrow way.

3 Days of darkness still may meet me,
    sorrow's paths my feet may tread;
but his presence still is with me,
    by his guiding hand I'm led.

4 He will keep me till the river
    rolls its waters at my feet:
then he'll bear me safely over,
    made by grace for glory meet.

F. H. ROWLEY (1854–1952)

383

ST DENIO　　11 11 11 11 Anapaestic

Welsh hymn melody, 1839
founded on a folk-tune

IMMORTAL, invisible, God only wise,
in light inaccessible hid from our eyes,
most blessed, most glorious, the ancient of days,
almighty, victorious, thy great name we praise.

2 Unresting, unhasting, and silent as light,
nor wanting, nor wasting, thou rulest in might;
thy justice like mountains high soaring above
thy clouds, which are fountains of goodness and love.

3 To all, life thou givest, to both great and small;
in all life thou livest, the true life of all;
we blossom and flourish as leaves on the tree,
and wither and perish: but nought changeth thee.

4 Great Father of glory, pure Father of light,
thine angels adore thee, all veiling their sight;
but of all thy rich graces this grace, Lord, impart:
take the veil from our faces, the veil from our heart.

5 All praise we would render; O help us to see,
'tis only the splendour of light hideth thee;
and so let thy glory, Almighty, impart,
through Christ in the story, thy Christ to the heart.

W. C. SMITH (1824–1908)
based on 1 Timothy 1: 17

384

DAVID J. MANSELL (b. 1936)
arr. A. S. COX (b. 1918)

JESUS IS LORD

REFRAIN

Je - sus is Lord! Je - sus is

Lord! Praise him with al-le - lu-ias for Je-sus is Lord!

JESUS is Lord! Creation's voice proclaims it,
    for by his power each tree and flower was planned and made.
Jesus is Lord! The universe declares it.
    Sun, moon and stars in heaven cry Jesus is Lord!

    Jesus is Lord! Jesus is Lord!
    Praise him with alleluias for Jesus is Lord!

2 Jesus is Lord! Yet from his throne eternal
    in flesh he came to die in pain on Calvary's tree.
Jesus is Lord! From him all life proceeding,
    yet gave his life a ransom thus setting us free.

3 Jesus is Lord! O'er sin the mighty conqueror,
    from death he rose and all his foes shall own his name.
Jesus is Lord! God sends his Holy Spirit
    to show by works of power that Jesus is Lord.

DAVID J. MANSELL (b. 1936)
based on Mark 10: 45, Romans 10: 9, and 1 Corinthians 12: 3

585

385

HIS NAME IS WONDERFUL

AUDREY MIEIR (b. 1916)
arr. NORMAN L. WARREN (b. 1934)

His name is wonderful,
his name is wonderful,
his name is wonderful,
Jesus my Lord;
he is the mighty King,
master of everything;
his name is wonderful,
Jesus my Lord!

He's the great shepherd,
the rock of all ages,
almighty God is he;
bow down before him,
love and adore him,
his name is wonderful,
Jesus my Lord!

Anon.

386

LIFE   78 78 77

A. S. COX (b. 1918)

JESUS, life of all the world,
  source and sum of all creation,
Son of God and Son of Man,
  only hope of our salvation,
    living Word for all our need,
    life you give is life indeed.

2 Life of freedom, gladness, truth,
  all our guilt and fear transcending;
life that leaps beyond the grave,
  God's own life that knows no ending;
    life eternal, gift unpriced,
    freely ours in Jesus Christ!

3 Yours is life that makes us stand
  firm for truth, all wrong defying;
yours the strength by which we strive,
  on your holy arm relying;
    yours the war we wage on sin,
    yours the power by which we win.

4 Jesus, life of all the world,
  you are Lord of every nation;
by your Holy Spirit's power
  make your Church your incarnation;
    till our lives of truth and grace
    show the world your human face.

MARGARET CLARKSON (b. 1915)

387

ALMSGIVING   888 4

J. B. DYKES (1823–76)

O LORD of heaven and earth and sea,
to you all praise and glory be;
who loved us from eternity
    and gave us all.

2 The golden sunshine, gentle air,
sweet flowers and fruit, your love declare;
when harvests ripen you are there;
    you give us all.

3 For peaceful homes and healthful days,
for all the blessings earth displays,
we owe you thankfulness and praise;
    you give us all.

4 Freely you gave your only Son,
who on the cross salvation won;
and in the life through him begun
    you give us all.

5 You sent your Spirit from above
as wind and fire and gentle dove;
and in his gifts of power and love
    you gave us all.

6 For souls redeemed, for sins forgiven,
for means of grace and hopes of heaven,
to you, O Lord, what can be given?
    You give us all.

CHRISTOPHER WORDSWORTH (1807–85)

388

MARTHAM LM

J. H. MAUNDER (1858–1920)

May also be sung to EISENACH, no. 207.

O LOVE of God, how strong and true,
eternal and yet ever new;
uncomprehended and unbought,
beyond all knowledge and all thought.

2 O heavenly love, how precious still,
in days of weariness and ill,
in nights of pain and helplessness,
to heal, to comfort, and to bless!

3 O wide-embracing, wondrous love,
we read you in the sky above;
we read you in the earth below,
in seas that swell and streams that flow.

4 We read you best in him who came
to bear for us the cross of shame,
sent by the Father from on high,
our life to live, our death to die.

5 We read your power to bless and save
within the darkness of the grave;
still more in resurrection-light,
we read the fulness of your might.

6 O love of God, our shield and stay
through all the perils of our way;
eternal love, in you we rest,
for ever safe, for ever blest.

HORATIUS BONAR (1808–89)
based on Romans 8: 38–9

389

ST ANNE   CM

WILLIAM CROFT (1678–1727)

Our God, our help in ages past,
  our hope for years to come,
our shelter from the stormy blast,
  and our eternal home.

2 Under the shadow of your throne
  your saints have lived secure;
sufficient is your arm alone,
  and our defence is sure.

3 Before the hills in order stood,
  or earth received her frame,
from everlasting you are God,
  to endless years the same.

4 A thousand ages in your sight
  are like an evening gone;
short as the watch that ends the night
  before the rising sun.

5 Time, like an ever-rolling stream,
  bears all its sons away;
they fly, forgotten as a dream
  dies at the opening day.

6 Our God, our help in ages past,
  our hope for years to come,
be now our guard while life shall last,
  and our eternal home.

ISAAC WATTS (1674–1748)
based on Psalm 90

390

NETTIE ROSE
arr. DAVID TRAFFORD (b. 1950)

PRAISE YOU, LORD

PRAISE you, Lord,
for the wonder of your healing;
praise you, Lord,
for your love so freely given;
outpouring, anointing,
flowing in to heal our wounds;
praise you, Lord, for your love for me.

2 Praise you, Lord,
for your gift of liberation;
praise you, Lord,
you have set the captives free;
the chains that bind are broken
by the sharpness of your sword;
praise you, Lord, you gave your life for me.

3 Praise you, Lord,
you have borne the depths of sorrow;
praise you, Lord,
for your anguish on the tree;
the nails that tore your body
and the pain that tore your soul;
praise you, Lord, your tears they fell for me.

4 Praise you, Lord,
you have turned our thorns to roses;
glory, Lord,
as they bloom upon your brow;
the path of pain is hallowed,
for your love has made it sweet;
praise you, Lord, and may I love you now.

NETTIE ROSE

391

WOODLANDS   10 10 10 10   WALTER GREATOREX (1877–1949)

TELL out, my soul, the greatness of the Lord:
    unnumbered blessings, give my spirit voice;
tender to me the promise of his word;
    in God my Saviour shall my heart rejoice.

2 Tell out, my soul, the greatness of his name:
make known his might, the deeds his arm has done;
his mercy sure, from age to age the same;
his holy name, the Lord, the Mighty One.

3 Tell out, my soul, the greatness of his might:
powers and dominions lay their glory by;
proud hearts and stubborn wills are put to flight,
the hungry fed, the humble lifted high.

4 Tell out, my soul, the glories of his word:
firm is his promise, and his mercy sure.
Tell out, my soul, the greatness of the Lord
to children's children and for evermore.

TIMOTHY DUDLEY-SMITH (b. 1926)
based on Luke 1: 46–55

392

THANK YOU JESUS

Words and music anon.
arr. MARGARET EVANS

CONFESSING THE FAITH

1. You went to Cal - va-ry,_____ and there you died for me:
2. You rose up from the grave,_____ to me new life you gave:_

_ thank you Lord_____ for lov-ing me._____
_ thank you Lord_____ for lov-ing me._____

_ You went to Cal - va-ry,_____ and there you died for
_ You rose up from the grave,_____ to me new life you

me: thank you Lord_____ for lov-ing me._____
gave: thank you Lord_____ for lov-ing me._____

393

AURELIA   76 76 D   S. S. WESLEY (1810–76)

THE Church's one foundation
    is Jesus Christ her Lord;
she is his new creation
    by water and the word:
from heaven he came and sought her
    to be his holy bride;
with his own blood he bought her,
    and for her life he died.

2 Elect from every nation,
    yet one o'er all the earth,
her charter of salvation
    one Lord, one faith, one birth;
one holy name she blesses,
    partakes one holy food,
and to one hope she presses,
    with every grace endued.

3 'Mid toil and tribulation,
    and tumult of her war,
she waits the consummation
    of peace for evermore;
till with the vision glorious
    her longing eyes are blest,
and the great Church victorious
    shall be the Church at rest.

4 Yet she on earth has union
    with God the three in one,
and mystic sweet communion
    with those whose rest is won:
O happy ones and holy!
    Lord, give us grace that we,
like them, the meek and lowly,
    on high may dwell with thee.

S. J. STONE (1839–1900)
based on 1 Corinthians 3: 11 and
Ephesians 5: 25–27

394

DOMINUS REGIT ME   87 87 Iambic   J. B. DYKES (1823–76)

ST COLUMBA   87 87 Iambic   Ancient Irish hymn melody

THE King of love my shepherd is,
   whose goodness fails me never;
I nothing lack if I am his
   and he is mine for ever.

2 Where streams of living water flow
   to rest my soul he leads me,
and, where the rich green pastures grow,
   with heavenly food he feeds me.

3 Perverse and foolish when I strayed,
   each time, in love he sought me,
and on his shoulder gently laid,
   and home, rejoicing, brought me.

4 In death's dark vale I fear no ill
   with you, dear Lord, beside me;
your rod and staff, my comfort still,
   your cross before to guide me.

5 You spread a table in my sight;
   your blessings grace bestowing;
you bid me taste the sweet delight
   from your pure chalice flowing!

6 And so through all my length of days
   your goodness fails me never.
Good Shepherd, may I sing your praise
   within your house for ever.

H. W. BAKER (1821–77) altd.
based on Psalm 23

395

CRIMOND   CM

Melody by JESSIE S. IRVINE (1836–87)

Second Tune

BROTHER JAMES' AIR   CM extended

JAMES LEITH MACBETH BAIN

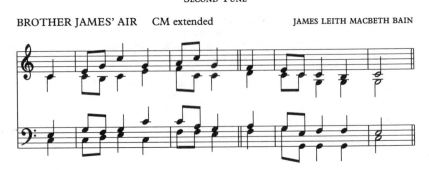

When sung to BROTHER JAMES' AIR, the last two lines of each verse are repeated.

THE Lord's my shepherd, I'll not want;
    he makes me down to lie
in pastures green; he leadeth me
    the quiet waters by.

2 My soul he doth restore again,
    and me to walk doth make
within the paths of righteousness,
    e'en for his own name's sake.

3 Yea, though I walk through death's dark vale,
    yet will I fear no ill;
for thou art with me, and thy rod
    and staff me comfort still.

4 My table thou hast furnishèd
    in presence of my foes;
my head thou dost with oil anoint,
    and my cup overflows.

5 Goodness and mercy all my life
    shall surely follow me;
and in God's house for evermore
    my dwelling-place shall be.

FRANCIS ROUS (1579–1659)
based on Psalm 23
revised, Scottish Psalter 1650

396

THERE'S NO GREATER NAME

MICHAEL BAUGHEN (b. 1930)

1. There's no great-er name than Je - sus, name of
3. In our minds, by faith pro - fess - ing, in our

him who came to save___ us; in that sav - ing
hearts, by in - ward bless - ing, on our tongues, by

name so gra - cious ev - ery knee___ shall bow.___
words con - fess - ing, Je - sus

Christ is Lord.___ 2. Let ev-ery-thing that's be - neath the

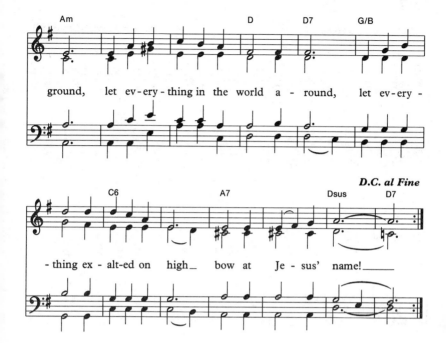

THERE'S no greater name than Jesus,
name of him who came to save us;
in that saving name so gracious
   every knee shall bow.

2 Let everything that's beneath the ground,
let everything in the world around,
let everything exalted on high
   bow at Jesus' name!

3 In our minds, by faith professing,
in our hearts, by inward blessing,
on our tongues, by words confessing,
   Jesus Christ is Lord.

MICHAEL BAUGHEN (b. 1930)
based on Philippians 2: 9–11

397

PALMYRA   86 86 88

JOSEPH SUMMERS (1843–1916)

THOU art the everlasting Word,
   the Father's only Son;
God manifestly seen and heard,
   and heaven's beloved one:

    Worthy, O Lamb of God, art thou,
    that every knee to thee should bow.

2 In thee most perfectly expressed
   the Father's glories shine;
of the full deity possessed,
   eternally divine:

3 True image of the infinite,
   whose essence is concealed;
brightness of uncreated light;
   the heart of God revealed:

4 But the high mysteries of thy name
   an angel's grasp transcend;
the Father only—glorious claim!
   the Son can comprehend:

5 Throughout the universe of bliss,
   the centre thou, and sun;
the eternal theme of praise is this,
   to heaven's beloved one:

JOSIAH CONDER (1789–1855)

398

Words by E. H. PLUMPTRE (1821–91)
based on Ephesians 4: 4–5
Music by BASIL HARWOOD (1859–1949)

THORNBURY   76 76 D

vv. 1, 4 *Unison*

1. Your hand, O God, has guid - ed your
4. Your mer - cy will not fail us, nor

flock from age to age; the won-drous tale is
leave your work un - done; with your right hand to

writ - ten, full clear, on ev - ery page. Our
help us, your vic - tory shall be won; and

fa - thers owned your good - ness, and we their deeds re -
then, by men and an - gels, your name shall be a -

- cord;   and both of___ this bear wit - ness, one
- dored,   and this shall___ be their an - them, one

Church,   one Faith,   one Lord._____
Church,   one Faith,   one Lord._____

vv. 2, 3 *Harmony*

2. Your her - alds brought glad tid - ings to
3. Through many a day of dark - ness, through

great-est, as___ to least;_____ they bade men rise, and
many a scene of strife,_____ the faith-ful few fought

609

399

> I have been put to death with Christ on his cross, so that it is no
> longer I who live, but it is Christ who lives in me.
> This life that I live now, I live by faith in the Son of God,
> who loved me and gave himself for me.

It is through faith that all of you are God's sons in union with
Christ Jesus. You were baptized into union with Christ, and now you
are clothed, so to speak, with the life of Christ himself.

> So there is no difference between Jews and Gentiles,
> between slaves and free men,
> between men and women;
> you are all one in union with Christ Jesus.

400

Thanks be to you, my Lord Jesus Christ,
  for all the benefits you have won for me,
  for all the pains and insults you have borne for me.
O most merciful Redeemer, Friend and Brother,
  may I know you more clearly,
  love you more dearly,
  and follow you more nearly,
for ever and ever. Amen.

401

FIRST TUNE

KILMARNOCK   CM

NEIL DOUGALL (1776–1862)

SECOND TUNE

LUCIUS   CM

attrib. *Templi Carmina*, 1829

ALL praise to our redeeming Lord
who joins us by his grace,
and bids us, each to each restored,
together seek his face.

2 He bids us build each other up;
and, gathered into one,
to our high calling's glorious hope
we hand in hand go on.

3 The gift which he on one bestows
we all delight to prove;
the grace through every vessel flows
in purest streams of love.

4 We all partake the joy of one,
the common peace we feel,
a peace to worldly minds unknown,
a joy unspeakable.

5 And if our fellowship below
in Jesus be so sweet,
what heights of rapture shall we know
when round his throne we meet!

CHARLES WESLEY (1707–88)
based on Ephesians 1: 15–23
and Philippians 1: 7

402

MIT FREUDEN ZART   87 87 887

Hymn melody of the
Bohemian Brethren, 1566

ALL who believe and are baptized
   shall see the Lord's salvation;
baptized into the death of Christ,
   they are a new creation.
      Through Christ's redemption they shall stand
      among the glorious heavenly band
   of every tribe and nation.

2 With one accord, O God we pray:
   grant us your Holy Spirit,
cleanse and forgive us day by day
   through Jesus' blood and merit.
      O keep us in baptismal grace,
      until at last we take our place
   with all who life inherit.

THOMAS HANSEN KINGO (1634–1703)
tr. GEORGE ALFRED TAYLOR RYGH (1860–1943) altd.
based on Romans 6: 3–4

403

Melody and bass (slightly altered)
probably by JEREMIAH CLARKE (1670–1707)

ST MAGNUS CM

A MIGHTY mystery we set forth,
    a wondrous sign and seal;
Lord, give our hearts to know its worth
    and all its truth to feel.

2 Death to the world we thus avow,
    death to each selfish lust;
the risen life is our life now,
    the risen Christ our trust.

3 Baptized into the Father's name,
    we're children of our God;
baptized into the Son, we claim
    the ransom of his blood.

4 Baptized into the Holy Ghost,
    in this accepted hour,
give us to own the Pentecost,
    and the descending power.

GEORGE RAWSON (1807–89)
based on Romans 6: 3–4

404

MORNING HYMN   LM   Melody by F. H. BARTHÉLÉMON (1741–1808)

AWAKE, awake: fling off the night!
for God has sent his glorious light;
and we who live in Christ's new day
must works of darkness put away.

2 Awake and rise, by God renewed
and with the Spirit's power endued,
the light of life in us must glow,
the fruits of truth and goodness show.

3 Let in the light; all sin expose
to Christ, whose life no darkness knows.
Before his cross for guidance kneel;
his light will judge and, judging, heal.

4 Awake, and rise up from the dead,
and Christ his light on you will shed.
His power will wrong desires destroy,
and your whole being fill with joy.

5 Then sing for joy, use all your days;
give thanks for everything, always.
Lift up your hearts; with one accord
praise God through Jesus Christ our Lord.

JOHN RAPHAEL PEACEY (1896–1971) altd.
based on Romans 13: 11–14
and Ephesians 5: 8–20

405

BEATITUDO   CM

J. B. DYKES (1823–76)

For this tune in A♭ major see no. 307.

SECOND TUNE

ST BERNARD   CM

Tochter Zion, Cologne, 1741

CHRIST, when for us you were baptized,
    God's Spirit on you came,
as peaceful as a dove, and yet
    as urgent as a flame.

2 God named you his beloved Son,
    named you his servant too;
his kingdom you were called to preach,
    his holy will to do.

3 At once, and faithful unto death,
    you then obeyed his call
freely as Son of Man to serve,
    and give your life for all.

4 Baptize us with your Spirit, Lord,
    your cross on us be signed,
that likewise in God's service we
    may perfect freedom find.

F. BLAND TUCKER (1895–1984) altd.
based on Mark 1: 9–11

406

LUX EOI   87 87 D   ARTHUR SULLIVAN (1842–1900)

CHURCH of God, elect and glorious,
　　holy nation, chosen race;
called as God's own special people,
　　royal priests and heirs of grace:
know the purpose of your calling,
　　show to all his mighty deeds;
tell of love which knows no limits,
　　grace which meets all human needs.

2 God has called you out of darkness
　　into his most marvellous light;
brought his truth to life within you,
　　turned your blindness into sight.
Let your light so shine around you
　　that God's name is glorified;
and all find fresh hope and purpose
　　in Christ Jesus crucified.

3 Once you were an alien people,
　　strangers to God's heart of love;
but he brought you home in mercy,
　　citizens of heaven above.
Let his love flow out to others,
　　let them feel a Father's care;
that they too may know his welcome
　　and his countless blessings share.

4 Church of God, elect and holy,
　　be the people he intends;
strong in faith and swift to answer
　　each command your master sends:
royal priests, fulfil your calling
　　through your sacrifice and prayer;
give your lives in joyful service,
　　sing his praise, his love declare.

JAMES E. SEDDON (1915–83)
based on 1 Peter 2: 9–11

407

AVE VIRGO VIRGINUM   76 76 D

Medieval melody from
J. Horn's *Gesangbuch*, 1544

For a different harmonization of this tune (in G major) see no. 248.

COME, God's people, sing for joy,
　shout your songs of gladness,
for the hope of Easter day
　overcomes our sadness.
Come with all God's people here,
　who with true affection
join again to celebrate
　Jesus' resurrection.

2 Years before, as Moses led
　Israel's sons and daughters
from their bonds to exodus
　through the Red Sea waters:
so the living Lord of life
　speaks through our baptism
of the new life which we share
　with him who is risen.

3 That first Easter he arose,
　his disciples greeting;
Christians now in every place
　still their Lord are meeting.
Christ, who died for all the world,
　in his death brings healing;
and his rising from the grave
　is God's power revealing.

KEITH D. PEARSON (b. 1925)
based on JOHN OF DAMASCUS (c.675–749)

407

GOOD KING WENCESLAS   76 76 D
(TEMPUS ADEST FLORIDUM)

English traditional carol
harm. J. STAINER (1840–1901)

COME, God's people, sing for joy,
  shout your songs of gladness,
for the hope of Easter day
  overcomes our sadness.
Come with all God's people here,
  who with true affection
join again to celebrate
  Jesus' resurrection.

2 Years before, as Moses led
  Israel's sons and daughters
from their bonds to exodus
  through the Red Sea waters:
so the living Lord of life
  speaks through our baptism
of the new life which we share
  with him who is risen.

3 That first Easter he arose,
  his disciples greeting;
Christians now in every place
  still their Lord are meeting.
Christ, who died for all the world,
  in his death brings healing;
and his rising from the grave
  is God's power revealing.

KEITH D. PEARSON (b. 1925)
based on JOHN OF DAMASCUS (c.675–749)

408

KRISTIN   7 7 7 5 with refrain

ROBIN MANN (b. 1949)

REFRAIN
Unison

Fa - ther wel-comes all__ his child-ren to__ his fam-ily through his Son; Fa - ther giv - ing his__ sal - va - tion, life__ for e - ver has been won.   won.

VERSES

1. Lit - tle child - ren, come to me,
2. In the wa - ter, in__ the word
3. Let us dai - ly die__ to sin,

626

for my king-dom is of these; life and love I
is his pro-mise, be as-sured, those who be-lieve and
let us dai - ly rise with him, walk in the love of

have to give, mer - cy for your sin.
are bap-tized shall be born a - gain.
Christ our Lord, live in the peace of God.

Father welcomes all his children
to his family through his Son;
Father giving his salvation,
life for ever has been won.

LITTLE children, come to me,
for my kingdom is of these;
life and love I have to give,
mercy for your sin.

2 In the water, in the word
is his promise, be assured,
those who believe and are baptized
shall be born again.

3 Let us daily die to sin,
let us daily rise with him,
walk in the love of Christ our Lord,
live in the peace of God.

ROBIN MANN (b. 1949)
based on Romans 6: 4

627

409

ABBOT'S LEIGH   87 87 D

CYRIL V. TAYLOR (1907–91)

JESUS CHRIST, my heart's true captain,
 yours I give myself to be.
All my strength is at your service
 who laid down your life for me.
Now, whatever fame or fortune
 comes my way for good or ill,
yours alone am I for ever,
 take and lead me where you will.

2 Here before you stands a sinner,
 bowed before your searching eyes.
Humbled, shamed, all sin confessing,
 trusting your command, 'Arise!'
My poor heart is all unworthy
 that my God should here abide,
yet alone by your indwelling
 can my soul be satisfied.

3 Peace cannot be bought or bartered,
 grace costs more than worlds of wealth.
Only in your glad adventure
 shall my searching heart find health.
Truest gain lies in self-giving,
 all I have I count but loss.
Let me spend it in your service
 for the glory of the cross.

4 God is rising up to judgement,
 earth is waking to your light.
Peoples yet shall be united,
 wrong be conquered by the right.
Tasks that call for tireless courage
 lie before us in the way.
Then together let us venture
 till our God has won the day.

GREVILLE COOKE (1894–1989)

409

MANOR HOUSE   87 87 D   FREDERICK GEORGE CARTER (b. 1913)

JESUS CHRIST, my heart's true captain,
    yours I give myself to be.
All my strength is at your service
    who laid down your life for me.
Now, whatever fame or fortune
    comes my way for good or ill,
yours alone am I for ever,
    take and lead me where you will.

2 Here before you stands a sinner,
    bowed before your searching eyes.
Humbled, shamed, all sin confessing,
    trusting your command, 'Arise!'
My poor heart is all unworthy
    that my God should here abide,
yet alone by your indwelling
    can my soul be satisfied.

3 Peace cannot be bought or bartered,
    grace costs more than worlds of wealth.
Only in your glad adventure
    shall my searching heart find health.
Truest gain lies in self-giving,
    all I have I count but loss.
Let me spend it in your service
    for the glory of the cross.

4 God is rising up to judgement,
    earth is waking to your light.
Peoples yet shall be united,
    wrong be conquered by the right.
Tasks that call for tireless courage
    lie before us in the way.
Then together let us venture
    till our God has won the day.

GREVILLE COOKE (1894–1989)

410

HOLY ROOD   SM

A. H. BROWN (1830–1926)

English traditional carol
from W. SANDYS' *Christmas Carols*, 1833

SANDYS   SM

FOR me to live is Christ:
  with him new life begins;
his loving touch renews the mind
  and takes away my sins.

2 For me to live is Christ:
    from him true living springs;
  he comes, and with his radiant love
    transforms all common things.

3 For me to live is Christ:
   to serve is now my aim;
   to help wherever there is need,
      and care in Jesus' name.

4 For me to live is Christ:
   and death itself is gain;
   for all who trust, beyond the grave
      with Christ the Lord will reign.

5 For me to live is Christ:
   on him my life I cast;
   my strength, my aim, my hope, reward,
      my Lord, from first to last.

PETER TONGEMAN (b. 1929)
based on Philippians 1: 21-2

411

ST MICHAEL   SM

Genevan Psalter, 1551
adpt. WILLIAM CROTCH (1775–1847)

LORD, in the strength of grace,
   with a glad heart and true,
myself and my remaining days,
   I consecrate to you.

2 Your ransomed servant, I
   restore to you your own;
and, from this moment, live or die
   to serve my God alone.

CHARLES WESLEY (1707–88) altd.

412

FARRANT   CM

Adpt. from an anthem
probably by JOHN HILTON (d. 1608)

LORD, let your grace descend on those
who, hoping in your word,
this day do publicly declare
that Jesus is their Lord.

2 With cheerful steps may they advance
and run the Christian race;
and through the troubles of the way
find all-sufficient grace.

JAMES NEWTON (1732–90)

413

CONFIRMATION   11 10 11 10   T. BRIAN COLEMAN (b. 1920)

1 LORD, we have come at your own invitation,
  chosen by you, to be counted your friends;
yours is the strength that sustains dedication,
  ours a commitment we know never ends.

2 Here, at your table, confirm our intention,
  give it your seal of forgiveness and grace;
teach us to serve, without pride or pretension,
  Lord, in your kingdom, whatever our place.

3 When, at your table, each time of returning,
  vows are renewed and our courage restored:
may we increasingly glory in learning
  all that it means to accept you as Lord.

4 So, in the world, where each duty assigned us
  gives us the chance to create or destroy,
help us to make those decisions that bind us,
  Lord, to yourself, in obedience and joy.

F. PRATT GREEN (b. 1903)

414

MARCHING   87 87

MARTIN SHAW (1875–1958)

SECOND TUNE

Russian folk melody
arr. NOËL TREDINNICK (b. 1949)

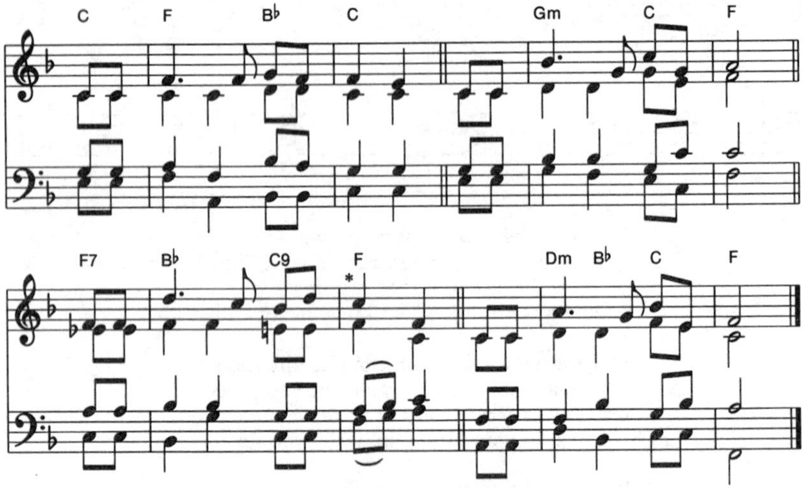

STENKA RAZIN   87 87

*Instead of the original, the more
familiar ending may be used:

Arrangement © Noël Tredinnick/Jubilate Hymns

636

PRAISE to God, almighty maker
of all things, below, above;
for his might is in redemption
manifest as holy love.

2 Praise the Son who thus revealed him,
love incarnate shown to us,
living, suffering, dying, risen,
love through death victorious.

3 Here, redemption's wondrous story
we set forth in mystic rite:
see him die, the grave receive him,
see him rise, by God's great might.

4 Here, within the pool we meet him;
here with him we buried lie;
here we plead his matchless merit;
here with him to sin we die.

5 Then, victorious through his passion,
from the grave with him we rise,
born again to do him service
in the strength his grace supplies.

6 Praise the Spirit, who is promised
here to be the gift divine,
making in our hearts his temple,
love, joy, peace, his holy sign.

7 Praise to Father, Son and Spirit,
sacred name of holy love;
here, baptized, the Church we enter,
realm on earth of heaven above.

8 Praise to God, almighty Saviour,
praises from the earth ascend;
praises join from saints in heaven,
alleluias without end.

WILLIAM ROBINSON (1888–1963)
based on Romans 6: 3–11

415

DEBBY KERNER
arr. A. S. COX (b. 1918)

WELCOME TO THE FAMILY

INTRODUCTION

REFRAIN
Unison

Wel-come to the fa — mi-ly, we're glad that you have come

to share your life with us,＿＿＿ as we

grow in love; and may we al-ways

BAPTISM AND MEMBERSHIP

be to you___ what God would have us be, a fam - 'ly

al - ways there,___ to be strong and

Last time **to Coda**

to lean on.___

VERSES

1. May we learn to love each o - ther more with each new day!
2. May we learn to help each o - ther, for each o - ther care;

639

Welcome to the family, we're glad that you have come
to share your life with us, as we grow in love;
and may we always be to you what God would have us be,
a family always there, to be strong and to lean on.

MAY we learn to love each other more with each new day!
may words of love be on our lips in everything we say;
may the Spirit melt our hearts and teach us how to pray,
that we may be a true family.

2 May we learn to help each other, for each other care;
may we laugh and learn together, each others' burdens share;
may the Spirit send us out, loving deeds to dare,
that we may be a true family.

DEBBY KERNER
V2. MICHAEL BALL (b. 1938)

416

RICHMOND CM

T. HAWEIS (1734–1820)
adpt. S. WEBBE (THE YOUNGER) (c.1770–1843)

May also be sung to CREATOR GOD, no. 133.

WITNESS, both earth and heaven now
  before the Lord we speak;
to him we make our solemn vow,
  a vow we dare not break:

2 As long as life itself shall last,
  ourselves to Christ we yield;
nor from his cause will we depart,
  or ever quit the field.

3 We trust not in our native strength,
  but on his grace rely,
that, with returning wants, the Lord
  will all our need supply.

4 O guide our doubtful steps aright,
  and keep us in your ways;
and while we turn our vows to prayers,
  Lord, turn our prayers to praise.

BENJAMIN BEDDOME (1717–95)

417

Surely you know that when we were baptized into union with
Christ Jesus, we were baptized into union with his death.
**By our baptism, we were buried with him and shared his death,
in order that, just as Christ was raised from death by the
glorious power of the Father, so also we might live a new life.**
For since we have become one with him in dying as he did,
**in the same way we shall be one with him
by being raised to life as he was.**

418

If we died with him, we shall live with him;
if we endure, we shall reign with him.
If we deny him, he will deny us.
**If we are faithless, he keeps faith,
for he cannot deny himself.**

419

Lord, we thank you that you chose to be one with us in the waters
of baptism. We ask that our baptism may make us one with you.

We are baptized into your death:
**may we die to what is selfish, impious, faithless, cowardly
and unworthy of your calling.**

We are baptized into your resurrection:
**may we carry the unwavering hope of eternal life within us,
and live this present life as those who have tasted the life to come.**

We are baptized into your Spirit:
may we continue to grow to maturity through his indwelling.

We are baptized into your Church:
**Lord, may we never disown those who are our brothers and
sisters in the faith, but always seek that unity and
compassion by which your family is to be recognized.**

Lord, in whom we are baptized,
**keep us faithful in the wilderness,
keep us brave at the cross,
keep us joyous in the resurrection.
In the name of Jesus. Amen.**

420

We believe in God
who, in the beginning, in love created all things
and, at the end, in love will gather all things to himself.

We believe in Jesus Christ
who came to earth,
one of us and one with us,
with whom, in baptism,
we die and are buried
that we may rise in his resurrection life.

We believe in the Holy Spirit,
who led us to Christ,
who is given to us again in baptism
that we may love and serve the Lord
with all our being.

We believe in the Church,
of which, through faith and baptism,
we are made members,
one with Christ in his body.

We believe in the Christian calling to live in the world;
to live under the obedience of Christ
in his love, his joy and his peace.

421

Father, we thank you for calling us to the way of Christ
and for making us members of your Church;
bless these who now join us in the fellowship of your body.
   May we enrich one another, support one another,
   love one another and encourage one another.
May we honour your house, be obedient to your word,
and come with expectancy to your table.
   May we together witness to your saving love,
   so that others may come to know and believe in Jesus Christ.
May we together be filled with your Holy Spirit
and the fullness of your love.
   Through Jesus Christ our Lord. Amen.

422

Teach us, good Lord, to serve you as you deserve:
   to give and not to count the cost;
   to fight and not to heed the wounds;
   to toil and not to seek for rest;
   to labour and to ask for no reward,
   save that of knowing that we do your will.
Amen.

423

We welcome you into the Lord's family.
We are members together of the body of Christ;
we are children of the same heavenly Father;
we are inheritors together of the kingdom of God.
We welcome you.

424 THE CONFESSION OF FAITH: THE APOSTLES' CREED

I believe in God the Father almighty,
maker of heaven and earth;
and in Jesus Christ, his only Son, our Lord,
who was conceived of the Holy Spirit,
born of the Virgin Mary,
suffered under Pontius Pilate,
was crucified, died and was buried.
He descended into hell.
The third day he rose again from the dead;
he ascended into heaven,
and sits at the right hand of God the Father almighty.
I believe in the Holy Spirit:
the holy, catholic Church,
the communion of saints,
the forgiveness of sins,
the resurrection of the body,
and the life everlasting.

425

God our Father, you have welcomed us home into your
    kingdom.
May your love surround those who have found their home
    in this church.
Help us to grow together:
to encourage one another,
to share our lives with one another,
to love one another.
Through Jesus Christ our Lord. Amen.

426

Lord, make us instruments of your peace:
    where there is hatred, let us sow love;
    where there is injury, pardon;
    where there is discord, union;
    where there is doubt, faith;
    where there is despair, hope;
    where there is darkness, light;
    where there is sadness, joy;
for your truth and mercy's sake. Amen.

427

VERMONT   LM

A. E. FLOYD (1877–1974)

SECOND TUNE

ANGELS' SONG   LM

ORLANDO GIBBONS (1583–1625)

May also be sung to YELLOW BITTERN, no. 229.

AMONG us our beloved stands,
and bids us see his nail-pierced hands,
points to his wounded feet and side,
blest emblems of the crucified.

2 When at his table sits the Lord,
what generous food adorns his board;
when Jesus comes his guests to meet,
the wine how rich, the bread how sweet!

3 If now with eyes earth-bound and dim,
we see the signs, but see not him,
then may his love the veil displace
and help us see him face to face.

C. H. SPURGEON (1834–92), altd.

428

First Tune

SPIRITUS VITAE   98 98

MARY JANE HAMMOND (1878–1964)

Second Tune

SACRAMENT   98 98

E. J. HOPKINS (1818–1901)

BREAD of the world, in mercy broken,
   wine of the soul, in mercy shed,
by whom the words of life were spoken,
   and in whose death our sins are dead,

2 Look on the heart by sorrow broken,
   look on the tears by sinners shed;
and be this feast to us the token
   that by your grace our souls are fed.

REGINALD HEBER (1783–1826)
based on John 6: 58

429

FOLKSONG (O WALY WALY)   98 98

English traditional melody
arr. JOHN WILSON (b. 1905)

*This may be repeated before v. 4, or before v. 3 if the hymn has been so divided.
If any of vv. 1–3 are sung by the choir alone, a soloist (or semichorus) may sing the melody,
with other voices humming or vocalizing the harmony.

AN upper room did our Lord prepare
    for those he loved until the end:
and his disciples still gather there
    to celebrate their risen friend.

2 A lasting gift Jesus gave his own—
    to share his bread, his loving cup.
Whatever burdens may bow us down,
    he by his cross shall lift us up.

3 And after supper he washed their feet,
    for service, too, is sacrament.
In him our joy shall be made complete—
    sent out to serve, as he was sent.

4 No end there is: we depart in peace.
    He loves beyond our uttermost:
in every room in our Father's house
    he will be there, as Lord and host.

F. PRATT GREEN (b. 1903)
based on Mark 14: 12–16, 22–4
and John 13: 3–5

430

AVE VIRGO VIRGINUM   76 76 D

Medieval melody from
J. HORN'S *Gesangbuch*, 1544

For a different harmonization of this tune (in G major) see no. 248.

CHRISTIAN people, raise your song,
  chase away all grieving;
sing your joy and be made strong,
  our Lord's life receiving.
Nature's gifts of wheat and vine
  now are set before us;
as we offer bread and wine
  Christ comes to restore us.

2 Come to welcome Christ today,
  God's great revelation.
He has pioneered the way
  of the new creation.
Greet him, Christ our risen King
  gladly recognizing,
as with joy we greet the spring
  out of winter rising.

COLIN P. THOMPSON (b. 1945)

431

ST HELEN   87 87 87

GEORGE C. MARTIN (1844–1916)

Small notes organ only.

CHRISTIANS, lift your hearts and voices,
　　let your praises be outpoured;
come with joy and exultation
　　to the table of the Lord;
come believing, come expectant,
　　in obedience to his word.

2 See, presiding at his table,
　　Jesus Christ our great high priest;
where he summons all his people,
　　none is greatest, none is least;
graciously he bids us welcome
　　to the eucharistic feast.

3 Lord, we offer in thanksgiving
　　life and work for you to bless;
yet unworthy is the offering
　　marred by pride and carelessness;
so, Lord, pardon our transgressions,
　　plant in us true holiness.

4 On the evening of his passion
　　Jesus gave the wine and bread,
so that all who love and serve him
　　shall for evermore be fed.
Taste and see the Lord is gracious,
　　feed upon the living bread.

JOHN E. BOWERS (b. 1923)

432

CATUROG NA NONOY 12 13 12 12

Bicolano folk melody (Philippines)
arr. LAWRENCE BARTLETT (b. 1933)

FAR beyond our mind's grasp
    and our tongue's declaring,
you are here in mystery,
    quietly, truly, without fail;
lifted once on Calvary,
    sin and weakness bearing,
O Lord, how wondrously
    you call us through the veil.

2 None of us is worthy
    of your gracious presence
in this meal together,
    yet the gift is yours by choice.
In the face of death,
    in you is safe dependence,
your promise is for life;
    we only can rejoice.

3 So our hearts are lifted
    to the realms above us,
nourished and united
    by the precious bread and wine:
here what sweet contentment,
    knowing that you love us!
We thank you for this feast,
    this fellowship divine.

4 Soon you bid us scatter,
    share what we inherit
from this home of blessing
    where we taste your peace and grace:
may our lives be altars
    glowing with your Spirit
to light the lamps of those
    who also seek your face.

FRANCISCO F. FELICIANO
para. JAMES MINCHIN (b. 1942)
tr. THE CHRISTIAN CONFERENCE OF ASIA

433

NETTLETON   87 87 D

American folk hymn
harm. ERIK ROUTLEY (1917–82)

Arrangement © Reformed Church in America

FATHER, it is right and fitting
   we should bring you thanks and praise.
Here we make our great thanksgiving,
   here our hearts to you we raise.
You alone are the creator
   of this world in which we live;
for its beauty and its splendour
   heartfelt thanks we freely give.

2 Thank you for the life of Jesus—
   son of Mary, child of God;
for the way he opened to us
   as our suffering path he trod;
for his fatal, firm obedience
   leading to that cross of wood;
and the joyful, hopeful radiance
   shining from our risen Lord.

3 On the night of his betrayal,
   this same Jesus gladly shared
with his friends his final meal,
   blessed the food they had prepared:
'In this wine my blood is given,
   and my body in this bread.
Eat and drink, proclaim my dying;
   do this till I come,' he said.

4 Here we keep our Lord's instruction,
   here his bitter death recall;
here proclaim his resurrection,
   in his service offer all.
Come, Lord come. Yes, through the Spirit
   may these people and this food
be Christ's body, here incarnate
   to sustain us in this world.

5 Here we join with all creation
   in the endless hymn of praise.
Every age and every nation
   all as one their voices raise:
'Holy, holy, Lord almighty,
   you are God of power and might.
Heaven and earth are filled with glory;
   through earth's darkness floods your light.'

DAVID GOODBOURN
based on 1 Corinthians 11: 23–6

434

SPIRITUS VITAE   98 98   MARY JANE HAMMOND (1878–1964)

Second Tune

SACRAMENT   98 98   E. J. HOPKINS (1818–1901)

FATHER, we thank you now for planting
　　your holy name within our hearts.
Knowledge and faith and life immortal
　　Jesus your Son to us imparts.

2 Lord, you have made us for your pleasure,
　　giving us food for all our days,
giving in Christ the bread eternal;
　　yours is the power, be yours the praise.

3 Over your Church, Lord, watch in mercy,
　　save it from evil, guard it still,
perfect it in your love, unite it,
　　cleansed in accordance with your will.

4 As grain, once scattered on the hillsides,
　　was in the broken bread made one,
so from all lands your Church be gathered
　　into the kingdom of your Son.

from the *Didache*, 2nd century
versified by F. BLAND TUCKER (1895–1984)

435

FIRST TUNE

SELFLESS LOVE   DCM

ANDREW MARIES (b. 1949)

HE gave his life in selfless love,
    for sinners once he came;
he had no stain of sin himself
    but bore our guilt and shame:
he took the cup of pain and death,
    his blood was freely shed;
we see his body on the cross,
    we share the living bread.

2 He did not come to call the good
    but sinners to repent;
it was the lame, the deaf, the blind
    for whom his life was spent:
to heal the sick, to find the lost—
    it was for such he came,
and round his table all may come
    to praise his holy name.

3 They heard him call his Father's name—
    then 'Finished!' was his cry;
like them we have forsaken him
    and left him there to die:
the sins that crucified him then
    are sins his blood has cured;
the love that bound him to a cross
    our freedom has ensured.

4 His body broken once for us
    is glorious now above;
the cup of blessing we receive,
    a sharing of his love:
as in his presence we partake,
    his dying we proclaim
until the hour of majesty
    when Jesus comes again.

CHRISTOPHER PORTEOUS (b. 1935)

435

COE FEN   DCM

KEN NAYLOR (b. 1931)

HE gave his life in selfless love,
　　for sinners once he came;
he had no stain of sin himself
　　but bore our guilt and shame:
he took the cup of pain and death,
　　his blood was freely shed;
we see his body on the cross,
　　we share the living bread.

2　He did not come to call the good
　　　but sinners to repent;
　it was the lame, the deaf, the blind
　　　for whom his life was spent:
　to heal the sick, to find the lost—
　　　it was for such he came,
　and round his table all may come
　　　to praise his holy name.

3　They heard him call his Father's name—
　　　then 'Finished!' was his cry;
　like them we have forsaken him
　　　and left him there to die:
　the sins that crucified him then
　　　are sins his blood has cured;
　the love that bound him to a cross
　　　our freedom has ensured.

4　His body broken once for us
　　　is glorious now above;
　the cup of blessing we receive,
　　　a sharing of his love:
　as in his presence we partake,
　　　his dying we proclaim
　until the hour of majesty
　　　when Jesus comes again.

CHRISTOPHER PORTEOUS (b. 1935)

436

TOULON   10 10 10 10

Genevan Psalter, 1551

Here, O my Lord, I see you face to face;
    here faith can touch and handle things unseen;
here I will grasp with firmer hand your grace,
    and all my helplessness upon you lean.

2 Here I will feed upon the bread of God,
    here drink with you the royal wine of heaven;
here I will lay aside each earthly load,
    here taste afresh the calm of sin forgiven.

3 Too soon we rise, the symbols disappear;
    the feast, though not the love, is past and gone;
the bread and wine remove, but you are here,
    nearer than ever; still my shield and sun.

4 Feast after feast thus comes and passes by,
    yet passing, points to the glad feast above,
giving sweet foretaste of the festal joy,
    the Lamb's great bridal feast of bliss and love.

HORATIUS BONAR (1808–89) altd.

437

First Tune

UNIVERSITY   CM

C. COLLIGNON (1725–85)

Second Tune

BARCHESTER FAIR   CM

CHRISTIAN STROVER (b. 1932)

Unison version

Harmony version

I COME with joy to meet my Lord,
   forgiven, loved and free,
in awe and wonder to recall
   his life laid down for me.

2 I come with Christians far and near,
   to find, as all are fed,
the new community of love
   in Christ's communion bread.

3 As Christ breaks bread and bids us share,
   each proud division ends.
The love that made us makes us one,
   and strangers now are friends.

4 And thus with joy we meet our Lord.
   His presence, always near,
is in such friendships better known:
   we see and praise him here.

5 Together met, together bound,
   we'll go our different ways,
and as his people in the world
   we'll live and speak his praise.

BRIAN A. WREN (b. 1936)

438

FIRST TUNE

ST ETHELWALD   SM

W. H. MONK (1823–89)

SECOND TUNE

BOD ALWYN   SM

DAVID JENKINS (1848–1915)

JESUS invites his saints
    to meet around his board;
here pardoned rebels sit and hold
    communion with their Lord.

2 Here we survey that love
    which spoke in every breath,
which crowned each action of his life,
    and triumphed in his death.

3 This holy bread and wine
    maintain our fainting breath,
by union with our living Lord,
    and interest in his death.

4 Our heavenly Father calls
    Christ and his members one;
we the young children of his love,
    and he the first-born Son.

5 We are but several parts
    of the same broken bread;
our body has its several limbs,
    but Jesus is the head.

6 Let all our powers be joined
    his glorious name to raise;
pleasure and love fill every mind
    and every voice be praise.

ISAAC WATTS (1674–1748)

439

HEREFORD   LM

S. S. WESLEY (1810–76)

JESUS, the joy of loving hearts,
 the fount of life, the light of men;
from the best bliss that earth imparts
 we turn unfilled to you again.

2 Your truth unchanged has ever stood;
 you save all those who on you call;
to those still seeking, you are good,
 to those who find you, all in all!

3 We taste of you, the living bread,
 and long to feast upon you still;
we drink of you, the fountain-head,
 our thirsty souls from you to fill.

4 Our restless spirits yearn for you,
 whichever way our lives are cast;
glad when your gracious smile we view,
 blest when our faith can hold you fast.

5 Jesus, forever with us stay,
 make all our moments calm and bright,
chase the dark night of sin away,
 shed on this world your holy light.

Latin, 12th century
tr. RAY PALMER (1808–87)

440

ST COLUMBA   87 87 Iambic   Ancient Irish hymn melody

HERE, Lord, we take the broken bread
  and drink the wine, believing
that by your life our souls are fed,
  your parting gifts receiving.

2 As you have given so we would give
    ourselves for others' healing;
  as you have lived, so we would live,
    the Father's love revealing.

CHARLES VENN PILCHER (1879–1961)

441

PICARDY 87 87 87

French traditional carol

LET all mortal flesh keep silence,
  and with awe and welcome stand;
harbour nothing earthly-minded;
  for, with blessing in his hand,
Christ our Lord with us is dwelling,
  loving homage to demand.

2 King of kings, yet born of Mary,
  as of old on earth he stood,
Lord of lords, in human vesture,
  in the body and the blood:
he will give to all the faithful
  his own self for heavenly food.

3 Rank on rank the hosts immortal
  sweep in joy before your face,
shining in the light exalted,
  friends and loved ones in embrace,
as the dark dissolves before you,
  light of all the human race.

4 At your feet the seraphs cluster,
  veil their faces in that light,
spirits of the just made perfect,
  now in timeless splendour bright,
saints and angels, all adore you,
  serve and praise you in the height.

Liturgy of St James
tr. PERCY DEARMER (1867–1936) altd.
v. 2 tr. GERARD MOULTRIE (1829–85)

442

ABINGDON   88 88 88

ERIK ROUTLEY (1917–82)

GREAT GOD, your love has called us here
as we, by love, for love were made.
Your living likeness still we bear,
though marred, dishonoured, disobeyed.
We come, with all our heart and mind
your call to hear, your love to find.

2 We come with self-inflicted pains
of broken trust and chosen wrong,
half-free, half-bound by inner chains,
by social forces swept along,
by powers and systems close confined
yet seeking hope for humankind.

3 Great God, in Christ you call our name
and then receive us as your own
not through some merit, right or claim
but by your gracious love alone.
We strain to glimpse your mercy seat
and find you kneeling at our feet.

4 Then take the towel, and break the bread,
and humble us, and call us friends.
Suffer and serve till all are fed
and show how grandly love intends
to work till all creation sings,
to fill all worlds, to crown all things.

5 Great God, in Christ you set us free
your life to live, your joy to share.
Give us your Spirit's liberty
to turn from guilt and dull despair
and offer all that faith can do
while love is making all things new.

BRIAN A. WREN (b. 1936)

443

LET US BREAK BREAD

American spiritual

When I   fall on my knees, with my

face to the ris- ing sun,   O   Lord, have mer-cy on   me.

LET us break bread together with the Lord;
let us break bread together with the Lord:

When I fall on my knees,
with my face to the rising sun,
O Lord, have mercy on me.

2 Let us drink wine together with the Lord . . .

3 Let us praise God together in the Lord . . .

based on an American spiritual

444

LIVING LORD   98 88 83

Words and music by
PATRICK APPLEFORD (b. 1925)

1. Lord Je-sus Christ,____ you____ have come to us,
2. Lord Je-sus Christ,____ now____ and ev-ery day
3. Lord Je-sus Christ,____ you____ have come to us,
4. Lord Je-sus Christ,____ I____ would come to you,

you____ are one with us, Ma - ry's son –____
teach____ us how to pray, Son of God.____
born____ as one of us, Ma - ry's son –____
live____ my life for you, Son of God;____

The unison version accompaniment is appropriate for the piano.
Organists may prefer to play the harmony version.
For a slightly different version of the guitar chords, see no. 547.

clean - sing our souls___ from all their sin,
You have com - mand - ed us to do
led out to die___ on Cal - va - ry,
all your com - mands___ I know are true;

pour - ing your love___ and good - ness in;
this in re - mem - brance, Lord, of you;
ri - sen from death___ to set us free;
your ma - ny gifts___ will make me new;

Je - sus, our love for you we sing,____
in - to our lives your power breaks through,_
liv - ing Lord Je - sus, help us see____
in - to my life your power breaks through,_

liv - ing__ Lord.
liv - ing__ Lord.
you are__ Lord.
liv - ing__ Lord.

679

445

CRESSWELL   88 97 with refrain

ANTHONY MILNER (b. 1925)

Rich-er than gold is the love of my Lord: bet-ter than splen-dour or wealth.

LOVE is his word, love is his way,
    feasting with men, fasting alone,
living and dying, rising again,
    love, only love, is his way.

    Richer than gold is the love of my Lord:
    better than splendour or wealth.

2 Love is his way, love is his mark,
    sharing his last Passover feast,
Christ at his table, host to the twelve,
    love, only love, is his mark.

3 Love is his mark, love is his sign,
    bread for our strength, wine for our joy,
'This is my body, this is my blood.'
    Love, only love, is his sign.

4 Love is his sign, love is his news;
    'Do this,' he said, 'lest you forget
all my deep sorrow, all my dear blood.'
    Love, only love, is his news.

5 Love is his news, love is his name,
    we are his own, chosen and called,
family, brethren, cousins and kin.
    Love, only love, is his name.

6 Love is his name, love is his law;
    hear his command, all who are his:
'Love one another, I have loved you.'
    Love, only love, is his law.

7 Love is his law, love is his word:
    love of the Lord, Father and Word,
love of the Spirit, God ever one.
    Love, only love, is his word.

LUKE CONNAUGHTON (1917–79)

446

FIRST TUNE

English traditional carol
from SANDYS' *Christmas Carols*, 1833

SANDYS SM

SECOND TUNE

From a melody in M. WEISSE'S
Ein Neu Gesengbuchlen, 1531

AUGUSTINE (GILDAS) SM

Now Jesus we obey
    your last and kindest word:
and in your own appointed way
    we come to meet our Lord.

2 Our hearts we open wide
    to make the Saviour room;
behold! the Lamb, the crucified,
    the sinner's friend has come.

3 Lord, in remembrance, we
    take now this bread and wine
as your own dying legacy
    and our redemption's sign.

4 Your presence makes the feast;
    now let our spirits feel
the glory not to be expressed,
    the joy unspeakable.

5 Now let our souls be fed
    with manna from above,
and over us your banner spread
    of everlasting love.

CHARLES WESLEY (1707–88)

447

WAS LEBET   12 10 12 10   *Reinhardt MS*, Üttingen, 1754

PASSOVER God, we remember your faithfulness,
　　God of the exodus, friend of the poor;
people bowed down with the burden of powerlessness,
　　sin in its ruthlessness making them slaves.

2 Still people shrivel, imprisoned in bitterness,
　　hemmed in by fear and diminished by hate;
tormented prisoners and perishing hungry ones,
　　broken humanity calls for your aid.

3 You summoned Moses to work for the freedom march,
　　you called the slaves to be people of hope;
set free from Egypt, you led them through desert lands,
　　loving commands gave them justice and truth.

4 You gave the travellers bread in the wilderness;
　　strengthen us now with the bread that we share:
bread for the struggle and wine for rejoicing;
　　in Christ you free us and teach us to care.

5 We are your people, still called to a promised land,
　　called for a purpose with Christ as the way;
grant us commitment to wholeness and liberty,
　　strength for the journey and grace for each day.

CHRISTOPHER ELLIS (b. 1949)

448

THE ASH GROVE   12 11 12 11 D   Welsh traditional melody

THE LORD'S SUPPER

SENT forth by God's blessing, our true faith confessing,
    the people of God from his table take leave.
The supper is ended: O now be extended
    the fruits of his service in all who believe.
The seed of his teaching, our hungry souls reaching,
    shall blossom in action for all humankind.
His grace shall incite us, his love shall unite us
    to work for his kingdom, his purpose to find.

2 With praise and thanksgiving to God ever-living
    the task of our everyday life we will face.
Our faith ever sharing, in love ever caring,
    embracing as neighbours all those of each race.
One feast that has fed us, one light that has led us,
    unite us as one in his life that we share.
Then may all the living, with praise and thanksgiving,
    give honour to Christ and his name that we bear.

OMER WESTENDORF (b. 1916)

449

GRAFTON   87 87 87

French church melody
from *Chants Ordinaires de l'Office Divin*,
Paris, 1881

SING, my tongue, the Saviour's glory,
    of his cross the mystery sing;
lift on high the wondrous trophy,
    tell the triumph of the King:
he, the world's Redeemer, conquers
    death, through death now vanquishing.

2 Born for us and for us given,
    Son of Man, like us below,
He as man with us abiding
    dwells, the seed of life to sow;
he, our heavy griefs partaking,
    thus fulfils his life of woe.

3 Word made flesh! His word life-giving,
    gives his flesh our meat to be,
bids us drink his blood believing,
    through his death, we life shall see:
blessèd they, who thus receiving
    are from death and sin set free.

4 Low in adoration bending,
    now our hearts our God revere;
faith her aid to sight is lending,
    though unseen the Lord is near;
ancient types and shadows ending,
    Christ our Paschal Lamb is here.

5 Praise for ever, thanks and blessing,
    yours, our gracious Father, be;
praise be yours, dear Christ, for bringing
    life and immortality;
praise be yours, God's quickening Spirit,
    praise through all eternity.

from THOMAS AQUINAS (*c.*1227–74)

450

FIRST TUNE

BUCKLAND   77 77

L. G. HAYNE (1836–83)

SECOND TUNE

CULBACH   77 77

SCHEFFLER'S, *Heilige Seelenlust*, 1657

SPREAD the table of the Lord,
    break the bread and pour the wine;
gathered at the sacred board,
    share in faith the feast divine.

2 Saints and martyrs of the faith
    to the cross have turned their eyes,
sharing, in their life and death,
    that eternal sacrifice.

3 Humbly now my place I claim
    in that glorious band and true,
proud confessors of the name,
    breaking bread, O Christ, with you.

4 By the memory of your love,
    to the glory of the Lord,
here I raise your cross above,
    and to arm me take your sword.

5 Guided by your mighty hand,
    all your mind I would fulfil,
loyal to your least command,
    serving you with steadfast will.

G. O. GREGORY (1881–1972)

451

KILLIBEGS   LM

WILLIAM DAVIES (b. 1921)

May also be sung to NIAGARA, no. 543.

Now let us from this table rise,
　renewed in body, mind and soul;
with Christ we die and live again;
　his selfless love has made us whole.

2 With minds alert, upheld by grace,
　　to spread the Word in speech and deed,
we follow in the steps of Christ,
　　at one with all in hope and need.

3 To fill each human house with love,
　　it is the sacrament of care;
the work that Christ began to do
　　we humbly pledge ourselves to share.

4 Then give us courage, Father God,
　　to choose again the pilgrim way,
and help us to accept with joy
　　the challenge of tomorrow's day.

FRED KAAN (b. 1929)

452

STAY WITH US

JACQUES BERTHIER
as sung at Taizé

Stay with us, O Lord Je - sus Christ: night will soon fall. Then stay with us, O Lord Je - sus Christ: light in our dark - ness.

453

ACH GOTT UND HERR   87 87 Iambic

Melody in
As Hymnodus Sacer, Leipzig, 1625
adpt. and harm. J. S. BACH (1685–1750)

SECOND TUNE

CURBAR EDGE (slightly modified)   87 87 Iambic   BRIAN R. HOARE (b. 1935)

Music © B. Hoare/Jubilate Hymns

STRENGTHEN for service, Lord, the hands
that holy things have taken;
let ears that now have heard your songs
to clamour never waken.

2 Lord, may the tongues which 'holy' sang
    keep free from all deceiving;
  the eyes which saw your love be bright,
    your blessed hope perceiving.

3 The feet that tread your holy courts,
    from light, Lord, never banish;
  the bodies by your body fed
    with your new life replenish.

Liturgy of Malabar
tr. C. W. HUMPHREYS (1840–1921)
PERCY DEARMER (1867–1936)

454

KYRIE ELEISON   From the liturgy of the Russian Orthodox Church

Ky - ri - e   e - lei - son,   Ky - ri - e   e - lei - son,

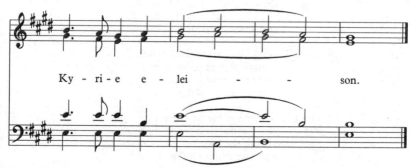

Ky - ri - e   e - lei   — —   son.

Best sung unaccompanied.

KYRIE eleison,
Kyrie eleison,
Kyrie eleison.

(*Lord have mercy.*)

455

BUCER   SM

Cantica Laudis, 1850

May also be sung to ST ETHELWALD, no. 438.

THE Son of God proclaim,
   the Lord of time and space;
the God who bade the light break forth
   now shines in Jesus' face.

2 He, God's creative word,
   the Church's Lord and head,
here bids us gather as his friends
   and share his wine and bread.

3 Behold his outstretched hands;
   though all was in his power
he took the towel and basin then,
   and serves us in this hour.

4 The Lord of life and death
   with wondering praise we sing;
we break the bread at his command,
   and name him God and King.

5 We take this cup in hope;
   for he, who gladly bore
the shameful cross, is risen again
   and reigns for evermore.

BASIL E. BRIDGE (b. 1927)

456

SANCTUS

JACQUES BERTHIER
as sung at Taizé

CANTOR

Ho - ly, ho - ly, ho - ly Lord, God of power____ and might,

(A) CONGREGATION (*in canon*) (B)

Sanc - tus, sanc - tus, sanc - tus Do - mi - nus,

CHOIR

(*hum*)

ACCOMPANIMENT

F   B♭   Gm   C   F   B♭   Gm   C

The congregational line may be sung as a simple melody or as a four-part canon, either with the printed accompaniment or unaccompanied. If there is a choir, it may hum the harmony provided. The cantor part is optional, and may be sung by a soloist or solo group while the congregation continue with the melody.

457

HOLY, HOLY, HOLY

Sanctus from *Deutsche Messe*, 1826
F. SCHUBERT (1797–1828)

Ho - ly, ho - ly, ho - ly, God al - migh - ty Lord! _____ Ho - ly, ho - ly, ho - ly, ev - ery - where a - dored! _____

Glo - ry to the Fa - ther, glo - ry to the Son _____ and the Ho - ly Spi - rit, e - ver three in one. _____

1. He with - out be - gin - ning, he th'e -
2. Power and love and won - der circ - ling

(*Fine*)

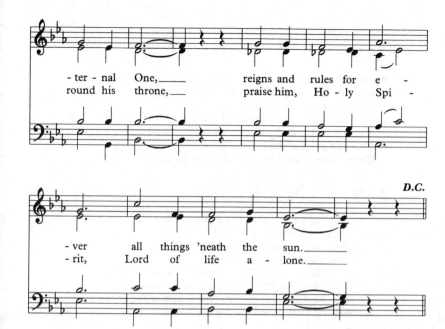

-ter-nal One,____ reigns and rules for e -
round his throne,____ praise him, Ho - ly Spi -

D.C.

-ver all things 'neath the sun.____
-rit, Lord of life a - lone.____

Holy, holy, holy,
God almighty Lord!
Holy, holy, holy,
everywhere adored!

HE without beginning,
he the eternal One,
reigns and rules for ever
all things 'neath the sun.

Glory to the Father,
glory to the Son
and the Holy Spirit,
ever three in one.

2 Power and love and wonder
circling round his throne,
praise him, Holy Spirit,
Lord of life alone.

Glory to the Father,
glory to the Son
and the Holy Spirit,
ever three in one.

based on the Sanctus

701

458

What shall we render to the Lord for all his bounty toward us?
We will lift up the cup of salvation
and call on the name of the Lord.
Christ our Passover is sacrificed for us.
Therefore let us keep the feast.
O taste and see that the Lord is good!
Happy are they who take refuge in him!

459

He grew up before the Lord like a young plant
whose roots are in parched ground;
he had no beauty, no majesty to draw our eyes,
no grace to make us delight in him;
his form, disfigured, lost all the likeness of a man,
his beauty changed beyond all human semblance.
He was despised, he shrank from the sight of men,
tormented and humbled by suffering.

After all his pains he shall be bathed in light,
after his disgrace he shall be fully vindicated;
so shall he enjoy long life and see his children's children,
and in his hands the Lord's cause shall prosper.

Alleluia! Christ is risen!
Alleluia! Alleluia! Alleluia!
Christ is risen indeed!

460

Father, we come to this table with gratitude, faith and hope.

Christ died for us:
accept our thanks and praise;
Christ is here:
give us faith to know his presence;
Christ is coming again:
may this hope lighten the dark world.

With thanksgiving we remember,
with joy we welcome our risen Lord,
with confidence we believe that the future is yours.
Through Christ our Lord. Amen.

461

We do not presume
to come to this your table, merciful Lord,
trusting in our own righteousness,
but in your manifold and great mercies.
We are not worthy
so much as to gather up the crumbs under your table.
But you are the same Lord,
whose nature is always to have mercy.
Grant us therefore, gracious Lord,
so to eat the flesh of your dear Son Jesus Christ,
and to drink his blood,
that we may evermore dwell in him,
and he in us. Amen.

462

Our Father God,
there is no place we would rather be,
no one whose presence we more desire,
no love that can compare with yours.
By your Spirit, make this holy ground,
and surround us with everlasting love.
Through Jesus Christ our Lord. Amen.

463

Lift up your hearts!
   We lift them to the Lord!
Let us give thanks to the Lord our God.
   It is right to give him thanks and praise.
It is not only right, it is our duty and our joy, at all times and in all places,
to give you thanks and praise, holy Father, heavenly King, almighty and
eternal God, through Jesus Christ, your only Son, our Lord.

(*Extempore prayer*)

Therefore with angels and archangels, and with all the company of heaven,
we proclaim your great and glorious name, for ever praising you and saying:

   Holy! Holy! Holy!
   God of power and might,
   heaven and earth are full of your glory.
   Hosanna in the highest!
   Blessed is he who comes in the name of the Lord!
   Hosanna in the highest!

God our Father, pour out the Holy Spirit
upon your people, that they may have faith,
and upon these gifts of bread and wine,
that they may be for us the body and blood
of our risen and ascended Lord;
may we, eating and drinking in faith,
receive Christ to ourselves again,
for the strengthening of our faith,
the assuring of our hope,
and the deepening of our love.
Through Jesus Christ our Lord. Amen.

464

Your death, O Lord, we commemorate.
Your resurrection we confess.
Your second coming we await.
Glory be to you, O Christ.

**Christ has died!
Christ is risen!
Christ will come again!**

465   A PERSONAL PRAYER WHEN RECEIVING COMMUNION

**Lord, unite me to yourself in this communion:
as you have given yourself to me,
may I give myself to you.
Use me, as you have used this bread and wine,
to share your life with the world.
For your name's sake. Amen.**

466

**Almighty God,
we thank you for feeding us
with the body and blood of your Son Jesus Christ.
Through him we offer you
our souls and bodies
to be a living sacrifice.
Send us out in the power of your Spirit,
to live and work to your praise and glory. Amen.**

467

We have seen your glory here, O Lord,
  may we see it in the world.
We have known your presence here, O Lord,
  may we know it everywhere.
We have received your love, O Lord,
  may we give you ours.
Through Christ our Lord. **Amen.**

468

We give thanks to the Father who has fitted us
to share the heritage of God's people in the realm of light.
  **He rescued us from the domain of darkness
  and brought us into the kingdom of his dear Son.**

In him, our release is secured and our sins forgiven.
  **He is the image of the invisible God;
  his is the primacy over all created things.**

The whole universe has been created through him and for him.
  **He exists before everything
  and all things are held together in him.**

Glory to the Father!
  Glory to the Son!
Glory to the Holy Spirit!
  One God, for ever. Amen.

469

Rejoice, our Redeemer has come!
  Our sins are washed away.

Rejoice, he shall renew the whole heaven and earth!
  Christ has come amongst us.

Rejoice, he has broken death and God has opened the gates of heaven.
  Alleluia! Christ is risen!

[*see also no. 81*]

470

A NEW COMMANDMENT

Music anon.
arr. ANTHONY F. CARVER (b. 1947)
Words based on John 13: 34–5

A new com - mand-ment I give un - to you: that you love___ one an - oth - er as I___ have loved you, that you love_ one an - oth-er as I have loved you. By this shall all know that

COMMUNITY IN CHRIST

you are my dis - ci - ples, if____ you have

love one for an - oth - er.____ By this shall

all know that you are my dis - ci - ples, if

you have love one for an - oth - er.

707

471

BIND US TOGETHER

B. GILLMAN
arr. DAVID TRAFFORD (b. 1950)

Bind us together, Lord,
bind us together
with cords that cannot be broken.
Bind us together, Lord,
bind us together,
O bind us together with love.

THERE is only one God,
there is only one King,
there is only one body,
that is why we sing:

2 Made for the glory of God,
purchased by his precious Son.
Born with the right to be clean,
for Jesus the victory has won.

3 You are the family of God,
you are the promise divine,
you are God's chosen desire,
you are the glorious new wine.

B. GILLMAN

472

FIRST TUNE

DENNIS   SM

H. G. NÄGELI (1773–1836)

SECOND TUNE

MYNYDD DU   SM

JOHN ELLIS (b. 1931)

BLEST be the tie that binds
    our hearts in Christian love;
the fellowship of kindred minds
    is like to that above.

2 Before our Father's throne
    we pour our ardent prayers;
our fears, our hopes, our aims are one,
    our comforts and our cares.

3 We share our mutual woes,
    our mutual burdens bear,
and often for each other flows
    the sympathizing tear.

4 When for a while we part,
    this thought will soothe our pain,
that we shall still be joined in heart,
    and hope to meet again.

5 This glorious hope revives
    our courage by the way,
while each in expectation lives,
    and longs to see the day.

6 From sorrow, toil, and pain,
    and sin we shall be free;
and perfect love and friendship reign
    through all eternity.

JOHN FAWCETT (1740–1817)

473

SERVANT SONG   87 87

RICHARD GILLARD (b. 1953)
arr. BETTY PULKINGHAM (b. 1928)

BROTHER, sister, let me serve you,
    let me be as Christ to you;
pray that I may have the grace to
    let you be my servant too.

2 We are pilgrims on a journey
    and companions on the road;
we are here to help each other
    walk the mile and bear the load.

3 I will hold the Christ-light for you
    in the night-time of your fear;
I will hold my hand out to you,
    speak the peace you long to hear.

4 I will weep when you are weeping;
    when you laugh I'll laugh with you;
I will share your joy and sorrow
    till we've seen this journey through.

5 When we sing to God in heaven
    we shall find such harmony,
born of all we've known together
    of Christ's love and agony.

6 Brother, sister, let me serve you,
    let me be as Christ to you;
pray that I may have the grace to
    let you be my servant too.

RICHARD GILLARD (b. 1953)

474

WESTMINSTER ABBEY   87 87 87

Adpt. from
HENRY PURCELL (1659–95)

COMMUNITY IN CHRIST

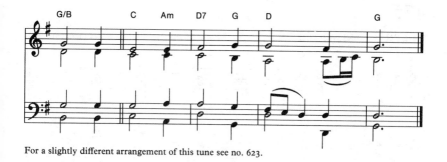

For a slightly different arrangement of this tune see no. 623.

CHRIST is made the sure foundation,
    Christ the head and corner-stone,
chosen of the Lord and precious,
    binding all the Church in one;
holy Zion's help for ever,
    and her confidence alone.

2 All within that holy city
    dearly loved of God on high,
in exultant jubilation
    sing, in perfect harmony;
God the one-in-three adoring
    in glad hymns eternally.

3 We as living stones implore you:
    come among us, Lord, today!
With your gracious loving kindness
    hear your children as we pray;
and the fullness of your blessing
    in our fellowship display.

4 Here entrust to all your servants
    what we long from you to gain,
that on earth and in the heavens
    we one people shall remain,
till, united in your glory,
    evermore with you we reign.

5 Praise and honour to the Father,
    praise and honour to the Son,
praise and honour to the Spirit,
    ever three and ever one;
one in power and one in glory
    while eternal ages run.

from Latin, 7th century
J. M. NEALE (1818–66)

475

VULPIUS   888 with alleluias   Melody from M. VULPIUS'S *Gesangbuch*, 1609

Al - le - lu - ia, al - le - lu - ia, al - le - lu - ia!

For a different arrangement of this tune (in C major) see no. 250.

CHRIST is the King! O friends rejoice;
brothers and sisters, with one voice
make each one know he is your choice.
   Alleluia!

2 O magnify the Lord, and raise
anthems of joy and holy praise
for Christ's brave saints of ancient days.

3 They with a faith for ever new
followed the King, and round him drew
thousands of faithful servants true.

4 O Christian women, Christian men,
all the world over, seek again
the way disciples followed then.

5 Christ through all ages is the same:
place the same hope in his great name;
with the same faith his word proclaim.

6 Let love's unconquerable might
your scattered companies unite
in service to the Lord of light.

7 So shall God's will on earth be done,
new lamps be lit, new tasks begun,
and the whole Church at last be one.

G. K. A. BELL (1883–1958)

476

First Tune

TALLIS'S CANON   LM

THOMAS TALLIS (*c*.1510–85)
adpt. T. RAVENSCROFT, *Psalmes*, 1621

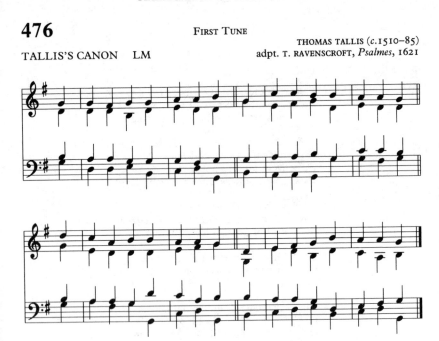

Second Tune

DUNEDIN   LM

VERNON GRIFFITHS (1894–1983)

Music © 1971 Faber Music Ltd. from the *New Catholic Hymnal*

COME, all who look to Christ today,
　　stretch out your hands, enlarge your mind,
together share his living way
　　where all who humbly seek will find.

2 Come, all who will from every race;
　　find here new powers of brotherhood,
accept the Spirit's strong embrace
　　which binds us to the common good.

3 Come, young and old from every Church,
　　bring all your treasures of prayer,
join the dynamic Spirit's search
　　to press beyond the truths we share.

4 Bring your traditions' richest store,
　　your hymns and rites and cherished creeds;
explore our visions, pray for more,
　　since God delights to meet fresh needs.

5 Come, trust in Christ and live in peace,
　　anticipate that final light
when strife and bigotry shall cease,
　　and faith be lost in praise and sight.

RICHARD G. JONES (b. 1926)

477

FIRST TUNE

Melody and bass by
ORLANDO GIBBONS (1583–1625)

SONG 1   10 10 10 10 10 10

ETERNAL Ruler of the ceaseless round
  of circling planets singing on their way;
guide of the nations from the night profound
  into the glory of the perfect day;
rule in our hearts, that we may ever be
guided and strengthened, and upheld by thee.

2 We are of thee, the children of thy love,
  the brothers of thy well-belovèd Son;
descend, O Holy Spirit, like a dove,
  into our hearts, that we may be as one:
as one with thee, to whom we ever tend;
as one with him, our brother and our friend.

3 We would be one in hatred of all wrong,
  one in our love of all things sweet and fair,
one with the joy that breaketh into song,
  one with the grief that trembles into prayer,
one in the power that makes thy children free
to follow truth, and thus to follow thee.

4 O clothe us with thy heavenly armour, Lord,
  thy trusty shield, thy sword of love divine;
our inspiration be thy constant word;
  we ask no victories that are not thine:
give or withhold, let pain or pleasure be;
enough to know that we are serving thee.

J. W. CHADWICK (1840–1904)

477

SECOND TUNE

UNDE ET MEMORES   10 10 10 10 10 10

W. H. MONK (1823–89)

ETERNAL Ruler of the ceaseless round
  of circling planets singing on their way;
guide of the nations from the night profound
  into the glory of the perfect day;
rule in our hearts, that we may ever be
guided and strengthened, and upheld by thee.

2 We are of thee, the children of thy love,
  the brothers of thy well-belovèd Son;
descend, O Holy Spirit, like a dove,
  into our hearts, that we may be as one:
as one with thee, to whom we ever tend;
as one with him, our brother and our friend.

3 We would be one in hatred of all wrong,
  one in our love of all things sweet and fair,
one with the joy that breaketh into song,
  one with the grief that trembles into prayer,
one in the power that makes thy children free
to follow truth, and thus to follow thee.

4 O clothe us with thy heavenly armour, Lord,
  thy trusty shield, thy sword of love divine;
our inspiration be thy constant word;
  we ask no victories that are not thine:
give or withhold, let pain or pleasure be;
enough to know that we are serving thee.

J. W. CHADWICK (1840–1904)

478

Music by R. VAUGHAN WILLIAMS (1872–1958)
Words by W. W. HOW (1823–97) altd.

SINE NOMINE
10 10 10 with alleluias

VERSES 1, 2, 6 and 7
Unison

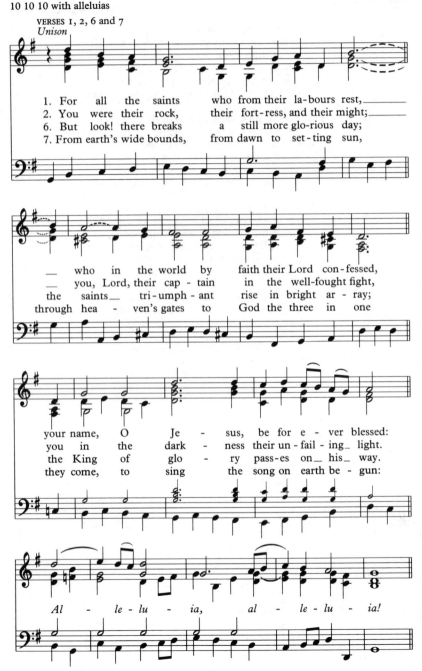

1. For all the saints who from their la-bours rest,_____
2. You were their rock, their fort-ress, and their might;_____
6. But look! there breaks a still more glo-rious day;
7. From earth's wide bounds, from dawn to set-ting sun,

___ who in the world by faith their Lord con-fessed,
___ you, Lord, their cap - tain in the well-fought fight,
the saints___ tri - umph - ant rise in bright ar - ray;
through hea - ven's gates to God the three in one

your name, O Je - sus, be for e - ver blessed:
you in the dark - ness their un - fail - ing_ light.
the King of glo - ry pass-es on_ his_ way.
they come, to sing the song on earth be - gun:

Al - le-lu - ia, al - le-lu - ia!

724

COMMUNITY IN CHRIST

VERSES 3, 4 and 5
Harmony

3. O blest com - mu - nion, fel - low-ship di - vine,
4. And when the fight is fierce, the war - fare long,
5. The gold - en eve - ning bright-ens in the west:

we fee - bly strug - gle, they in glo - ry shine,
far off we hear the dis - tant tri - umph - song;
soon, soon to faith - ful war - riors comes their rest,

yet all are__ yours and__ all in praise com - bine,__
and hearts are__ brave a - gain, and arms are_ strong._
the peace - ful_ calm of__ pa - ra -dise_ the_ blessed._

Al - le - lu - ia,__ al - le - lu - ia!

479

MOUNTAIN CHRISTIANS
76 76 D (Irregular)

Attrib. JOHN MANNIN (1802–65)
in the *Fellowship Hymn Book*, 1909

REFRAIN

For the might of your arm we___ bless you, our   God, our fa-thers' God.

FOR the might of your arm we bless you,
  our God, our fathers' God;
you have kept your pilgrim people
  by the strength of your staff and rod;
you have called us to the journey
  which faithless feet ne'er trod;

  For the might of your arm we bless you,
  our God, our fathers' God.

2 For the love of Christ constraining
    that bound their hearts as one;
  for the faith in truth and freedom,
    in which their work was done:
  for the peace of God's evangel
    wherewith their feet were shod;

3 We are watchers of a beacon
    whose light must never die;
  we are guardians of an altar
    that shows you ever nigh;
  we are children of the freemen
    who have gained your rest, O God;

4 May the shadow of your presence
    around our camp be spread;
  baptize us with the courage
    with which you blessed our dead;
  O keep us in the pathway
    their saintly feet have trod;

C. SILVESTER HORNE (1865–1914)

479

STOKESAY CASTLE   76 76 D (Irregular)   ERIC H. THIMAN (1900–75)

might of your arm we _ *bless you, our God, our fa-thers' God.*

*Optional soprano and tenor parts for v. 4.

FOR the might of your arm we bless you,
　　our God, our fathers' God;
you have kept your pilgrim people
　　by the strength of your staff and rod;
you have called us to the journey
　　which faithless feet ne'er trod;

　　　For the might of your arm we bless you,
　　　our God, our fathers' God.

2 For the love of Christ constraining
　　that bound their hearts as one;
for the faith in truth and freedom,
　　in which their work was done:
for the peace of God's evangel
　　wherewith their feet were shod;

3 We are watchers of a beacon
　　whose light must never die;
we are guardians of an altar
　　that shows you ever nigh;
we are children of the freemen
　　who have gained your rest, O God;

4 May the shadow of your presence
　　around our camp be spread;
baptize us with the courage
　　with which you blessed our dead;
O keep us in the pathway
　　their saintly feet have trod;

C. SILVESTER HORNE (1865–1914)

729

480

ABBOT'S LEIGH   87 87 D

CYRIL V. TAYLOR (1907–91)

GLORIOUS things of you are spoken,
  Zion, city of our God!
He whose word cannot be broken,
  formed you for his own abode:
On the rock of ages founded,
  what can shake your sure repose?
With salvation's wall surrounded,
  you may smile at all your foes.

2 See, the streams of living waters,
    springing from eternal love,
  well supply your sons and daughters,
    and all fear of want remove:
  who can faint, while such a river
    ever flows their thirst to assuage—
  grace which like the Lord the giver
    never fails from age to age?

3 Blest inhabitants of Zion,
    washed in the Redeemer's blood,
  Jesus, whom their souls rely on,
    makes them kings and priests to God.
  'Tis his love his people raises
    over self to reign as kings;
  and as priests, his solemn praises
    each for a thank-offering brings.

4 Saviour, since of Zion's city
    I, through grace, a member am,
  let the world deride or pity,
    I will glory in your name:
  fading is the worldling's pleasure,
    all his boasted pomp and show;
  solid joys and lasting treasure
    none but Zion's children know.

JOHN NEWTON (1725–1807)
based on Psalm 46: 4
and Psalm 87: 3

480

AUSTRIA   87 87 D

F. J. HAYDN (1732–1809)

GLORIOUS things of you are spoken,
  Zion, city of our God!
He whose word cannot be broken,
  formed you for his own abode:
On the rock of ages founded,
  what can shake your sure repose?
With salvation's wall surrounded,
  you may smile at all your foes.

2 See, the streams of living waters,
  springing from eternal love,
well supply your sons and daughters,
  and all fear of want remove:
who can faint, while such a river
  ever flows their thirst to assuage—
grace which like the Lord the giver
  never fails from age to age?

3 Blest inhabitants of Zion,
  washed in the Redeemer's blood,
Jesus, whom their souls rely on,
  makes them kings and priests to God.
'Tis his love his people raises
  over self to reign as kings;
and as priests, his solemn praises
  each for a thank-offering brings.

4 Saviour, since of Zion's city
  I, through grace, a member am,
let the world deride or pity,
  I will glory in your name:
fading is the worldling's pleasure,
  all his boasted pomp and show;
solid joys and lasting treasure
  none but Zion's children know.

JOHN NEWTON (1725–1807)
based on Psalm 46: 4
and Psalm 87: 3

481

GRAND ISLE Irregular   J. H. HOPKINS (1861–1945)

I SING a song of the saints of God,
    patient and brave and true,
who toiled and fought and lived and died
    for the Lord they loved and knew.
And one was a doctor, and one was a queen,
and one was a shepherdess on the green:
they were all of them saints of God; and I mean,
    God helping, to be one too.

2 They loved their Lord so good and dear,
    and his love made them strong;
and they followed the right, for Jesus' sake,
    the whole of their good lives long.
And one was a soldier, and one was a priest,
and one was slain by a fierce wild beast:
and there's not any reason, no, not the least,
    why I shouldn't be one too.

3 They lived not only in ages past,
    there are hundreds of thousands still;
the world is bright with the joyous saints
    who love to do Jesus' will.
You can meet them in school, or in lanes, or at sea,
in church, or in trains, or in shops, or at tea,
for the saints of God began just like me,
    and I mean to be one too.

LESBIA SCOTT (1898–1986)

482

ST STEPHEN   CM   WILLIAM JONES (1726–1800)

SECOND TUNE

ST BERNARD   CM   *Tochter Zion*, Cologne, 1741

In Christ there is no east or west,
    in him no south or north,
but one great fellowship of love
    throughout the whole wide earth.

2 In him shall true hearts everywhere
    their high communion find:
his service is the golden cord
    close-binding all mankind.

3 Join hands then, people of the faith,
    whate'er your race may be!
Who serves my Father as his child
    is surely kin to me.

4 In Christ now meet both east and west,
    in him meet south and north,
all Christian souls are one in him,
    throughout the whole wide earth.

JOHN OXENHAM (1852–1941)

483

FOR I'M BUILDING

D. RICHARDS

For I'm build-ing a peo-ple of po-wer and I'm mak-ing a peo-ple of praise, that will move through this land by my Spi-rit,— and will glo-ri-fy my pre-cious name. Build your Church, Lord, make us strong, Lord, join our hearts, Lord, through your Son. Make us one, Lord, in your bo-dy, in the king-dom of your Son.—

484

LET THERE BE LOVE

DAVE BILBROUGH

LET there be love shared among us,
let there be love in our eyes,
may now your love sweep this nation,
cause us, O Lord, to arise.

Give us a fresh understanding
of brotherly love that is real,
let there be love shared among us,
let there be love.

DAVE BILBROUGH

485

TICHFIELD   77 77 D

J. RICHARDSON (1816–79)

COMMUNITY IN CHRIST

MAIDSTONE   77 77 D

W. B. GILBERT (1829–1910)

Lord from whom all blessings flow,
perfecting the Church below,
steadfast may we cleave to thee,
love the mystic union be:
join our faithful spirits, join
each to each, and all to thine;
lead us through the paths of peace
on to perfect holiness.

2 Move and actuate and guide;
various gifts to each divide;
placed according to thy will,
let us all our work fulfil;
never from our calling move;
needful to each other prove;
use the grace on each bestowed,
tempered by the art of God.

3 Lovingly may we agree;
filled with understanding be;
there is neither bond nor free,
great nor servile, Lord, in thee:
love, like death, hath all destroyed,
rendered all distinctions void;
names and sects and parties fall,
thou, O Christ, art all in all.

CHARLES WESLEY (1707–88)

486

LONDONDERRY AIR   11 10 11 10 D

Irish traditional melody
arr. DONALD DAVISON (b. 1937)

For another arrangement of this tune see no. 381.

Lord of the Church, we pray for our renewing:
  Christ over all, our undivided aim;
fire of the Spirit, burn for our enduing,
  wind of the Spirit, fan the living flame!
We turn to Christ amid our fear and failing,
  the will that lacks the courage to be free,
the weary labours, all but unavailing,
  to bring us nearer what a Church should be.

2 Lord of the Church, we seek a Father's blessing,
    a true repentance and a faith restored,
  a swift obedience and a new possessing,
    filled with the Holy Spirit of the Lord!
  We turn to Christ from all our restless striving,
    unnumbered voices with a single prayer—
  the living water for our souls' reviving,
    in Christ to live, and love and serve and care.

3 Lord of the Church, we long for our uniting,
    true to one calling, by one vision stirred;
  one cross proclaiming and one creed reciting,
    one in the truth of Jesus and his word;
  so lead us on till toil and trouble ended,
    one Church triumphant one new song shall sing
  to praise his glory, risen and ascended,
    Christ over all, the everlasting King!

TIMOTHY DUDLEY-SMITH (b. 1926)

743

487

South African traditional melody
arr. A. NYBERG

SIYAHAMBA   Irregular

1. We are march - ing in the light of God, __ we are march-ing in the light of God, __ we are march-ing in the light of, the light of God. __ We are march-ing, march-ing, we are march-ing, oh, __ march-ing, we are march-ing in the light of God. __

We are march - ing, We are march-ing, march-ing, we are

WE are marching in the light of God,
we are marching in the light of God,
we are marching in the light of God,
we are marching in the light of God.

> We are marching, oh,
> we are marching in the light of God.
> We are marching, oh,
> we are marching in the light of God.

2 We are living in the love of God.

3 We are moving in the power of God.

South African traditional
tr. A NYBERG

488

THE GOLDEN CHAIN   87 87 887

J. BARNBY (1836–96)

WE come unto our fathers' God:
   their rock is our salvation;
the eternal arms, their dear abode,
   we make our habitation;
we bring you, Lord, the praise they brought;
we seek you as the saints have sought
   in every generation.

2 The fire divine, their steps that led,
   still travels bright before us;
the heavenly shield, around them spread,
   is still held high above us;
the grace those sinners that subdued,
the strength those weaklings that renewed,
   now vanquishes, restores us.

3 Their joy unto their Lord we bring,
   their song to us descending;
the Spirit who in them did sing
   his music now is lending.
His song in them, in us, is one:
we raise it high, we send it on—
   the song that has no ending.

4 You saints to come, take up the strain,
   the same sweet theme endeavour;
unbroken be the golden chain,
   keep on the song for ever!
Safe in the same dear dwelling-place,
rich with the same eternal grace,
   bless the same boundless giver!

T. H. GILL (1819–1906) altd.

488

LUTHER'S HYMN   87 87 887

Geistliche Lieder, Wittenberg, 1535

WE come unto our fathers' God:
    their rock is our salvation;
the eternal arms, their dear abode,
    we make our habitation;
we bring you, Lord, the praise they brought;
we seek you as the saints have sought
    in every generation.

2 The fire divine, their steps that led,
    still travels bright before us;
the heavenly shield, around them spread,
    is still held high above us;
the grace those sinners that subdued,
the strength those weaklings that renewed,
    now vanquishes, restores us.

3 Their joy unto their Lord we bring,
    their song to us descending;
the Spirit who in them did sing
    his music now is lending.
His song in them, in us, is one:
we raise it high, we send it on—
    the song that has no ending.

4 You saints to come, take up the strain,
    the same sweet theme endeavour;
unbroken be the golden chain,
    keep on the song for ever!
Safe in the same dear dwelling-place,
rich with the same eternal grace,
    bless the same boundless giver!

T. H. GILL (1819–1906) altd.

489

THE PEOPLE OF GOD

Words and music by ESTELLE WHITE (b. 1925)

Unison

1. 'Mo - ses, I know you're the man,' the Lord said;
2. 'Don't get too set in your ways,' the Lord said;
3. 'No mat - ter what you may do,' the Lord said,
4. 'Look at the birds in the air,' the Lord said;
5. 'Fox - es have pla - ces to go,' the Lord said,

'you're going to work out my plan,' the Lord said.
'each step is on - ly a phase,' the Lord said.
'I shall be faith - ful and true,' the Lord said.
'they fly un - ham - pered by care,' the Lord said;
'but I've no home here be - low,' the Lord said;

COMMUNITY IN CHRIST

'Lead all the Is - rael - ites out of sla - ve -
'I'll go be - fore you and I shall be a
'My love will strength - en you as you go a -
'you will move ea - sier if you're tra - vel - ling
'so if you want to be with me all your

- ry, and I shall
sign to guide my
- long, for you're my
light, for you're a
days, keep up the

make them a wan-der-ing race called the peo-ple of God.'
tra - vel-ling, wan-der-ing race; you're the peo-ple of God.'
tra - vel-ling, wan-der-ing race, you're the peo-ple of God.'
wan - der-ing, va - ga-bond race, you're the peo-ple of God.'
mov - ing and tra - vel-ling on, you're the peo-ple of God.'

490

MAINZER LM

J. MAINZER (1801–51)

WE praise, we worship you, O God,
your sovereign power we sound abroad;
all nations bow before your throne,
and you the eternal Father own.

2 Loud alleluias to your name
angels and seraphim proclaim:
the heavens and all the powers on high
in ceaseless songs of joy do cry:

3 'O holy, holy, holy Lord!
the God of hosts, by all adored;
in earth and heaven your majesty,
your light, your power, your glory be.'

4 Apostles join the glorious throng
and swell the loud immortal song;
prophets enraptured hear the sound
and spread the alleluia round.

5 Victorious martyrs join their praise
and shout the omnipotence of grace,
while Christians all, throughout the earth
acknowledge and extol your worth.

6 Glory to you, O God most high!
Father, we praise your majesty,
the Son, the Spirit, we adore:
one Godhead, blest for evermore.

PHILIP GELL'S *Psalms and Hymns*, 1815

491

MOUNTAIN CHRISTIANS
76 76 D (Irregular)

Attrib. JOHN MANNIN (1802–65)
in the *Fellowship Hymn Book*, 1909

WE thank you for the memories
    that fill our minds today;
for the Church that once received us
    and kept us in your way;
for the ones that introduced us
    to Jesus Christ our Lord;
for the saints who have known and loved us,
    our God you are adored.

2 We thank you for those others
    whom we have never known,
with whose courage and devotion
    the Christian Church has grown;
who lived in different ages,
    and thought in different ways;
but whose Lord is the same as our Lord,
    to whom be all our praise.

3 We thank you for the present
    in which we know your care;
for the life we now are given
    in which your work to share;
for the witness and the service
    of your people here these days;
for the saints with whom we worship,
    we offer, Lord, our praise.

4 We thank you for the future
    to which your Spirit leads,
that in every moment of it
    he will satisfy our needs.
Your love can never fail us
    through all eternity;
so may we, and all your people,
    fulfil our destiny.

DAVID J. HARDING

492

If you confess that Jesus is Lord and believe that God raised
him from death, you will be saved.
  **For it is by our faith that we are put right with God;
  it is by our confession that we are saved.**

God is the same Lord of all and richly blesses all who call to him.
  **As the scripture says, 'Everyone who calls out to the Lord
  for help will be saved.'**

But how can they call to him for help if they have not believed?
  And how can they hear if the message is not proclaimed?

And how can the message be proclaimed if the messengers are not sent out?
  **As the scripture says, 'How wonderful is the coming of
  messengers to bring good news.'**

493   THE MISSIONARY CALL

Jesus said: I have been given all authority in heaven and on earth.
Go, then, to all peoples everywhere and make them my disciples;
baptize them in the name of the Father, the Son, and the Holy Spirit,
and teach them to obey everything I have commanded you.
And I will be with you always, to the end of the age.

  **Jesus said: Go throughout the world and preach the gospel
  to all mankind. Whoever believes and is baptized will be saved;
  whoever does not believe will be condemned.**

Jesus said: This is what is written: the Messiah must suffer and must rise
from the dead three days later, and in his name the message about repentance
and the forgiveness of sins must be preached to all nations, beginning in
Jerusalem. You are witnesses of these things. But you must wait in the city
until the power from above comes down upon you.

  **Jesus said to them again: Peace be with you. As the Father
  sent me, so I send you. Then he breathed on them and said:
  Receive the Holy Spirit.**

Paul said: God gave us the task of making others his friends also.
Our message is that God was making all mankind his friends through
Christ. God did not keep an account of their sins, and he has given us the
message which tells how he makes them his friends.

  **Here we are, speaking for Christ, as though God himself were
  making his appeal through us. We plead on Christ's behalf:
  let God change you from enemies into his friends!**

494

Lord, you have called us to be your witnesses in the world:
give us grace to hear and obey your call.
Release us from the bondage of anxiety and fear;
restore us to love, joy and peace as we trust in you;
and so strengthen us by your Holy Spirit
that, by word and good example,
we may glorify you in our daily lives;
through Jesus Christ our Lord.

495

You who bring good tidings to Zion,
go up on a high mountain.
> **You who bring good tidings to Jerusalem,**
> **lift up your voice with a shout.**

See, the sovereign Lord comes with power
and his arm rules for him.
> **See, his reward is with him,**
> **and his recompense accompanies him.**

Awake, awake, O Zion, clothe yourself with strength.
> **Put on your garments of splendour, O Jerusalem.**

'Your God reigns!'
> **Burst into songs together,**
> **for the Lord has comforted his people.**

He has redeemed Jerusalem.
> **The Lord will lay bare his holy arm**
> **in the sight of all nations,**
and all the ends of the earth
will see the salvation of our God.

496

Almighty God, we long for the time when your kingdom shall
come on earth;
when men and nations shall acknowledge your sovereignty,
seek your glory, and serve your good and righteous will.
Help us not only to pray but also to work for that new day;
and enable us by your grace to promote the cause of justice
and peace, truth and freedom,
both in our own society and in the life of the world;
for the honour of Christ, our Saviour and our Lord.

497

SHARON   87 87

Adpt. from WILLIAM BOYCE (1711–79)

For a different version of this tune (in D major) see no. 110.

CHRIST who welcomed little children
    to thine arms in Galilee,
lovingly we bring this baby
    that *he* too be blessed by thee.

2 Lord, accept the parents' praises,
    help them by thy grace divine;
may their tender care and nurture
    train and lead *him* to be thine.

3 In their home may thine own presence
    guide and guard from day to day,
filling life with love and gladness
    throughout all *his* childhood's way.

4 Then in strength of mind and body
    may *he* own thee Lord and King,
tread the paths of Christian service,
    all *his* heart's allegiance bring.

5 Christ who welcomes little children
    bid this baby welcome too.
May thy mighty arms protect *him*
    all life's varied journey through.

HUGH MARTIN (1890–1964)
based on Mark 9: 36–7

498

QUEM PASTORES LAUDAVERE
888 7

14th-century German carol melody
arr. R. VAUGHAN WILLIAMS (1872–1958)

FATHER, in your presence kneeling,
all our heart's desire revealing,
to your love, in faith, appealing—
for our children, Lord, we pray.

2 Grant us wisdom so to train them
that no mortal evil stain them;
young for Jesus would we gain them—
for our children, Lord, we pray.

3 Keep them onward, upward pressing;
courage, self-control possessing;
bravely Christ their King confessing—
for our children, Lord, we pray.

4 Strengthen them for high endeavour,
to your will unfaithful never,
God and neighbour serving ever—
for our children, Lord, we pray.

5 Lord, on life's adventure guide them;
in your secret presence hide them;
to your love we now confide them—
all we ask in Jesus' name.

CHARLES VENN PILCHER (1879–1961)

499

ST MATTHIAS   88 88 88

W. H. MONK (1823–89)

FATHER on high to whom we pray
   and lift our thankful hearts above,
for all your mercies day by day,
    for gifts of hearth and home and love—
      protect them still beneath your care:
      Lord, in your mercy, hear our prayer.

2 O Christ who came as man to earth,
   and chose in Egypt's land to be
a homeless child of alien birth,
    an exile and a refugee—
      for homeless people everywhere,
      Lord, in your mercy, hear our prayer.

3 Spirit divine, whose work is done
   in souls renewed and lives restored:
strive in our hearts to make us one,
    one faith, one family, one Lord—
      till at the last one home we share:
      Lord, in your mercy, hear our prayer.

TIMOTHY DUDLEY-SMITH (b. 1926)

500

PHILIPPINE   LM

R. E. ROBERTS (1878–1940)

LORD of the home, your only Son
    received a mother's tender love;
and from an earthly father won
    his vision of your home above.

2 Help us, O Lord, our homes to make
    your Holy Spirit's dwelling place;
our hands and hearts' devotion take
    to be the servants of your grace.

3 Pray we that all who with us dwell,
    your love and joy and peace may know;
and while our lips your praises tell,
    may faithful lives your glory show.

4 Teach us to keep our homes so fair,
    that were our Lord a child once more,
he might be glad our hearth to share,
    and find a welcome at our door.

5 Lord, may your Spirit sanctify
    each household duty we fulfil,
may we our Master glorify
    in glad obedience to your will.

ALBERT F. BAYLY (1901–84)

501

The Lord is our God, one Lord,
 and you must love the Lord your God
 with all your heart and soul and strength.
The commandments which I give you this day are to be kept in your heart;
 you shall repeat them to your children,
 and speak of them indoors and out of doors,
 when you lie down and when you rise.

502

Jesus said: Unless you turn round and become like children,
you will never enter the kingdom of heaven.
 Let a man humble himself till he is like a child,
 and he will be greatest in the kingdom of heaven.

503

Husbands, love your wives just as Christ loved the Church
and gave his life for it.
 Every husband must love his wife as himself,
 and every wife must respect her husband.

Children, it is your Christian duty to obey your parents,
for this is the right thing to do.
 Parents, do not treat your children in such a way as to make
 them angry.
 Instead, bring them up with Christian discipline
 and instruction.

You must clothe yourselves with compassion, kindness, humility,
gentleness and patience.
 Be tolerant with one another and forgive one another
 whenever any of you has a complaint against someone else.

You must forgive one another just as the Lord has forgiven you.
 And to all these qualities add love,
 which binds all together in perfect unity.

504 A PRAYER BY THE PARENTS AND THE CHURCH

God our Father, together as parents and as a Church we bring
this baby N to you.

> **We want to show N the welcome that Jesus gave to children
> in the gospel story.
> We want to give her/him the strong support of the
> family of God in friendship, instruction and prayer.
> Please accept the commitment of ourselves to her/his nurture.**

(PARENTS) *We recognize that N is a gift from you and has been placed in our care
as a serious and loving responsibility. We ask that, with your help, we will be able
to provide her/him with a Christian home and to bring her/him up in the faith of
the gospel and the fellowship of the Church.*

Father, these are our prayers in this sacred and solemn moment
of dedication. Grant that through the careful concern of this Church,
and the patient love of the parents, N will come to accept Christ's
saving and enriching presence in her/his life. May she/he confess
Jesus as Lord and, through faith and baptism, enter her/his
inheritance in the eternal kingdom of God, in the fellowship of the Spirit.
Amen.

505

**In faith and hope, O Lord, we commit to you this child's future life
as it stretches out before him/her.
Protect him/her in moments of danger.
Reassure him/her in moments of doubt.
Strengthen him/her as (s)he passes from childhood to adolescence
and from adolescence to adulthood.
Surround him/her with your love expressed in people who will
care for him/her, and give him/her those with whom that love
can be shared.
And grant that when the years of discretion shall have come (s)he
may confess you as Lord and Saviour in the waters of baptism.**

506

SUSSEX CAROL   888 D

English traditional carol
arr. R. VAUGHAN WILLIAMS (1872–1958)

As man and woman we were made
  that love be found and life begun;
so praise the Lord who made us two
  and praise the Lord when two are one:
praise for the love that comes to life
through child or parent, husband, wife.

2 Now Jesus lived and gave his love
  to make our life and loving new;
so celebrate with him today
  and drink the joy he offers you
that makes the simple moment shine
and changes water into wine.

3 And Jesus died to live again;
  so praise the love that, come what may,
can bring the dawn and clear the skies,
  and waits to wipe all tears away;
and let us hope for what shall be,
believing where we cannot see.

4 Then spread the table, clear the hall
  and celebrate till day is done;
let peace go deep between us all
  and joy be shared by everyone:
laugh and make merry with your friends
and praise the love that never ends!

BRIAN A. WREN (b. 1936)

507

MARYTON LM

H. P. SMITH (1825–98)

May also be sung to FULDA, no. 585.

JESUS, the Lord of love and life,
draw near to bless this man and wife;
as they are now in love made one,
let your good will for them be done.

2 Give them each day your peace and joy,
let no dark clouds these gifts destroy;
in growing trust may love endure,
to keep their marriage-bond secure.

3 As they have vowed to have and hold,
each by the other be consoled;
in wealth or want, in health or pain,
till death shall part, let love remain.

4 Deepen, O Lord, their love for you,
and in that love, their own renew;
each in the other find delight,
as lives and interests now unite.

5 Be to them both a guide and friend,
through all the years their home defend;
Jesus, the Lord of love and life,
stay near and bless this man and wife.

JAMES E. SEDDON (1915–83)

508

DONCASTER   SM

S. WESLEY (1766–1837)

O GOD, by whose design
  as partners here we stand,
bless now the bonds of love and trust
  that join us hand to hand.

2 Give strength to keep each vow
  we mutually declare,
that faithfulness and loyalty
  may grace the life we share.

3 In sickness or in health
  let each one dwell secure;
may patient, kind, forgiving love
  our partnership mature.

4 If children should be born,
  grant wisdom and delight;
let words and deeds then both combine
  commending truth and right.

5 In thankfulness and praise
  we worship now and pray,
O Holy Spirit, walk with us
  along our future way.

PETER TONGEMAN (b. 1929)

509

O PERFECT LOVE   11 10 11 10

J. BARNBY (1838–96)

O PERFECT love, all human thought transcending,
  lowly we kneel in prayer before your throne,
that theirs may be the love which knows no ending
  whom now for evermore you join in one.

2 O perfect life, be their full strong assurance
    of tender charity and steadfast faith,
  of patient hope and quiet brave endurance,
    with childlike trust that fears nor pain nor death.

3 Grant them the joy which brightens earthly sorrow;
    grant them the peace which calms all earthly strife,
  and to life's day the glorious unknown morrow
    that dawns upon eternal love and life.

DOROTHY GURNEY (1858–1932)

510

LOVE UNKNOWN   66 66 88   JOHN IRELAND (1879–1962)

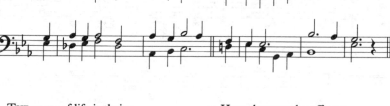

THE grace of life is theirs
 who on this wedding day
delight to make their vows,
 and for each other pray.
May they, O Lord, together prove
the lasting joy of Christian love.

2 Where love is, God abides;
 and God shall surely bless
a home where trust and care
 give birth to happiness.
May they, O Lord, together prove
the lasting joy of such a love.

3 How slow to take offence
 love is! How quick to heal!
How ready in distress
 to know how others feel!
May they, O Lord, together prove
the lasting joy of such a love.

4 And when time lays its hand
 on all we hold most dear,
and life, by life consumed,
 fulfils its purpose here,
may we, O Lord, together prove
the lasting joy of Christian love.

F. PRATT GREEN (b. 1903)

511

GRACIAS   67 67 66 66

GEOFFREY BEAUMONT (1903–70)

WE give you thanks, dear Lord,
   for human love and kindness,
that we may find your joy
   surmounting all our sadness;
that daily in our lives
   your guiding hand we know,
and in each other's love
   our love for you will grow.

2 We thank you that we find
   in mutual love and caring
a richer way of life;
   by giving and in sharing,
in joining of our loves,
   in blessings richly poured,
the meaning of your love;
   we give you thanks, dear Lord.

PETER TURNBULL (1931–71)

512

THAXTED   13 13 13 13 13 13   GUSTAV HOLST (1874–1934)

WE pledge to one another,
 before the Lord above,
entire and whole and perfect,
 this union of our love—
a love that will be patient,
 a love that will be wise,
that will not twist with envy,
 nor lose itself in lies;
a love that will not falter,
 a love to hold us fast,
and bind us to each other
 as long as life shall last.

2 We pray that God will guide us
 through all the years to be,
our lives be shaped by courage,
 hope and serenity.
Through joy and celebration,
 through loneliness and pain,
may loyalty, compassion
 and tenderness remain,
that those who share the blessing
 of love that cannot cease
may walk the paths of gentleness
 into the place of peace.

JILL JENKINS (b. 1937)

513

Blessed are you, O Lord our God, King of the universe,
who created the fruit of the vine.
Blessed are you, O Lord our God, King of the universe,
who created all things for your glory.

Blessed are you, O Lord our God, King of the universe,
who made man and woman in your image.
Make these loved companions greatly to rejoice,
even as you gladdened the hearts of your creatures in Eden.

Blessed are you, O Lord, who make bride and bridegroom to rejoice.
May these, your children, establish a home to glorify
    your name.
Blessed are you, O Lord, who love all your children.

Blessed are you, O Lord our God, King of the universe,
who has created joy and gladness, love and humanity, joy and fellowship.
Blessed are you, O Lord our God, King of the universe,
who fills the hearts of bride and bridegroom with joy.

O give thanks to the Lord for he is good,
for his loving kindness endures forever.

514

LITTLE CORNARD   66 66 88   MARTIN SHAW (1875–1958)

LORD of our growing years,
with us from infancy,
laughter and quick-dried tears,
freshness and energy:

your grace surrounds us all our days—
for all your gifts we bring our praise.

2 Lord of our strongest years,
   stretching our youthful powers,
lovers and pioneers
   when all the world seems ours:

3 Lord of our middle years,
   giver of steadfastness,
courage that perseveres
   when there is small success:

4 Lord of our older years,
   steep though the road may be,
rid us of foolish fears,
   bring us serenity:

5 Lord of our closing years,
   always your promise stands;
hold us when death appears,
   safely within your hands:

DAVID MOWBRAY (b. 1938)

Words © D. Mowbray/Jubilate Hymns

515

EVENTIDE   10 10 10 10

W. H. MONK (1823–89)

ABIDE with me: fast falls the eventide;
the darkness deepens: Lord, with me abide;
when other helpers fail, and comforts flee,
help of the helpless, O abide with me.

2 Swift to its close ebbs out life's little day;
earth's joys grow dim, its glories pass away;
change and decay in all around I see:
you never change, O Lord abide with me.

3 I need your presence every passing hour;
what but your grace can foil the tempter's power?
Who like yourself my guide and stay can be?
Through cloud and sunshine, O abide with me.

4 I fear no foe, with you at hand to bless;
ills have no weight, and tears no bitterness;
where, death, your sting? where, grave, your victory?
I triumph still if you abide with me.

5 Hold now your cross before my closing eyes,
shine through the gloom, and point me to the skies:
heaven's morning breaks, and earth's vain shadows flee:
in life, in death, O Lord, abide with me.

H. F. LYTE (1793–1847)

516

CRÜGER   76 76 D

J. CRÜGER (1598–1662)
adpt. W. H. MONK (1823–89)

I KNOW that my Redeemer
    lives crowned upon the throne;
Lord over earth and heaven
    he saves, and he alone;
he conquered death by dying
    upon the accursèd tree,
and from his death sprang glorious
    eternal life for me.

2 I think upon my Saviour,
    I trust his power to keep,
his mighty arm enfolds me
    awaking and in sleep.
Christ is my rock, my courage;
    Christ is my soul's true life;
and Christ (my heart still knows it)
    will bear me through the strife.

3 In Jesus' name I'm living;
    in Jesus' name I'll die;
I'll fear not, though life's vigour
    from death's cold shadow fly.
O grave, where is your triumph?
    O death, where is your sting?
Come when you will, and welcome!
    Secure in Christ I sing.

From an Icelandic burial hymn
tr. CHARLES VENN PILCHER (1879–1961)

517

SLANE   10 11 11 11*

Irish traditional melody
harm. MARTIN SHAW (1875–1958) adpt.

*10 11 11 12 here.

LORD of all hopefulness, Lord of all joy,
whose trust, ever child-like, no care could destroy,
be there at our waking, and give us we pray,
your bliss in our hearts, Lord, at the break of the day.

2 Lord of all eagerness, Lord of all faith,
whose strong hands were skilled at the plane and the lathe,
be there at our labours, and give us, we pray,
your strength in our hearts, Lord, at the noon of the day.

3 Lord of all kindliness, Lord of all grace,
your hands swift to welcome, your arms to embrace,
be there at our homing, and give us, we pray,
your love in our hearts, Lord, at the eve of the day.

4 Lord of all gentleness, Lord of all calm,
whose voice is contentment, whose presence is balm,
be there at our sleeping, and give us, we pray,
your peace in our hearts, Lord, at the end of the day.

JAN STRUTHER (1901–53)

518

Since it was a man who brought death into the world,
a man also brought resurrection of the dead.
As in Adam all die,
so in Christ all will be brought to life.

519

Now we see only puzzling reflections in a mirror,
but then we shall see, face to face.
My knowledge now is partial;
then it will be whole, like God's knowledge of me.
In a word, there are three things that last for ever:
faith, hope and love;
but the greatest of them all is love.

520

Father, we thank you for the life of *N*:
for the life we lived together,
for the love we shared,
for the truths that shaped our lives,
for the memories that remain.

Father, we thank you for Christ our Lord:
for the death he died,
for the grave in which he was laid,
for the victory he won,
for his resurrection on the third day.

Father, we thank you for what you have promised:
for the eternal life you give us,
for the heaven you have opened to *N*,
for the day we shall see each other,
for holding us together until then.

In Jesus' name.
Amen.

4. LIVING THE GOSPEL

521

Irish traditional melody
harm. MARTIN SHAW (1875–1958) adpt.

SLANE   10 11 11 11

Be thou my vision, O Lord of my heart;
be all else but nothing, except what thou art;
be thou my best thought in the day and the night,
both waking and sleeping, thy presence my light.

2 Be thou my wisdom, be thou my true word;
be thou ever with me, and I with thee, Lord;
be thou my great Father, and I thy true son;
be thou in me dwelling, and I with thee one.

3 Be thou my breastplate, my sword for the fight;
be thou my whole armour, be thou my true might;
be thou my soul's shelter, be thou my strong tower;
O raise thou me heavenward, great power of my power.

4 Be thou my true riches, not man's empty praise;
be thou mine inheritance, now and always;
be thou and thou only the first in my heart;
O sovereign of heaven, my treasure thou art.

5 High King of heaven, thou heaven's bright sun,
O grant me its joys, after victory is won;
great heart of my own heart, whatever befall,
still be thou my vision, O ruler of all.

Ancient Irish, tr. MARY BYRNE (1881–1931)
Versified by ELEANOR HULL (1861–1935) altd.

522

ADSUM   64 64 10 10

E. B. LESLIE (CAREY BONNER) (1859–1938)

Second Tune

SURSUM CORDA   64 64 10 10

GEORGE LOMAS (1834–84)

CHRIST of the upward way,
　my guide divine,
where you have set your feet
　may I place mine;
and move and march wherever you have trod,
keeping face forward up the hill of God.

2 Give me the heart to hear
　your voice and will,
that without fault or fear
　I may fulfil
your purpose with a glad and holy zest,
like one who would not bring less than the best.

3 Give me the eye to see
　each chance to serve,
then send me strength to rise
　with steady nerve,
and leap at once with kind and helpful deed
to the sure comfort of a soul in need.

4 Give me the good strong arm
　to shield the right,
and wield your sword of truth
　with all my might,
that in faith's warfare I may ever be
more than a conqueror through your victory.

5 Christ of the upward way,
　my guide divine,
where you have set your feet,
　may I place mine;
and when your last call comes serene and clear,
calm may my answer be, 'Lord, I am here.'

W. J. MATHAMS (1853–1931)

523

FIRST TUNE

English traditional melody
adpt. and harm. R. VAUGHAN WILLIAMS (1872–1958)

SUSSEX   87 87

SECOND TUNE

GOTT WILL'S MACHEN   87 87

J. L. STEINER (1688–1761)

FATHER, hear the prayer we offer:
  not for ease that prayer shall be,
but for strength, that we may ever
  live our lives courageously.

2 Not for ever in green pastures
  do we ask our way to be;
but by steep and rugged pathways
  would we seek you fearlessly.

3 Not for ever by still waters
   would we idly quiet stay;
  but would smite the living fountains
   from the rocks along our way.

4 Be our strength in hours of weakness,
   in our wanderings be our guide;
  through endeavour, failure, danger,
   Father, be there at our side.

LOVE MARIA WILLIS (1824–1908)

524

DUKE STREET   LM

JOHN HATTON (d. 1793)

FIGHT the good fight with all your might;
Christ is your strength, and Christ your right;
lay hold on life, and it shall be
your joy and crown eternally.

2 Run the straight race through God's good grace,
lift up your eyes and seek his face;
life with its path before us lies;
Christ is the way, and Christ the prize.

3 Cast care aside, lean on your guide;
his boundless mercy will provide;
trust, and your trusting soul shall prove
Christ is its life, and Christ its love.

4 Faint not, nor fear: his arm is near;
he changes not, and you are dear;
only believe and Christ shall be
your all-in-all eternally.

J. S. B. MONSELL (1811–75)
based on 1 Timothy 6: 11–12

525

ST MICHAEL   SM

Genevan Psalter, 1551
arr. WILLIAM CROTCH (1775–1847)

May also be sung to CARLISLE, no. 635.

COME, we that love the Lord,
   and let our joys be known;
join in a song with sweet accord,
   and thus surround the throne.

2 The sorrows of the mind
   be banished from the place;
religion never was designed
   to make our pleasures less.

3 Let those refuse to sing
   who never knew our God;
but children of the heavenly King
   must speak their joys abroad.

4 Then let our songs abound,
   and every tear be dry;
we're marching through Immanuel's ground
   to fairer worlds on high.

ISAAC WATTS (1674–1748) altd.

526

ANGELS' SONG   LM   ORLANDO GIBBONS (1583–1625)

FORTH in your name, O Lord, I go,
　my daily labour to pursue;
you, Lord, alone I choose to know
　in all I think or speak or do.

2 The task your wisdom has assigned
　　here let me cheerfully fulfil;
　in all my work your presence find
　　and prove your good and perfect will.

3 You I would set at my right hand,
　　whose eyes my inmost secrets view;
　and labour on at your command
　　and offer all my work to you.

4 Help me to bear your easy yoke
　　and every moment watch and pray;
　and still to things eternal look,
　　and hasten to that glorious day.

5 Gladly for you may I employ
　　all that your generous grace has given;
　and run my earthly course with joy,
　　and closely walk with you to heaven.

CHARLES WESLEY (1707–88)

© in this version Jubilee Hymns

527

RACHIE   65 65 D with refrain

CARADOG ROBERTS (1879–1935)

(1.) For-ward through the de-sert, through the toil and fight:_

(1.) For-ward through the de-sert, through the toil and fight:_

'FORWARD!' be our watchword,
    steps and voices joined;
seek the things before us,
    not a look behind;
burns the fiery pillar
    at our army's head:
who shall dream of shrinking,
    by our captain led?
Forward through the desert,
    through the toil and fight:
Jordan flows before us,
    Zion beams with light.

2 Forward, flock of Jesus,
    salt of all the earth,
till each yearning purpose
    spring to glorious birth.
Sick, they ask for healing,
    blind, they grope for day;
pour upon the nations
    wisdom's loving ray.
Forward out of error,
    leave behind the night;
forward through the darkness,
    forward into light.

3 Glories upon glories
    has our God prepared,
by the souls that love him
    one day to be shared.
Eye has not beheld them,
    ear has never heard;
nor of these has uttered,
    thought or speech, a word.
Forward, marching forward,
    where the heaven is bright,
till the veil is lifted,
    till our faith be sight.

HENRY ALFORD (1810–71)

528

FROM STRENGTH TO STRENGTH   DSM

E. W. NAYLOR (1867–1934)

FREEDOM and life are ours
for Christ has set us free!
Never again submit to powers
that lead to slavery:
Christ is the Lord who breaks
our chains, our bondage ends,
Christ is the rescuer who makes
the helpless slaves his friends.

2 Called by the Lord to use
our freedom and be strong,
not letting liberty excuse
a life of blatant wrong:
freed from the law's stern hand
God's gift of grace to prove,
know that the law's entire demand
is gladly met by love.

3 Spirit of God, come, fill,
emancipate us all!
Speak to us, Word of truth, until
before his throne we fall:
glory and liberty
our Father has decreed,
and if the Son shall make us free
we shall be free indeed!

CHRISTOPHER IDLE (b. 1938)

529

THE SERVANT KING

GRAHAM KENDRICK (b. 1950)

This is our God,____ the Ser-vant King,____ he calls us

now to fol-low him,____ to bring our lives as a dai-ly of-fer-

-ing____ of wor-ship to____ the Ser-vant King. King.

FROM heaven you came, helpless babe,
entered our world, your glory veiled;
not to be served but to serve,
and give your life that we might live.

This is our God, the Servant King,
he calls us now to follow him,
to bring our lives as a daily offering
of worship to the Servant King.

2 There in the garden of tears,
my heavy load he chose to bear;
his heart with sorrow was torn,
'Yet not my will but yours,' he said.

3 Come see his hands and his feet,
the scars that speak of sacrifice,
hands that flung stars into space
to cruel nails surrendered.

4 So let us learn how to serve,
and in our lives enthrone him;
each other's needs to prefer,
for it is Christ we're serving.

GRAHAM KENDRICK (b. 1950)

530

Traditional melody
arr. GERALD L. BARNES (b. 1935)

SING HOSANNA   10 8 10 9 with refrain

Sing ho - san - na, sing ho - san - na,

sing ho-san-na to the King of kings! Sing ho-san-na,

sing ho-san-na, sing ho-san-na to the King.

GIVE me oil in my lamp, keep me burning,
   give me oil in my lamp, I pray;
give me oil in my lamp, keep me burning,
   keep me burning till the break of day.

   Sing hosanna, sing hosanna,
      sing hosanna to the King of kings!
   Sing hosanna, sing hosanna,
      sing hosanna to the King.

2 Give me joy in my heart, keep me singing,
   give me joy in my heart, I pray;
give me joy in my heart, keep me singing,
   keep me singing till the break of day.

3 Give me love in my heart, keep me serving,
   give me love in my heart, I pray;
give me love in my heart, keep me serving,
   keep me serving till the break of day.

Traditional

531

GATESCARTH 86886

CARYL MICKLEM (b. 1925)

HARMONY VERSION

GIVE to me, Lord, a thankful heart
   and a discerning mind:
give, as I play the Christian's part,
the strength to finish what I start
   and act on what I find.

2 When, in the rush of days, my will
   is habit-bound and slow,
help me to keep in vision still
what love and power and peace can fill,
   a life that trusts in you.

3 By your divine and urgent claim,
   and by your human face,
kindle our sinking hearts to flame
and as you teach the world your name
   let it become your place.

4 Jesus, with all your Church I long
   to see your kingdom come:
show me your way of righting wrong
and turning sorrow into song
   until you bring me home.

CARYL MICKLEM (b. 1925)

532

I KNOW WHOM I HAVE BELIEVED
CM with refrain

JAMES MCGRANAHAN (1840–1907)

But 'I know whom_ I have be - liev - èd;__ and am per - suad - ed__ that he is ab - le to

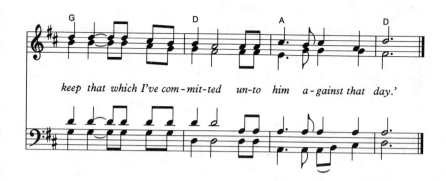

keep that which I've com-mit-ted un-to him a-gainst that day.'

I KNOW not why God's wondrous grace
    to me has been made known;
nor why—unworthy as I am—
    he claimed me for his own.

> *But 'I know whom I have believèd;*
> *and am persuaded that he is able*
> *to keep that which I've committed*
> *unto him against that day.'*

2 I know not how this saving faith
    to me he did impart;
nor how believing in his word
    wrought peace within my heart.

3 I know not how the Spirit moves,
    convincing men of sin;
revealing Jesus through the word,
    creating faith in him.

4 I know not what of good or ill
    may be reserved for me—
of weary ways or golden days
    before his face I see.

D. W. WHITTLE (1840–1901)
based on 2 Timothy 1: 12

533

FIRST TUNE

I NEED YOU   10 10 with refrain

R. LOWRY (1826–99)

REFRAIN

I need you, O I need you; ev - ery hour I need you;

O bless me now, my Sav-iour! I come___ to you.

SECOND TUNE

GARDEN   10 10

English traditional melody
adpt. ERIC DAWES (1902–74)

I NEED you every hour, most gracious Lord:
no tender voice like yours can peace afford.

I need you, O I need you;
every hour I need you;
O bless me now, my Saviour!
I come to you.

2 I need you every hour: Lord stay nearby;
   temptations lose their power when you are nigh.

3 I need you every hour, in joy or pain;
   come quickly and abide, or life is vain.

4 I need you every hour; teach me your will,
   and your rich promises in me fulfil.

5 I need you every hour, most holy one;
   O make me yours indeed, God's blessèd Son.

ANNIE S. HAWKS (1835–1918)

The refrain is omitted when sung to the tune GARDEN.

534

NOËL NOUVELET   11 11 10 11

French traditional carol

For a different arrangement of this tune (in F minor) see no. 257.

JESUS CHRIST is waiting,
 waiting in the streets;
no one is his neighbour,
 all alone he eats.
Listen, Lord Jesus,
 I am lonely too:
make me, friend or stranger,
 fit to wait on you.

2 Jesus Christ is raging,
 raging in the streets,
where injustice spirals
 and real hope retreats.
Listen, Lord Jesus,
 I am angry too:
in the kingdom's causes
 let me rage with you.

3 Jesus Christ is healing,
 healing in the streets,
curing those who suffer,
 touching those he greets.
Listen, Lord Jesus,
 I have pity too:
let my care be active,
 healing just like you.

4 Jesus Christ is dancing,
 dancing in the streets,
where each sign of hatred
 he, with love, defeats.
Listen, Lord Jesus,
 I should triumph too:
on suspicion's graveyard
 let me dance with you.

5 Jesus Christ is calling,
 calling in the streets,
'Who will join my journey?
 I will guide their feet.'
Listen, Lord Jesus,
 let my fears be few:
walk one step before me;
 I will follow you.

     Iona Community

535

LORD OF THE YEARS   11 10 11 10

MICHAEL BAUGHEN (b. 1930)
arr. DAVID ILIFF (b. 1939)

LORD, for the years your love has kept and guided,
urged and inspired us, cheered us on our way,
sought us and saved us, pardoned and provided:
Lord of the years, we bring our thanks today.

2 Lord, for that word, the word of life which fires us,
speaks to our hearts and sets our souls ablaze,
teaches and trains, rebukes us and inspires us:
Lord of the word, receive your people's praise.

3 Lord, for our land, in this our generation,
spirits oppressed by pleasure, wealth and care:
for young and old, for commonwealth and nation,
Lord of our land, be pleased to hear our prayer.

4 Lord, for our world, where men disown and doubt you,
loveless in strength, and comfortless in pain,
hungry and helpless, lost indeed without you:
Lord of the world, we pray that Christ may reign.

5 Lord, for ourselves, in living power remake us—
self on the cross and Christ upon the throne,
past put behind us, for the future take us:
Lord of our lives, to live for Christ alone.

TIMOTHY DUDLEY-SMITH (b. 1926)

536

MAGISTER   87 87 77   LOWELL MASON (1792–1872)

MASTER, speak! Your servant's listening,
  waiting for your gracious word,
for your gladdening voice I'm longing;
  Master, let it now be heard.
As I listen, Lord, I pray:
  'Speak your word to me today!'

2 Speak to me by name, dear Master!
  Let me know it is to me;
speak, that I may follow faster,
  with a step more firm and free,
where the shepherd leads the flock
  in the shadow of the rock.

3 Master, speak! Though least and lowest,
  let me not unheard depart;
Master, speak! You know the deepest
  fears and longings of my heart;
fully know my truest need;
  speak, and make me blest indeed.

4 Master, speak! and make me ready,
  when your voice is truly heard,
with obedience glad and steady
  still to follow every word.
As I listen, Lord, I pray:
  'Master, speak to me today!'

FRANCES RIDLEY HAVERGAL (1836–79) altd.
based on 1 Samuel 3: 10

537

ST LEONARDS 87 85   A. C. BARHAM GOULD (1891–1953)

MAY the mind of Christ my Saviour
  live in me from day to day,
by his love and power controlling
  all I do or say.

2 May the word of God dwell richly
  in my heart from hour to hour,
so that all may see I triumph
  only through his power.

3 May the peace of God my Father
  rule my life in everything,
that I may be calm to comfort
  sick and sorrowing.

4 May the love of Jesus fill me,
  as the waters fill the sea:
him exalting, self abasing,
  this is victory.

5 May I run the race before me,
  strong and brave to face the foe,
looking only unto Jesus
  as I onward go.

6 May his beauty rest upon me
  as I seek to make him known,
so that all may look to Jesus,
  seeing him alone.

KATIE B. WILKINSON (1859–1928)
v. 6 Jubilate Hymns
based on Philippians 2: 5 and Hebrews 12: 1–2

538

ABRIDGE   CM

I. SMITH (1734–1805)

O FOR a heart to praise my God,
    a heart from sin set free;
a heart that's sprinkled with the blood
    so freely shed for me:

2 A heart resigned, submissive, meek,
    my great Redeemer's throne;
where only Christ is heard to speak,
    where Jesus reigns alone:

3 A humble, lowly, contrite heart,
    believing, true and clean,
which neither life nor death can part
    from him who dwells within:

4 A heart in every thought renewed,
    and full of love divine;
perfect and right, and pure and good,
    your life revealed in mine.

5 Your nature, gracious Lord, impart,
　　come quickly from above;
　write your new name upon my heart,
　　your own great name of love.

CHARLES WESLEY (1707–88)

539

FIRST TUNE

FESTUS　LM

Adpt. from a melody in
FREYLINGHAUSEN'S *Gesangbuch*, 1704

O HAPPY day, that fixed my choice
　　on you, my Saviour and my God!
Well may this glowing heart rejoice,
　　and tell its rapture all abroad.

2 It's done, the great transaction's done;
　　I am my Lord's and he is mine;
　he drew me, and I followed on,
　　charmed to confess the voice divine.

3 Now rest, my long-divided heart,
　　fixed on this blissful centre, rest;
　nor ever from your Lord depart,
　　with him of every good possessed.

4 High heaven, that heard my solemn vow,
　　that vow renewed shall daily hear,
　till in life's latest hour I bow,
　　and bless in death a bond so dear.

PHILIP DODDRIDGE (1702–51)

539

O HAPPY DAY   LM with refrain

RON JONES

RENEWED COMMITMENT

O HAPPY day, that fixed my choice
on you, my Saviour and my God!
Well may this glowing heart rejoice,
and tell its rapture all abroad.

O happy day, O happy day,
when Jesus washed my sins away;
he taught me how to watch and pray,
and live rejoicing every day;
O happy day, O happy day,
when Jesus washed my sins away.

2 It's done, the great transaction's done;
I am my Lord's and he is mine;
he drew me, and I followed on,
charmed to confess the voice divine.

3 Now rest, my long-divided heart,
fixed on this blissful centre, rest;
nor ever from your Lord depart,
with him of every good possessed.

4 High heaven, that heard my solemn vow,
that vow renewed shall daily hear,
till in life's latest hour I bow,
and bless in death a bond so dear.

PHILIP DODDRIDGE (1702–51)

540

WAVENEY CM

RICHARD REDHEAD (1820–1901)

CAITHNESS CM

Scottish Psalter, 1635

O Jesus Christ, within me grow
   and all things else recede;
more of your nature may I know,
   from sin be daily freed.

2 Each day may your supporting might
   my weakness still embrace;
my darkness vanish in your light,
   your life my death efface.

3 Make this poor self grow less and less,
   be both my life and aim;
and make me daily through your grace,
   more fit to bear your name.

4 Daily more filled with love my heart,
   daily from self more free;
Lord to whom prayer did strength impart,
   of my prayer hearer be.

5 Fill me with gladness from above,
   hold me by strength divine;
Lord, let the glow of your great love
   through my whole being shine.

J. C. LAVATER (1741–1801)
tr. ELIZABETH LEE SMITH (1817–98)

541

ST MARGARET   88 886   A. L. PEACE (1844–1912)

BAX   88 886   JOHN LOCK (b. 1937)

O LOVE that will not let me go,
  I rest my weary soul in thee;
I give thee back the life I owe,
that in thine ocean depths its flow
  may richer, fuller be.

2 O light that follows all my way,
    I yield my flickering torch to thee;
  my heart restores its borrowed ray,
  that in thy sunshine's blaze its day
    may brighter, fairer be.

3 O joy that seeks for me through pain,
    I cannot close my heart to thee;
  I trace the rainbow through the rain,
  and feel the promise is not vain
    that morn shall tearless be.

4 O cross that raises up my head,
    I dare not ask to fly from thee;
  I lay in dust life's glory dead,
  and from the ground there blossoms red
    life that shall endless be.

GEORGE MATHESON (1842–1906)

542

FOLLOW MY LEADER

VALERIE COLLISON (b. 1933)

Will you ride, ride, ride with the King of kings, will you

RENEWED COMMITMENT

fol-low my lea - der true; will you shout ho - san-na to the

low-ly Son of God, who died for __ me __ and you?

THE journey of life may be easy, may be hard,
  there'll be dangers on the way;
with Christ at my side I'll do battle as I ride
  'gainst the foe that would lead me astray.

  Will you ride, ride, ride with the King of kings,
    will you follow my leader true;
  will you shout hosanna to the lowly Son of God,
    who died for me and you?

2 My burden is light and a song is in my heart,
    as I travel on life's way;
  for Christ is my Lord and he's given me his word,
    that by my side he'll stay.

3 When doubts arise and when tears are in my eyes,
    when all seems lost to me,
  with Christ as my guide I can smile whate'er betide,
    for he my strength will be.

4 I'll follow my leader wherever he may go,
    for Jesus is my friend;
  he'll lead me on to the place where he has gone,
    when I come to my journey's end.

VALERIE COLLISON (b. 1933)

823

543

NIAGARA LM

R. JACKSON (1840–1914)

CHURCH TRIUMPHANT LM

J. W. ELLIOTT (1833–1915)

THE Lord is King! I own his power,
his right to rule each day and hour;
I own his claim on heart and will,
and his demands I would fulfil.

2 He claims my heart, to keep it clean,
from all the stains of human sin;
he claims my will, that I may prove
how swift obedience answers love.

3 He claims my hand for active life
in noble deeds and worthy strife;
he claims my feet, that in his ways
I may walk boldly all my days.

4 He claims my lips, that purest word
in all my speaking may be heard;
my motives, feelings, thoughts, that these,
my inner life, my King may please.

5 He claims the brightness of my youth,
my earnest strivings after truth,
my joys, my toil, my craftsman's skill;
all have their place, and serve his will.

6 To you, O Lord my King, I turn,
your holy purpose to discern.
My daily task your name to own,
for heart and will are yours alone.

DARLEY TERRY (1848–1934) altd.

544

WILTSHIRE   CM

G. T. SMART (1776–1867)

THROUGH all the changing scenes of life,
    in trouble and in joy,
the praises of my God shall still
    my heart and tongue employ.

2 Of his deliverance I will boast,
    till all that are distressed,
from my example comfort take,
    and charm their griefs to rest.

3 The hosts of God encamp around
    the dwellings of the just;
protection he affords to all
    who make his name their trust.

4 O magnify the Lord with me,
    with me exalt his name;
when in distress to him I called
    he to my rescue came.

5 O make but trial of his love,
    experience will decide
how blest are they, and only they,
    who in his truth confide.

6 Fear him, you saints, and you will then
    have nothing else to fear;
make but his service your delight;
    your wants shall be his care.

NAHUM TATE (1652–1715) and
NICHOLAS BRADY (1659–1726)
based on Psalm 34

545

AJALON*   77 77 77   RICHARD REDHEAD (1820–1901)

ROCK of ages, cleft for me,
hide me now, my refuge be;
let the water and the blood
from your wounded side which flowed,
be of sin the double cure;
cleanse me from its guilt and power.

2 Not the labours of my hands
can fulfil your law's demands:
could my zeal no respite know,
could my tears for ever flow,
all for sin could not atone;
you must save and you alone.

3 Nothing in my hand I bring,
simply to your cross I cling;
naked, come to you for dress,
helpless, look to you for grace;
stained by sin, to you I cry:
'Wash me, Saviour, or I die!'

4 While I draw this fleeting breath,
when my eyelids close in death,
when I soar through realms unknown,
bow before the judgement throne:
hide me then, my refuge be,
Rock of ages, cleft for me.

A. M. TOPLADY (1740–78)
based on Exodus 33: 21–3

*Also known as PETRA and REDHEAD NO. 76.

© in this version Jubilate Hymns

546

MARCHING   87 87

MARTIN SHAW (1875–1958)

THROUGH the night of doubt and sorrow
  onward goes the pilgrim band,
singing songs of expectation,
  marching to the promised land.

2 Clear before us through the darkness
    gleams and burns the guiding light;
  clasping hands with one another,
    we step fearless through the night.

3 One the light of God's own presence
    o'er his ransomed people shed,
  chasing far the gloom and terror,
    brightening all the path we tread;

4 One the object of our journey,
    one the faith that never tires,
  one the earnest looking forward,
    one the hope our God inspires;

5 One the strain that lips of thousands
    lift as from the heart of one;
  one the conflict, one the peril,
    one the march in God begun;

6 One the gladness of rejoicing
    on the far eternal shore,
  where the one almighty Father
    reigns in love for evermore.

B. S. INGEMANN (1789–1862)
tr. SABINE BARING-GOULD (1834–1924)

829

547

LIVING LORD   98 88 83

PATRICK APPLEFORD (b. 1925)

For a harmony arrangement of this tune (with a slightly different set of guitar chords) see no. 444.

To him we come—
    Jesus Christ our Lord,
    God's own living Word,
        his dear Son:
in him there is no east and west,
in him all nations shall be blessed;
to all he offers peace and rest—
    loving Lord!

2 In him we live—
    Christ our strength and stay,
    life and truth and way,
        friend divine:
his power can break the chains of sin,
still all life's storms without, within,
help us the daily fight to win—
    living Lord!

3 For him we go—
    soldiers of the cross,
    counting all things loss
        him to know;
going to every land and race,
preaching to all redeeming grace,
building his Church in every place—
    conquering Lord!

4 With him we serve—
    his the work we share
    with saints everywhere,
        near and far;
one in the task which faith requires,
one in the zeal which never tires,
one in the hope his love inspires—
    coming Lord!

5 Onward we go—
    faithful, bold, and true,
    called his will to do,
        day by day,
till, at the last, with joy we'll see
Jesus, in glorious majesty;
live with him through eternity—
    reigning Lord!

JAMES E. SEDDON (1915–83)

548

TRUST AND OBEY   669 D with refrain

DANIEL B. TOWNER (1850–1919)
arr. A. S. COX (b. 1918)

REFRAIN

Trust and o - bey,   for there's   no   oth - er   way   to be

hap - py   in   Je - sus,   but   to   trust   and   o - bey.

WHEN we walk with the Lord
in the light of his word,
   what a glory he sheds on our way!
While we do his good will,
he abides with us still,
   and with all who will trust and obey.

> *Trust and obey,*
> *for there's no other way*
> *to be happy in Jesus,*
> *but to trust and obey.*

2 Not a burden we bear,
  not a sorrow we share,
    but our toil he will richly repay;
  not a grief nor a loss,
  not a frown nor a cross,
    but is blest if we trust and obey.

3 But we never can prove
  the delights of his love
    until all on the altar we lay;
  for the favour he shows,
  and the joy he bestows,
    are for them who will trust and obey.

4 Then in fellowship sweet
  we will sit at his feet,
    or we'll walk by his side in the way;
  what he says we will do,
  where he sends we will go—
    never fear, only trust and obey.

J. H. SAMMIS (1846–1919)

549

WILL YOUR ANCHOR HOLD?
Irregular with refrain

W. J. KIRKPATRICK (1838–1921)

REFRAIN

We have an an-chor that keeps the soul

stead-fast and sure while the bil-lows roll; fast-ened to the rock which

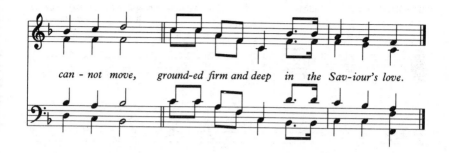

can - not move, ground-ed firm and deep in the Sav-iour's love.

WILL your anchor hold in the storms of life,
when the clouds unfold their wings of strife?
When the strong tides lift, and the cables strain,
will your anchor drift, or firm remain?

We have an anchor that keeps the soul
steadfast and sure while the billows roll;
fastened to the rock which cannot move,
grounded firm and deep in the Saviour's love.

2 Will your anchor hold in the straits of fear,
when the breakers roar and the reef is near?
While the surges rave, and the wild winds blow,
shall the angry waves then your boat o'erflow?

3 Will your anchor hold in the floods of death,
when the waters cold chill your fading breath?
On the rising tide you can safely stay,
while your anchor holds in life's ebbing day.

4 Will your eyes behold through the morning light
the city of gold and the harbour bright?
Will you anchor safe by the heavenly shore,
when life's storms are past for evermore?

PRISCILLA OWENS (1829–99)
based on Hebrews 6: 19

550

AMAZING GRACE   CM

American folk hymn
Melody arr. E. O. EXCELL (1851–1921)
harm. A. S. COX (b. 1918)

AMAZING grace! How sweet the sound
    that saved a wretch like me!
I once was lost, but now am found,
    was blind, but now I see.

2 'Twas grace that taught my heart to fear,
    and grace my fears relieved;
how precious did that grace appear,
    the hour I first believed!

3 My rebel soul, that once withstood
    the Saviour's kindest call,
rejoices now, by grace subdued,
    to serve him with its all.

4 Through many dangers, toils and snares,
    I have already come;
'tis grace has brought me safe thus far,
    and grace will lead me home.

5 What thanks I owe you, and what love—
    a boundless, endless store—
shall echo through the realms above
    when time shall be no more.

JOHN NEWTON (1725–1807)
v.5 WILLIAM COWPER (1731–1800)
based on Ephesians 2: 4–8

551

ARIZONA LM

R. H. EARNSHAW (1856–1929)

WHAT purpose burns within our hearts
　　that we together here should stand,
pledging each other mutual vows,
　　and ready hand to join in hand?

2 We see in vision fair a time
　　when evil shall have passed away;
and thus we dedicate our lives
　　to hasten on that blessed day;

3 To seek the truth whate'er it be,
　　to follow it where'er it leads;
to turn to facts our dreams of good,
　　and coin our lives in loving deeds:

4 For this we gather here today;
　　to such a Church of God we bring
our utmost love and loyalty,
　　and make our souls an offering.

MINOT JUDSON SAVAGE (1841–1918)

552

WINCHESTER NEW   LM

From a chorale in the
Musikalisches Handbuch, Hamburg, 1690
arr. W. H. HAVERGAL (1793–1870)

GREAT GOD, we sing your guiding hand
by which supported still we stand;
the opening year your mercy shows;
that mercy crowns it till its close.

2 By day, by night, at home, abroad,
still are we guarded by our God;
by his incessant bounty fed,
by his unerring counsel led.

3 With grateful hearts the past we own;
the future, all to us unknown,
we to your guardian care commit,
and peaceful leave before your feet.

4 In scenes exalted or depressed,
you are our joy, you are our rest;
your goodness all our hopes shall raise,
adored through all our changing days.

5 When death shall interrupt these songs,
and seal in silence mortal tongues,
our helper God, in whom we trust,
shall keep our souls and guard our dust.

PHILIP DODDRIDGE (1702–51)
based on Acts 26: 22

553

FAITHFULNESS   11 10 11 10 with refrain   W. M. RUNYAN (1870–1957)

REFRAIN

Great is your faith-ful-ness!   Great is your   faith-ful-ness!   Morn-ing by

GOD'S GRACE

morn-ing new mer-cies I see; all I have need-ed your

hand has pro-vid-ed— great is your faith-ful-ness, Fa-ther, to me.

GREAT is your faithfulness, O God my Father,
    you have fulfilled all your promise to me;
you never fail and your love is unchanging,
    all you have been you for ever will be.

> *Great is your faithfulness!*
> *Great is your faithfulness!*
> *Morning by morning new mercies I see;*
> *all I have needed your hand has provided—*
> *great is your faithfulness, Father, to me.*

2 Summer and winter, and springtime and harvest,
    sun, moon and stars in their courses above
join with all nature in eloquent witness
    to your great faithfulness, mercy and love.

3 Pardon for sin, and a peace everlasting,
    your living presence to cheer and to guide;
strength for today, and bright hope for tomorrow—
    these are the blessings your love will provide.

T. O. CHISHOLM (1866–1960)
based on Lamentations 3: 22–3 and Genesis 8: 22

554

SOUTHWELL (IRONS)   CM

H. S. IRONS (1834–1905)

Second Tune

English traditional melody
arr. R. VAUGHAN WILLIAMS (1872–1958)

KINGSFOLD   DCM

HE lives in us, the Christ of God,
　his Spirit joins with ours;
he brings to us the Father's grace
　with powers beyond our powers.
And if enticing sin grows strong,
　when human nature fails,
God's Spirit in our inner self
　fights with us, and prevails.

2 Our pangs of guilt and fears of death
　are Satan's stratagems—
by Jesus Christ who died for us
　God pardons; who condemns?
And when we cannot feel our faith,
　nor bring ourselves to pray,
the Spirit pleads with God for us
　in words we could not say.

3 God gave his Son to save us all—
　no greater love is known!
And shall that love abandon us
　who have become Christ's own?
For God has raised him from the grave,
　in this we stand assured;
so none can tear us from the love
　of Jesus Christ our Lord.

MICHAEL PERRY (b. 1942)
based on Romans 8

555

PENLAN   76 76 D   DAVID JENKINS (1848–1915)

IN heavenly love abiding,
    no change my heart shall fear;
and safe is such confiding,
    for nothing changes here.
The storm may roar without me,
    my heart may low be laid,
but God is round about me,
    and can I be dismayed?

2 Wherever he may guide me,
    no want shall turn me back;
my shepherd is beside me,
    and nothing can I lack.
His wisdom ever waketh,
    his sight is never dim,
he knows the way he taketh,
    and I will walk with him.

3 Green pastures are before me,
    which yet I have not seen;
bright skies will soon be o'er me,
    where dark the clouds have been.
My hope I cannot measure,
    my path to life is free,
my Saviour has my treasure
    and he will walk with me.

ANNA LAETITIA WARING (1823–1910)

556

FIRST TUNE

GLENFINLAS   65 65

K. G. FINLAY (1882–1974)

SECOND TUNE

EXAUDI DEUS   65 65

ALISTAIR BERWICK (b. 1964)

*Last verse

LISTEN to my prayer, Lord,
  hear my humble cry;
when my heart is fainting,
  to your throne I fly.

2 In earth's farthest corner
    you will hear my voice:
  set me on your rock, Lord,
    then I shall rejoice.

3 You have been my shelter
    when the foe was near,
  as a tower of refuge
    shielding me from fear.

4 I will rest for ever
    in your care and love,
  guarded and protected
    as by wings above.

5 All that I have promised,
    help me to fulfil;
  and in all who love you
    work your perfect will.

6 May your truth and mercy
    keep me all my days;
  let my words and actions
    be my songs of praise!

JAMES E. SEDDON (1915–1983)
based on Psalm 61

557

CROFT'S 136th   66 66 88

Melody and bass by
WILLIAM CROFT (1678–1727)

For a different version of this tune see no. 72.

JOIN all the glorious names
   of wisdom, love and power,
that ever mortals knew,
   that angels ever bore:
all are too mean to speak his worth,
too mean to set my Saviour forth.

2   Great prophet of my God,
   my tongue would bless your
      name;
by you the joyful news
   of our salvation came:
the joyful news of sins forgiven,
of hell subdued, and peace with
      heaven.

3   Jesus, my great high priest,
   offered his blood and died;
my guilty conscience seeks
   no sacrifice beside:
his powerful blood did once atone,
and now it pleads before the throne.

4   My Saviour and my Lord,
   my conqueror and my King!
Your sceptre and your sword,
   your reign of grace I sing:
yours is the power; behold I sit
in willing bonds before your feet.

ISAAC WATTS (1674–1748) altd.

558

SAXBY   LM

T. R. MATTHEWS (1826–1910)

LORD, I was blind, I could not see
  in your marred features any grace;
  but now the beauty of your face
in radiant vision dawns on me.

2 Lord, I was deaf, I could not hear
  the thrilling music of your voice;
  but now I hear you and rejoice,
and mighty are your words, and dear.

3 Lord, I was dumb, I could not speak
  the grace and glory of your name;
  but now, as touched with living flame,
my lips your eager praises wake.

4 Lord, I was dead, I could not move
  my lifeless soul from sin's dark grave;
  but now the power of life you gave
has raised me up to know your love.

5 Lord, you have made the blind to see,
  the deaf to hear, the dumb to speak,
  the dead to live; and now, I break
the chains of my captivity.

W. T. MATSON (1833–99)
vv. 4 & 5 Jubilate Hymns
based on John 9: 25

559

BLAENWERN   87 87 D

W. P. ROWLANDS (1860–1937)

LOVE divine, all loves excelling,
   joy of heaven, to earth come down,
fix in us your humble dwelling,
   all your faithful mercies crown.
Jesus, you are all compassion,
   boundless love that makes us whole;
visit us with your salvation,
   enter every trembling soul.

2 Come, almighty to deliver,
   let us all your grace receive;
suddenly return, and never,
   never more your temples leave.
You we would be always blessing,
   serve you as your hosts above,
pray, and praise you without ceasing,
   glory in your perfect love.

3 Finish then your new creation:
   pure and sinless let us be;
let us see your great salvation,
   perfect in eternity:
changed from glory into glory
   till in heaven we take our place,
till we cast our crowns before you,
   lost in wonder, love and praise!

CHARLES WESLEY (1707–88)

559   Second Tune

BETHANY   87 87 D   Henry Smart (1813–79)

For this tune in E major see no. 639.

Love divine, all loves excelling,
   joy of heaven, to earth come down,
fix in us your humble dwelling,
   all your faithful mercies crown.
Jesus, you are all compassion,
   boundless love that makes us whole;
visit us with your salvation,
   enter every trembling soul.

2 Come, almighty to deliver,
   let us all your grace receive;
suddenly return, and never,
   never more your temples leave.
You we would be always blessing,
   serve you as your hosts above,
pray, and praise you without ceasing,
   glory in your perfect love.

3 Finish then your new creation:
   pure and sinless let us be;
let us see your great salvation,
   perfect in eternity:
changed from glory into glory
   till in heaven we take our place,
till we cast our crowns before you,
   lost in wonder, love and praise!

CHARLES WESLEY (1707–88)

560

ALL SAINTS   87 87 77

Melody from *Darmstadt Gesangbuch*, 1698
adpt. W. H. MONK (1823–29)

Second Tune

GOUNOD   87 87 77

C. GOUNOD (1818–93)

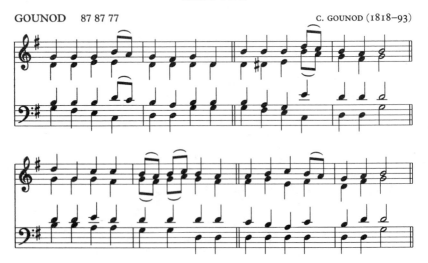

ONE there is, above all others,
  well deserves the name of friend.
His is love beyond a brother's,
  costly, free, and knows no end:
    they who once his kindness prove,
    find it everlasting love.

2 Which of all our friends, to save us,
    could, or would, have shed his blood?
  But the Saviour died to have us
    reconciled in him to God:
      this was boundless love indeed!
      Jesus is a friend in need.

3 When he lived on earth abasèd,
    friend of sinners was his name;
  now, above all glory raisèd,
    he rejoices in the same;
      still he calls them brethren, friends,
      and to all their wants attends.

4 Could we bear from one another
    what he daily bears from us?
  Yet this glorious friend and brother
    loves us though we treat him thus;
      though for good we render ill,
      he accounts us brethren still.

5 O for grace our hearts to soften!
    Teach us, Lord, at length to love.
  We, alas, forget too often
    what a friend we have above:
      but, when home our souls are brought,
      we shall love you as we ought.

JOHN NEWTON (1725–1807) altd.

561

FIRST TUNE

SONG 46   10 10

ORLANDO GIBBONS (1583–1625)

SECOND TUNE

G. T. CALDBECK (1852–1918)
and C. J. VINCENT (1852–1934)

PAX TECUM   10 10

PEACE, perfect peace,
   in this dark world of sin?
The blood of Jesus whispers peace within.

2 Peace, perfect peace,
   by thronging duties pressed?
To do the will of Jesus, this is rest.

3 Peace, perfect peace,
   with sorrows surging round?
With Jesus present, his true calm is found.

4 Peace, perfect peace,
   with loved ones far away?
In Jesus' keeping we are safe, and they.

5 Peace, perfect peace,
   our future all unknown?
Jesus we know, and he is on the throne.

6 Peace, perfect peace,
   death shadowing us and ours?
Jesus has vanquished death and all its powers.

7 It is enough;
   earth's troubles soon shall cease,
and Jesus call us to heaven's perfect peace.

E. H. BICKERSTETH (1823–1906)

562

GERONTIUS   CM

J. B. DYKES (1823–76)

BILLING   CM

R. R. TERRY (1865–1938)

PRAISE to the Holiest in the height,
  and in the depth be praise;
in all his words most wonderful,
  most sure in all his ways.

2 O loving wisdom of our God!
    when all was sin and shame,
  a second Adam to the fight
    and to the rescue came.

3 O wisest love! that flesh and blood,
    which did in Adam fail,
  should strive afresh against the foe,
    should strive and should prevail;

4 And that the highest gift of grace
    should flesh and blood refine:
  God's presence, and his very self,
    and essence all divine.

5 O generous love! that he, who smote
    in Man for man the foe,
  the double agony in Man
    for man should undergo;

6 And in the garden secretly,
    and on the cross on high,
  should teach his brethren, and inspire
    to suffer and to die!

7 Praise to the Holiest in the height,
    and in the depth be praise;
  in all his words most wonderful,
    most sure in all his ways.

J. H. NEWMAN (1801–90)

563

EBENEZER   87 87 D

T. J. WILLIAMS (1869–1944)

TELL his praise in song and story,
   bless the Lord with heart and voice;
in my God is all my glory—
   come before him and rejoice:
join to praise his name together,
   he who hears his people's cry;
tell his praise, come wind or weather,
   shining faces lifted high.

2 To the Lord whose love has found them
   poor men cry in their distress;
swift his angels camped around them,
   prove him sure to save and bless:
God it is who hears our crying
   though the spark of faith be dim;
taste and see! beyond denying
   blest are those who trust in him.

3 Taste and see! in faith draw near him,
   trust the Lord with all your powers;
seek and serve him, love and fear him,
   life and all its joys are ours—
true delight in holy living,
   peace and plenty, length of days:
come, my children, with thanksgiving
   bless the Lord in songs of praise.

4 In our need he walks beside us,
   ears alert to every cry;
watchful eyes to guard and guide us,
   love that whispers, 'It is I'.
Good shall triumph, wrong be righted,
   God has pledged his promised word;
so with ransomed saints united
   join to praise our living Lord!

TIMOTHY DUDLEY-SMITH (b. 1926)
based on Psalm 34

564

GONFALON ROYAL   LM   P. C. BUCK (1871–1947)

A - - - men.

LORD, you have searched and known my ways
    and understood my thought from far;
how can I rightly sound your praise
    or tell how great your wonders are?

2 Besetting me, before, behind,
    upon my life your hand is laid;
caught in the compass of your mind
    are all the creatures you have made.

3 Such knowledge is too wonderful,
    too high for me to understand—
enough that the Unsearchable
    has searched my heart and held my hand.
                    (Amen.)

PETER G. JARVIS (b. 1925)
based on Psalm 139: 1–6

565

THERE ARE HUNDREDS OF SPARROWS   11 12 12 10   JOHN LARSSON

THERE are hundreds of sparrows, thousands, millions,
    they're two a penny, far too many there must be;
there are hundreds and thousands, millions of sparrows,
    but God knows every one and God knows me.

2 There are hundreds of flowers, thousands, millions,
    and flowers fair the meadows wear for all to see;
there are hundreds and thousands, millions of flowers,
    but God knows every one and God knows me.

3 There are hundreds of planets, thousands, millions,
    way out in space each has a place by God's decree;
there are hundreds and thousands, millions of planets,
    but God knows every one and God knows me.

4 There are hundreds of children, thousands, millions,
    and yet their names are written on God's memory;
there are hundreds and thousands, millions of children,
    but God knows every one and God knows me.

JOHN GOWANS

566

TO GOD BE THE GLORY   11 11 11 11 with refrain   W. H. DOANE (1832–1915)

REFRAIN

Praise the Lord!   Praise the Lord!   Let   the earth hear   his   voice!

GOD'S GRACE

Praise the Lord! Praise the Lord! Let the peo - ple re - joice!

O come__ to the Fa - ther, through Je - sus the Son,

and give him the glo - ry! Great things he has done!

To God be the glory! Great things he has done!
So loved he the world that he gave us his Son;
who yielded his life an atonement for sin,
and opened the life gate that all may go in.

Praise the Lord! Praise the Lord!
  Let the earth hear his voice!
Praise the Lord! Praise the Lord!
  Let the people rejoice!
O come to the Father, through Jesus the Son,
and give him the glory! Great things he has done!

2 O perfect redemption, the purchase of blood,
  to every believer the promise of God;
  for every offender who truly believes,
  that moment from Jesus a pardon receives.

3 Great things he has taught us, great things he has done,
  and great our rejoicing through Jesus the Son;
  but purer and higher and greater will be
  the joy and the wonder when Jesus we see.

FRANCES VAN ALSTYNE (1820–1915)
based on Revelation 15: 3–4

567

YOU CAN'T STOP RAIN

JOHN LARSSON

You can't stop rain from falling down,
    prevent the sun from shining;
you can't stop spring from coming in,
    or winter from resigning,
or still the waves or stay the winds,
    or keep the day from dawning;
you can't stop God from loving you,
    his love is new each morning.

2 You can't stop ice from being cold,
    you can't stop fire from burning,
or hold the tide that's going out,
    delay its sure returning,
or halt the progress of the years,
    the flight of fame and fashion;
you can't stop God from loving you,
    his nature is compassion.

3 You can't stop God from loving you,
    though you may disobey him;
you can't stop God from loving you,
    however you betray him:
from love like this no power on earth
    the human heart can sever;
you can't stop God from loving you,
    not God, not now, nor ever.

JOHN GOWANS

568

COLOURS OF DAY

SUSAN McCLELLAN, JOHN PAC, and
KEITH RYECROFT

So light up the fire and let the flame burn, o-pen the door, let Je-sus re-turn, take seeds of his Spi-rit,

let the fruit grow, tell the peo-ple of Je - sus, let his love show.

COLOURS of day dawn into the mind,
the sun has come up, the night is behind.
Go down in the city, into the street,
and let's give the message to the people we meet.

So light up the fire and let the flame burn,
open the door, let Jesus return,
take seeds of his Spirit, let the fruit grow,
tell the people of Jesus, let his love show.

2 Go through the park, on into the town;
the sun still shines on, it never goes down.
The light of the world is risen again;
the people of darkness are needing our friend.

3 Open your eyes, look into the sky,
the darkness has come, the sun came to die.
The evening draws on, the sun disappears,
but Jesus is living, his Spirit is near.

SUSAN MCCLELLAN, JOHN PAC, and KEITH RYECROFT

569

FIRST TUNE

RICHMOND   CM

Adpt. from T. HAWEIS (1734–1820)
by S. WEBBE (THE YOUNGER) (c.1770–1843)

SECOND TUNE

ST FULBERT   CM

H. J. GAUNTLETT (1805–76)

FILL now my life, O Lord my God,
    in every part with praise,
that my whole being may proclaim
    your being and your ways.

2 Not for the lips of praise alone,
    nor yet the praising heart
I ask, but for a life made up
    of praise in every part.

3 Praise in the common things of life,
    its goings out and in;
praise in each duty and each deed,
    exalted or unseen.

4 Fill every part of me with praise;
    let all my being speak
of you and of your love, O Lord,
    poor though I be and weak.

5 Then, Lord, from me you shall receive
    the praise and glory due;
and so shall I begin on earth
    the song for ever new.

6 So shall no part of day or night
    from sacredness be free;
but all my life, with you my God,
    in fellowship shall be.

HORATIUS BONAR (1808–89)

570

GO FORTH   10 10 10 10

MICHAEL BAUGHEN (b. 1930)

May also be sung to WOODLANDS, no. 391.

Go forth and tell! O Church of God awake!
God's saving news to all the nations take;
proclaim Christ Jesus, Saviour, Lord, and King,
that all the world his worthy praise may sing.

2 Go forth and tell! God's love embraces all;
he will in grace respond to all who call:
how shall they call if they have never heard
the gracious invitation of his word?

3 Go forth and tell where still the darkness lies;
in wealth or want, the sinner surely dies:
give us, O Lord, concern of heart and mind,
a love like yours which cares for all mankind.

4 Go forth and tell! The doors are open wide:
share God's good gifts—let no one be denied;
live out your life as Christ your Lord shall choose,
your ransomed powers for his sole glory use.

5 Go forth and tell! O Church of God, arise!
go in the strength which Christ your Lord supplies;
go till all nations his great name adore
and serve him Lord and King for evermore.

JAMES E. SEDDON (1915–83)

571

GO TELL IT ON THE MOUNTAIN

American folk melody
arr. GERALD L. BARNES (b. 1935)

REFRAIN
Unison

Go, tell it on the moun - tain, o-ver the hills and ev-ery-where;

Fine

go, tell it on the moun - tain that Je - sus is his name.

VERSES
Harmony

D.C. al Fine

Go, tell it on the mountain,
over the hills and everywhere;
go, tell it on the mountain
that Jesus is his name.

HE possessed no riches,
    no home to lay his head;
he fasted in the desert,
    he gave to others bread:

2 He reached out and touched them,
    the blind, the deaf, the lame;
he spoke and listened gladly
    to anyone who came:

3 Some turned away in anger,
    with hatred in their eye;
they tried him and condemned him,
    then led him out to die:

4 'Father, now forgive them,'
    upon the cross he said;
in three more days he was alive
    and risen from the dead:

5 He still comes to people,
    his life moves through the lands;
he uses us for speaking,
    he touches with our hands:

GEOFFREY MARSHALL-TAYLOR altd.

572

RHUDDLAN   87 87 87

Welsh traditional melody
harm. in *The English Hymnal*, 1906

May also be sung to WESTMINSTER ABBEY, no. 623(*ii*).

GOD of grace and God of glory,
  on your people pour your power;
crown your ancient Church's story,
  bring her bud to glorious flower.
    Grant us wisdom,
    grant us courage
  for the facing of this hour.

2 See the hosts of evil round us
    scorn your Christ, attack his ways!
  Fears and doubts too long have bound us;
    free our hearts to work and praise.
      Grant us wisdom,
      grant us courage
    for the living of these days.

3 Heal your children's warring madness,
    bend our pride to your control;
  shame our wanton, selfish gladness,
    rich in things and poor in soul.
      Grant us wisdom,
      grant us courage
    lest we miss your kingdom's goal.

4 Save us from weak resignation
    to the evils we deplore;
  let the search for your salvation
    be our glory evermore.
      Grant us wisdom,
      grant us courage
    serving you whom we adore.

H. E. FOSDICK (1878–1969) altd.

573

ST MABYN   87 87

A. H. BROWN (1830–1926)

THERE'S a wideness in God's mercy,
 like the wideness of the sea;
there's a kindness in his justice,
 which is more than liberty.

2 There is no place where earth's
   sorrows
  are more felt than up in heaven;
 there is no place where earth's failings
  have such kindly judgement given.

3 For the love of God is broader
  than the measures of man's mind;
 and the heart of the Eternal
  is most wonderfully kind.

4 But we make his love too narrow
   by false limits of our own;
 and we magnify his strictness
  with a zeal he will not own.

5 There is plentiful redemption
  in the blood that has been shed;
 there is joy for all the members
  in the sorrows of the head.

6 If our love were but more simple,
  we should take him at his word;
 and our lives be filled with gladness,
  from the presence of the Lord.

F. W. FABER (1814–63)

574

GO TELL EVERYONE   88 85 with refrain

HUBERT RICHARDS (b. 1921)
BETTY PULKINGHAM (b. 1926)
Words by ALAN DALE (1902–79)
based on Luke 4: 18
and Matthew 10: 9–10, 19–20

1. God's Spi-rit is in___ my heart,___ he has called me and set me a - part,_____ this is what I have to do,_____ what I have to
2. Just as the Fa-ther sent me___ so I'm send-ing you out to be_____ my wit - ness through-out___ the world,_____ the whole of the
3. Don't car-ry a load in your pack,___ you don't need two shirts on your back;_____ a work-man can earn his own keep,_____ can earn his own
4. Don't wor-ry what you have to say,___ don't wor - ry be - cause on that day_____ God's Spi - rit will speak in your heart,_____ will speak in your

575

CRUCIFER   10 10 with refrain   S. H. NICHOLSON (1875–1947)

REFRAIN
Unison

Lift high the cross, the love of Christ pro - claim till all the world____ a - dores____ his sac - red name!

VERSES
Harmony

Lift high the cross, the love of Christ proclaim
till all the world adores his sacred name!

COME, Christians, follow where the captain trod,
the King victorious, Christ the Son of God:

2 Saved by the cross on which their Lord was slain,
see Adam's children their lost home regain:

3 From north and south, from east and west they raise
in growing unison their songs of praise:

4 Let every race and every language tell
of him who saves our souls from death and hell!

5 O Lord, once lifted on the tree of pain,
draw all the world to seek you once again:

6 Set up your throne, that earth's despair may cease
beneath the shadow of its healing peace:

G. W. KITCHEN (1827–1912) and
M. R. NEWBOLT (1874–1956)

576

SPRINGFIELD   11 10 11 10 Dactylic   H. J. GAUNTLETT (1805–76)

SECOND TUNE

CRUDWELL   11 10 11 10 Dactylic   W. K. STANTON (1891–1978)

LORD, you have given yourself for our healing;
    poured out your life that our souls might be freed;
love from the heart of the Father, revealing
    light for our darkness and grace for our need.

2 Saviour of men, our humanity sharing,
    give us a passion for souls that are lost;
help us to follow, your gospel declaring;
    daily to serve you and count not the cost.

3 Pray we for those who today in their blindness
    wander from you and your kingdom of truth;
grant them a sight of your great loving-kindness,
    Lord of their years and the guide of their youth.

4 Come, Holy Spirit, to cleanse and renew us:
    purge us from evil and fill us with power:
thus shall the waters of healing flow through us;
    so shall revival be born in this hour.

5 Give to your Church, as she tells forth the story,
    strength for her weakness and trust for her fears:
make her a channel of grace for your glory,
    answer her prayers in the midst of the years.

R. D. BROWNE (b. 1905) altd.

577

EVERTON   87 87 D   HENRY SMART (1813–79)

Lord, thy Church on earth is seeking
    thy renewal from above;
teach us all the art of speaking
    with the accent of thy love.
We will heed thy great commission:
    Go ye into every place—
preach, baptize, fulfil my mission,
    serve with love and share my grace.

2 Freedom give to those in bondage,
    lift the burdens caused by sin.
Give new hope, new strength and courage,
    grant release from fears within:
light for darkness; joy for sorrow;
    love for hatred; peace for strife.
These and countless blessings follow
    as the Spirit gives new life.

3 In the streets of every city
    where the bruised and lonely dwell,
let us show the Saviour's pity,
    let us of his mercy tell.
In all lands and with all races
    let us serve, and seek to bring
all the world to render praises,
    Christ, to thee, Redeemer, King.

H. SHERLOCK (b. 1905)

578

STUTTGART   87 87   Melody by C. F. WITT (1660–1716)

LORD, your kingdom bring
  triumphant,
    give this world your liberty;
may your Spirit's strong compulsion
  rule our tides of energy:

2 Where the vessel cleaves the ocean,
    or the pilot steers the plane;
  where the miner toils in darkness,
    and the farmer sows the grain.

3 Consecrate your people's labour
    at the airfield, mill and port;
  with the gladness of your presence
    bless our homes and grace our sport.

4 Let your mercy and your wisdom
    rule our courts and parliament,
  and to soldier, sage and scholar
    may your light and truth be sent.

5 By the pioneer's endeavour,
    by the word of printed page,
  by the martyr's dying witness,
    and your saints in every age:

6 By the living voice of preacher,
    by the skill of surgeon's hand,
  by the far borne broadcast tidings
    speaking peace from land to land:

7 Lord, your kingdom bring triumphant,
    visit us this living hour,
  let your toiling, sinning children
    see your kingdom come in power.

ALBERT F. BAYLY (1901–84)

579

MAINZER LM

J. MAINZER (1801–51)

May also be sung to DUKE STREET, no. 313.

O SPIRIT of the living God,
  in all the fullness of your grace,
wherever human feet have trod,
  descend on our apostate race.

2 Give tongues of fire and hearts of love
  to preach the reconciling word;
give power and blessing from above,
  each time the joyful sound is heard.

3 Be darkness, at your coming, light;
  confusion, order in your path;
souls without strength inspire with might;
  bid mercy triumph over wrath.

4 O Spirit of the Lord, prepare
  all the round earth her God to meet;
breathe now abroad like morning air
  till hearts of stone begin to beat.

5 Baptize the nations; far and nigh,
  the triumphs of the cross record;
the name of Jesus glorify,
  till all the people call him Lord.

JAMES MONTGOMERY (1771–1854)
based on Acts 2: 3–4

580

FROM STRENGTH TO STRENGTH   DSM   E. W. NAYLOR (1867–1934)

SOLDIERS of Christ, arise,
    and put your armour on,
strong in the strength which God supplies
    through his eternal Son.
Strong in the Lord of hosts,
    and in his mighty power;
who in the strength of Jesus trusts
    is more than conqueror.

2 Stand then in his great might,
    with all his strength endued;
and take, to arm you for the fight,
    the panoply of God.
To keep your armour bright
    attend with constant care,
still walking in your captain's sight,
    and watching unto prayer.

3 From strength to strength go on;
    wrestle and fight and pray;
tread all the powers of darkness down,
    and win the well-fought day.
Then having all things done,
    and every conflict passed,
you may o'ercome through Christ alone,
    and stand complete at last.

CHARLES WESLEY (1707–88)

581

LLANGLOFFAN   76 76 D

Welsh hymn melody
harm. DAVID EVANS (1874–1948)

May also be sung to THORNBURY, no. 582, or CRÜGER, no. 142.

SPEAK forth your word, O Father,
 our hungry minds to feed:
the people starve and perish,
 and cannot name their need;
for Lord, you have so made us
 that not alone by bread,
but by your word of comfort
 our hunger must be fed.

2 To each one in their language,
 to each one in their home,
by many paths and channels
 the faith of Christ may come:
the printed word on paper,
 the wave that spans the air,
the screen, the stage, the picture
 may all its truth declare.

3 How shall they hear your message
 if there are none to preach?
How shall they learn your lesson
 if there are none to teach?
Take us, then, Lord, and use us
 to tell what we have heard,
and all the minds of millions
 shall feed upon your word.

CHARLES JEFFRIES (1896–1972)

582

THORNBURY   76 76 D   BASIL HARWOOD (1859–1949)

TELL all the world of Jesus,
  our Saviour, Lord and King;
and let the whole creation
  of his salvation sing:
proclaim his glorious greatness
  in nature and in grace;
Creator and Redeemer,
  the Lord of time and space.

2 Tell all the world of Jesus,
  that everyone may find
the joy of his forgiveness—
  true peace of heart and mind:
proclaim his perfect goodness,
  his deep, unfailing care;
his love so rich in mercy,
  a love beyond compare.

3 Tell all the world of Jesus,
  that everyone may know
of his almighty triumph
  defeating every foe:
proclaim his coming glory,
  when sin is overthrown,
and he shall reign in splendour—
  the King upon his throne!

JAMES E. SEDDON (1915–83)

583

Russian folk melody
arr. DAVID TRAFFORD (b. 1950)

FESTIVAL   87 87 D

WE are called to be God's people
  showing by our lives his grace,
one in heart and one in spirit,
  sign of hope for every race.
Let us show how he has changed us,
  and remade us as his own;
let us share our life together
  as we shall around his throne.

2 We are called to be God's servants,
  working in his world today;
taking his own task upon us,
  all his sacred words obey.
Let us rise, then, to his summons,
  dedicate to him our all,
that we may be faithful servants,
  quick to answer now his call.

3 We are called to be God's prophets,
  speaking for the truth and right;
standing firm for godly justice,
  bringing evil into light.
Let us seek the courage needed,
  our high calling to fulfil,
that mankind may know God's blessing
  in the doing of his will.

THOMAS A. JACKSON (b. 1931)

584

OMBERSLEY   LM   W. H. GLADSTONE (1840–91)

SEND forth the gospel! Let it run
   southward and northward, east and west:
tell all the earth Christ died and lives,
   and gives his pardon, life and rest.

2 Send forth your gospel, mighty Lord!
   Out of the chaos bring to birth
your own creation's promised hope;
   the better days of heaven on earth.

3 Send forth your gospel, gracious Lord!
   Yours was the blood for sinners shed;
your voice still pleads in human hearts;
   to you let other sheep be led.

4 Send forth your gospel, holy Lord!
   kindle in us love's sacred flame;
love giving all and grudging naught
   for Jesus' sake, in Jesus' name.

5 Send forth the gospel! Tell it out!
   Go, Christians, at the Master's call;
prepare his way, who comes to reign
   the King of kings and Lord of all.

H. E. FOX (1841–1926)

585

FULDA (WALTON)   LM

GARDINER'S *Sacred Melodies*, 1815

WE have a gospel to proclaim,
   good news for all throughout the earth;
the gospel of a Saviour's name:
   we sing his glory, tell his worth.

2 Tell of his birth at Bethlehem,
   not in a royal house or hall
but in a stable dark and dim,
   the Word made flesh, a light
      for all.

3 Tell of his death at Calvary,
   hated by those he came to save,
in lonely suffering on the cross;
   for all he loved his life he gave.

4 Tell of that glorious Easter morn:
   empty the tomb, for he was free.
He broke the power of death and hell
   that we might share his victory.

5 Tell of his reign at God's right hand,
   by all creation glorified.
He sends his Spirit on his Church
   to live for him, the Lamb who died.

6 Now we rejoice to name him King:
   Jesus is Lord of all the earth.
This gospel-message we proclaim:
   we sing his glory, tell his worth.

EDWARD J. BURNS (b. 1938)

586

MESSAGE   10 8 87 with refrain   H. E. NICHOL (1862–1926)

For the dark-ness shall turn to dawn - ing, and the

dawn-ing to noon-day bright,___ and Christ's great king-dom shall come on earth, the king - dom of love and light.

WE'VE a story to tell to the nations,
    that shall turn their hearts to the right;
a story of truth and goodness,
    a story of peace and light:

> *For the darkness shall turn to dawning,*
>   *and the dawning to noonday bright,*
> *and Christ's great kingdom shall come on earth,*
>   *the kingdom of love and light.*

2 We've a song to be sung to the nations,
    that shall lift their hearts to the Lord;
a song that shall conquer evil,
    and shatter the spear and sword:

3 We've a message to give to the nations,
    that God who is reigning above
has sent us his Son to save us,
    and show us that God is love:

4 We've a Saviour to show to the nations,
    who the path of sorrow has trod,
that all of the world's great peoples
    might come to the truth of God:

COLIN STERNE (1862–1926)

587

MELITA   88 88 88

J. B. DYKES (1823–76)

ETERNAL Father, strong to save,
whose arm hath bound the restless wave,
who bidd'st the mighty ocean deep
its own appointed limits keep;
   O hear us when we cry to thee
   for those in peril on the sea.

2 O Christ, whose voice the waters heard,
and hushed their raging at thy word,
who walkedst on the foaming deep,
and calm amid the storm didst sleep:
   O hear us when we cry to thee
   for those in peril on the sea.

3 O Holy Spirit, who didst brood
upon the chaos dark and rude,
and bid its angry tumult cease,
and give, for wild confusion, peace:
   O hear us when we cry to thee
   for those in peril on the sea.

4 O Trinity of love and power
our brethren shield in danger's hour,
from rock and tempest, fire and foe,
protect them wheresoe'er they go;
   thus evermore shall rise to thee
   glad hymns of praise from land and sea.

WILLIAM WHITING (1825–78)

588

FRANCONIA SM

KÖNIG'S *Harmonischer Liederschatz*, 1738
adpt. W. H. HAVERGAL (1793–1870)

BLEST are the pure in heart,
    for they shall see their God;
the secret of the Lord is theirs;
    their soul is Christ's abode.

2 The Lord who left the heavens,
    our life and peace to bring,
to dwell in lowliness with men,
    their pattern and their king:

3 Still to the lowly soul
    himself he will impart;
and for his dwelling and his throne
    chooses the pure in heart.

4 Lord, we your presence seek:
    we ask this blessing too;
give us a pure and lowly heart,
    a temple fit for you.

JOHN KEBLE (1792–1866)
WILLIAM JOHN HALL (1793–1861)
based on Matthew 5: 8

589

KUM BA YAH   88 85

West Indian traditional melody
arr. DAVID PEACOCK (b. 1949)

FATHER God in heaven,
  Lord most high:
hear your children's prayer,
  Lord most high:
hallowed be your name,
  Lord most high—
    O Lord, hear our prayer.

2 May your kingdom come
    here on earth;
  may your will be done
    here on earth,
  as it is in heaven
    so on earth—
      O Lord, hear our prayer.

3 Give us daily bread
    day by day,
  and forgive our sins
    day by day,
  as we too forgive
    day by day—
      O Lord, hear our prayer.

4 Lead us in your way,
    make us strong;
  when temptations come
    make us strong;
  save us from all sin,
    keep us strong—
      O Lord, hear our prayer.

5 All things come from you,
    all are yours—
  kingdom, glory, power,
    all are yours;
  take our lives and gifts,
    all are yours—
      O Lord, hear our prayer.

JAMES E. SEDDON (1915–83)
from the Lord's Prayer (Matthew 6: 9–13)

590

Gaelic melody
harm. *New Church Praise*, 1975

BUNESSAN   55 54 D

For an alternative arrangement of this tune (in D major) see no. 249.

FATHER in heaven,
be your name hallowed;
bring in your kingdom,
    reign here in love;
help us to give you
joyful obedience,
as they obey you
    in heaven above.

2 Give to us daily
food for our bodies;
grant us forgiveness
    as we forgive;
you know our weakness,
spare us the testing,
save us from evil
    each day we live.

3 Yours is the kingdom,
Father eternal;
yours is the power,
    maker of men;
worship we offer,
praises we bring you,
yours is the glory
    for ever. Amen.

STELLA READ
from the Lord's Prayer (Matthew 6: 9–13)

591

MOSCOW   664 6664   Adpt. from F. DE GIARDINI (1716–96)

FATHER whose mighty word
chaos and darkness heard
   and took their flight,
hear us, we humbly pray,
and where the gospel day
sheds not its glorious ray,
   let there be light.

2 Saviour who came to bring
on your redeeming wing
   healing and sight,
health to the sick in mind,
sight to the inly blind,
O now to all mankind
   let there be light.

3 Spirit of truth and love,
life-giving, holy dove,
   speed forth your flight;
move on the water's face,
bearing the lamp of grace,
and in earth's darkest place
   let there be light.

4 Blessed and holy three
most glorious Trinity,
   wisdom, love, might,
boundless as ocean's tide
rolling in fullest pride,
through the world far and wide
   let there be light.

JOHN MARRIOTT (1780–1825)

592

GOD BE IN MY HEAD   Irregular   H. WALFORD DAVIES (1869–1941)

God be in my head, and in my un-der-stand-ing; God be in my eyes, and in my look-ing; God be in my mouth, and in my speak - ing;

God be in my heart, and in my think - ing; God be at my ___ end, and at my de - part - ing.

GOD be in my head,
   and in my understanding;
God be in my eyes,
   and in my looking;
God be in my mouth,
   and in my speaking;
God be in my heart,
   and in my thinking;
God be at my end,
   and at my departing.

PYNSON'S *Horae*, 1514

593

CWM RHONDDA   87 87 47 extended   JOHN HUGHES (1873–1932)

For this tune in A♭ major see no. 652.

GUIDE me, O thou great Jehovah,
  pilgrim through this barren land;
I am weak, but thou art mighty;
  hold me with thy powerful hand:
    bread of heaven,
  feed me now and evermore.

2 Open now the crystal fountain,
    whence the healing stream doth flow;
  let the fiery, cloudy pillar
    lead me all my journey through:
      strong deliverer,
    be thou still my strength and shield.

3 When I tread the verge of Jordan,
    bid my anxious fears subside:
  death of death, and hell's destruction,
    land me safe on Canaan's side:
      songs of praises
    I will ever sing to thee.

WILLIAM WILLIAMS (1717–91)
based on Exodus 13: 21–2; 14: 26–31;
16: 4–18; 17: 4–6

594

SOLOTHURN LM   Swiss traditional melody

GIVE us, O God, the grace to see
   your smile within the morning light,
your signature upon the sea,
   your shadow in the blackest night.

2 Give us, O God, the grace to hear
   your word when marble turns to clay,
your voice when thunder clouds appear,
   your answer when the mountains sway.

3 Give us, O God, the grace to feel
   your breath upon the winds of change,
your kiss in sacraments that heal,
   your hand in what the years arrange.

4 Give us, O God, the grace to be
   convinced when miracles are rare,
your truth when stars turn ebony,
   your saints till earth has no despair.

Chinese Christian Literature Council

595

DAVOS   98 97

MICHAEL BAUGHEN (b. 1930)
and ELISABETH CROCKER (b. 1950)

I LIFT my eyes
to the quiet hills
in the press of a busy day;
    as green hills stand
    in a dusty land
so God is my strength and stay.

2 I lift my eyes
to the quiet hills
to a calm that is mine to share;
    secure and still
    in the Father's will
and kept by the Father's care.

3 I lift my eyes
to the quiet hills
with a prayer as I turn to sleep;
    by day, by night,
    through the dark and light
my shepherd will guard his sheep.

4 I lift my eyes
to the quiet hills
and my heart to the Father's throne;
    in all my ways
    to the end of days
the Lord will preserve his own.

TIMOTHY DUDLEY-SMITH (b. 1926)
based on Psalm 121

913

596

H. WALFORD DAVIES (1869–1941)
arr. JOHN WILSON (b. 1905)

VISION   15 15 15 6 (7)

Je-sus, my ex - am - ple be!

as I seek to fol - low you, fol - low you.

In your glad obedience to your
    Father's will to set us free,
in your singleness of purpose,
    Lord, throughout your ministry,
in your calm determination
    as you faced your Calvary,
        Jesus, my example be!

2 In your friendship for the lonely,
    your compassion for the sad,
in your stern denunciation
    of the shabby, mean and bad,
in your absolute preparedness
    to give God all you had,
        Jesus, my example be!

3 In your tenderness with children,
    your desire to help the old,
in your stand for honest dealings
    by all those who bought and sold,
in your call for kingdom values,
    worth far more than gems or gold,
        Jesus, my example be!

4 As I hope to shape my life
    on your supreme example, Lord,
drawing strength and inspiration
    from the study of your word,
may your Spirit give me power
    to live and share the truth I've heard,
        as I seek to follow you,
            follow you.

EILEEN D. ABBOTT (b. 1912)

597

MANNHEIM 87 87 87

F. FILITZ (1804–76)

LEAD us, heavenly Father, lead us
o'er the world's tempestuous sea;
guard us, guide us, keep us, feed us,
for we have no help but thee,
yet possessing every blessing,
if our God our Father be.

2 Saviour, breathe forgiveness o'er us;
all our weakness thou dost know;
thou didst tread this earth before us,
thou didst feel its keenest woe;
Son of Mary, lone and weary,
victor through this world didst go.

3 Spirit of our God descending,
fill our hearts with heavenly joy,
love with every passion blending,
pleasure that can never cloy.
Thus provided, pardoned, guided,
nothing can our peace destroy.

JAMES EDMESTON (1791–1867)

916

598

WAREHAM   LM

W. KNAPP (1698–1768)

LORD JESUS, once you spoke to men,
   upon the mountain, in the plain:
O help us listen now, as then,
   and wonder at your words again.

2 We all have secret fears to face,
   our minds and motives to amend;
we seek your truth, we need your grace,
   our living Lord and present friend.

3 The gospel speaks—and we receive
   your light, your love, your own command:
O help us live what we believe
   in daily work of heart and hand.

H. C. A. GAUNT (1902–83)

599

SALZBURG CM

J. M. HAYDN (1737–1806)

O God of Bethel, by whose hand
   your people still are fed;
who through this earthly pilgrimage
   your people safely led;

2 Our vows, our prayers, we now present
   before your gracious throne;
as you have been their faithful God,
   so always be our own!

3 Through each perplexing path of life
   our wandering footsteps guide;
give us today our daily bread,
   and for our needs provide.

4 O spread your covering wings around
   till all our wanderings cease;
and at our heavenly Father's home
   we shall arrive in peace.

PHILIP DODDRIDGE (1702–51)
based on Genesis 28: 10–22

600

O LORD HEAR MY PRAYER

JACQUES BERTHIER
as sung at Taizé
Words based on Psalm 55: 1–2

O Lord, hear my prayer, O Lord, hear my prayer,
when I call, an-swer me. O Lord, hear my prayer, O
Lord, hear my prayer, come and lis-ten to me.

601

TILAK   88

CAREY BONNER (1859–1938)

PRAYER to a heart of lowly love
opens the gate of heaven above.

2 Ah, prayer is God's high dwelling-place,
wherein his children see his face.

3 From earth to heaven we build a stair,
the name by which we call it, prayer.

4 Prayer is the gracious Father's knee;
on it the child climbs lovingly.

5 Love's rain, the Spirit's holy ray,
and tears of joy are theirs who pray.

6 Prayer to a heart of lowly love
opens the gate of heaven above.

NARAYAN VAMAN TILAK (1862–1919)
tr. N. MACNICOL (1870–1952)
based on Genesis 28: 12 and Psalm 103: 13

602

BUTTERMERE   LM

JOHN BARNARD (b. 1948)

UNTO the silent hills I raise
my weary eyes, that they may gaze
and feast upon the peaceful scene
that makes my soul content, serene.

2 Yet for my strength and help I seek
the one who made the mountain peak;
the Lord who formed the heavens and earth,
and gave created man his birth.

3 He is my keeper and my guide
when I walk closely by his side;
no evil thing beneath the sky
escapes his wise, discerning eye.

4 His loving hand will shield by day
from scorching heat of sun's hot ray;
he will not sleep by day or night,
his children's good is his delight.

5 Unto the silent hills I raise
my eyes, my heart, my soul in praise;
to him may alleluias soar,
who keeps my life for ever more!

MOLLIE KNIGHT
based on Psalm 121

603

CONVERSE   87 87 D

C. C. CONVERSE (1832–1918)
harm. BERNARD S. MASSEY (b. 1927)

WHAT a friend we have in Jesus,
  all our sins and griefs to bear!
What a privilege to carry
  everything to God in prayer!
O what peace we often forfeit,
  O what needless pain we bear,
all because we do not carry
  everything to God in prayer!

2 Have we trials and temptations?
  Is there trouble anywhere?
We should never be discouraged:
  take it to the Lord in prayer!
Can we find a friend so faithful,
  who will all our sorrows share?
Jesus knows our every weakness,
  take it to the Lord in prayer!

3 Are we weak and heavy-laden,
  cumbered with a load of care?
Jesus only is our refuge:
  take it to the Lord in prayer!
Do your friends despise, forsake you?
  Take it to the Lord in prayer!
In his arms he'll take and shield you;
  you will find a solace there.

JOSEPH SCRIVEN (1819–86)

604

SLANE   10 11 11 11

Irish traditional melody
harm. MARTIN SHAW (1875–1958) adpt.

For a version with guitar chords see no. 521.

CHEDWORTH   10 11 11 11

JOHN BARNARD (b. 1948)

© John Barnard/Jubilate Hymns

FATHER of glory, whose heavenly plan
was wholly made flesh in the life of a man,
your image of splendour we see in the face
of every known child of the whole human race:

2 Darkest to lightest, created as one,
all made for each other, set free by your Son.
No language or colour can hinder your care;
the failures and pains of the whole world you bear.

3 Barriers, divisions, no longer we see;
in Christ are no colours, no slaves now nor free,
no outcasts, no favourites, no Gentile, no Jew,
but one human family, united in you.

4 Give us the courage to mean what we say,
treat people as equals, their full rights to pay—
employment, enjoyment and freedom from fear,
to know, when in danger, that justice is near.

5 Give us the vision of all things made new,
of enmity ended, your promise come true;
that while in this city as neighbours we live,
we may to each other true dignity give.

KEITH W. CLEMENTS (b. 1943)

605

DUKE STREET LM   JOHN HATTON (d. 1793)

PONT STREET LM   GERALD L. BARNES (b. 1935)

GLORY to God, within the Church:
   let congregations gladly sing,
in faith uphold his glorious name,
   and honour bring to Christ our King.

2 Glory to God, within the world:
   let people join of every race
to live together in the Lord,
   divinely moved by Jesus' grace.

3 Glory to God, within the home:
   let every family feel his love;
should sadness, strife and discord reign,
   refresh and heal them from above.

4 Glory to God, in daily work:
   let all for him their best powers give,
to labour well in honest toil
   and for their Saviour gladly live.

5 Glory to God, in leisure time:
   let every hour his honour claim,
in loving care and service given
   to glorify his splendid name.

6 Glory to God, let angels sing,
   let people join in one accord,
with heart and voice, in word and deed,
   to praise and glorify the Lord.

PETER TONGEMAN (b. 1929)

606

CHEREPONI   779 with refrain

Ghanaian
adpt. TOM COLVIN, 1963

REFRAIN
Unison

Ye - su,_____ Ye - su,_____ fill

us with your love,   show   us   how   to   serve   the

(*Fine*)

neigh-bours   we   have   from   you._____

VERSES

D.C.

May be sung unaccompanied.

Yesu, Yesu, fill us with your love,
show us how to serve
the neighbours we have from you.

KNEELS at the feet of his friends,
silently washes their feet;
master who acts as a slave to them.

2 Neighbours are both rich and poor,
neighbours are black, brown and white,
neighbours are nearby and far away.

3 These are the ones we should serve,
these are the ones we should love,
all these are neighbours to us and you.

4 Loving puts us on our knees,
serving as though we are slaves,
this is the way we should live with you.

TOM COLVIN, 1963

607

ANGELS' SONG   LM   ORLANDO GIBBONS (1583–1625)

FORTH in the peace of Christ we go,
     Christ to the world with joy we bring;
Christ in our minds, Christ on our lips,
     Christ in our hearts, the world's true King.

2 King of our hearts, Christ makes us kings:
     kingship with him his servants gain;
with Christ, the Servant-Lord of all,
     Christ's world we serve to share Christ's reign.

3 Priests of the world, Christ sends us forth
     the world of time to consecrate,
the world of sin by grace to heal,
     Christ's world in Christ to re-create.

4 Christ's are our lips, his words we speak;
     prophets are we whose deeds proclaim
Christ's truth in love, that we may be
     Christ in the world, to spread Christ's name.

5 We are the Church; Christ bids us show
     that in his Church all nations find
their hearth and home, where Christ restores
     true peace, true love, to humankind.

JAMES QUINN (b. 1919)

608

CLOISTERS   11 11 11 5

J. BARNBY (1838–96)

LORD, as we rise to leave this shell of worship,
called to the risk of unprotected living,
willing to be at one with all your people,
   we ask for courage.

2 For all the strain with living interwoven,
for the demands each day will make upon us,
and for the love we owe the modern city,
   Lord, make us cheerful.

3 Give us an eye for openings to serve you;
make us alert when calm is interrupted,
ready and wise to use the unexpected:
   sharpen our insight.

4 Lift from our life the blanket of convention;
give us the nerve to lose our life to others,
be with your Church in death and resurrection,
   Lord of all ages!

FRED KAAN (b. 1929)

609

BENTLEY　　76 76 D

JOHN HULLAH (1812–84)

May also be sung to ELLACOMBE, no. 297.

LORD JESUS we must know you
    if we would make you known,
for how can we proclaim you
    but by your grace alone?
We long to know your fullness,
    your life of risen power,
for you alone can answer
    the challenge of this hour.

2 Our broken world is seeking
    what only you can give;
our words may go unheeded,
    but not the way we live.
O Saviour, live within us
    your life so strong, so true,
that others, touched with wonder,
    may seek and worship you!

3 Lord Jesus, by your Spirit
    renew your Church, we pray,
till what we are makes valid
    the truth of what we say.
So truly may we know you,
    so make your life our own,
that we become so like you
    our lives must make you known.

MARGARET CLARKSON (b. 1915)

610

RUSTINGTON   87 87 D

C. H. H. PARRY (1848–1918)

Fa-ther, as in high-est hea-ven, so on earth your will be done.

LORD of light, your name outshining
    all the stars and suns of space,
calling all to be co-workers
    in the kingdom of your grace;
use us to fulfil your purpose
    in the gift of Christ your Son:

Father, as in highest heaven,
so on earth your will be done.

2 By the toil of lonely workers
    in some far outlying field;
by the courage where the radiance
    of the cross is still revealed;
by the victories of meekness,
    through reproach and suffering won:

3 Grant that knowledge, still increasing,
    at your feet may lowly kneel;
with your grace our triumphs hallow,
    with your charity our zeal;
lift the nations from the shadows
    to the gladness of the sun:

4 By the prayers of faithful watchmen,
    never silent day or night;
by the cross of Jesus bringing
    peace to all, and healing light;
by the love that passes knowledge,
    making all your children one:

H. ELVET LEWIS (1860–1953)

611

WHITBURN   LM

H. BAKER (1835–1910)

Second Tune

LLEF   LM

G. H. JONES (1849–1919)

LORD, speak to me, that I may speak
    in living echoes of your tone;
as you have sought, so let me seek
    your erring children, lost, alone.

2 O lead me, Lord, that I may lead
    the stumbling and the straying feet;
and feed me Lord, that I may feed
    your hungry ones with manna sweet.

3 O strengthen me, that while I stand
    firm on the rock, secure but free,
I may stretch out a loving hand
    to wrestlers with the troubled sea.

4 O teach me, Lord, that I may teach
    the precious truths which you impart;
and wing my words that they may reach
    the hidden depths of many a heart.

5 O use me, Lord, use even me,
    just as you will, and when, and where,
until at last your face I see,
    your rest, your joy, your glory share.

FRANCES RIDLEY HAVERGAL (1836–79) altd.

612

HARVEST   98 98

MICHAEL METCALF (b. 1937)

Now join we, to praise the creator,
  our voices in worship and song;
we stand to recall with thanksgiving
  that to him all seasons belong.

2 We thank you, O God, for you goodness,
    for the joy and abundance of crops,
  for food that is stored in our larders,
    for all we can buy in the shops.

3 But also of need and starvation
    we sing with concern and despair,
  of skills that are used for destruction,
    of land that is burnt and laid bare.

4 We cry for the plight of the hungry
    while harvests are left on the field,
  for orchards neglected and wasting,
    for produce from markets withheld.

5 The song grows in depth and in wideness;
    the earth and its people are one,
  there can be no thanks without giving,
    no words without deeds that are done.

6 Then teach us, O Lord of the harvest,
    to be humble in all that we claim;
  to share what we have with the nations,
    to care for the world in your name.

FRED KAAN (b. 1929)

613

HERONGATE   LM

English traditional melody
arr. R. VAUGHAN WILLIAMS (1872–1958)

THE Church of Christ in every age
    beset by change, but Spirit-led,
must claim and test its heritage
    and keep on rising from the dead.

2 Across the world, across the street,
    the victims of injustice cry
for shelter and for bread to eat,
    and never live until they die.

3 Then let the servant Church arise,
    a caring Church that longs to be
a partner in Christ's sacrifice,
    and clothed in Christ's humanity.

4 For he alone, whose blood was shed,
    can cure the fever in our blood,
and teach us how to share our bread
    and feed the starving multitude.

5 We have no mission but to serve
    in full obedience to our Lord:
to care for all, without reserve,
    and spread his liberating word.

F. PRATT GREEN (b. 1903)

614

FIRST TUNE

CUDDESDON   65 65 D

W. H. FERGUSON (1874–1950)

WHEN the Church of Jesus
    shuts its outer door,
lest the roar of traffic
    drown the voice of prayer:
may our prayers, Lord, make us
    ten times more aware
that the world we banish
    is our Christian care.

2 If our hearts are lifted
    where devotion soars
high above this hungry
    suffering world of ours:
lest our hymns should drug us
    to forget its needs,
forge our Christian worship
    into Christian deeds.

3 Lest the gifts we offer,
    money, talents, time,
serve to salve our conscience
    to our secret shame:
Lord, reprove, inspire us
    by the way you give;
teach us, dying Saviour,
    how true Christians live.

F. PRATT GREEN (b. 1903)

614

SUTTON TRINITY   65 65 D

F. PRATT GREEN (b. 1903)

WHEN the Church of Jesus
   shuts its outer door,
lest the roar of traffic
   drown the voice of prayer:
may our prayers, Lord, make us
   ten times more aware
that the world we banish
   is our Christian care.

2 If our hearts are lifted
   where devotion soars
high above this hungry
   suffering world of ours:
lest our hymns should drug us
   to forget its needs,
forge our Christian worship
   into Christian deeds.

3 Lest the gifts we offer,
   money, talents, time,
serve to salve our conscience
   to our secret shame:
Lord, reprove, inspire us
   by the way you give;
teach us, dying Saviour,
   how true Christians live.

F. PRATT GREEN (b. 1903)

615

ARMAGEDDON   65 65 D with refrain (65 65)

German melody
adpt. J. GOSS (1800–80)

WHO is on the Lord's side?
  Who will serve the King?
Who will be his helpers
  other lives to bring?
Who will leave the world's side?
  Who will face the foe?
Who is on the Lord's side?
  Who for him will go?
    By thy call of mercy,
      by thy grace divine,
    we are on the Lord's side;
    Saviour, we are thine.

2 Not for weight of glory,
    not for crown and palm,
  enter we the army,
    raise the warrior-psalm;
  but for love that claimeth
    lives for whom he died:
  he whom Jesus nameth
    must be on his side.
      By thy love constraining,
        by thy grace divine,
      we are on the Lord's side;
      Saviour, we are thine.

3 Fierce may be the conflict,
    strong may be the foe,
  but the King's own army
    none can overthrow.
  Round his standard ranging,
    victory is secure,
  for his truth unchanging
    makes the triumph sure.
      Joyfully enlisting,
        by thy grace divine,
      we are on the Lord's side;
      Saviour, we are thine.

4 Chosen to be soldiers
    in an alien land,
  chosen, called and faithful,
    for our captain's band;
  in the service royal
    let us not grow cold;
  let us be right loyal,
    noble, true and bold.
      Master, thou wilt keep us,
        by thy grace divine,
      always on the Lord's side,
      Saviour, always thine.

FRANCES RIDLEY HAVERGAL (1836–79)

616

ANGELUS   LM

Founded on a melody in
SCHEFFER'S *Heilige Seelenlust*, 1657

AT evening, when the sun had set,
    the sick, O Lord, around you lay;
O with what differing pains they met,
    O with what joy they went away!

2 Like them we seek you, Lord, and we,
    oppressed with various ills, draw near;
although your form we cannot see
    we know and feel that you are here.

3 O Saviour Christ, our woes dispel:
    for some are sick and some are sad,
and some have never loved you well,
    and some have lost the love they had.

4 And none, O Lord, have perfect rest,
    for none are wholly free from sin;
and they who long to serve you best
    are conscious most of wrong within.

5 O Saviour Christ, you too are man;
    you have been troubled, tempted, tried;
your kind but searching glance can scan
    the very wounds that shame would hide.

6 Your touch still has its ancient power,
    no word from you can fruitless fall;
hear in this solemn worship hour,
    and in your mercy heal us all.

HENRY TWELLS (1823–1900)
based on Mark 1: 32–4

617

Melody from T. MOORE'S
*Psalm-Singer's Pocket Companion, c.*1756

GLASGOW   CM

BEHOLD, the mountain of the Lord
 in latter days shall rise
on mountain tops, above the hills,
 and draw the wondering eyes.

2 To this the joyful nations round,
 all tribes and tongues, shall flow;
up to the hill of God, they'll say,
 and to his house we'll go.

3 The beam that shines from Zion's hill
 shall lighten every land;
the King who reigns in Salem's towers
 shall all the world command.

4 No strife shall vex, nor hostile feuds
 disturb those peaceful years;
to ploughshares men shall beat their swords,
 to pruning-hooks their spears.

5 No longer hosts encountering hosts
 their millions slain deplore;
they hang the trumpet in the hall
 and study war no more.

6 Come, then, O come, from every land
 to worship at his shrine;
and walking in the light of God
 with holy beauties shine.

Scottish Paraphrases, 1781
based on Isaiah 2: 2–5

618

First Tune

Adpt. from a melody by
J. CRÜGER (1598–1662)

NUN DANKET 67 67 66 66

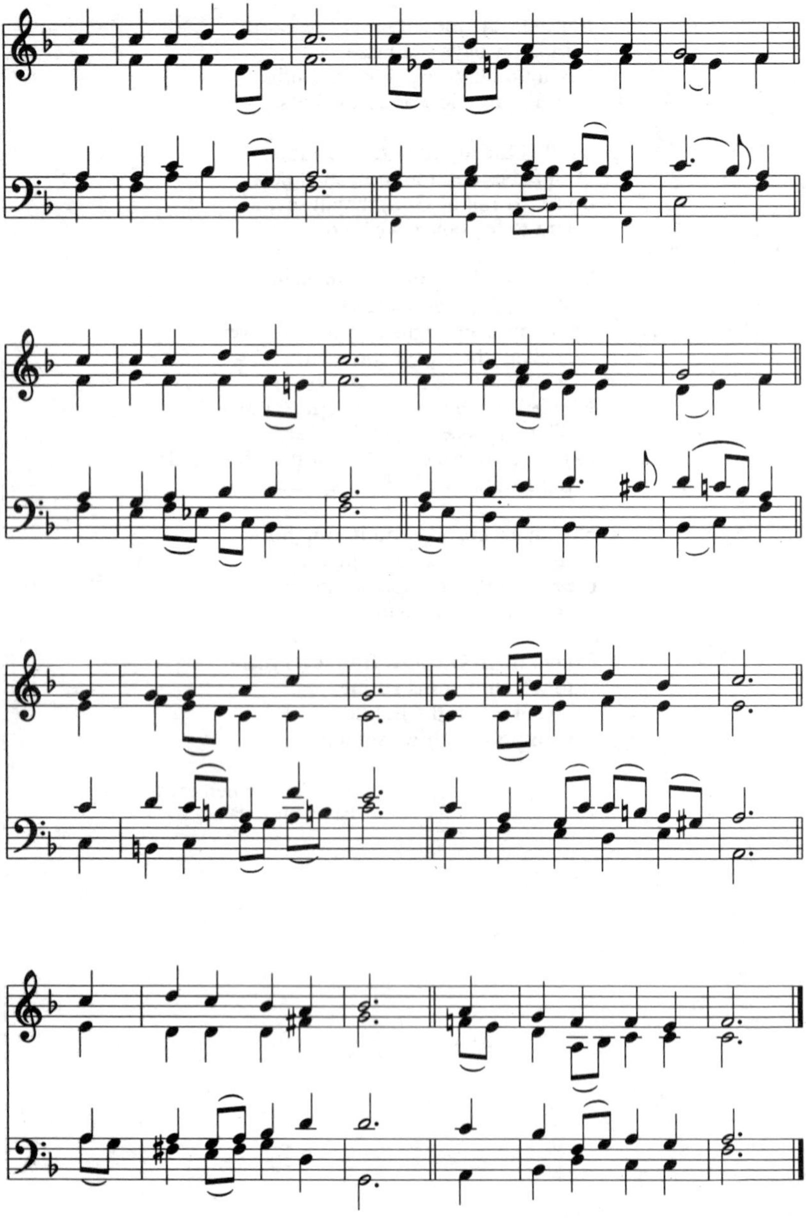

CHRIST is the world's true light,
    its captain of salvation,
the daystar clear and bright
    of every man and nation;
new life, new hope awakes,
    where people own his sway:
freedom her bondage breaks,
    and night is turned to day.

2 In Christ all races meet,
    their ancient feuds forgetting,
the whole round world complete,
    from sunrise to its setting.
When Christ is throned as Lord,
    men shall forsake their fear,
to ploughshare beat the sword,
    to pruning-hook the spear.

3 One Lord, in one great name
    unite us all who own you;
cast out our pride and shame
    that hinder to enthrone you.
The world has waited long,
    has travailed long in pain;
to heal its ancient wrong,
    come, Prince of peace, and reign.

G. W. BRIGGS (1875–1959)
based on John 8:12 and Isaiah 2: 4–5

618
SECOND TUNE

RINKART   67 67 66 66

J. S. BACH (1685–1750)

CHRIST is the world's true light,
　　its captain of salvation,
the daystar clear and bright
　　of every man and nation;
new life, new hope awakes,
　　where people own his sway:
freedom her bondage breaks,
　　and night is turned to day.

2　In Christ all races meet,
　　　their ancient feuds forgetting,
　the whole round world complete,
　　　from sunrise to its setting.
　When Christ is throned as Lord,
　　　men shall forsake their fear,
　to ploughshare beat the sword,
　　　to pruning-hook the spear.

3　One Lord, in one great name
　　　unite us all who own you;
　cast out our pride and shame
　　　that hinder to enthrone you.
　The world has waited long,
　　　has travailed long in pain;
　to heal its ancient wrong,
　　　come, Prince of peace, and reign.

G. W. BRIGGS (1875–1959)
based on John 8:12 and Isaiah 2: 4–5

619

SPRINGFIELD   11 10 11 10 Dactylic   H. J. GAUNTLETT (1805–76)

Second Tune

MELISSA   11 10 11 10 Dactylic   JOHN LOCK (b. 1937)

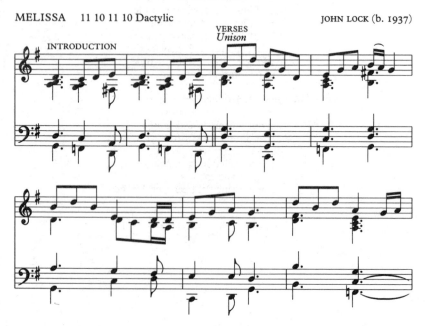

Optional ending after last verse

CRADLE, O Lord, in your arms everlasting,
  one that we love and for whom we now pray:
graces and gifts which in *him* we acknowledge
  come from the God who rules both night and day.

2 Cradle, O Lord, in your arms everlasting,
    those who now suffer sore anguish and pain:
  warmed may they be by true human affection;
    by love surrounded, in your care remain.

3 Cradle, O Lord, in your arms everlasting,
    all who seek here for your *comfort** today:
  make of our lives prayers of joyful self-giving,
    offered to Christ who is light for the way.

CHRISTOPHER T. BRADNOCK (b. 1942)

*Or *healing*, as appropriate.

620

FIRST TUNE

ODE TO JOY 87 87 D

L. VAN BEETHOVEN (1770–1827)

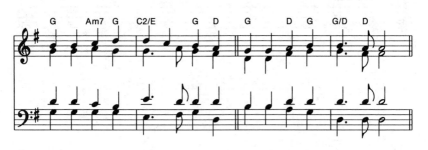

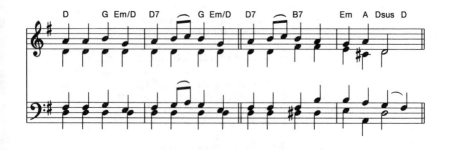

FATHER, Lord of all creation,
　　ground of being, life and love;
height and depth beyond description
　　only life in you can prove:
you are mortal life's dependence:
　　thought, speech, sight are ours by grace;
yours is every hour's existence,
　　sovereign Lord of time and space.

2 Jesus Christ, the man for others,
　　we, your people, make our prayer:
give us grace to love as brothers
　　all whose burdens we can share.
Where your name binds us together
　　you, Lord Christ, will surely be;
where no selfishness can sever
　　there your love may all men see.

3 Holy Spirit, rushing, burning
　　wind and flame of Pentecost,
fire our hearts afresh with yearning
　　to regain what we have lost.
May your love unite our action,
　　nevermore to speak alone:
God, in us abolish faction,
　　God, through us your love make known.

STEWART CROSS (1928–89)

620

SECOND TUNE

Melody by
CHARLES VENN PILCHER (1879–1961)

HERMON   87 87 D

FATHER, Lord of all creation,
 ground of being, life and love;
height and depth beyond description
 only life in you can prove:
you are mortal life's dependence:
 thought, speech, sight are ours by grace;
yours is every hour's existence,
 sovereign Lord of time and space.

2 Jesus Christ, the man for others,
 we, your people, make our prayer:
give us grace to love as brothers
 all whose burdens we can share.
Where your name binds us together
 you, Lord Christ, will surely be;
where no selfishness can sever
 there your love may all men see.

3 Holy Spirit, rushing, burning
 wind and flame of Pentecost,
fire our hearts afresh with yearning
 to regain what we have lost.
May your love unite our action,
 nevermore to speak alone:
God, in us abolish friction,
 God, through us your love make known.

STEWART CROSS (1928–89)

621

CORINTH   87 87 87

S. WEBBE (THE ELDER) (1740–1816)

FOR the healing of the nations,
   Lord, we pray with one accord;
for a just and equal sharing
   of the things that earth affords.
To a life of love in action
   help us rise and pledge our word.

2 Lead us, Father, into freedom,
   from despair your world release,
that, redeemed from war and hatred,
   all may come and go in peace.
Show us how through care and goodness
   fear will die and hope increase.

3 All that kills abundant living,
   let it from the earth be banned;
pride of status, race or schooling,
   dogmas that obscure your plan.
In our common quest for justice
   may we hallow life's brief span.

4 You, Creator-God, have written
   your great name on humankind;
for our growing in your likeness
   bring the life of Christ to mind;
that by our response and service
   earth its destiny may find.

FRED KAAN (b. 1929)

622

FREEDOM IS COMING

South African traditional song
as sung by the Iona Community

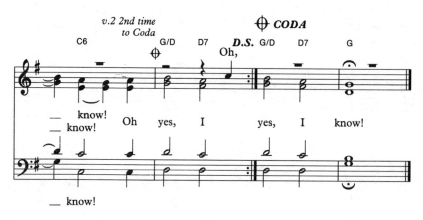

FREEDOM is coming,
Oh yes, I know!

2 Jesus is coming,
Oh yes, I know!

Iona Community

623

First Tune

TREDEGAR 87 87 87 GUTHRIE FOOTE (1897–1972)

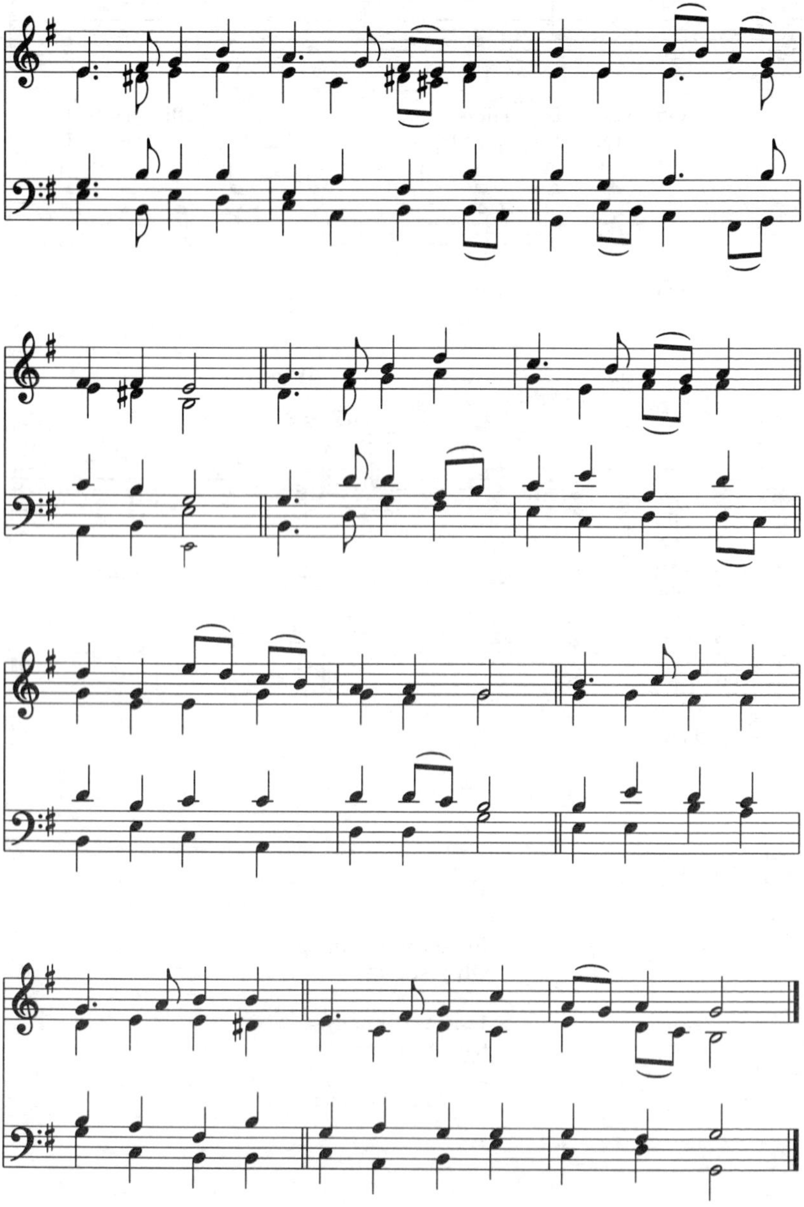

God of freedom, God of justice,
   God whose love is strong as death,
God who saw the dark of prison,
   God who knew the price of faith:
touch our world of sad oppression
   with your Spirit's healing breath.

2 Rid the earth of torture's terror,
   you whose hands were nailed to wood;
hear the cries of pain and protest,
   Christ who shed the tears and blood;
move in us the power of pity
   restless for the common good.

3 Make in us a captive conscience
   quick to hear, to act, to plead;
make us truly sisters, brothers
   of whatever race or creed;
teach us to be fully human,
   open to each other's need.

SHIRLEY ERENA MURRAY (b. 1931)

623

SECOND TUNE

WESTMINSTER ABBEY   87 87 87

Adpt. from
HENRY PURCELL (1659–95)

For a slightly different arrangement of this tune see no. 474.

GOD of freedom, God of justice,
  God whose love is strong as death,
God who saw the dark of prison,
  God who knew the price of faith:
touch our world of sad oppression
  with your Spirit's healing breath.

2 Rid the earth of torture's terror,
    you whose hands were nailed to wood;
  hear the cries of pain and protest,
    Christ who shed the tears and blood;
  move in us the power of pity
    restless for the common good.

3 Make in us a captive conscience
    quick to hear, to act, to plead;
  make us truly sisters, brothers
    of whatever race or creed;
  teach us to be fully human,
    open to each other's need.

SHIRLEY ERENA MURRAY (b. 1931)

624

TOULON   10 10 10 10

Genevan Psalter, 1551

SECOND TUNE

E. J. HOPKINS (1818–1901)
arr. ARTHUR SULLIVAN (1842–1900)

ELLERS   10 10 10 10

GRANT us your peace, for you alone can bend
our faltering purpose to a nobler end;
you Lord alone can teach our hearts to know
the fellowship that through your love can grow.

2 Grant us your peace, for we have filled the years
with greed and envy and with foolish fears,
with squandered treasures and ignoble gain,
and fruitless harvests that we reap in vain.

3 Grant us your peace, till all our strife shall seem
the hateful memory of some evil dream;
till that new song ring out that shall not cease,
'In heaven your glory and on earth your peace!'

J. H. B. MASTERMAN (1867–1933)

625

HE COMES TO US   86 886   NORMAN WARREN (b. 1934)

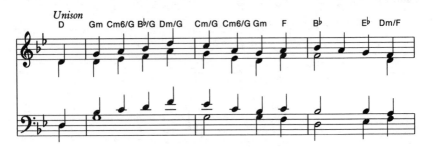

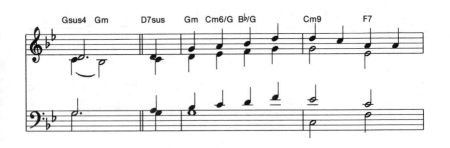

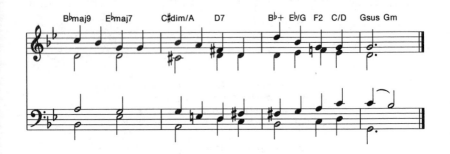

'I HAVE a dream,' a man once said,
  'where all is perfect peace:
where men and women, black and white,
stand hand in hand, and all unite
  in freedom and in love.'

2 But in this world of bitter strife
  the dream can often fade:
reality seems dark as night,
we catch but glimpses of the light
  Christ sheds on humankind.

3 Fierce persecution, war and hate
  are raging everywhere:
through struggles and through sacrifice
God's people pay the costly price
  of standing for the right.

4 So dream your dreams and sing your songs,
  but never be content;
for thoughts and words don't ease the pain:
unless there's action, all is vain;
  faith proves itself in deeds.

5 Lord, grant us vision, make us strong,
  and help us do your will;
nor let us rest until we see
your love throughout humanity
  uniting us in peace.

PAM PETTITT

626

FULDA (WALTON)   LM   GARDINER'S *Sacred Melodies*, 1815

WHERE cross the crowded ways of life,
    where sound the cries of race and clan,
above the noise of selfish strife,
    we hear your voice, O Son of Man!

2 In haunts of wretchedness and need,
    on shadowed thresholds dark with fears,
from paths where hide the lures of greed,
    we catch the vision of your tears.

3 The cup of water given for you
    still holds the freshness of your grace;
yet long these multitudes to view
    the strong compassion of your face.

4 O Master, from the mountain side
    make haste to heal those hearts of pain;
among these restless throngs abide;
    O tread the city's streets again;

5 Till humankind shall learn your love,
    and follow where your feet have trod;
till glorious from your heaven above
    shall come the city of our God.

FRANK MASON NORTH (1850–1935)

627

RHUDDLAN   87 87 87

Welsh traditional melody
harm. in *The English Hymnal*, 1906

JUDGE eternal, throned in splendour,
   Lord of hosts and King of kings,
with your living fire of judgement
   purge this realm of bitter things;
solace all its wide dominion
   with the healing of your wings.

2 Still the weary folk are pining
   for the hour that brings release,
and the city's crowded clangour
   cries aloud for sin to cease,
and the homesteads and the woodlands
   plead in silence for their peace.

3 Crown, O God, your own endeavour;
   cleave our darkness with your sword;
feed the faint and hungry heathen
   with the richness of your word;
cleanse the body of this nation
   through the glory of the Lord.

H. SCOTT HOLLAND (1847–1918)

628

FIRST TUNE

STEEPLE ASHTON   SM

JOHN BARNARD (b. 1948)

Music © J. Barnard/Jubilate Hymns

SECOND TUNE

SHERE   SM

ERIC H. THIMAN (1900–75)

LEAD me from death to life,
 from falsehood into truth;
and may I keep, through all my years,
 the hopefulness of youth.

2 From dark despair to hope,
 from fear to trust in God,
from hate to love, from war to peace,
 still lead me on, dear Lord.

3 Let peace enfold my heart;
 in peace my soul immerse;
and may God's peace pervade the world,
 then fill the universe.

adapted from the paraphrase
by RAE E. WHITNEY (b. 1927)
of the *World Peace Prayer*

Author's prefered version:
 v. 1 line 4: the wondrous joy of youth
 v. 2 line 4: keep leading me, dear Lord

629

LET THERE BE PEACE ON EARTH

Words and music by
SY MILLER and JILL JACKSON

1. Let there be peace on earth and let it be-gin with me; let there be peace on earth, the peace that was meant to be. With God as our Fa-ther, bro-thers and sis-ters are we.

2. Let peace be-gin with me, let this be the mo-ment now; With ev-ery step I take, let this be my sol-emn vow: to

2nd time to Coda

HARMONY AND HEALING

Let us walk with each o - ther___ in per - fect har - mo -

- ny.___

CODA

take each mo - ment, and live each

mo - ment in peace e - ter - nal - ly.___ Let there be

peace on earth and let it be - gin with me.___

630

CONCORD   47 76

ROBERT J. B. FLEMING (b. 1921)

LET there be light,
let there be understanding,
let all the nations gather,
let them be face to face;

2 Open our lips,
open our minds to ponder,
open the way to concord
opening into grace;

3 Perish the sword,
perish the angry judgement,
perish the bombs and hunger,
perish the fight for gain;

4 Hallow our love,
hallow the deaths of martyrs,
hallow their holy freedom,
hallowèd be your name;

5 Your kingdom come,
your spirit turn to language,
your people speak together,
your spirit never fade;

6 Let there be light,
open our hearts to wonder,
perish the way of terror,
hallow the world God made.

FRANCES WHEELER DAVIS (b. 1936)

631

REGENT SQUARE   87 87 87   HENRY SMART (1813–79)

LET us sing the King Messiah,
  King of righteousness and peace;
hail him, all his happy subjects,
  never let his praises cease:
    ever hail him;
  never let his praises cease.

2 How transcendent are your glories,
    fairer than the sons of men,
  while your blessed mediation
    brings us back to God again:
      blest Redeemer,
    how we triumph in your reign!

3 Gird your sword on, mighty hero
    ride for truth in word and deed;
  prosper in your course majestic;
    till your glorious cause succeed:
      gracious victor,
    let mankind before you bow.

4 Majesty combined with meekness,
    righteousness and peace unite
  to ensure your blessed conquests;
    on, great Prince, assert your right:
      ride triumphant
    all around the conquered globe.

5 Blest are all who touch your sceptre;
    blest are all who own your reign,
  freed from sin, that worst of tyrants,
    rescued from its galling chain:
      saints and angels,
    all who know you bless your reign.

JOHN RYLAND (1753–1825) altd.
based on Psalm 45

632

OLD YEAVERING   888 7

NOËL TREDINNICK (b. 1949)

Music © N. Tredinnick/Jubilate Hymns

Second Tune

QUEM PASTORES LAUDAVERE
888 7

14th-century German carol melody
arr. R. VAUGHAN WILLIAMS (1872–1958)

LIKE a mighty river flowing,
like a flower in beauty growing,
far beyond all human knowing
   is the perfect peace of God.

2 Like the hills serene and even,
like the coursing clouds of heaven,
like the heart that's been forgiven
   is the perfect peace of God.

3 Like the summer breezes playing,
like the tall trees softly swaying,
like the lips of silent praying
   is the perfect peace of God.

4 Like the morning sun ascended,
like the scents of evening blended,
like a friendship never ended
   is the perfect peace of God.

5 Like the azure ocean swelling,
like the jewel all-excelling,
far beyond our human telling
   is the perfect peace of God.

MICHAEL PERRY (b. 1942)
based on Philippians 4: 7

633

COMPTON ABDALE   54 54 54 64   JOHN BARNARD (b. 1948)

MADE in God's image:
　woman and man;
here is the wholeness:
　God's human plan.
Brother and sister,
　daughter and son,
here is a family
　made to be one.

2　We need each other,
　old folk and young,
sharing together
　life from the Son.
This is the meaning,
　prize to be won,
here is a family
　made to be one.

3　Dappled creation,
　diverse its ways,
colours and cultures
　offer their praise.
Gathered together
　under the sun,
here is a family
　made to be one.

4　Praise to the Father
　and to the Son,
praise to the Spirit:
　our God is one.
Here is our vision,
　new world begun,
here is a family
　made to be one.

CHRISTOPHER ELLIS (b. 1949)

634

A CHANNEL OF YOUR PEACE

SEBASTIAN TEMPLE (b. 1928)
arr. BETTY PULKINGHAM (b. 1928)
Words based on the Prayer of St Francis

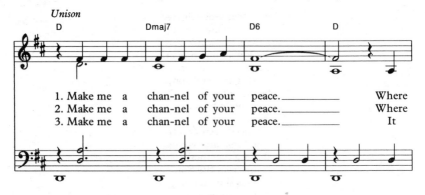

1. Make me a chan-nel of your peace._____ Where
2. Make me a chan-nel of your peace._____ Where
3. Make me a chan-nel of your peace._____ It

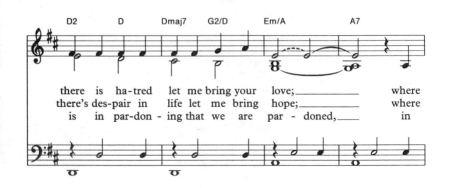

there is ha-tred let me bring your love;_____ where
there's des-pair in life let me bring hope;_____ where
is in par-don - ing that we are par - doned,___ in

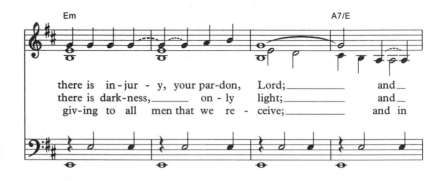

there is in-jur - y, your par-don, Lord;_____ and__
there is dark-ness,_____ on - ly light;_____ and__
giv-ing to all men that we re - ceive;_____ and in

HARMONY AND HEALING

* Voices may sing in two-part harmony.

635

FIRST TUNE

CARLISLE   SM

C. LOCKHART (1745–1815)

SECOND TUNE

Genevan Psalter, 1551
adpt. WILLIAM CROTCH (1775–1847)

ST MICHAEL   SM

O DAY of God, draw near
in beauty and in power,
come with your timeless judgement now
to match our present hour.

2 Bring to our troubled minds,
uncertain and afraid,
the quiet of a steadfast faith,
calm of a call obeyed.

3 Bring justice to our land,
that all may dwell secure,
and finely build for days to come
foundations that endure.

4 Bring to our world of strife
your sovereign word of peace,
that war may haunt the earth no more
and desolation cease.

5 O day of God, draw near,
as at creation's birth,
let there be light again, and set
your judgements in the earth.

R. B. Y. SCOTT (1899–1987)

636

O LORD ALL THE WORLD BELONGS TO YOU   PATRICK APPLEFORD (b. 1925)

O Lord, all the world belongs to you,
and you are always making all things new;
   what is wrong you forgive
   and the new life you give
is what's turning this world upside down.

2 The world's only loving to its friends,
but your way of loving never ends;
   loving enemies too,
   and this loving with you
is what's turning this world upside down.

3 The world lives divided and apart,
you draw us together and we start
   in your body to see
   that in fellowship we
can be turning this world upside down.

4 The world wants the wealth to live in state,
but you showed a new way to be great;
   like a servant you came
   and if we do the same
we'll be turning this world upside down.

5 O Lord, all the world belongs to you,
and you are always making all things new;
   send your Spirit on all
   in your Church whom you call
to be turning this world upside down.

PATRICK APPLEFORD (b. 1925)

637

ST COLUMBA   87 87 Iambic   Ancient Irish hymn melody

PUT peace into each other's hands
    and like a treasure hold it;
protect it like a candle-flame,
    with tenderness enfold it.

2 Put peace into each other's hands
    with loving expectation;
be gentle in your words and ways,
    in touch with God's creation.

3 Put peace into each other's hands
    like bread we break for sharing;
look people warmly in the eye:
    our life is meant for caring.

4 As at communion shape your hands
    into a waiting cradle;
the gift of Christ receive, revere,
    united round the table.

5 Put Christ into each other's hands,
    he is love's deepest measure;
in love make peace, give peace a chance
    and share it like a treasure.

FRED KAAN (b. 1929)

638   First Tune

SIMEON   LM   S. STANLEY (1767–1822)

Second Tune

BROADMEAD   LM   WALTER WEBBER (b. 1893)

SING we a song of high revolt;
make great the Lord, his name exalt!
Sing we the song that Mary sang
of God at war with human wrong.

2 Sing we of him who deeply cares,
and still with us our burden bears;
he who with strength the proud disowns,
brings down the mighty from their thrones.

3 By him the poor are lifted up;
he satisfies with bread and cup
the hungry ones of many lands;
the rich must go with empty hands.

4 He calls us to revolt and fight
with him for what is just and right,
to sing and live Magnificat
in crowded street and council flat.

FRED KAAN (b. 1929)

639

BETHANY   87 87 D

HENRY SMART (1813–79)

For this tune in F major see no. 559(*ii*).
May also be sung to EVERTON, no. 577.

Son of God, eternal Saviour,
    source of life and truth and grace;
Son of Man, whose birth among us
    hallows all our human race;
Christ our head, for all your people
    you have never ceased to plead;
fill us with your love and pity,
    heal our wrongs, and help our need.

2 As you, Lord, have lived for others,
    so may we for others live;
freely have your gifts been granted,
    freely may your servants give;
yours the gold and yours the silver,
    all the wealth of sea and land;
we but stewards of your riches
    held in trust at your command.

3 Come, O Christ, and reign among us,
    King of love, and Prince of peace;
hush the storm of strife and passion,
    bid its cruel discords cease;
by your patient years of toiling,
    by your silent hours of pain,
quench our fevered thirst for pleasure,
    shame our selfish greed of gain.

4 Son of God, eternal Saviour,
    source of life and truth and grace;
Son of Man, whose birth among us
    hallows all our human race:
you have prayed and you have purposed
    that your people shall be one;
grant to us our hope's fulfilment:
    here on earth your will be done!

S. C. LOWRY (1855–1932)

640

LOVE IS THE FULFILLING
11 10 11 10 with refrain

RICHARD CONNOLLY (b. 1927)

The law of Christ a-lone can make us free, and

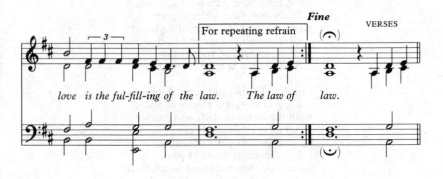

love is the ful-fill-ing of the law. The law of law.

The law of

The refrain may be sung first by a soloist or small group and then repeated by the congregation.
The verses may be sung either by the group or by the congregation.

The law of Christ alone can make us free,
and love is the fulfilling of the law.
The law of Christ alone can make us free,
and love is the fulfilling of the law.

WE are the sons of God, sisters and brothers;
    but will the fatherhood of God be known
if we do not reflect his love to others?
    In charity and justice God is shown:

2 Millions believe the law of life is cunning
    within a world of cruelty and greed;
how can they know God's charity and justice
    if helping hands have never reached their need?

3 Christ is at work through us who are his body:
    he chooses us to witness and to teach,
to heal and raise and liberate and strengthen,
    to be his hands and eyes, his heart and speech:

4 There is no promise that we shall not suffer,
    no promise that we shall not need to fight;
only the word that love is our redemption,
    and freedom comes by turning to the light:

J. P. MCAULEY (1917–76) altd.
based on Romans 13: 8–10

641

INTERCESSOR   11 10 11 10   C. H. H. PARRY (1848–1918)

May also be sung to FINLANDIA, no. 117.

WE turn to you, O God of every nation,
    giver of good and origin of life;
your love is at the heart of all creation,
    your hurt is people's pain in war and death.

2 We turn to you that we may be forgiven
    for crucifying Christ on earth again.
We know that we have never wholly striven,
    to share with all the promise of your reign.

3 Free every heart from pride and self-reliance,
    our ways of thought inspire with simple grace;
break down among us barriers of defiance,
    speak to the soul of all the human race.

4 On all who rise on earth for right relations
    we pray the light of love from hour to hour.
Grant wisdom to the leaders of the nations,
    the gift of carefulness to those in power.

5 Teach us, good Lord, to serve the need of others,
    help us to give and not to count the cost.
Unite us all to live as sisters, brothers;
    defeat our Babel with your Pentecost!

FRED KAAN (b. 1929)

642

BENTLEY   76 76 D

JOHN HULLAH (1812–84)

For this tune in D major see no. 312.
May also be sung to PENLAN, no. 555, or LLANGLOFFAN, no. 581.

WHERE restless crowds are thronging
　　along the city ways,
where pride and greed and turmoil
　　consume the fevered days,
where vain ambitions banish
　　all thoughts of praise and prayer,
the people's spirits waver:
　　but you, O Christ, are there.

2　In scenes of want and sorrow
　　　and haunts of flagrant wrong,
　in homes where kindness falters,
　　　and strife and fear are strong,
　in busy street of barter,
　　　in lonely thoroughfare,
　the people's spirits languish:
　　　but you, O Christ, are there.

3　O Christ, behold your people:
　　　they press on every hand!
　Bring light to all the cities
　　　of our beloved land.
　May all our bitter striving
　　　give way to visions fair
　of righteousness and justice:
　　　for you, O Christ, are there.

THOMAS CURTIS CLARK (1877–1953)

643

THANK YOU LORD   777 4

DIANE ANDREW

THANK you, Lord, for this new day,
thank you, Lord, for this new day,
thank you, Lord, for this new day,
right where we are.

Alleluia, praise the Lord,
right where we are.

2 Thank you, Lord, for food to eat,

3 Thank you, Lord, for clothes to wear,

4 Thank you, Lord, for all your gifts.

DIANE ANDREW
words adpt. GEOFFREY MARSHALL-TAYLOR

644

ST CECILIA   66 66

L. G. HAYNE (1836–83)

YOUR kingdom come, O God,
  your rule, O Christ, begin;
break with your iron rod
  the tyrannies of sin.

2 Where is your reign of peace
    and purity and love?
  When shall all hatred cease,
    as in the realms above?

3 When comes the promised time,
    that war shall be no more,
  and lust, oppression, crime
    shall flee your face before?

4 We pray you, Lord, arise,
    and come in your great might;
  revive our longing eyes
    which languish for your sight.

5 Scorned is your sacred name,
    and wolves devour your fold;
  by many deeds of shame
    we learn that love grows cold.

6 O'er lands both near and far
    darkness is brooding yet:
  arise, O morning star,
    arise, and never set!

LEWIS HENSLEY (1824–1905)

645   THE ALLELUIAS OF HEAVEN

After this I heard what sounded like the roar of a great multitude in heaven
shouting: 'Alleluia! Salvation and glory and power belong to our God,
for true and just are his judgements.'
   **Then a voice came from the throne, saying: 'Praise to our God,
all you his servants, you who fear him, small and great.'**

Then I heard what sounded like a great multitude, like the roar of
rushing waters and like loud peals of thunder, shouting:
   **'Alleluia! For our Lord God Almighty reigns.
Let us rejoice and be glad and give him the glory!'**

646   THE NEW JERUSALEM

Then I saw a new heaven and a new earth. The first heaven and the
first earth disappeared, and the sea vanished.
   **And I saw the holy city, the New Jerusalem, coming down out
of heaven from God, prepared and ready, like a bride dressed
to meet her husband.**

I heard a loud voice speaking from the throne: 'Now God's home is
with mankind! He will live with them, and they will be his people.
God himself will be with them, and he will be their God.
   **'He will wipe away all tears from their eyes. There will be no
more death, no more grief or crying or pain. The old things
have disappeared.'**

Then the one who sits on the throne said: 'And now I shall make all
things new!'

647   MORE THAN CONQUERORS

We know that in all things God works for good with those who love him,
those whom he has called according to his purpose.
   **In view of all this, what can we say?
If God is for us, who can be against us?**

Certainly not God, who did not even keep back his own Son, but
offered him up for us all!
   He gave us his Son—will he not also freely give us all things?

Who, then, can separate us from the love of Christ?
   **Can trouble do it, or hardship or persecution
or hunger or poverty or danger or death?**

No, in all these things we have complete victory
through him who loved us!
   Nothing can separate us from his love:

neither death nor life, nor angels nor other heavenly rulers or powers,
neither the present nor the future, neither the world above
nor the world below—
   **there is nothing in all creation that will ever be able to separate
us from the love of God, which is ours through Christ our Lord.**

5. HYMNS IN WELSH

648

ARWELFA   87 87 D   JOHN HUGHES (1896–1968)

ARGLWYDD, gad im dawel orffwys
    dan gysgodau'r palmwydd clyd,
lle yr eistedd pererinion
    ar eu ffordd i'r nefol fyd;
lle'r adroddant dy ffyddlondeb
    iddynt yn yr anial cras,
nes anghofio'u cyfyngderau
    wrth foliannu nerth dy ras.

2 O! mor hoff yw cwmni'r brodyr
    sydd a'u hwyneb tua'r wlad,
heb un tafod yn gwenieithio—
    heb un fron yn meithrin brad:
gwlith y nefoedd ar eu profiad,
    atsain hyder yn eu hiaith;
teimlant hiraeth am eu cartref,
    carant sôn am ben eu taith.

3 Arglwydd, dal ni nes mynd adref,
    nid yw'r llwybyr eto'n faith;
gwened heulwen ar ein henaid,
    wrth nes'u at ben y daith;
doed y nefol awel dyner
    i'n cyfarfod yn y glyn,
nes in deimlo'n traed yn sengi
    ar uchelder Seion fryn.

WILLIAM AMBROSE (EMRYS) (1813–73)

GRANT, O Lord, a peaceful respite
    in the tranquil shade of palms,
where the pilgrims on their sojourn
    sing of solace in the psalms;
where in thankfulness they ponder
    and your faithful blessings name,
where all fears and woes they conquer
    as your mercies they proclaim.

2 O, how sweet is our communion
    with God's people homeward bound,
where no flattering word is spoken
    and no treacherous heart is found.
Heavenly dew on life's rich story,
    strong resolve in all their song,
as with joy they talk of heaven
    and the home for which they long.

3 Lord, support us with your mercies
    while our homeward path we wend;
let your rays our souls encourage
    as we near our journey's end;
may the gentle heavenly breezes
    bless us till the vale is past
and our feet are firmly planted
    high on Zion's hill at last.

WILLIAM AMBROSE (EMRYS) (1813–73)
tr. RAYMOND WILLIAMS (1928–90)

649

MAWLGAN Irregular

J. H. ROBERTS (1848–1924)

(1.) hun,_____ yn ei - ddo i - ddo'i hun.
(1.) yn ei - ddo, yn

BENDIGEDIG fyddo'r Iesu!
Yr hwn sydd yn ein caru,
ein galw o'r byd a'n prynu,
ac yn ei waed ein golchi,
   yn eiddo iddo'i hun.

   Haleliwia, Haleliwia,
   Moliant iddo byth, Amen.
   Haleliwia, Haleliwia,
   Moliant iddo byth, Amen.

2 Bendigedig fyddo'r Iesu!
Fe welir ei Ddyweddi
heb un brycheuyn arni
yn lân fel y goleuni,
   ar ddelw Mab y Dyn.

J. SPINTHER JAMES (1837–1914)

LET us praise the Lord triumphant
   who from the grave is risen:
his life and death so glorious
shall make his Church victorious,
   that we might all be free.

   Alleluia, Alleluia,
   praise him now and evermore.
   Alleluia, Alleluia,
   praise him now and evermore.

2 Let us praise the Lord triumphant
   who from the grave is risen:
his love is great, unending,
all earthly bounds transcending.
   O come, and praise his name.

tr. JOHN HUGHES (1896–1968)

650

TYDI A RODDAIST   86 86 88   ARWEL HUGHES (1909–88)

*Optional Amen, after final verse only

A - men, A - men, A - men, A - men.

TYDI, a roddaist liw i'r wawr
  a hud i'r machlud mwyn;
tydi a luniaist gerdd a sawr
  a gwanwyn yn y llwyn:
O! cadw ni rhag colli'r hud
  sydd heddiw'n crwydro drwy'r holl fyd.

2 Tydi, a luniaist gân i'r nant,
    a'i si i'r goedwig werdd;
  tydi a roist i'r awel dant,
    ac i'r ehedydd gerdd:
  O! cadw ni rhag dyfod dydd
    na yrr ein calon gân yn rhydd.

3 Tydi, a glywaist lithriad traed
    ar ffordd Calfaria gynt;
  tydi, a welaist ddafnau gwaed
    y gŵr ar ddieithr hynt;
  O! cadw ni rhag dyfod oes
    heb goron ddrain na chur na chroes.
                                    (Amen.)

                  T. ROWLAND HUGHES (1903–49)

O LORD, who gave the dawn its glow,
  and charm to close of day,
you made all song and fragrance flow,
  gave spring its magic sway:
deliver us, lest none should praise
  for glories that all earth displays.

2 O Lord, who caused the streams to sing,
    gave joy to forest trees,
  you gave a song to lark on wing,
    and chords to gentlest breeze:
  deliver us, lest we should see
    a day without a song set free.

3 O Lord, who heard the lonely tread
    on that strange path of old,
  you saw the Son of Man once shed
    his blood from love untold:
  deliver us, lest one age dawn
    without a cross or crown of thorn.
                                    (Amen.)

                  T. ROWLAND HUGHES (1903–49)
                  tr. RAYMOND WILLIAMS (1928–90)

651

PANTYFEDWEN   10 10 10 10 D   M. EDDIE EVANS (1890–1984)

REFRAIN

TYDI a wnaeth y wyrth, O! Grist, Fab Duw,
tydi a roddaist imi flas ar fyw;
fe gydiaist ynof trwy dy Ysbryd Glân,
ni allaf, tra bwyf byw, ond canu'r gân;
'rwyf heddiw'n gweld yr harddwch sy'n parhau,
'rwy'n teimlo'r ddwyfol ias sy'n bywiocáu;

> *Mae'r Haleliwia yn fy enaid i*
> *a rhoddaf, Iesu, fy mawrhad i ti.*

2 Tydi yw Haul fy nydd, O! Grist y Groes,
yr wyt yn harddu holl orwelion f'oes;
lle'r oedd cysgodion nos mae llif y wawr,
lle'r oeddwn gynt yn ddall 'rwy'n gweld yn awr;
mae golau imi yn dy Berson hael,
penllanw fy ngorfoledd yw dy gael;

3 Tydi sy'n haeddu'r clod, Ddihalog Un,
mae ystyr bywyd ynot Ti dy Hun;
yr wyt yn llanw'r gwacter trwy dy Air,
daw'r pell yn agos ynot, O! Fab Mair;
mae melodïau'r cread er dy fwyn,
mi welaf dy ogoniant ar bob twyn;

W. RHYS NICHOLAS

YOU did this mighty deed, O Christ, God's Son,
you gave me joy anew, the race to run;
your Spirit held and guided me along,
for evermore, I'll sing the glorious song;
I see the beauty now that can survive,
I feel the touch divine that makes alive.

> *The alleluia has possessed my soul,*
> *to you, O Christ, I give my praises all.*

2 You are the sun, O Christ of Calvary,
you beautify the whole of life for me;
the gleaming dawn makes all the shadows flee,
I now have sight, where once I could not see;
your gracious life upon my path sheds light,
to cherish you is my supreme delight.

3 To you belongs all honour, Holy One,
life's purpose can be found in you alone;
your word sustains and moves in every sphere,
O Mary's Son, in you the far is near;
to you belongs the praise creation sings,
and I behold your glory in all things.

tr. J. H. GRIFFITHS (1815–85)

652

CWM RHONDDA   87 87 47 extended   JOHN HUGHES (1873–1932)

For this tune in G major see no. 593.

ARGLWYDD, arwain drwy'r anialwch
fi, bererin gwael ei wedd,
nad oes ynof nerth na bywyd,
fel yn gorwedd yn y bedd:
hollalluog,
ydyw'r un a'm cwyd i'r lan.

2 Colofn dân rho'r nos i'm harwain,
a rho golofn niwl y dydd;
dal fi pan fwy'n teithio'r mannau
geirwon yn fy ffordd y sydd;
rho i mi fanna,
fel na bwyf yn llwfwrhau.

3 Agor y ffynhonnau melys
sydd yn tarddu o'r graig i maes;
'r hyd yr anial mawr canlyned
afon iachawdwriaeth gras:
rho i mi hynny;
dim i mi ond dy fwynhau.

WILLIAM WILLIAMS (1717–91)

For the English version of this hymn see no. 593.

6. PSALMS

653 *Psalm 1*

1 Blessed is the man
  who does not walk in the counsel
  of the wicked
    or stand in the way of sinners
    or sit in the seat of mockers.

2 But his delight is in the law of the Lord,
    and on his law he meditates
    day and night.

3 He is like a tree planted by streams of water,
  which yields its fruit in season
  and whose leaf does not wither.
    Whatever he does prospers.

4 Not so the wicked!
    They are like chaff
    that the wind blows away.

5 Therefore the wicked will not
  stand in the judgement,
    nor sinners in the assembly
    of the righteous.

6 For the Lord watches over
  the way of the righteous,
    but the way of the wicked will perish.

NIV

654 *Psalm 5*

1 Hear my words O Lord,
  give heed to my groaning;
    listen to my cry,
    you that are my King and my God.

2 In the morning when I pray to you
  surely you will hear my voice;
    at daybreak I lay my prayers before you,
    and look up.

3 For you are not a God
  who takes pleasure in wickedness,
    nor can any evil dwell with you.

6 But because of your great goodness
  I will come into your house;
  **I will bow down toward your holy temple
  in awe and fear of you.**

7 Lead me O Lord in your righteousness,
  for my enemies lie in wait;
  make straight your way before me.

11 But let all who put their trust in you rejoice;
  let them shout with joy for ever.

12 Be the defender of those who love your name;
  let them exult because of you.

13 For you will bless O Lord
  the man that is righteous;
  **you will cover him with your favour
  as with a shield.**

ASB

655   *Psalm 8*

1 How great is your name, O Lord our God,
  through all the earth!
2 **Your majesty is praised above the heavens;
  on the lips of children and of babes
  you have found praise to foil your enemy,
  to silence the foe and the rebel.**

3 When I see the heavens, the work of your hands,
  the moon and the stars which you arranged,
4 what is man that you should keep him in mind,
  mortal man that you care for him?
5 **Yet you have made him little less than a god;
  with glory and honour you crowned him,**
6 **gave him power over the works of your hand,
  put all things under his feet.**

7 All of them, sheep and cattle,
  yes, even the savage beasts,
8 birds of the air, and fish
  that make their way through the waters.
9 **How great is your name, O Lord our God,
  through all the earth!**

The Grail

656 *Psalm 15*

1 Lord, who may enter your temple?
  Who may worship on Zion, your sacred hill?

2 A person who obeys God in everything
  and always does what is right,

  whose words are true and sincere,
3   **and who does not slander others.**

  He does no wrong to his friends
  and does not spread rumours about his neighbours.

4 He always does what he promises,
  no matter how much it may cost.

5 He makes loans without charging interest
  and cannot be bribed
  to testify against the innocent.

  Whoever does these things will always be secure.

GNB

657 *Psalm 16*

1 Preserve me, God, I take refuge in you.
2   **I say to the Lord: 'You are my God.**
  My happiness lies in you alone.'

5 O Lord, it is you who are my portion and cup;
  it is you yourself who are my prize.
6   **The lot marked out for me is my delight:**
  welcome indeed the heritage that falls to me!

7 I will bless the Lord who gives me counsel,
  who even at night directs my heart.
8   **I keep the Lord ever in my sight:**
  since he is at my right hand, I shall stand firm.

9 And so my heart rejoices, my soul is glad;
  even my body shall rest in safety.
10   **For you will not leave my soul among the dead,**
  nor let your beloved know decay.

11 You will show me the path of life,
  the fullness of joy in your presence,
  at your right hand happiness for ever.

The Grail

658 *Psalm 19*

1 The heavens declare the glory of God;
   the skies proclaim the work of his hands.

2 Day after day they pour forth speech;
   night after night they display knowledge.

3 There is no speech or language
   where their voice is not heard.
4 **Their voice goes out into all the earth,**
   their words to the ends of the world.

   In the heavens he has pitched a tent for the sun,
5 which is like a bridegroom coming forth from his pavilion,
   like a champion rejoicing to run his course.

6 It rises at one end of the heavens
   and makes its circuit to the other;
   nothing is hidden from its heat.

7 The law of the Lord is perfect,
   reviving the soul.
   The statutes of the Lord are trustworthy,
   making wise the simple.

8 The precepts of the Lord are right,
   giving joy to the heart.
   The commands of the Lord are radiant,
   giving light to the eyes.

9 The fear of the Lord is pure,
   enduring for ever.
   The ordinances of the Lord are sure
   and altogether righteous.

10 They are more precious than gold,
   than much pure gold;
   they are sweeter than honey,
   than honey from the comb.

11 By them is your servant warned;
   in keeping them there is great reward.
12 **Who can discern his errors?**
   Forgive my hidden faults.

13 Keep your servant also from wilful sins;
   may they not rule over me.
   Then will I be blameless,
   innocent of great transgression.
14 **May the words of my mouth**
   and the meditation of my heart
   be pleasing in your sight,
   O Lord, my Rock and my Redeemer.

NIV

659 *Psalm 23*

1 The Lord is my shepherd,
  therefore can I lack nothing.

2 He will make me lie down in green pastures
  and lead me beside still waters.

3 He will refresh my soul
  and guide me in right pathways
  for his name's sake.

4 Though I walk through the valley
  of the shadow of death, I will fear no evil;
  for you are with me
  your rod and your staff comfort me.

5 You spread a table before me
  in the face of those who trouble me;
  you have anointed my head with oil,
  and my cup will be full.

6 Surely your goodness and loving-kindness
  will follow me all the days of my life,
  and I shall dwell in the house
  of the Lord for ever.

ASB

660 *Psalm 24*

1 The world and all that is in it belong to the Lord;
  the earth and all who live on it are his.

3 Who has the right to go up the Lord's hill?
  Who may enter his holy temple?
4 **Those who are pure in act and in thought,**
  who do not worship idols or make false promises.

5 The Lord will bless them and save them;
  God will declare them innocent.
6 **Such are the people who come to God,**
  who come into the presence of the God of Jacob.

7 Fling wide the gates, open the ancient doors,
  and the great King will come in.

8 Who is this great King?
   He is the Lord, strong and mighty,
   the Lord, victorious in battle.

9 Fling wide the gates, open the ancient doors,
   and the great King will come in.

10 Who is this great King?
   The triumphant Lord—he is the great King!

GNB

661 *Psalm 25*

4 Lord, make me know your ways.
   Lord, teach me your paths.
5 **Make me walk in your truth, and teach me:**
   for you are God my Saviour.

In you I hope all day long
because of your goodness, O Lord.

6 Remember your mercy, Lord,
   and the love you have shown from of old.

7 Do not remember the sins of my youth.
   In your love remember me.

8 The Lord is good and upright.
   He shows the path to those who stray.
9 **He guides the humble in the right path;**
   he teaches his way to the poor.

11 Lord, for the sake of your name
   forgive my guilt; for it is great.
16 **Turn to me and have mercy**
   for I am lonely and poor.

17 Relieve the anguish of my heart
   and set me free from my distress.
18 **See my affliction and my toil**
   and take all my sins away.

20 Preserve my life and rescue me.
   Do not disappoint me, you are my refuge.

The Grail

662 *Psalm 27*

1 The Lord is my light and my salvation—
whom shall I fear?
**The Lord is the stronghold of my life—
of whom shall I be afraid?**

3 Though an army besiege me,
my heart will not fear;
**though war break out against me,
even then will I be confident.**

4 One thing I ask of the Lord,
this is what I seek:

that I may dwell in the house of the Lord
all the days of my life,
**to gaze upon the beauty of the Lord
and to seek him in his temple.**

5 For in the day of trouble
he will keep me safe in his dwelling;
**he will hide me
in the shelter of his tabernacle
and set me high upon a rock.**

7 Hear my voice when I call, O Lord;
be merciful to me and answer me.
9 **Do not hide your face from me,
do not turn your servant away in anger;
you have been my helper.**

Do not reject me or forsake me,
O God my Saviour.
10 **Though my father and mother forsake me,
the Lord will receive me.**

13 I am still confident of this:
I will see the goodness of the Lord
in the land of the living.
14 **Wait for the Lord;
be strong and take heart
and wait for the Lord.**

NIV

663 *Psalm 29*

1 Praise the Lord, you heavenly beings;
  praise his glory and power.
2 **Praise the Lord's glorious name;**
  bow down before the Holy One
  when he appears.

3 The voice of the Lord is heard on the seas;
  the glorious God thunders,
  and his voice echoes over the ocean.
4 **The voice of the Lord is heard**
  in all its might and majesty.

10 The Lord rules over the deep waters;
  he rules as King for ever.
11 **The Lord gives strength to his people**
  and blesses them with peace.

GNB

664 *Psalm 30*

1 I praise you, Lord, because you have saved me
  and kept my enemies from gloating over me.
2 **I cried to you for help, O Lord my God,**
  and you healed me;
3 **you kept me from the grave.**

I was on my way to the depths below,
  but you restored my life.
4 **Sing praise to the Lord,**
  all his faithful people!

Remember what the Holy One has done,
  and give him thanks!
5 **His anger lasts only a moment,**
  his goodness for a lifetime.

Tears may flow in the night,
  but the joy comes in the morning.
11 **You have changed my sadness**
  into a joyful dance;
  you have taken away my sorrow
  and surrounded me with joy.

12 So I will not be silent;
  I will sing praise to you.
  Lord, you are my God,
  I will give you thanks for ever.

GNB

665 *Psalm 31*

1 I come to you, Lord, for protection;
 never let me be defeated.
   You are a righteous God;
   save me, I pray!

3 You are my refuge and defence;
 guide me and lead me as you have promised.
5 **I place myself in your care.**
   You will save me, Lord;
   you are a faithful God.

19 How wonderful are the good things
 you keep for those who honour you!
   Everyone knows how good you are,
   how securely you protect those who trust you.

24 Be strong, be courageous,
 all you that hope in the Lord.

GNB

666 *Psalm 32*

1 Happy are those whose sins are forgiven,
 whose wrongs are pardoned.
2 **Happy is the man**
   whom the Lord does not accuse of doing wrong
   and who is free from all deceit.

3 When I did not confess my sins,
 I was worn out from crying all day long.
4 **Day and night you punished me, Lord;**
   my strength was completely drained,
   as moisture is dried up by the summer heat.

5 Then I confessed my sins to you;
 I did not conceal my wrongdoings.
   I decided to confess them to you,
   and you forgave all my sins.

11 You that are righteous, be glad and rejoice
 because of what the Lord has done.
   You that obey him, shout for joy!

GNB

667 *Psalm 33*

8   Worship the Lord, all the earth!
    Honour him, all peoples of the world!
9   **When he spoke, the world was created;**
    at his command everything appeared.

10 The Lord frustrates the purposes of the nations;
    he keeps them from carrying out their plans.
11 **But his plans endure for ever;**
    his purposes last eternally.

12 Happy is the nation whose God is the Lord;
    happy are the people he has chosen for his own!
20 **We put our hope in the Lord;**
    he is our protector and our help.

21 We are glad because of him;
    we trust in his holy name.
22 **May your constant love be with us, Lord,**
    as we put our hope in you.

GNB

668 *Psalm 34*

11 Come, my children, listen to me;
    I will teach you the fear of the Lord.
12 Whoever of you loves life
    and desires to see many good days,
13 **keep your tongue from evil**
    and keep your lips from speaking lies.

14 Turn from evil and do good;
    seek peace and pursue it.
15 **The eyes of the Lord are on the righteous**
    and his ears are attentive to their cry;

16 the face of the Lord is against those who do evil,
    to cut off the memory of them from the earth.
17 **The righteous cry out,**
    and the Lord hears them;
    he delivers them from all their troubles.

18 The Lord is close to the broken-hearted
    and saves those who are crushed in spirit.

NIV

669 *Psalm 36*

5 Lord, your constant love reaches the heavens;
your faithfulness extends to the skies.

6 **Your righteousness is towering like the mountains;**
your justice is like the depths of the sea.
Men and animals are in your care.

7 How precious, O God, is your constant love!
We find protection under the shadow of your wings.

8 **We feast on the abundant food you provide;**
you let us drink from the river of your goodness.

9 You are the source of all life,
and because of your light we see the light.

10 **Continue to love those who know you**
and to do good to those who are righteous.

GNB

670 *Psalm 37*

1 Don't be worried on account of the wicked;
don't be jealous of those who do wrong.

2 **They will soon disappear like the grass that dries up;**
they will die like plants that wither.

3 Trust in the Lord and do good;
live in the land and be safe.

4 **Seek your happiness in the Lord,**
and he will give you your heart's desire.

5 Give yourself to the Lord;
trust in him, and he will help you;

6 **he will make your righteousness**
shine like the noonday sun.

7 Be patient and wait for the Lord to act;
don't be worried about those who prosper
or those who succeed in their evil plans.

8 **Don't give in to worry or anger;**
it only leads to trouble.

9 Those who trust in the Lord will possess the land,
but the wicked will be driven out.

27 **Turn away from evil and do good,**
and your descendants will always live in the land;

28 for the Lord loves what is right
and does not abandon his faithful people.

GNB

671 *Psalm 40*

1 I waited patiently for the Lord's help;
   then he listened to me and heard my cry.
2 **He pulled me out of a dangerous pit,**
   out of the deadly quicksand.

   He set me safely on a rock
   and made me secure.
3 **He taught me to sing a new song,**
   a song of praise to our God.

   Many who see this will take warning
   and will put their trust in the Lord.
4 **Happy are those who trust the Lord,**
   who do not turn to idols
   or join those who worship false gods.

5 You have done many things for us, O Lord our God;
   there is no one like you!
   You have made many wonderful plans for us.
   I could never speak of them all—
   their number is so great!

                                                      GNB

672 *Psalm 42*

1 As the deer pants for streams of water,
   so my soul pants for you, O God.
2 **My soul thirsts for God, for the living God.**
   When can I go and meet with God?

3 My tears have been my food day and night,
   while men say to me all day long,
   'Where is your God?'
4 **These things I remember as I pour out my soul:**
   how I used to go with the multitude,
   leading the procession to the house of God,
   with shouts of joy and thanksgiving
   among the festive throng.

5 Why are you downcast, O my soul?
   Why so disturbed within me?
   Put your hope in God,
   for I will yet praise him,
   my Saviour and my God.

                                                      NIV

673 *Psalm 46*

1 God is our refuge and strength,
an ever present help in trouble.
2 **Therefore we will not fear,**
though the earth give way
and the mountains fall into the heart of the sea,
3 **though its waters roar and foam**
and the mountains quake with their surging.

4 There is a river whose streams
make glad the city of God,
the holy place where the Most High dwells.
5 **God is within her, she will not fall;**
God will help her at break of day.

6 Nations are in uproar, kingdoms fall;
he lifts his voice, the earth melts.
7 **The Lord Almighty is with us;**
the God of Jacob is our fortress.

8 Come and see the works of the Lord,
the desolations he has brought on the earth.
9 **He makes wars cease to the ends of the earth;**
he breaks the bow and shatters the spear,
he burns the shields with fire.

10 'Be still, and know that I am God;
I will be exalted among the nations,
I will be exalted in the earth.'
11 **The Lord Almighty is with us;**
the God of Jacob is our fortress.

NIV

674 *Psalm 47*

1 Clap your hands for joy, all peoples!
Praise God with loud songs!
2 **The Lord, the Most High, is to be feared;**
he is a great King, ruling over all the world.

5 God goes up to his throne.
There are shouts of joy and the blast of trumpets,
as the Lord goes up.
6 **Sing praise to God;**
sing praise to our King!

7 God is King over all the world;
praise him with songs!
8 **God sits on his sacred throne;**
he rules over the nations.

9 More powerful than all armies is he;
he rules supreme.

GNB

675 *Psalm 48*

1 The Lord is great and is to be highly praised
  in the city of our God, on his sacred hill.
2 **Zion, the mountain of God,**
  is high and beautiful;
  the city of the great King
  brings joy to all the world.

3 God has shown that there is safety with him
  inside the fortresses of the city.
9 **Inside your temple, O God,**
  we think of your constant love.

10 You are praised by people everywhere,
  and your fame extends over all the earth.
  You rule with justice;
11 **let the people of Zion be glad!**
  You give right judgements;
  let there be joy in the cities of Judah!

12 People of God, walk round Zion and count the towers;
13 take notice of the walls and examine the fortresses,
  so that you may tell the next generation:
14 **'This God is our God for ever and ever;**
  he will lead us for all time to come.'

GNB

676 *Psalm 51*

1 Have mercy upon me, O God,
  according to your unfailing love;
  according to your great compassion
  blot out my transgressions.
2 **Wash away all my iniquity**
  and cleanse me from my sin.

3 For I know my transgressions,
  and my sin is always before me.
4 **Against you, you only, have I sinned**
  and done what is evil in your sight,
  so that you are proved right when you speak
  and justified when you judge.

9 Hide your face from my sins
  and blot out all my iniquity.
10 **Create in me a pure heart, O God,**
  and renew a steadfast spirit within me.

11 Do not cast me from your presence
   or take your Holy Spirit from me.
12   **Restore to me the joy of your salvation**
      and grant me a willing spirit, to sustain me.

13 Then I will teach transgressors your ways,
   and sinners will turn back to you.
15   **O Lord, open my lips,**
      and my mouth will declare your praise.

16 You do not delight in sacrifice, or I would bring it;
   you do not take pleasure in burnt offerings.
17   **The sacrifices of God are a broken spirit;**
      a broken and contrite heart,
      O God, you will not despise.

NIV

677   *Psalm 62*

1 I wait patiently for God to save me;
   I depend on him alone.
2   **He alone protects and saves me;**
      he is my defender,
      and I shall never be defeated.

5 I depend on God alone;
   I put my hope in him.
6   **He alone protects and saves me;**
      he is my defender,
      and I shall never be defeated.

7 My salvation and honour depend on God;
   he is my strong protector;
   he is my shelter.
8   **Trust in God at all times, my people.**
      Tell him all your troubles,
      for he is our refuge.

10 Don't put your trust in violence;
   don't hope to gain anything by robbery;
   even if your riches increase,
   don't depend on them.
11   **More than once I have heard God say**
      that power belongs to him
      and that his love is constant.

12 You yourself, O Lord, reward everyone
   according to his deeds.

GNB

678 *Psalm 63*

1 O God, you are my God, earnestly I seek you;
my soul thirsts for you, my body longs for you,
in a dry and weary land where there is no water.

2 **I have seen you in the sanctuary**
and beheld your power and your glory.

3 Because your love is better than life,
my lips will glorify you.

4 **I will praise you as long as I live,**
and in your name I will lift up my hands.

5 My soul will be satisfied as with the richest of foods;
with singing lips my mouth will praise you.

6 **On my bed I remember you;**
I think of you through the watches of the night.

7 Because you are my help
I sing in the shadow of your wings.

8 **I stay close to you;**
your right hand upholds me.

NIV

679 *Psalm 65*

1 O God, it is right for us to praise you in Zion
and keep our promises to you,

2 because you answer prayers.
People everywhere will come to you

3 **on account of their sins.**
Our faults defeat us,
but you forgive them.

4 Happy are those whom you choose,
whom you bring to live in your sanctuary.
We shall be satisfied
with the good things of your house,
the blessings of your sacred temple.

6 You set the mountains in place by your strength,
showing your mighty power.

7 **You calm the roar of the seas**
and the noise of the waves;
you calm the uproar of the peoples.

9 You show your care for the land by sending rain;
   you make it rich and fertile.
   You fill the streams with water;
   you provide the earth with crops.
   This is how you do it:
10   **you send abundant rain**
     on the ploughed fields
     and soak them with water.

   You soften the soil with showers
   and cause the young plants to grow.
11   **What a rich harvest your goodness provides!**
     Wherever you go there is plenty.

12 The pastures are filled with flocks;
   the hillsides are full of joy.
13   **The fields are covered with sheep;**
     the valleys are full of wheat.
     Everything shouts and sings for joy.

GNB

680 *Psalm 66*

1 Praise God with shouts of joy, all people!
2   **Sing to the glory of his name;**
     offer him glorious praise!

3 Say to God,
   'How wonderful are the things you do!
   Your power is so great that your enemies
   bow down in fear before you.
4   **Everyone on earth worships you;**
     they sing praises to you,
     they sing praises to your name.'

16 Come and listen, all who honour God,
   and I will tell you what he has done for me.
17   **I cried to him for help;**
     I praised him with songs.

18 If I had ignored my sins,
   the Lord would not have listened to me.
19   **But God has indeed heard me;**
     he has listened to my prayer.
20   **I praise God,**
     because he did not reject my prayer
     or keep back his constant love from me.

GNB

681 *Psalm 67*

1 God, be merciful to us and bless us;
   look on us with kindness,
2   **so that the whole world may know your will;**
   so that all nations may know your salvation.

3 May the peoples praise you, O God;
   may all the peoples praise you!
4   **May the nations be glad and sing for joy,**
   because you judge the peoples with justice
   and guide every nation on earth.

5 May the peoples praise you, O God;
   may all the peoples praise you!
6   **The land has produced its harvest;**
   God, our God, has blessed us.
7   **God has blessed us;**
   may people everywhere honour him.

GNB

682 *Psalm 72*

1 Teach the king to judge
   with your righteousness, O God;
   share with him your own justice,
2   **so that he will rule over your people with justice**
   and govern the oppressed with righteousness.

3 May the land enjoy prosperity;
   may it experience righteousness.
4   **May the king judge the poor fairly;**
   may he help the needy
   and defeat their oppressors.

15 Long live the king!
   May prayers be said for him at all times;
   may God's blessings be on him always!

GNB

683 *Psalm 75*

1 We give thanks to you, O God,
   we give thanks to you!
   We proclaim how great you are
   and tell of the wonderful things you have done.

2 'I have set a time for judgement,' says God,
'and I will judge with fairness.
3 **Though every living creature tremble**
and the earth itself be shaken,
I will keep its foundations firm.
4 **I tell the wicked not to be arrogant;**
5 **I tell them to stop their boasting.'**

6 Judgement does not come
from the east or from the west,
from the north or from the south;
7 **it is God who is the judge,**
condemning some and acquitting others.

8 The Lord holds a cup in his hand,
filled with the strong wine of his anger.
He pours it out, and all the wicked drink it;
they drink it down to the last drop.

9 But I will never stop speaking of the God of Jacob
or singing praises to him.
10 **He will break the power of the wicked,**
but the power of the righteous will be increased.

GNB

684 *Psalm 84*

1 How lovely is your dwelling-place,
O Lord Almighty!
2 **My soul yearns, even faints**
for the courts of the Lord;
my heart and my flesh cry out
for the living God.

3 Even the sparrow has found a home,
and the swallow a nest for herself,
where she may have her young—
a place near your altar,
O Lord Almighty, my King and my God.
4 **Blessed are those who dwell in your house;**
they are ever praising you.

5 Blessed are those whose strength is in you,
who have set their hearts on pilgrimage.
6 **As they pass through the Valley of Baca,**
they make it a place of springs;
the autumn rains also cover it with pools.

7 They go from strength to strength
   till each appears before God in Zion.
10 **Better is one day in your courts**
   than a thousand elsewhere;

   I would rather be a doorkeeper
   in the house of my God
   than dwell in the tents of the wicked.
11 **For the Lord God is a sun and shield;**
   the Lord bestows favour and honour;
   no good thing does he withhold
   from those whose walk is blameless.
12 **O Lord Almighty,**
   blessed is the man who trusts in you.

NIV

685 *Psalm 86*

1 Listen to me, Lord, and answer me,
   for I am helpless and weak.
4 **Make your servant glad, O Lord,**
   because my prayers go up to you.

5 You are good to us and forgiving,
   full of constant love for all who pray to you.
6 **Listen, Lord, to my prayer;**
   hear my cries for help.

7 I call to you in times of trouble,
   because you answer my prayers.
8 **There is no god like you, O Lord,**
   not one has done what you have done.

9 All the nations that you have created
   will come and bow down to you;
   they will praise your greatness.
10 **You are mighty and do wonderful things;**
   you alone are God.

11 Teach me, Lord, what you want me to do,
   and I will obey you faithfully;
   teach me to serve you with complete devotion.
12 **I will praise you with all my heart,**
   O Lord my God;
   I will proclaim your greatness for ever.

13 How great is your constant love for me!
You have saved me from the grave itself.
15 **But you, O Lord, are a merciful and loving God,
always patient, always kind and faithful.**

16 Turn to me and have mercy on me;
strengthen me and save me,
because I serve you, just as my mother did.
17 **Show me proof of your goodness, Lord;
those who hate me will be ashamed
when they see that you
have given me comfort and help.**

GNB

686 *Psalm 90*

1 O Lord, you have always been our home.
2 **Before you created the hills
or brought the world into being,
you were eternally God,
and will be God for ever.**

3 You tell man to return to what he was;
you change him back to dust.
4 **A thousand years to you are like one day;
they are like yesterday, already gone,
like a short hour in the night.**

5 You carry us away like a flood;
we last no longer than a dream.
We are like weeds that sprout in the morning,
6 **that grow and burst into bloom,
then dry up and die in the evening.**

10 Seventy years is all we have—
eighty years, if we are strong;
yet all they bring us is trouble and sorrow;
life is soon over, and we are gone.
12 **Teach us how short our life is,
so that we may become wise.**

14 Fill us each morning with your constant love,
so that we may sing and be glad all our life.
17 **Lord our God,
may your blessings be with us.
Give us success in all we do!**

GNB

687 *Psalm 91*

1 Whoever goes to the Lord for safety,
  whoever remains under the protection of the Almighty,
2 can say to him,
  'You are my defender and protector.
  You are my God; in you I trust.'

3 He will keep you safe from all hidden dangers
  and from all deadly diseases.
4 **He will cover you with his wings;**
  you will be safe in his care;
  his faithfulness will protect and defend you.

5 You need not fear any dangers at night
  or sudden attacks during the day
6 **or the plagues that strike in the dark**
  or the evils that kill in daylight.

9 You have made the Lord your defender,
  the Most High your protector,
10 **and so no disaster will strike you,**
  no violence will come near your home.

11 God will put his angels in charge of you
  to protect you wherever you go.
12 **They will hold you up with their hands**
  to keep you from hurting
  your feet on the stones.

14 God says, 'I will save those who love me
  and will protect those who acknowledge me as Lord.
15 **When they call to me, I will answer them;**
  when they are in trouble, I will be with them.
  I will reward them with long life;
  I will save them.'

GNB

688 *Psalm 95*

1 Come! Let us raise a joyful song to the Lord,
  a shout of triumph to the rock of our salvation.
2 **Let us come into his presence with thanksgiving,**
  and sing him psalms of triumph.
3 For the Lord is a great God,
  a great King over all gods;
4 **the farthest places of the earth are in his hands,**
  and the folds of the hills are his;
5 the sea is his, he made it;
  the dry land fashioned by his hands is his.
6 **Come! let us throw ourselves at his feet in homage,**
  let us kneel before the Lord who made us;
7 for he is our God,
  we are his people, we the flock he shepherds.

NEB

689 *Psalm 96*

1 Sing to the Lord a new song,
   sing to the Lord, all the earth.

2 Sing to the Lord, praise his name;
   proclaim his salvation day after day.

3 Declare his glory among the nations,
   his marvellous deeds among all peoples.

4 For great is the Lord and most worthy of praise;
   he is to be feared above all gods.

5 For all the gods of the nations are idols,
   but the Lord made the heavens.

6 Splendour and majesty are before him;
   strength and glory are in his sanctuary.

7 Ascribe to the Lord, O families of nations,
   ascribe to the Lord glory and strength.

8 Ascribe to the Lord the glory due to his name,
   bring an offering and come into his courts.

9 Worship the Lord in the splendour of his holiness;
   tremble before him, all the earth.

10 Say among the nations, 'The Lord reigns.'
   The world is firmly established, it cannot be moved;
   he will judge the peoples with equity.

11 Let the heavens rejoice, let the earth be glad;
   let the sea resound, and all that is in it;

12 let the fields be jubilant, and everything in them.
   Then all the trees of the forest will sing for joy;

13 they will sing before the Lord, for he comes,
   he comes to judge the earth.

   He will judge the world in righteousness
   and the peoples in his truth.

NIV

690 *Psalm 98*

1 Sing a new song to the Lord,
for he has worked wonders.
  **His right hand and his holy arm
  have brought salvation.**

2 The Lord has made known his salvation:
has shown his justice to the nations.
3 **He has remembered his truth and love
  for the house of Israel.**

All the ends of the earth have seen
the salvation of our God.
4 **Shout to the Lord all the earth,
  ring out your joy.**

5 Sing psalms to the Lord with the harp,
with the sound of music.
6 **With trumpets and the sound of the horn
  acclaim the King, the Lord.**

7 Let the sea, and all within it, thunder;
the world, and all its peoples.
8 **Let the rivers clap their hands
  and the hills ring out their joy**

9 at the presence of the Lord: for he comes,
he comes to rule the earth.
  **He will rule the world with justice
  and the peoples with fairness.**

The Grail

691 *Psalm 100*

1 Shout for joy to the Lord, all the earth.
2 **Worship the Lord with gladness;
  come before him with joyful songs.**

3 Know that the Lord is God.
  **It is he who made us, and we are his;
  we are his people, the sheep of his pasture.**

4 Enter his gates with thanksgiving
and his courts with praise;
  give thanks to him and praise his name.

5 For the Lord is good and his love endures for ever;
  his faithfulness continues through all generations.

NIV

692 *Psalm 103*

1 My soul, give thanks to the Lord,
all my being, bless his holy name.
2 **My soul, give thanks to the Lord**
and never forget all his blessings.

3 It is he who forgives all your guilt,
who heals every one of your ills,
4 **who redeems your life from the grave,**
who crowns you with love and compassion,
5 who fills your life with good things,
renewing your youth like an eagle's.

8 The Lord is compassion and love,
slow to anger and rich in mercy.
9 **His wrath will come to an end;**
he will not be angry for ever.
10 He does not treat us according to our sins
nor repay us according to our faults.

13 As a father has compassion on his sons,
the Lord has pity on those who fear him;
14 **for he knows of what we are made,**
he remembers that we are dust.

15 As for man, his days are like grass;
he flowers like the flower of the field;
16 **the wind blows and he is gone**
and his place never sees him again.

17 But the love of the Lord is everlasting
upon those who hold him in fear;
his justice reaches out to children's children
18 **when they keep his covenant in truth,**
when they keep his will in their mind.

20 Give thanks to the Lord, all his angels,
mighty in power, fulfilling his word,
who heed the voice of his word.
21 **Give thanks to the Lord, all his hosts,**
his servants who do his will.

22 Give thanks to the Lord, all his works,
in every place where he rules.
My soul, give thanks to the Lord!

The Grail

693 *Psalm 108*

1 My heart is steadfast, O God;
  I will sing and make music with all my soul.
2 **Awake, harp and lyre!**
  I will awaken the dawn.

3 I will praise you, O Lord, among the nations;
  I will sing of you among the peoples.
4 **For great is your love,**
  higher than the heavens;
  your faithfulness reaches to the skies.

5 Be exalted, O God, above the heavens,
  and let your glory be over all the earth.
6 **Save us and help us with your right hand,**
  that those you love may be delivered.

12 Give us aid against the enemy,
  for the help of man is worthless.
13 **With God we shall gain the victory,**
  and he will trample down our enemies.

NIV

694 *Psalm 111*

1 I will thank the Lord with all my heart
  in the meeting of the just and their assembly.
2 **Great are the works of the Lord;**
  to be pondered by all who love them.

3 Majestic and glorious his work,
  his justice stands firm for ever.
4 **He makes us remember his wonders.**
  The Lord is compassion and love.

5 He gives food to those who fear him;
  keeps his covenant ever in mind.
6 **He has shown his might to the people**
  by giving them the lands of the nations.

7 His works are justice and truth:
  his precepts are all of them sure,
8 **standing firm for ever and ever:**
  they are made in uprightness and truth.

9 He has sent deliverance to his people
and established his covenant for ever.
Holy his name, to be feared.

10 To fear the Lord is the first stage of wisdom;
all who do so prove themselves wise.
His praise shall last for ever!

The Grail

695 *Psalm 116*

1 I love the Lord, for he heard my voice;
he heard my cry for mercy.
2 **Because he turned his ear to me,
I will call on him as long as I live.**

5 The Lord is gracious and righteous;
our God is full of compassion.
6 **The Lord protects the simple-hearted;
when I was in great need, he saved me.**

8 For you, O Lord,
have delivered my soul from death,
my eyes from tears, my feet from stumbling,
9 **that I may walk before the Lord
in the land of the living.**
12 **How can I repay the Lord
for all his goodness to me?**
13 **I will lift up the cup of salvation
and call on the name of the Lord.**

14 I will fulfil my vows to the Lord
in the presence of all his people.
17 **I will sacrifice a thank-offering to you
and call on the name of the Lord.**

18 I will fulfil my vows to the Lord
in the presence of all his people,
19 **in the courts of the house of the Lord—
in your midst, O Jerusalem.
Praise the Lord.**

NIV

696 *Psalm 118*

1   Give thanks to the Lord, for he is good;
    his love endures forever.
2   **Let Israel say:**
    'His love endures for ever.'

3   Let the house of Aaron say:
    'His love endures for ever.'
4   **Let those who fear the Lord say:**
    'His love endures for ever.'

13 I was pushed back and about to fall,
    but the Lord helped me.
14 **The Lord is my strength and my song;**
    he has become my salvation.

15 Shouts of joy and victory
    resound in the tents of the righteous:
    'The Lord's right hand has done mighty things!

16 The Lord's right hand is lifted high;
    the Lord's right hand has done mighty things!'

22 The stone the builders rejected
    has become the capstone;
23 **the Lord has done this,**
    and it is marvellous in our eyes.

24 This is the day the Lord has made;
    let us rejoice and be glad in it.

26 Blessed is he who comes in the name of the Lord.
    From the house of the Lord we bless you.

27 The Lord is God,
    and he has made his light shine upon us.

28 You are my God, and I will give thanks;
    you are my God, and I will exalt you.

29 Give thanks to the Lord, for he is good;
    his love endures for ever.

NIV

697 *Psalm 119*

33 Teach me the demands of your statutes
    and I will keep them to the end.

34 Train me to observe your law,
    to keep it with my heart.

35 Guide me in the path of your commands;
    for there is my delight.

36 Bend my heart to your will
   and not to love of gain.

37 Keep my eyes from what is false:
   by your word give me life.

38 Keep the promise you have made
   to the servant who fears you.

39 Keep me from the scorn I dread,
   for your decrees are good.

40 See, I long for your precepts:
   then in your justice, give me life.

The Grail

698 *Psalm 121*

1 I lift up my eyes to the hills—
   where does my help come from?
2 **My help comes from the Lord,**
   the maker of heaven and earth.

3 He will not let your foot slip—
   he who watches over you will not slumber;
4 **indeed, he who watches over Israel**
   will neither slumber nor sleep.

5 The Lord watches over you—
   the Lord is your shade at your right hand;
6 **the sun will not harm you by day,**
   nor the moon by night.

7 The Lord will keep you from all harm—
   he will watch over your life;
8 **the Lord will watch over your**
   coming and going
   both now and for evermore.

NIV

699 *Psalm 122*

1 I was glad when they said to me,
   'Let us go to the Lord's house.'
6 **Pray for the peace of Jerusalem:**
   'May those who love you prosper.

7 May there be peace inside your walls
   and safety in your palaces.'
8 **For the sake of my relatives and friends**
   I say to Jerusalem, 'Peace be with you!'

9 For the sake of the house of the Lord our God,
   I pray for your prosperity.

GNB

700 *Psalm 126*

1 When the Lord brought back the captives to Zion,
we were like men who dreamed.
2 **Our mouths were filled with laughter,
our tongues with songs of joy.**

Then it was said among the nations,
'The Lord has done great things for them.'
3 **The Lord has done great things for us,
and we are filled with joy.**

5 Those who sow in tears
will reap with songs of joy.
6 **He who goes out weeping,
will return with songs of joy.**

NIV

701 *Psalm 130*

1 From the depths of my despair
I call to you, Lord.
2 **Hear my cry, O Lord;**

listen to my call for help!
3 **If you kept a record of our sins,
who could escape being condemned?**

4 But you forgive us,
so that we should stand in awe of you.
5 **I wait eagerly for the Lord's help,**

and in his word I trust.
6 **I wait for the Lord
more eagerly than watchmen wait for the dawn—**

than watchmen wait for the dawn.

GNB

702 *Psalm 136*

1 Give thanks to the Lord,
because he is good;
his love is eternal.
2 **Give thanks to the greatest of all gods;
his love is eternal.**

1045

3 Give thanks to the mightiest of all lords;
   his love is eternal.
4 **He alone performs great miracles;**
   his love is eternal.

5 By his wisdom he made the heavens;
   his love is eternal;
6 **he built the earth on the deep waters;**
   his love is eternal.

7 He made the sun and the moon;
   his love is eternal;
8 **the sun to rule over the day;**
   his love is eternal;

9 the moon and the stars to rule over the night;
   his love is eternal.
24 **he freed us from our enemies;**
   his love is eternal.

26 Give thanks to the God of heaven;
   his love is eternal.

GNB

703 *Psalm 137*

1 By the rivers of Babylon we sat down;
   there we wept when we remembered Zion.
2 **On the willows near by**
   we hung up our harps.

3 Those who captured us told us to sing;
   they told us to entertain them:
   'Sing us a song about Zion.'

4 How can we sing a song to the Lord
   in a foreign land?
5 **May I never be able to play the harp again**
   if I forget you, Jerusalem!

6 May I never be able to sing again
   if I do not remember you,
   if I do not think of you as my greatest joy!

GNB

704 *Psalm 138*

1 I will praise you, O Lord, with all my heart;
    I will sing your praise,
2   **and will praise your name
        for your love and your faithfulness.**

3 When I called, you answered me;
    you made me bold and stout-hearted.
4   **May all the kings of the earth
        praise you, O Lord,
        when they hear the words of your mouth.**

5 May they sing of the ways of the Lord,
    for the glory of the Lord is great.
6   **Though the Lord is on high,
        he looks upon the lowly,
        but the proud he knows from afar.**

7 Though I walk in the midst of trouble,
    you preserve my life;
        **you stretch out your hand
        against the anger of my foes,
        with your right hand you save me.**

8 The Lord will fulfil his purpose for me;
        **your love, O Lord, endures for ever—
        do not abandon the works of your hands.**

                                                        NIV

705 *Psalm 139*

1 O Lord, you have searched me
    and you know me.
2   **You know when I sit and when I rise;
        you perceive my thoughts from afar.**

3 You discern my going out and my lying down;
    you are familiar with all my ways.
4   **Before a word is on my tongue
        you know it completely, O Lord.**

5 You hem me in—behind and before;
    you have laid your hand upon me.
6   **Such knowledge is too wonderful for me,
        too lofty for me to attain.**

7 Where can I go from your Spirit?
 Where can I flee from your presence?

8 If I go up to the heavens, you are there;
 if I make my bed in the depths, you are there;

9 if I rise on the wings of the dawn,
 if I settle on the far side of the sea,

10 even there your hand will guide me,
 your right hand will hold me fast.

11 If I say, 'Surely the darkness will hide me
 and the light become night around me,'
12 **even the darkness will not be dark to you;**
 the night will shine like the day,
 for darkness is as light to you.

13 For you created my inmost being;
 you knit me together in my mother's womb.

14 I praise you because I am fearfully and wonderfully made;
 your works are wonderful,
 I know that full well.

15 My frame was not hidden from you
 when I was made in the secret place.
 When I was woven together
 in the depths of the earth,
16 **your eyes saw my unformed body.**

 All the days ordained for me
 were written in your book
 before one of them came to be.
17 **How precious to me are your thoughts, O God!**

 How vast is the sum of them!
18 **Were I to count them,**
 they would outnumber the grains of sand.

23 Search me, O God, and know my heart;
 test me and know my anxious thoughts.

24 See if there is any offensive way in me,
 and lead me in the way everlasting.

NIV

706 *Psalm 140*

1 Rescue me, O Lord, from evil men;
   protect me from men of violence.

3 They make their tongues as sharp as a serpent's;
   the poison of vipers is on their lips.

6 O Lord, I say to you, 'You are my God.'
   Hear, O Lord, my cry for mercy.

7 O sovereign Lord, my strong deliverer,
8 do not grant the wicked their desires, O Lord;
   do not let their plans succeed.

12 I know that the Lord secures justice for the poor
   and upholds the cause of the needy.

13 Surely the righteous will praise your name
   and the upright will live before you.

NIV

707 *Psalm 145*

1 I will exalt you, my God the King;
   I will praise your name for ever and ever.

2 Every day I will praise you
   and extol your name for ever and ever.

3 Great is the Lord and most worthy of praise;
   his greatness no one can fathom.

4 One generation will commend your works to another;
   they will tell of your mighty acts.

5 They will speak of the glorious splendour of your majesty,
   and I will meditate on your wonderful works.

6 They will tell of the power of your awesome works,
   and I will proclaim your great deeds.

7 They will celebrate your abundant goodness
and joyfully sing of your righteousness.

8 The Lord is gracious and compassionate,
slow to anger and rich in love.

9 The Lord is good to all;
he has compassion on all he has made.

10 All you have made will praise you, O Lord;
your saints will extol you.

11 They will tell of the glory of your kingdom
and speak of your might.

13 Your kingdom is an everlasting kingdom,
and your dominion endures through all generations.

The Lord is faithful to all his promises
and loving towards all he has made.

14 The Lord upholds all those who fall
and lifts up all who are bowed down.

15 The eyes of all look to you,
and you give them their food at the proper time.

16 You open your hand
and satisfy the desires of every living thing.

17 The Lord is righteous in all his ways
and loving towards all he has made.

18 The Lord is near to all who call on him,
to all who call on him in truth.

19 He fulfils the desires of those who fear him;
he hears their cry and saves them.

20 The Lord watches over all who love him,
but all the wicked he will destroy.

21 My mouth will speak in praise of the Lord.
**Let every creature praise his holy name
for ever and ever.**

NIV

708 *Psalm 146*

1 Praise the Lord.
   Praise the Lord, O my soul.

2 I will praise the Lord all my life;
   I will sing praise to my God as long as I live.

3 Do not put your trust in princes,
   in mortal men, who cannot save.

5 Blessed is he whose help is the God of Jacob,
   whose hope is in the Lord his God,

   the Lord, who remains faithful for ever.
7 **He upholds the cause of the oppressed**
   and gives food to the hungry.
   The Lord sets prisoners free,

8 the Lord gives sight to the blind,
   the Lord lifts up those who are bowed down,

   the Lord loves the righteous.
9 **The Lord watches over the alien**

   and sustains the fatherless and the widow,
   but he frustrates the ways of the wicked.

10 The Lord reigns for ever.
   Praise the Lord.

NIV

709 *Psalm 147*

1 How good it is to sing praises to our God,
   how pleasant and fitting to praise him!

3 He heals the broken-hearted
   and binds up their wounds.

4 He determines the number of the stars
   and calls them each by name.

5   Great is our Lord and mighty in power;
    his understanding has no limit.

7   Sing to the Lord with thanksgiving;
    make music to our God on the harp.

8   He covers the sky with clouds;
    **he supplies the earth with rain
    and makes grass grow on the hills.**

9   He provides food for the cattle
    and for the young ravens when they call.

19 He has revealed his word to Jacob,
    his laws and decrees to Israel.

20 Praise the Lord.

                                          NIV

710   *Psalm 148*

1   Praise the Lord.
    Praise the Lord from the heavens,
    praise him in the heights above.

2   Praise him, all his angels,
    praise him, all his heavenly hosts.

3   Praise him, sun and moon,
    praise him, all you shining stars.

5   Let them praise the name of the Lord,
    for he commanded and they were created.

6   He set them in place for ever and ever;
    he gave a decree that will never pass away.

7   Praise the Lord from the earth,
    you great sea creatures and all ocean depths,

8   lightning and hail, snow and clouds,
    stormy winds that do his bidding,

9 you mountains and all hills,
   fruit trees and all cedars,

10 wild animals and all cattle,
   small creatures and flying birds,

11 kings of the earth and all nations,
   you princes and all rulers on earth,

12 young men and maidens,
   old men and children.

13 Let them praise the name of the Lord,
   for his name alone is exalted;
   his splendour is above the earth and the heavens.
14 Praise the Lord.

NIV

711 *Psalm 150*

1 Praise the Lord.
   Praise God in his sanctuary;
   praise him in his mighty heavens.

2 Praise him for his acts of power;
   praise him for his surpassing greatness.

3 Praise him with the sounding of the trumpet,
   praise him with the harp and lyre,

4 praise him with tambourine and dancing,
   praise him with the strings and flute,

5 praise him with the clash of cymbals,
   praise him with resounding cymbals.

6 Let everything that has breath praise the Lord.
   Praise the Lord.

NIV

712

NATIONAL ANTHEM   664 6664   Anon.

GOD save our gracious Queen,
long live our noble Queen,
  God save the Queen!
Send her victorious,
happy and glorious,
long to reign over us;
  God save the Queen!

2 Lord be our nation's light,
  guide us in truth and right:
    in you we stand;
  give us your faithfulness,
  keep us from selfishness,
  raise us to godliness:
    God save our land!

3 Lord make your mercies known
  not on this land alone
    but on each shore.
  Soon may the nations be
  in love and unity,
  and form one family
    the whole world o'er.

v. 1 Anon.
v. 2 Jubilate Hymns
v. 3 WILLIAM EDWARD HICKSON (1803–70) altd.

INDEXES

INDEX OF SECTIONAL CROSS-REFERENCES

Many hymns are suitable for use in a variety of contexts, and this list cross-references additional hymns for the various sections of the book.

397 Thou art the everlasting Word
404 Awake, awake: fling off the night
441 Let all mortal flesh keep silence
635 O day of God, draw near
    See also Proclaiming the Gospel: God's
    Reign

Christmas

55 Jesus, name above all names
58 Meekness and majesty
192 Shepherds came, their praises bringing
199 In a byre near Bethlehem
209 Search for the infant
315 Joy to the world
391 Tell out my soul, the greatness of the Lord
441 Let all mortal flesh keep silence
529 *The Servant King*
585 We have a gospel to proclaim
638 Sing we a song of high revolt

Epiphany

22 Worship the Lord in the beauty of holiness
34 Christ is the world's light, he and none
    other
441 Let all mortal flesh keep silence
618 Christ is the world's true light

Our Lord's Ministry

37 Crown him with many crowns
83 Forgive our sins as we forgive
84 Dear Lord and Father of mankind
89 You gave us, Lord, by word and deed
98 Break now the bread of life
109 Lo, I am with you to the end of the world
112 Peace, perfect peace, is the gift of Christ
    our Lord
218 Forty days and forty nights
234 When he was baptized in Jordan
316 O Lord of the kingdom where losing is
    winning
321 The kingdom of God is justice and joy
333 *Sing hey*
337 Dear Master, in whose life I see
350 'Man of sorrows', wondrous name
357 Seek ye first the kingdom of God
381 I cannot tell why he, whom angels worship
396 There's no greater name than Jesus
397 Thou art the everlasting Word
405 Christ, when for us you were baptized
406 Church of God, elect and glorious
470 A new commandment
560 One there is, above all others
562 Praise to the holiest in the height
571 Go, tell it on the mountain
574 God's Spirit is in my heart
585 We have a gospel to proclaim
589 Father God in heaven
590 Father in heaven
596 In your glad obedience to your Father's
    will
598 Lord Jesus, once you spoke to men
606 Kneels at the feet of his friends
616 At evening, when the sun had set
639 Son of God, eternal Saviour

Lent and Passiontide

34 Christ is the world's light, he and none
    other
58 Meekness and majesty
204 My song is love unknown
205 My dear Redeemer and my Lord
207 O love, how deep, how broad, how high
208 Pull back the veil on the dawn of creation
209 Search for the infant
344 In the cross of Christ I glory
350 'Man of sorrows', wondrous name
351 O dearest Lord
392 Thank you Jesus
529 *The Servant King*
542 The journey of life may be easy, may be
    hard
545 Rock of ages
562 Praise to the holiest in the height
566 To God be the glory
575 Lift high the cross
585 We have a gospel to proclaim

Easter

21 This is the day
31 Alleluia, alleluia, give thanks to the risen
    Lord
88 Jesus stand among us
111 Now may he, who from the dead
199 In a byre near Bethlehem
207 O love, how deep, how broad, how high
208 Pull back the veil on the dawn of creation
209 Search for the infant
378 He is Lord, he is Lord
379 He lives, he lives, Christ Jesus lives today
392 Thank you Jesus
404 Awake, awake: fling off the night
407 Come, God's people, sing for joy
444 Lord Jesus Christ

Ascension

4 At your feet we fall
6 Come let us join our cheerful songs
20 The King is among us
29 All hail the power of Jesus' name
34 Christ is the world's light, he and none
    other
37 Crown him with many crowns
46 God of gods, we sound his praises
74 You are the King of glory
75 You are worthy, you are worthy
254 Led like a lamb to the slaughter
306 Christ triumphant ever reigning
318 Sing we the King who is coming to reign
370 At the name of Jesus
378 He is Lord, he is Lord
560 One there is, above all others

The Holy Spirit

5 Be still, for the presence of the Lord
20 The King is among us
21 This is the day
88 Jesus stand among us
97 Come, Holy Ghost, our hearts inspire

SECTIONAL CROSS-REFERENCES

380 How firm a foundation
387 O Lord of heaven and earth and sea
395 The Lord's my shepherd
415 Welcome to the family
478 For all the saints
542 The journey of life may be easy, may be hard
544 Through all the changing scenes of life
552 Great God, we sing your guiding hand
555 In heavenly love abiding
565 There are hundreds of sparrows
592 God be in my head
619 Cradle, O Lord, in your arms everlasting
633 Made in God's image

4. LIVING THE GOSPEL

Renewed Commitment

9 God of the morning, at whose voice
53 King of glory, King of peace
87 Now let us see your beauty, Lord
224 Lord Jesus, for my sake you come
327 All my hope on God is founded
358 Take my life, and let it be
592 God be in my head
596 In your glad obedience to your Father's will
602 Unto the silent hills I raise
607 Forth in the peace of Christ we go
608 Lord, as we rise to leave this shell of worship
615 Who is on the Lord's side?

God's Grace

8 At your feet, our God and Father
47 Give to our God immortal praise
65 Praise, my soul, the King of heaven
71 Bright the vision that delighted
102 Lord, your word shall guide us
117 By gracious powers so wonderfully sheltered
122 God moves in a mysterious way
394 The King of love
395 The Lord's my shepherd
510 The grace of life is theirs
594 Give us, O God, the grace to see

Witnessing

9 God of the morning, at whose voice
53 King of glory, King of peace
224 Lord Jesus, for my sake you come
448 Sent forth by God's blessing
526 Forth in your name
528 Freedom and life are ours
537 May the mind of Christ my Saviour
607 Forth in the peace of Christ we go
608 Lord, as we rise to leave this shell of worship
611 Lord, speak to me
613 The Church of Christ in every age
614 When the Church of Jesus

The Life of Prayer

84 Dear Lord and Father of mankind
148 Wait for the Lord
221 Jesus, remember me
227 Stay with me
275 With joy we meditate the grace
282 Breathe on me, breath of God
292 Holy Spirit, truth divine
294 O Holy Spirit breathe on me
298 Spirit of the living God, fall afresh on me
299 Spirit of the living God, move among us all
326 Abba Father, let me be
337 Dear Master, in whose life I see
351 O dearest Lord
360 Take this moment, sign and space
452 Stay with us
517 Lord of all hopefulness
536 Master, speak! Your servant's listening
537 May the mind of Christ my Saviour
610 Lord of light, your name outshining
634 Make me a channel of your peace
641 We turn to you, O God of every nation

The Life of Service

45 God is love: his the care
60 O God of all creation
197 How blest the poor who love the Lord
300 There's a spirit in the air
351 O dearest Lord
358 Take my life, and let it be
453 Strengthen for service
473 Brother, sister, let me serve you
481 I sing a song of the saints of God
484 Let there be love shared among us
487 *Marching in the light of God*
522 Christ of the upward way
523 Father, hear the prayer we offer
534 Jesus Christ is waiting
537 May the mind of Christ my Saviour
569 Fill now my life
572 God of grace and God of glory
577 Lord, your Church on earth is seeking
578 Lord, your kingdom bring triumphant
583 We are called to be God's people
638 Sing we a song of high revolt
642 Where restless crowds are thronging

Harmony and Healing

42 For beauty of meadows
84 Dear Lord and Father of mankind
112 Peace, perfect peace, is the gift of Christ our Lord
318 *Come let us sing*
373 God is hope and God is now
390 Praise you, Lord
471 Bind us together, Lord
472 Blest be the tie that binds
475 Christ is the King! O friends rejoice
477 Eternal Ruler of the ceaseless round
482 In Christ there is no east or west
551 What purpose burns within our hearts
576 Lord, you have given yourself for our healing

SELECT THEMATIC INDEX

SELECT THEMES

517 Lord of all hopefulness
553 Great is your faithfulness
568 Colours of day dawn into the mind
594 Give us, O God, the grace to see

Evening
108 Glory to you my God, this night
319 The day you gave us
515 Abide with me
517 Lord of all hopefulness
616 At evening, when the sun had set

The Lord's Day
21 This is the day
84 Dear Lord and Father of mankind
88 Jesus stand among us
249 Early on Sunday
319 The day you gave us
335 Father of all, whose laws have stood

Old and New Year
8 At your feet, our God and Father
16 Lord Christ, whose love has brought us here
40 Fill your hearts with joy and gladness
117 By gracious powers so wonderfully sheltered
128 Now thank we all our God
356 One more step along the world I go
535 Lord, for the years your love has kept and guided
544 Through all the changing scenes of life
552 Great God, we sing your guiding hand
553 Great is your faithfulness

Mothering Sunday
121 For the beauty of the earth
128 Now thank we all our God
134 Think of a world without any flowers
498 Father, in your presence kneeling
500 Lord of the home

Harvest Festival
28 All creatures of our God and King
40 Fill your hearts with joy and gladness
48 God of mercy, God of grace
116 All things bright and beautiful
120 Come, you thankful people, come
123 For the fruits of his creation
124 God, whose farm is all creation
135 We plough the fields and scatter
387 O Lord of heaven and earth and sea
553 Great is your faithfulness
612 Now join we, to praise the creator

Remembrance Sunday and Peace Services
114 Shalom, my friends
318 *Come let us sing*
389 Our God, our help in ages past
482 In Christ there is no east or west
604 Father of glory, whose heavenly plan
617 Behold, the mountain of the Lord
618 Christ is the world's true light
621 For the healing of the nations
624 Grant us your peace
625 'I have a dream,' a man once said
628 Lead me from death to life
629 Let there be peace on earth
630 Let there be light
634 Make me a channel of your peace
635 O day of God, draw near
637 Put peace into each other's hands
641 We turn to you, O God of every nation
644 Your kingdom come, O God
712 *National Anthem*

Aid and Development
300 There's a spirit in the air
316 O Lord of the kingdom where losing is winning
447 Passover God, we remember your faithfulness
581 Speak forth your word
612 Now join we, to praise the creator
626 Where cross the crowded ways of life
638 Sing we a song of high revolt

Church Anniversary
10 How pleased and blest was I
16 Lord Christ whose love has brought us here
17 O Lord, how lovely is the sight
30 Bring to the Lord a glad new song
319 The day you gave us
389 Our God, our help in ages past
398 Your hand, O God, has guided
406 Church of God, elect and glorious
413 Lord, we have come at your own invitation
450 Spread the table of the Lord
471 Bind us together, Lord
472 Blest be the tie that binds
474 Christ is made the sure foundation
478 For all the saints
479 For the might of your arm
481 I sing a song of the saints of God
488 We come unto our fathers' God
491 We thank you for the memories
535 Lord, for the years your love has kept and guided
547 To him we come
551 What purpose burns within our hearts
572 God of grace and God of glory
583 We are called to be God's people

INDEX OF HYMNS FOR FAMILY WORSHIP

Since there is no section of Hymns for Children, this index lists those which are suitable for all ages and can be enjoyed by children and adults alike at occasions of family worship.

INDEX OF BIBLICAL REFERENCES

References listed relate to hymns only and include either the biblical passage on which a hymn is based or one to which it is closely related. Psalms are in numerical order beginning at no. 653, and biblical references in responsive prayers and readings are not included.

INDEX OF AUTHORS, TRANSLATORS, AND SOURCES OF WORDS

This index does not include sources for the prayers and readings, which can be found in the Copyright Acknowledgements.

INDEX OF COMPOSERS, ARRANGERS, AND SOURCES OF MUSIC

An asterisk indicates a harmonization, adaptation, or other arrangement.

ALPHABETICAL INDEX OF TUNES

INDEXES

TUNES (ALPHABETICAL)

METRICAL INDEX OF TUNES

Irregular and non-metrical settings are not included here. Neither are those song tunes for which the metre is particularly unusual, even though it may be regular.

TUNES (METRICAL)

INDEX OF FIRST LINES AND TITLES

This index does not include psalms, prayers, and readings. Psalms can be found in numerical order from no. 653 onwards in the main body of the book. Prayers, readings, and other non-musical worship material appear at the end of the appropriate theme-section. Where titles differ from first lines, they are shown in *italic*.

INDEXES